What others are saying about *The Paradigm Co*

"This book is a must read for anyone who values family and freedom."
—Russell Means, activist, actor, and co-author of *Where White Mean Fear to Tread*

"This is an absolutely fantastic book . . . a five star, one in a decade, keep it on the shelf to refer back to forever, water mark for the end of the 20th Century, great goddamned book!"
—Brad Blanton, author of *Radical Honesty and Radical Being*

"*The Paradigm Conspiracy* presents a full-tilt attack on the soul-violating institutions in America which seek to control our lives. Their stifling of our independence and creativity spawns addictions of all types. [The authors] argue that a paradigm shift away from the domination model which encourages lies, secrets, restrictions, and cover-ups is the best path to recovery on both a personal and societal level. . . . *The Paradigm Conspiracy* is a philosophic masterwork that will enable you to see yourself and the world with fresh eyes."
—Frederic A. Brussat, co-author of *Spiritual Literacy: Reading the Sacred in Everyday Life.*

"A comprehensive survey of the changing paradigm and the need to increase the rate of change. We can only hope that we will find ourselves on the positive side of the tidal wave that now confronts us. There is a synthesis here that we need to understand—and support—if we are to survive."
—Vino Deloria, Jr., professor of history, religious studies, and law, University of Colorado, Boulder, and author of *Custer Died for Your Sins: An Indian Manifesto* and *Red Earth, White Lies: Native Americans and the Myth of Scientific Fact*

"Finally, a book that provides a political and economic context for personal recovery work. *The Paradigm Conspiracy* gives us a total view of how control systems work and why we need to change our governing paradigms. The book is wide-ranging, clarifying, and practical. It helps us move beyond victim blaming and towards system transformation."
—Paul Kivel, author of *Men's Work: How to Stop the Violence that Tears Our Lives Apart* and *Uprooting Racism: How White People Can Work for Radical Justice*

"We all feel the quiet anguish; *The Paradigm Conspiracy* names the perpetrator: our toxic, old-paradigm social/political systems, which survive at the price of our souls. But it doesn't have to be that way. This book teaches us how to map out a different, soul-affirming path for our lives, one that will allow us to walk with the powerful new healing that is moving into the world."
—Bill Kauth, co-founder of the New Warrior Training Adventure and author of *A Circle of Men: The Original Manual for Men's Support Groups*

"*The Paradigm Conspiracy* lays bare the faulty architecture of our society, the unassailable 'facts of life' that drive us crazy, and gives us some tools by which to navigate ourselves out of the maze. . . . [The book] is a very welcome addition to a library of precious voices reminding us that things can be better."
—Roderic Sorrell and Amy Max Sorrell, authors of *The I Ching Made Easy*

The Paradigm Conspiracy

Why Our Social Systems Violate Human Potential— And How We Can Change Them

Denise Breton
Christopher Largent

Hazelden
Center City, Minnesota 55012-0176

Library of Congress Cataloging-in-Publication Data
Breton, Denise.
    The paradigm consipiracy : why our social systems violate human
potential—and how we can change them / Denise Breton and Christopher
Largent.
        p. cm.
    Includes bibliographical references and index.
    ISBN 1-56838-106-9 (cloth)
    ISBN 1-56838-208-1 (paper)
    1. Social systems. 2. Social movements. 3. Social psychology. 4.
Paradigms (Social sciences) 5. Mind and body. 6. Change (Psychology) I.
Largent, Christopher. II. Title.
HM131.B688   1996   96-10895
301—dc20   CIP

Editor's note
Hazelden offers a variety of information on chemical dependency and related
areas. Our publications do not necessarily represent Hazelden's programs, nor do
they officially speak for any Twelve Step organization.

To
Mary Joy Breton

CONTENTS

ACKNOWLEDGMENTS

It wasn't our idea to write this book. The book evolved through the help—or conspiracy—of many people. Bob Italia, whom we met at a *Publishers Weekly* party for small publishers in the spring of 1991, first asked us to write on spirituality and recovery for the young teens in his treatment program, using the Twelve Steps of Alcoholics Anonymous as a framework. Although writing for young teens wasn't our forte, our background in comparative spirituality made the Twelve Steps jump out at us as expressing a universal process of transformation—a twelvefold process we'd encountered in other forms. We don't know where Bob is these days, but he got us going, and we're grateful to him for that—at least we think we're grateful.

As we worked on the twelvefold recovery process from a philosophical and spiritual perspective—as well as from the perspective of our personal lives—we realized there was no way recovery could be limited to individuals. Systems are involved, and not only family systems. That's when Judy Delaney, who we think of as one of the "saints of Hazelden" took hold of the idea and kept the book going through its years of development but especially through the tough "recovery books are dead" period, the dark ages of recovery publishing. Although "recovery as fad" has passed, "recovery as personal and cultural transformation interlinked" is just beginning. Judy felt this in her bones, and because of her vision, the project didn't die.

As far as we can tell, Hazelden is fully staffed with saints (or conspirators), as the next person we met was Hazelden's associate publisher, Dan Odegard. He's the one who came up with the book's attention-grabbing title—the ones we'd come up with had all the pizazz of "The Dull Memoirs of Two Philosophers." Both Dan and we thank Marilyn Ferguson for the title of her book, *The Aquarian Conspiracy*, which inspired Dan to purloin it (if you check the dictionary on *purloin*, we prefer "filch" to "steal").

In choosing the word *paradigm* in the title, Dan let our genies out of the bottle. On feedback from others ("it's too technical" or "it's too faddish" or "could you remind me what 'paradigm' means?"), we'd avoided the term, though both of us cut our philosophical teeth in college on Thomas Kuhn's *The Structure of Scientific Revolutions*. Not only being "allowed" but positively goaded into using the term, we were able to push our exploration of the issues further than we'd hoped. Working with Dan has been like coming home to philosophy in the marketplace in the true Socratic spirit: exploring "the perennial philosophy" in relation to the profoundly challenging personal and social issues we're all facing.

Steve Lehman, our editor, is one of those grounding saint/conspirators who wouldn't let us get away with abstractions but wanted to know the specifics. Thanks to him, we had to write about sex (we're not telling which chapter) and statistics (you don't want to know which chapter), names and cases. While doing research on what's going on in our society—the details are more grisly than the generalities—one of us got so depressed that we had to scrap one chapter and struggle with how not to get overwhelmed by today's problems (the results are chapter 9). But researching specifics has also been inspiring. Thanks to Steve, we learned about Aaron Feuerstein of Malden Mills in Methuen, Massachusetts—an extraordinary human being, especially given current business norms. Steve's enthusiasm and big vision has kept us going, even egged us on. We knew he was a kindred spirit when he kept quoting Dickens' *A Christmas Carol* in his letters.

Whenever we've thanked Judy, Dan, or Steve for their encouragement and support, they've typically replied that many others at Hazelden shared their enthusiasm and participated in exploring recovery issues from system, cultural, and paradigm perspectives. This means a great deal to us, as Hazelden has stood for recovery—healing, transformation, and restoration on soul levels—for decades. When we've mentioned to people that Hazelden is the publisher of our book, faces soften and light up, as if we've just mentioned a close friend of theirs. The many saint/conspirators on Hazelden's team are committed long-term to the inner health of the planet, and we're honored to work with them.

All along, we've been inspired by the thirteenth-century Sufi saint, sage, and poet, Jelaluddin Rumi, and the wonderful translations of his poetry by poet Coleman Barks. When we read the poems, we're always amazed at how immediately Rumi touches the soul and captures the essence of recovery.

Coleman Barks has been most generous in allowing us to use his translations, as has Threshold Books (RD 4 Box 600, Putney, Vermont 05346), Maypop Books (196 Westview Drive, Athens, Georgia 30606), and HarperSanFrancisco, a division of HarperCollins, which in 1995 published a beautiful compilation of his translations, entitled *The Essential Rumi.*

We also want to acknowledge our debt to all the thinkers and writers who are doing such interesting "new paradigm" work in so many different fields. Though we haven't met most of these people, we love their books, and we've been transformed, enriched, and helped by their insights. Thanks to the fair use law in publishing—so important to the free exchange of ideas—we're able to include the insights of many of these excellent thinkers and researchers, often in their own words.

We're also grateful for our readers, for whom we believe most if not all of the book will feel like an affirmation of what they've already been thinking. One woman to whom Steve gave a chapter commented after reading it, "So I'm not crazy." The paradigm dimension of recovery is in the air. So is the social system piece of addiction. We know at least one author whose original manuscript on addiction included much more on the social system dynamics that feed personal addictions, but whose publisher required her to take out those sections. Publishers play a critical role in deciding the direction of public discourse. Fortunately, many encourage cutting-edge writers, even though this can be a headache/challenge to their marketing departments—new perspectives don't fit easily into established marketing niches. In the end, though, books succeed by word of mouth, so it's readers who keep both authors and publishers on that cutting edge.

On the home front, we've been greatly assisted both in research and in exploring ideas by many friends and colleagues. In particular, we'd like to thank Linda Brackin, Jeannine Breton, Barbara Cohen, Kim Ewing, Alice Fredericks, Gerard Lennon, Ruth Newman, Carolyn Pontius, John Rudd, Rochelle Samuels, Ashley Wiper, and Helen Woodhull. Helen is our resource for animal rights issues and for alternatives to animal and human testing. Another special thanks goes to Ernie Breton, who, along with providing research assistance, ran up a $200 bill on a computer network trying to find a specific study on management he'd read several years ago claiming that the single character trait the CEOs in the study had in common was their drive, even need, to control. He never did locate the particular article, the main reason being that 16,000 references to management and control popped up. A huge thanks to Laura Holt for keeping us organized—or at least trying.

Most of all, we're grateful to Mary Joy Breton, the book's patron saint. It's no overstatement to say that this book would not exist without her partnership, support, encouragement, hard work, organizational talents, and extraordinary research skills. Beyond that, her profound commitment to consciousness change has both inspired and exemplified the ideas we explore.

And for our sanity—what there is of it—bless you, P. G. Wodehouse, wherever you are.

The following publishers have generously given permission to use extended quotations from copyrighted works. From *Birdsong*, translated by Coleman Barks. ©1993. Reprinted by permission of Maypop, 196 Westview Drive, Athens, GA 30606. From *Delicious Laughter*, translated by Coleman Barks. ©1990. Reprinted by permission of Maypop, 196 Westview Drive, Athens, GA 30606. From *Feeling the Shoulder of the Lion*, translated by Coleman Barks. ©1991. Reprinted by permission of Threshold Books, RD 4 Box 600, Putney, VT 05346. From *One-Handed Basket Weaving*, translated by Coleman Barks. ©1991. Reprinted by permission of Maypop, 196 Westview Drive, Athens, GA 30606. From *Say I Am You*, translated by Coleman Barks. ©1994. Reprinted by permission of Maypop, 196 Westview Drive, Athens, GA 30606. From *We Are Three*, translated by Coleman Barks. ©1987. Reprinted by permission of Maypop, 196 Westview Drive, Athens, GA 30606. From *A Cosmic Book* by Itzhak Bentov with Mirtala, published by Destiny Books, an imprint of Inner Traditions International, Rochester, VT 05767 USA, ©1988 by Mirtala. From *Healing the Shame That Binds You* by John Bradshaw. ©1988. Reprinted by permission of Health Communications. From *Recovering the Soul* by Larry Dossey, M.D. ©1989 by Larry Dossey, M.D. Used by permission of Bantam Books, a division of Bantam Doubleday Dell Publishing Group, Inc. From *Space, Time, and Medicine* by Larry Dossey; ©1982. Reprinted by arrangement with Shambhala Publications, Inc., 300 Massachusetts Avenue, Boston, MA 02115. From Peter Eisner, "Tobacco's Chokehold," *The Nation* magazine. ©1995 by The Nation Company, Inc. Used by permission. From *Adult Children: The Secrets of Dysfunctional Families* by John Friel and Linda Friel. ©1988. Reprinted by permission of Health Communications. From *Dumbing Us Down: The Hidden Curriculum of Compulsory Schooling* by John Taylor Gatto. ©1992. Reprinted by permission of New Society Publishers. From "Out of Bounds" in *Common Boundary* magazine, July/August 1995. ©1995 by Miriam Greenspan. Reprinted by permission. From "When Students Help Run the Schools" by Kevin Kennedy. Winter 1995. ©1995. Reprinted by permission of American News Service. From *When Corporations Rule the World* by David Korten. ©1995. Reprinted by permission of Kumarian Press, Inc., 14 Oakwood Avenue, West Hartford, CT 06119-2127 and Berrett-Koehler Publishers, Inc., 155 Montgomery Street, San Francisco, CA

94104. From *Doing Democracy* by Frances Moore Lappe and Paul Martin Du Bois. Winter 1995. ©1995. Reprinted by permission of Center for Living Democracy. From *Regression Therapy: A Handbook for Professionals, Vol. II* by Winafred Blake Lucas. Reprinted by permission of Deep Forest Press and Winafred Lucas, Ph.D. Reprinted from *World As Lover, World As Self* by Joanna Macy (1991) with permission of Parallax Press, Berkeley, California. From *Twelve-Tribe Nations and the Science of Enchanting the Landscape* by John Michell and Christine Rhone. ©1991. Reprinted by permission of Phanes Press. From *The Light Beyond* by Raymond A. Moody, Jr. ©1988 by Raymond A. Moody, Jr. Used by permission of Bantam Books, a division of Bantam Doubleday Dell Publishing Group, Inc. From *Mutant Message Down Under* by Marlo Morgan. ©1991, 1994 by Marlo Morgan. Reprinted by permission of HarperCollins Publishers, Inc. From *Open Secret: Versions of Rumi*, translated by John Moyne and Coleman Barks. ©1984. Reprinted by permission of Threshold Books, RD 4 Box 600, Putney, VT 05346. From *This Longing*, translated by John Moyne and Coleman Barks. ©1988. Reprinted by permission of Threshold Books, RD 4 Box 600, Putney, VT 05346. From *Unseen Rain*, translated by John Moyne and Coleman Barks. ©1986. Reprinted by permission of Threshold Books, RD 4 Box 600, Putney, VT 05346. From "You Can't High-Jump If the Bar Is Set Low" in *Newsweek*, November 6, 1995. ©1995, Newsweek, Inc. All rights reserved. Reprinted by permission. From "Interview with Deepak Chopra" in *The Noetic Sciences Review*, Winter 1993. Reprinted by permission. 12 Cycles of Truth used as epigraphs from *Sacred Path Cards* by Jamie Sams. ©1990 by Jamie Sams and Linda Childers. Reprinted by permission of HarperCollins Publishers, Inc. From *I Am Wind, You Are Fire: The Life and Works of Rumi* by Annemarie Schimmel. ©1992. Reprinted by arrangement with Shambhala Publications, Inc., 300 Massachusetts Avenue, Boston, MA 02115. From *The Fifth Discipline* by Peter M. Senge. ©1990 by Peter M. Senge. Used by permission of Doubleday, a division of Bantam Doubleday Dell Publishing Group, Inc. From *The Sufis* by Idries Shah. ©1964 by Idries Shah. Used by permission of Doubleday, a division of Bantam Doubleday Dell Publishing Group, Inc. From *Co-Dependence: A Paradoxical Dependency, in Co-Dependence: An Emerging Issue* by Robert Subby and John Friel. ©1984. Reprinted by permission of Health Communications. From *Zen Mind, Beginner's Mind* by Shunrya Suzuki. ©1970. Reprinted by permission of Weatherhill, Inc. Reprinted from *The Heart of Understanding: Commentaries on the Prajñaparamita Heart Sutra* by Thich Nhat Hanh (1988) by permission of Parallax Press, Berkeley, California. From *Co-Dependence: Healing the Human Condition* by Charles Whitfield. ©1991. Reprinted by permission of Health Communications. From *The Tao of Power* by R. L. Wing. ©1986 by Immedia. Used by permission of Doubleday, a division of Bantam Doubleday Dell Publishing Group, Inc.

Hazelden Publishing and Education is a division of the Hazelden Foundation, a not-for-profit organization. Since 1949, Hazelden has been a leader in promoting the dignity and treatment of people afflicted with the disease of chemical dependency.

The mission of the foundation is to improve the quality of life for individuals, families, and communities by providing a national continuum of information, education, and recovery services that are widely accessible; to advance the field through research and training; and to improve our quality and effectiveness through continuous improvement and innovation.

Stemming from that, the mission of the publishing division is to provide quality information and support to people wherever they may be in their personal journey—from education and early intervention, through treatment and recovery, to personal and spiritual growth.

Although our treatment programs do not necessarily use everything Hazelden publishes, our bibliotherapeutic materials support our mission and the Twelve Step philosophy upon which it is based. We encourage your comments and feedback.

The headquarters of the Hazelden Foundation is in Center City, Minnesota. Additional treatment facilities are located in Chicago, Illinois; New York, New York; Plymouth, Minnesota; St. Paul, Minnesota; and West Palm Beach, Florida. At these sites, we provide a continuum of care for men and women of all ages. Our Plymouth facility is designed specifically for youth and families.

*For more information on Hazelden, please call **1-800-257-7800**. Or you may access our World Wide Web site on the Internet at **http://www.Hazelden.org**.*

Recovery:
The Art of Paradigm Shifts

> It's time for us to join the line
> of your madmen, all chained together.
>
> Time to be totally free,
> and estranged....
>
> To set fire to structures
> and run out in the street.
>
> Time to ferment. How else
> can we leave the world-vat
> and go to the lip?
>
> We must die to become
> true human beings.
>
> Rumi[1]

THE GLOBAL CRISIS OF ADDICTIONS

Caught in deadly processes. Recovery: it's not just for "addicts" anymore. It's not even just for persons, not when addictive processes permeate every social system we've got, from schools to churches to workplaces to governments. We're up to our ears in addict-making processes, and we can't take two steps out of bed without running into them.

Substance addictions. Substance addictions—alcohol, drugs, nicotine, food, caffeine—are just the surface, the outward and visible ways addictive processes come get us. And they do get us. Drugs, alcohol, and tobacco

1

constitute the world's biggest economic empire. Only the weapons industry rivals it. Journalist James Mills writes in *The Underground Empire:*

> The inhabitants of earth spend more money on illegal drugs than they spend on food. More than they spend on housing, clothes, education, medical care, or any other product or service. The international narcotics industry is the largest growth industry in the world. Its annual revenues exceed half a trillion dollars—three times the value of all United States currency in circulation, more than the gross national products of all but a half dozen major industrialized nations.*

That's just illegal drugs. How about the money involved in dependence on prescribed drugs, alcohol, and nicotine? It seems we can't afford not to be substance dependent; our economies certainly are.

Process addictions. Next in the line of killers are process addictions, the ones society applauds: addiction to working, winning, high stress, fast-track jobs, perfectionism, relationships, making money, spending and debting, gaining power, getting fame or notoriety, living out family dramas, or—brace yourself—shopping. Sex can be another process addiction, but it's not one society looks kindly on, however much advertising promotes insatiable and manipulative sex as the solution to life's challenges.† Gambling is an old addiction which, with all the state lotteries, is coming back now with a vengeance, especially among young people.

Even the most lauded activities—religion, scientific study, academic inquiry, and government service—may take on classic addictive patterns. Religion turns into obsession. Scientific study turns into dogma, as if collecting enough facts will make up for a narrow worldview. Academic inquiry becomes an in-your-head addiction—quibbling esoterica with rabid acrimony, fiddling while Rome burns. As for government service, it's power

---

*James Mills, *The Underground Empire: Where Crime and Governments Embrace* (New York: Doubleday, 1986), 3. His figures being over ten years old, we can only imagine what they may be now. Statistics on this global empire are hard to come by, many estimates being filed away in secret and classified government documents (see p. 7).

†Patrick Carnes has pioneered the understanding of sexual addiction, which has a wide spectrum of manifestations. See *Out of the Shadows: Understanding Sexual Addiction* (Center City, MN: Hazelden, 1992) and *Contrary to Love: Helping the Sexual Addict* (Center City, MN: Hazelden, 1989).

addiction from the bureaucrats who throw around their paper-pushing weight to the big-timers who become brokers for corporate conglomerates.

Process addictions are every bit as deadly as substance addictions, because they underlie substance addictions—as well as just about every social and global ill we've got. They're the invisible killers, the ones we don't suspect, but the ones that made *millionaire* Ivan Boesky raid savings and loans to become a *billionaire*, leaving in his wake thousands who saw their life savings disappear. As Boesky was later to admit, "It's a sickness I have in the face of which I am helpless." Nor was Boesky alone in his sickness. Since the eighties, we've witnessed an army of greed-addicted corporate raiders, who made the jobs and pension funds of millions vanish overnight.*

Process addictions aren't limited to movers and shakers though. Ordinary folks following the right diet and the right exercise program are dropping dead at age thirty-five from workaholism, relationship addiction, anxiety, and stress.

If all these substance and process addictions don't afflict us, they nonetheless affect us. While addictions to drugs, food, alcohol, sex, or work hit us one by one, addictions to money,† control, divisiveness, status, and official-think oppress us together. We can't have power addicts running the world and not experience the consequences. Even when we try to claim it's business or government as usual, we find ourselves suffering from global plagues made invisible by their familiarity.

But a familiar plague is no less deadly. As Anne Wilson Schaef points out, a deadly virus is a deadly virus, even if the entire population has it. Alcoholics Anonymous (AA) holds that addiction is a "progressive, fatal disease." Schaef believes—and we agree—that this is true, no matter what form the addiction takes.² Our lungs may give out from tar and nicotine, or our hearts may give out from stress. We may die from the greed that destroys the environment or from a nuclear chain reaction set off by someone's power

---

*In *When Corporations Rule the World*, David C. Korten reports: "Nearly 2,000 cases have been identified in which the new owners [corporate raiders] have virtually stolen a total of $21 billion of what they often declare to be 'excess' funding from company pension accounts to apply to debt repayment" (West Hartford, CT: Kumarian Press, 1995), 209.

†See Donna Boundy's excellent analysis of this in *When Money Is the Drug: The Compulsion for Credit, Cash, and Chronic Debt* (San Francisco: HarperSanFrancisco, 1993).

play. Addiction—substance or process, acted out privately or on the world stage—is a fatal illness that we ignore at our peril.

Not that this is news. We can't read the papers or watch TV without wondering, What on earth is going on? We have the knowledge and technology. We have the resources, human and natural. We even have the desire. Why can't our social, economic, and environmental problems be solved? Why do we live from crisis to crisis?

Addict-making systems. Neither substance nor process addictions are limited to one race, sex, economic class, region, or occupation. Rich and poor, conservative and liberal, male and female, Hispanic, European, African, Asian, and Native Americans share the same disease.

When something so deadly cuts across society, we have to look at what we share: our social systems. In her 1987 ground-breaking book *When Society Becomes an Addict*, Anne Wilson Schaef suggests family dynamics, school rules, workplace policies and practices, corporate hierarchies, government workings, media messages, as well as cultural and religious belief structures all operate in ways that set us up to behave addictively. In fact, society itself, Schaef writes, "is an addictive system."[3]

That's a strong statement, yet the more we understand addiction, the more it seems like an understatement. Award-winning teacher John Taylor Gatto, for instance, pulls no punches about the messages schools send through their structure: "I began to realize that the bells and the confinement, the crazy sequences, the age-segregation, the lack of privacy, the constant surveillance, and all the rest of the national curriculum of schooling were designed exactly as if someone had set out to *prevent* children from learning how to think and act, to coax them into addiction and dependent behavior."[4]

In *When Money Is the Drug*, counselor and writer Donna Boundy sketches a similarly addict-making picture for corporations. The level of thinking distortion that takes over people in these systems is astonishing:

> For money-accumulators, huge sums take on an unreal quality, become distorted. One commodities trader reportedly flew into a rage when he got his monthly bonus check, stormed into his boss's office, threw the check on the floor, and spat on it. The check was for $2.1 million, but he thought it wasn't enough. Even J. Paul Getty once admitted, "I've never felt rich—in

the oil business others were all much richer than I was."

Even corporations sometimes behave as if their thinking has become distorted. While the Wall Street firm of Drexel Burnham Lambert was nearing bankruptcy, some executives still received million-dollar bonuses every month. In fact, as the firm's condition worsened, the bonuses grew larger. Less than a month before the firm filed bankruptcy, one executive received a bonus of $16.6 million. The company itself was acting like an addict, denying and defying reality.[5]

THE PARADIGM CONSPIRACY

What's going on? Why are systems betraying their service to us? Instead of performing their rightful functions of educating (schools), nurturing (families), promoting public good (governments), managing the shared household (businesses), and inspiring us to find and fulfill our life's purpose (religious institutions), they're abusing us and turning us into people we never wanted to be. Why?

Enter "paradigms." Back in 1962—so long ago John Kennedy was still alive—historian and philosopher of science Thomas Kuhn gave an analysis of how systems change (or don't) in his book *The Structure of Scientific Revolutions* that rocked the intellectual world. He wasn't talking about addictive systems but about the system of scientific research, which has its own brand of obsessive-compulsive behavior.

Introducing the term "paradigm," Kuhn said that scientists operate from mental models—paradigms—that shape everything they think, feel, and do. How scientists perceive and interpret experience is shaped by their internal structure of beliefs and concepts—their paradigm. If something is wrong, the paradigm is the place to look to find out why.

To raise paradigm issues is to reflect on the ideas or concepts we're using as our map of reality—our worldview, life perspective, philosophy, or mental model. Whatever we call it, it's powerful stuff. To look at our paradigm is to look at the blueprint we're using to build our worlds.*

---

*For instance, in his 1995 social critique *Opposing the System*, Charles Reich suggests that "the System" presents us with a paradigm through the use of images: the "free market," the "private sector," the "welfare mother," the "predatory criminal." Reich maintains that "an entire ideology can be rendered as a series of pictures making up a comprehensive

How do paradigms start? They usually begin with some exemplary model—"Newtonian science" or "Einsteinian relativity"—that weaves together theories, standards, and methods in a way that makes better sense than anything else. To share a paradigm is to share a commitment to rules that define how a scientist acts and reacts. No part of scientific activity is outside the reach of the paradigm's influence. It's as if scientists' energies get poured through the paradigm's mold, and whatever comes out is stamped by that all-encompassing model.

In the decades since Kuhn's paradigm concept was introduced, it has been applied to every discipline, from the arts to business. And rightly so. We experience our lives the way we do because of the paradigms we carry around. In computer terms, paradigms function like the central operating system of consciousness—the supra-program that transforms undefined perceptions into something we call our experience. They give us the mental tools to make sense of life and survive in it. We may not be able to summarize our paradigm in ten words or less, but our every thought is paradigm connected, even paradigm created.

Development within a paradigm. Given the power of paradigms, two kinds of development follow. The first occurs within the paradigm's framework. The second chucks the paradigm and forges a new one.

"Normal science," as Kuhn calls it, is the first kind of development. Practitioners operate within their mental model and pursue its implications to the nth degree. Working inside the prevailing paradigm is the secure, accepted, and well-rewarded way to do science.

In fact, the paradigm gets so comfortable that scientists forget that it's there; it becomes functionally invisible. The way they see things is just the way things are. For them, there is no paradigm between their ideas and reality.

Applied to life, the normal-science phase is business as usual, families as usual, politics, churches, schools, and professions as usual. When we're ticking away within a paradigm's framework, the norm is well defined, and we conform. Coping skills mean finding ways to fit into the norm, whether it's

---

map of reality. Constantly repeated without rebuttal or dissent, these pictures and the map [paradigm] they form set the parameters of debate and imagination" Charles Reich, *Opposing the System* (New York: Crown Publishers, 1995), 154.

healthy or not. In fact, "healthy" is whatever the paradigm says it is. Becoming healthy means adjusting to the paradigm's definition.

Paradigm shifts. The revolutionary development comes when the paradigm reaches a crisis. It doesn't solve problems the way it once did. Anomalies—things that the paradigm can't explain—start accumulating. Paradigm health starts making us sick. More and more, the paradigm doesn't work. That's when scientists are challenged to shift paradigms by moving into a phase Kuhn calls "extraordinary science."

But "extraordinary science" isn't easy. In language suited to academia, Kuhn describes how scientists essentially freak out. Everything they ever learned is called into question. During the revolutions in physics early in this century, even Einstein, no slouch in forward thinking, wrote, "It was as if the ground had been pulled out from under one, with no firm foundation to be seen anywhere, upon which one could have built."[6]

The more the paradigm fails to do its job, the more old-paradigm scientists try to make it work. The paradigm is ripe for a revolution, but because they've forgotten that they even have a paradigm, scientists conclude instead that their world is falling apart. Solutions—alternative ways of doing science—don't exist. As far as they're concerned, they've explored all the possibilities, and the only options they see don't help. They're too paradigm-bound to notice that they're stumbling over the limits of their own models.

The paradigm cause of soul-abusive systems. "Extraordinary science" describes the situation we face today. We're not experiencing paradigm norms as healthy, either personally or globally. The blueprint for our families, schools, businesses, and governments isn't working. It's causing our shared social systems to function abusively and to make us sick as a result. Happy people and healthy systems don't turn addictive, life-destroying substances into the biggest growth industry on the planet.

We'd think changing a paradigm that's not working would be easy, but it's not. As Kuhn observed, the paradigm cause of crises remains invisible to old-paradigm practitioners. We don't need a new paradigm, they believe, we just need to make the one we have work better. Nothing is wrong with our social systems, since that would call the underlying paradigm into question. Instead, when things don't work, something must be wrong with us.

"Blame certain people and label them as the troublemakers. We need more discipline, more restraints," old-paradigm experts advise us, "more tests and tougher grading systems, more hard-nosed business management practices, more God-fearing, sex-repressing piety, and more laws with stricter enforcement."

In other words, according to the prevailing paradigm, coming down hard on people isn't abuse. It's how we create healthy families, schools, businesses, governments, and churches, because it rids us of the sinful, ignorant, or otherwise unruly souls that muck up the social machinery. If things don't work, the solution is to take away more rights, stifle more creativity, intimidate more people, build more prisons, and bring back the death penalty. More fear keeps people in line.

This paradigm touches every part of our lives—but invisibly. We don't realize that the paradigm is there, which means we don't recognize its role in creating our social institutions. As long as the paradigm remains hidden, we don't see what's causing system-wide suffering, which means we can't stop it.

The paradigm of control and power-over. What kind of paradigm requires that we blame individuals, intimidate, and punish them in order to keep our social systems "healthy"? Like a complex tapestry, the paradigm has many threads, but the overall pattern has to do with control: Who has power over whom, and how is a power-over relation maintained?* Riane Eisler, in her pioneering work *The Chalice and the Blade* calls this the "dominator model," contrasting it with the "partnership way." Domination is the paradigm's driving issue, and for a reason: in this worldview, top-down control is necessary for social order.

According to the power-over model—what we refer to as the control paradigm—if somebody doesn't control us, our social systems will fall into chaos. Archaeologist John Romer notes, for instance, that the Roman Emperor Diocletian, in an attempt to hold "a ramshackle empire" together, "made a state where animals, land and people were all tightly organized and

---

*Riane Eisler's books, *The Chalice and the Blade* (HarperSanFrancisco, 1988) and (with David Loye) *The Partnership Way* (HarperSanFrancisco, 1990) contrast the dominator model with the partnership model, suggesting as we do that the former makes humans suffer, while the latter, both historically and culturally, allows humans to thrive.

controlled; one writer complained that there were more tax collectors than tax payers."[7] Like Diocletian, authorities of today believe that nothing would work if we each did our own thing. To have order, we must do what the authorities tell us to do.

Soul: The big threat. Now come the threads: to be controlled, we have to be unplugged from competing sources of control. The major threat to external control is our internal guidance system—our souls.

A clear definition of "soul" isn't easy to come by, since it's not an object we can measure or photograph. But "inner identity" or the "core of who we are" are good places to start. Soul refers to our deep presence. It's our inner connectedness to whatever we take to be Being, God, the One, the whole, or the ground of creation (to paraphrase theologian Paul Tillich). Physician Larry Dossey describes the soul as "some aspect of ourselves that is infinite, beyond the limits of space and time."[8] It's our direct link to reality.

This whole-connected core is the source of our talents and the wellspring of creativity. It's also what gives us the conviction that our lives have meaning. When we live from our souls, we feel alive and vital, and we take seriously the idea that we're here for a purpose.

To us, our souls are our best friends and most trusted guides. But to the control paradigm, they're the enemy—what has to be removed in order for external control to work. Only when we're sufficiently disconnected from our inner compass will we follow outer demands.

"Get rid of the troublemakers." For fear of chaos, social systems adopt the control paradigm and run with it. Through all sorts of institutionalized policies, we get the message that we're unacceptable as we are, but that if we surrender ourselves to the social system (the family, school, business, profession, or religion), we'll become acceptable. Our souls are sloppy and unmanageable troublemakers; they clog the system's efficient workings, and we're better off without them.

This isn't reality talking; it's a paradigm—an old one. Maybe sometime in the dim, dark recesses of human evolution a control-based paradigm may have served the species (we're skeptical about that), but it's not serving us now. The more power-over systems zap our inner lives, the less social order we have. It's a paradigm in crisis, and it's creating neither personal nor global health.

Two paradigm conspiracies. As long as the paradigm remains invisible, we're stuck. The prevailing model stymies change. Every time we try to move in a new direction, the old paradigm kicks in and intimidates us into doing the same old, soul-diminishing stuff.

That's the first paradigm conspiracy, the one that blocks our best efforts to confront crises and change.

But one paradigm conspiracy deserves another—the leap into "extraordinary science." True, paradigm shifts are full of uncertainties, trials and errors, hiccups and false starts, not to mention soul-searching forays into the unknown. We never know if we've come up with the "right" paradigm or even if there is such a thing. In extraordinary science, we let everything go into flux. Yet nothing conspires to change our world so completely as doing precisely that.

The most conspiratorial part of a paradigm shift is that it lies within the power of each of us to do it. Paradigms aren't Godzilla monsters; they're ideas. Their power comes from our shared commitment to them. The minute one person starts to explore alternative models, the paradigm no longer holds the same power.

As Marilyn Ferguson explained in *The Aquarian Conspiracy*, the word *conspiracy* comes from *conspirare*, which means "to breathe together." A new cultural paradigm begins with each person stepping out of the old and daring to breathe something new. The "movers and shakers" are powerless to prevent a paradigm shift once we together breathe a paradigm revolution into being.

MAKING THE SHIFT: BY DEATH OR BY RECOVERY?

Paradigm shifts are scary precisely because we don't know what's next. Control-paradigm authorities claim that soul-guided worlds aren't possible—that they degenerate into anarchy. Challenging this cultural belief involves a leap of faith. Our souls are what the old paradigm systematically pushed out of our lives, and we're not sure what it means to get them back or how our lives together would work if we did.

Given all these uncertainties, how are we ever going to make the paradigm shift that's needed? Are we stuck with the old model?

Plan A: Death. Kuhn believed that paradigms permeate our consciousness so thoroughly that the only way to get rid of them is for old-paradigm practitioners to die off. Kuhn wasn't recommending drastic measures; as a historian he was just describing what happens.

We can appreciate his observation, especially when we run head-on into control-paradigm types in power-over positions. But as a method, it lacks practicality, particularly if you buy the notion of reincarnation, e.g., what if Hitler was Caligula or Genghis Khan reborn? A power addict's death may not be the long-term solution it seems. If that's Plan A, what's Plan B?

Plan B: Recovery. In a way, Alcoholics Anonymous agrees with Kuhn. Addict-making paradigms lead to death. Either we let a paradigm die, or we die under the addictive model. One way or another, as the apostle Paul said, "I die daily," or as Jelaluddin Rumi (1207–1273 C.E.), the great Sufi mystic, sage, and poet, observed, "We must die to become true human beings."

But what kind of death will it be? Physical death is one way to experience a paradigm shift. Dying to a deadening paradigm is another.

For decades, AA—joined now by a host of programs focusing on specific addictions—has pioneered recovery through support groups and a Twelve Step process with a better track record than any other treatment program. It's not a crutch or for losers; it's a healing process for people committed to inner transformation. The reason it works is that it invites people to experience their personal paradigm in crisis and then to embark on the journey of "extraordinary science"—to evolve their own new models.

The limits of micro recovery. But there's a snag with doing recovery on the personal level alone. How can we get healthy when our systems are sick? In paradigm language, how can we make the paradigm revolution that our souls require as long as our cultural paradigm conspires to sabotage our shift?

As it is, our social systems reward soul-negating habits—those that blast our innate worth, creativity, and spirituality—and penalize people who put inner-directedness first. To take a common example, salaried employees who work on weekends get top performance ratings, while those who choose to spend that time with their families or, heaven forbid, to "have a life" are evaluated as mediocre by comparison. They're not "going the extra mile" for the company, which means their choice *not* to be workaholics costs them career advancement.

As long as social systems operate on a control paradigm, they reinforce habits that put soul needs last, because that's how we're controllable. Those who are "hungry enough" rise to the top; those less insatiable stay down in the ranks, though their battered self-esteem often leads to addiction as well.

No matter how committed we are to making a personal paradigm shift, how can we do it if our shared systems don't come with us? Sick paradigms make sick institutions that make sick people—and then reward us for not noticing how sick we've become.

One Nazi doctor, for example, spoke of his relationship to the system and the overpowering "authority of the regime," especially when he contemplated getting out. We've heard the same message, whether the system was a family, a church, a nonprofit, or a corporation: "The whole system radiated that authority. Like it or not, I was part of it.... I had no choice. I was in this web—this network of authority.... If you talk to people [in general terms about possibly leaving], they would say, you have to stay wherever you are,... where you are needed. Don't disturb the organization."[9]

Getting to the paradigm cause of social illness. AA's response to the dilemma between personal recovery and social illness has been to conceive of recovery as a lifelong process—a point on which it's been criticized, as if AA labels people as lifelong addicts. But who's being chronic here? People do their best to break out of addictive habits. It's the social systems that resist, because the control paradigm hiding in the shadows won't allow system-wide transformation to occur.

Micro recovery is undoubtedly where paradigm revolution starts. Exploring our own internalized habits of self-abuse is how we understand abusive processes and trace them to their origins. Getting to the root of these patterns, we question the paradigm behind them and move away from it.

But even if every traumatized person on earth were in a recovery program, global addiction still would not stop. The social systems requiring us to behave in soul-disconnected ways must also change. And no matter how hard we try to change social systems, they won't budge until we tackle the belief structures, rules, methods, and goals—the paradigm—that require "soul loss," as shamanic traditions call it, to create a "healthy" society.

Micro without macro recovery is where most recovery people are these days. We're dealing with original-family as well as self-esteem issues, which means we're challenging the power-over, soul-be-damned messages we got while growing up. We're doing our best to make a personal paradigm shift and to honor our souls in ways that were never modeled for us.

But as if this personal work isn't hard enough, we're living in systems that persist in the soul-excising model. Personal recovery can feel like one step forward and two steps back because, as we reconnect with our souls, we feel the soul-demeaning messages coming from institutions that much more intensely. Messages that, for instance, constantly measure our worth according to dollars, sales, deals, commissions, productivity but never in terms of fairness, compassion, responsibility, honesty, or integrity grind away at us. In control-paradigm systems, we're not human beings on quests for meaning; we're money-making, job-doing machines.

It's time all the wisdom gained from wrestling with personal abuse is focused on the root of the problem: addictive social systems and the control paradigm behind them. Recovery won't bring wholeness until it percolates down to the paradigm level, because recovery is nothing less than the art of making a paradigm shift.

As Kuhn observed, such a shift is revolutionary not to a piece of life but to all of it. The social system piece can't sit this one out.

WHAT RECOVERY IS AND ISN'T

What have we learned about paradigm shifting from our recovery experiences on the micro level?

It's holistic. Above all, that it's holistic. We're learning to conceive of ourselves as processes related to wider processes related to the big picture—the whole of creation. Our personal traumas are not unrelated to the systems around us, because we've adopted their paradigm as our own. How our social systems "think" has become how we think as well. The illness we experience from a sick paradigm is not therefore our personal problem alone, though we suffer personally. It's system-born.

It's not about fixing bad people. As a result, though each of us experiences recovery differently, it's safe to say recovery is not about making flawed or defective people okay again. There's not something wrong with us that we feel soul loss. There's something right with us that we notice the wounding of our inner lives and that we can't tolerate it.

It's not about getting rid of bad habits. Neither is recovery about correcting a few bad habits. That's a fragmented view, one that misses the paradigm perspective entirely. The symptoms of soul loss are precisely that: symptoms. We can drug them away, but the drugging won't restore our inner connectedness. Nor will it address the system issue. Drugging away the symptoms of a paradigm in crisis enables a sick paradigm to stay in power.

It's not about becoming "normal." Recovery is certainly not about going back to normal, since "normal" is defined by the very paradigm that causes soul sickness. If anything, family, school, church, or business life "as usual" causes addictions.

Not blame but accountability

Blame vs. responsibility. Nor is recovery—and this is a biggie—about blaming other people or systems to avoid personal responsibility. In fact, the paradigm approach addresses this issue head-on. By looking at our own and society's behavior from a paradigm perspective, we name who does what and why on all levels. That means we take responsibility for our participation in abusive processes. But it also means that we name the abusive processes that we've experienced around us.

On a personal level, if we catch ourselves acting out our own abuse, we take responsibility for our actions. We work to discover what we need to resolve and what amends we need to make.

At the same time, we recognize that we've been abused by others, and we name the abusers. Just as we claim responsibility for what we've done, we hold others accountable for what they've done. We're responsible and they're responsible. And the people who abused them are responsible.

To this personal level, a paradigm approach adds two other levels: *the systems that create interpersonal abuse and the paradigm that creates abusive systems.* With this approach, nothing gets off the hook. We name what's responsible as deeply as the responsibility goes.

There's a reason for doing this. Identifying abusive systems and the control paradigm behind them gives us leverage to change the entire lot. We expose the paradigm behind our social systems and challenge the system-wide abuse that it creates.

The blame dodge. Of course, to get off the hook, control-paradigm systems claim that they're being "blamed." But as Alice Miller points out in *Banished Knowledge*, that's a dodge. It's like calling journalists who tell the truth about corporate and governmental misconduct "muckrakers." Systems and their authorities protect themselves by taking no responsibility for the consequences of their behavior. They don't want the consequences known, and if it becomes known, they're not responsible.

The cry "You're just blaming others!" is therefore a trick for keeping control-paradigm systems in place. Like "Do you still beat your spouse?" the cry builds on two fallacious assumptions: (1) that in any situation, only one person or institution can be held accountable, and (2) if we hold someone *else* accountable besides ourselves, that gets *us* off the hook. In fact, more than one person or institution may be responsible—and often is—and just because we want accountability from the people and systems around us doesn't mean we are evading our personal responsibility.

A paradigm approach considers responsibility all around.

The infamous Triangle Shirtwaist Company fire. For example, in March 1911 a fire in New York's Triangle Shirtwaist Company killed 146 young women and seriously injured another 70. Isaac Harris and Max Blanck's non-union business on the eighth, ninth, and tenth floors of the Asch Building housed 600 cutters and seamstresses, packed together on floors littered with cloth and tissue paper soaked in oil from the sewing machines. There were no adequate fire exits on the eighth and ninth floors, only narrow staircases leading to two ground-level exits, a single hose (rotten, as it turned out) and one water bucket on each floor for fire prevention, a narrow fire escape and—most telling—bolts on the *outside* of the doors to keep "the girls from slipping out of the workroom for a few minutes' rest break and thus wasting the company's time." This was a typical loft factory, which Fire Chief Edward Croker had repeatedly warned city authorities about, especially since his fire department's ladders extended only six floors.

Shortly after the fire started, most of the escape routes failed, especially for ninth-floor workers. A passing policeman saved many eighth-floor employees by forcing open a door that, bodies pressed against it, had rendered unopenable from within. From the tenth-floor management office, Blanck and his visiting family, warned by a switchboard operator, easily escaped by taking a ladder to an adjoining roof. Though New York University students from a next-door building tried to help the trapped workers, Blanck was nowhere to be seen. He made no effort to unlock the bolt on the outside, and many workers died in the stairwell.

"A shock of horror hit the American public when the story of this disaster became known," wrote Hugh Clevely, one of many journalists to write books on the fire. "At once the question was asked, who was to blame? The answer seemed to be that everybody was to blame, and nobody was to blame."

While officials scrambled to pass the buck, Blanck and Harris were acquitted of first-degree manslaughter, the judge instructing the jury that the two could not be found guilty unless it was proven that they knew of the locked door at the time of the fire. After their acquittal, Blanck and Harris said that "they'd done all that was legally required, and if that wasn't enough, it wasn't their fault. It was the fault of the city government."*

---

*Hugh Clevely, *Famous Fires* (New York: John Day, 1958), 46–53. Though famous for no one's accepting responsibility, the 1911 fire isn't just ancient history. The first 1992 issue of the *National Fire Protection Association (NFPA) Journal* lamented a 1991 North Carolina chicken-processing-plant fire which killed twenty-five and injured fifty-four of the estimated ninety occupants. The October 1991 issue of *Occupational Health & Safety* added, "As workers tried to escape the fire, they found most of the fire exits locked or blocked. … According to witnesses, the door of the plant canteen was locked and had to be smashed so those inside could escape, the loading dock door was blocked by a truck, and a reporter found a padlock on a door labeled 'Fire Door—Do Not Block.'"

The operations manager of the plant—also the son of the owner—said he "was unaware of any locked doors." Was this just something that hadn't come up before? *Occupational Health & Safety's* November 1991 issue reported that the company "had been fined $2,560 in 1987 for safety violations that included inadequate fire exits that were either poorly marked or blocked." Unfortunately for workers, Peg Seminario, director of safety and health for the AFL-CIO, added that the "deplorable conditions" in the plant "are not unique to...the poultry industry...(or) North Carolina. The awful truth is that such unsafe and unhealthful working conditions exist in work places in every state in this country." *Occupational Health & Safety* first covered this in October 1991 (vol. 60, no. 10), p. 10; Seminario is quoted in the November 1991 issue (vol. 60, no. 11), pp. 10–11; the fate of the owner—plea bargaining a twenty-year sentence to get his son off, but eligible for parole in three years—is described in the April 1992 (vol. 61, no. 14) issue, p. 8, and the October 1992 issue (vol. 61, no. 10), pp. 20–21. The *NFPA* journal's analysis of the fire by Thomas Klem with comments by fire data specialist Alison Miller is in the January/February 1992 issue (vol. 86, no. 1), pp. 29–34. Our thanks to John Rudd for research on this section.

Paradigm accountability. A paradigm approach doesn't buy it. Accountability goes all around: individuals are held accountable, social institutions are held accountable, and the paradigm inspiring inhuman practices is held accountable.

But the paradigm most of all, since that's the root. It creates the context in which such tragedies become inevitable: the profit-at-all-costs business philosophy, the cynical attitude of owners and bureacrats toward "the working masses," and the Scrooge-like contempt of owners like Blanck and Harris, whose inhumanity springs from being treated inhumanly themselves. The paradigm that creates abuse is dragged onto center stage. If a paradigm requires doing emotional violence to individuals from the time they're born and institutionalizes humiliation as the way to achieve social order, then tragedies are bound to follow.

With a paradigm approach, we understand the likes of Blanck and Harris. This doesn't mean they're not accountable. It means that all of us, including the perpetrators, have been abused into accepting an abusive model and bear responsibility for how we've acted under it.

PERSONAL RECOVERY AS A PERSONAL PARADIGM SHIFT

But with responsibility comes choice. We can choose to shift models, and that's what recovery as a paradigm shift is all about.

At a personal level, recovery means making a profound shift in our personal operating system—our own personal paradigm. This shift includes at least three stages:

1. Experiencing soul pain as our paradigm in crisis and acknowledging it as such. Shifts in our model of consciousness usually start with pain. We become aware that something is hurting us. Acknowledging pain, not pushing it aside, is the first step in transformation.

Granted, this doesn't sound like fun. But if we don't feel pain in the body, for instance, we can't protect ourselves, much less heal. Pain gives us the feedback we need to get self-healing processes going. It tells us there's something wrong, even when the people and systems around us say everything is okay.

The trick with recovery is to trace pain back not to people or to circumstances but to a paradigm that makes all of us less than who we are. In

Kuhn's language, pain invites us to question our paradigm—to make the leap from normal to extraordinary science. It's the fire-alarm bell to life as usual. When it goes off, we can either blame the bell and muffle it with a towel (normal science), or we can see there's a fire in the house and get the hell out (extraordinary science).

Feeling pain is especially important to the paradigm shift that recovery involves. Pain connects us with something real—something genuinely us. Soul-ties are exactly what the control paradigm tries to sever by telling us that our deep feelings are unacceptable. By acknowledging our pain—feeling what we feel and accepting the wisdom of our feelings—we go against control-paradigm conditioning. The moment we listen to our souls, even if it's pain they're communicating, we're no longer under the old paradigm's control. The shift is already starting to happen.

What kind of pain are we talking about? Deep, gut stuff—the pain we experience as a result of being poured through the control paradigm's mold. When external demands take precedence over our right to be soul connected, outer noises drown out inner voices—to borrow African American studies scholar Na'im Akbar's theme in *The Community of Self*—and we lose touch with our core being. We even "come to fear the inner voices," Akbar writes, "because they tell the truth about us."[10] This is soul pain, the pain of being disconnected from who we are.

Psychotherapist Charles L. Whitfield describes relationship addiction, for instance, as "a disease of lost selfhood....When we focus so much outside of ourselves, we lose touch with what is inside of us."[11] One of our clients who came to us depressed, verging on suicidal, and on eleven different prescribed drugs complained that he couldn't convince his psychiatrists that he hadn't lost his mind; he'd lost his soul. That's soul pain pushing for a paradigm shift, with a team of "normal scientists" throwing towels over the alarm bell.

Unfortunately, soul loss is hard to escape—and even harder to acknowledge—in a society dominated by a paradigm that regards our souls as the enemy. When we're in pain, we don't mind a few towels thrown our way. To survive in families, schools, churches, and businesses, we put aside who we are and become what people and systems expect. For the sake of measuring up to the control paradigm's notion of health, we sacrifice our soul-connectedness.

When the pain gets to us, we resort to addictions. Feeling pain is threatening—it threatens our commitment to the control paradigm—so we're trained to silence it: "Buck up and do your duty!" "Fit in!" "What's wrong with you today?" "Be happy!" "Smile!" There's no place for feelings, especially so-called unpleasant ones, in rules/roles/systems-governed life. To avoid them, we plunge ourselves into work, hobbies, churches, and families, numbing any rumblings of discontent with food, alcohol, shopping, or drugs. We try to make up for what's missing—to dull the pain of soul loss. Maybe we can make the control paradigm work.

But it doesn't work, and the pain doesn't go away. We struggle with addictive behavior not because we're bad but because we're good: our inner core is good, and we've lost access to it. We feel pain because we've been coerced into surrendering our souls to systems that demand power over us, and we don't like it.

Even when we comply, we can't surrender our souls and not notice the loss. If anything, it's the sensitive, intelligent part of us that feels soul denial most and tolerates it least. With our inner lives driven into hiding, we experience our paradigm in crisis.

Accepting pain and what it says about the paradigm we're living is the first step in making a paradigm shift.

2. Spiritual awakening. But the shift doesn't stop there. Recovery is also about soul awakening. Spiritual teachings insist that the greatest treasures in the world lie within. Through our inner lives, we have access both to the wisdom of the universe and to the wisdom embedded within our own consciousness and bodies.

The recovery process connects us with our inner wisdom resources. In paradigm language, it introduces us to a paradigm that puts soul at the center—not the control-paradigm-created ego, but the soul that's one with All That Is.

In a now-famous letter to Bill Wilson, the co-founder of Alcoholics Anonymous, Carl Jung wrote: "Craving for alcohol [is] the equivalent, on a low level, of the spiritual thirst of our being for wholeness, expressed in medieval language: the union with God."[12] We thirst for who we are in the whole context, not as a control paradigm defines us.

Recovery, then, is the profound shift to a paradigm that honors who we are and unveils our truth underneath the roles we've assumed. Supported by a paradigm of soul-connectedness, we come to trust our inner self enough to follow it on a path of spiritual awakening.

By going within, we do the very thing forbidden by the control paradigm. If we no longer look outside ourselves for riches, we're no longer controllable.

3. Creativity. As we make a paradigm shift, we experience an explosion of creativity. The old-paradigm lid is off. Options aren't automatically excluded for control reasons. Old mental tapes that tell us how inadequate we are, how we'll never amount to anything, or how we have to behave to survive are silenced.

Stepping out of the control-defined norm, we start doing what we love and following our inner light. Without the control paradigm shutting us down, we discover what it is to participate in creative processes. Inner resources emerge that we didn't know we had. Instead of forcing our energies into established, soul-excluding channels, we allow our innate creativity to reshape our lives from the ground up.

Not stopping with personal paradigm shifts

Social systems: The means of control. But again, there's a snag to the success of personal paradigm shifting—the system snag. We aren't the only ones that the control paradigm affected. Human beings were the objects of control, but social systems became the means of control. Their purpose has been subverted just as much as ours has been. Instead of supporting our spiritual awakening, our social systems—families, schools, professions, governments, religions—function as emissaries of the control paradigm, sent to render us controllable.

Starting life at their mercy, we become insecure, driven by fear and shame, and dependent on external approval for self-worth. There's little room for individuality in a control model, since individuality is potentially threatening to the established order. It's up to our social systems to drive it out of us—to make us obedient and compliant.

Consequently, being stuck in self-abusive patterns isn't our doing. This isn't passing the buck; it's thinking holistically and understanding the interconnectedness of systems. Rosemary's baby excepted, human beings don't set out to be abusers, either of themselves or of others. They're not born sexist, racist, greedy, or power-obsessed. As Lieutenant Cable says in *South*

Pacific, "It's not born in you. It comes after you're born."

Soul-violating family systems. Since the recovery movement has emerged from a psychotherapeutic background, the main system-abuser that's been analyzed is the family system. By studying family dynamics, therapists have discovered the processes that lead to addiction. After all, families play a major role in shaping our personalities. It's the logical place to start looking for causes.

Psychologist Irwin Hyman reports that "very violent children are almost always frequent recipients of severe corporal punishment at home....The old saw that violence breeds violence is supported by this finding."[13] Hitler and Stalin, for example, were both beaten by their fathers, as family systems analyst Alice Miller documents in her study of Hitler's childhood* and as HBO revealed in its 1994 docudrama *Stalin*. Little Adolf and Joseph didn't become Hitler and Stalin on their own. Neither do mass murderers. Miller analyzed how one notorious German killer murdered his child victims. The horrific details mirrored precisely the horrors visited on him by his parents.[14]

For that matter, abusive CEOs and corporate raiders don't exploit employees and customers without help from their original family experiences: the win-or-else maxims, the do-this-and-I'll-reward-you training, as well as the shaming they experienced when they didn't obey the ruthless paradigm norm. Dictators of every ilk pass soul loss on to others through the roles they assume in social structures; soul loss is what they know, what they experienced in their family systems. Through their actions, they perpetuate the paradigm—the attitudes, rules, roles, and methods—that abused them from day one.

Not everyone's family experience is horrific, thank God. Most people mean well when they raise their children. They love their kids and want to do the best for them. But it's confusing being a parent. Out of the blue, new parents can hear their own parents' shaming responses coming out of their mouths.

---

*Alice Miller, *For Your Own Good* (New York: Noonday/Farrar, Straus, Giroux, 1983), 142–97. She discovered similar beatings in the life of Romanian dictator Nicolae Ceausescu; see *Breaking Down the Wall of Silence* (New York: Meridian/Penguin, 1983), 97–113. Gloria Steinem also discovered severe beatings in the childhood of Saddam Hussein; see *Ms.*, November/December 1991, 25–26.

Our present family system does many things for people and society, but it's not set up to nurture our souls, precisely because its underlying paradigm is suspicious of soul energies. The overwhelming response to John Bradshaw's synthesis of forty years of family systems research shows how deeply insights into control-paradigm family systems resonate with his readers. The reaction is, "How can he describe my family so accurately? He's never met them."

Soul-violating social systems. But just as individuals don't become who they are in isolation, so too families don't perpetuate soul-violating patterns in isolation. They're the first emissary we encounter from the control paradigm, but they're not the last.

Economic, religious, educational, political, and professional systems control what goes on in families just as powerfully as family systems control individuals. Just as we each mirror our family system, so families mirror our social systems. Families assimilate all the invisible control-paradigm baggage that these systems communicate, and then they use the control messages to mold family life.

Families are a dress rehearsal for what's to come, and they're designed to function that way. They prepare us emotionally to fit into society as it is. They're our first encounter with society's control paradigm.

Example: democracy or power-over? This encounter isn't made up of words but of practices. Think back to when you first heard about democracy, for instance: Was it a familiar or a foreign concept? Was it something you'd experienced firsthand in either family or school life? The words may have been democracy, but the practices were power-over: obeying authorities, submitting to control, conforming, ignoring one's inner touchstone.

Power-over, not democracy, is in fact what we find when we go into society. As Charles Reich notes, "We are told that democracy is the best form of government,...Yet the democratic model is losing out to the authoritarian model in our daily lives. Following the corporate lead, virtually all of our institutions, from schools and colleges to Little League, are based on the top-down model. If we spend most of our time working under authority, how can we say we are a democratic society? When and where do we practice democracy?"[15]

What we take with us on the job isn't, therefore, the democratic rhetoric we hear around election time but the lifelong practice of taking orders and obeying. If we don't, we can lose the job, which is why families trained us as they did.

Example: economies stacked to favor the few. On a broader scale, we're trained to go along with structures that concentrate power to the few, even at cost to ourselves—literally. In the economic sphere, the rise of debtor psychology—"buy now, pay later"—combined with crushingly high interest rates that would once have been forbidden as "usurious" have served to concentrate wealth at the top. New-paradigm researchers Willis Harman and John Hormann explain:

> The *combined effect* of a debtor psychology and high interest rates has a particularly pernicious consequence in the long run. The immediate effect has been that for every dollar a household spends, 30 to 50 cents go to debt servicing, most of it hidden. Everybody, rich and poor alike, gives out a third to half of total expenditures in direct and indirect interest payments. However, a small minority have excess money to lend out so that they *receive* interest. The net effect is of a pervasive and pernicious redistribution system, steadily shifting money from the working and middle classes to the rich. Over time, this unfair tendency of the economy to concentrate wealth is bound to result in mass discontent and political instability. A similar mechanism operates between nations, where its effect is already apparent in the fact that for many developing countries the transfer of wealth from poor nation to rich in the form of debt servicing far exceeds the transfer in the reverse direction through trade and development aid.[16]

Our economies are rigged to concentrate wealth and to keep it that way, and we're stumped as to what we can do about it. We're so stumped, in fact, that we don't even want to think about it. We just keep going to work and paying the bills—and paying and paying. How many family quarrels start over money? Family members don't even have to disagree to fight. Money stresses just come out and take their toll on close relationships.

We can't recover alone. If recovery is about making a paradigm shift away from soul-violating models, this process can't stop with families. All the systems that shape our world play a role in creating addiction, and these systems must be rethought if we're going to break out of addictive cycles.

This is a tall order, but we don't have much choice if we're serious about healing personal and global addiction. We're back to the micro-macro issue: How can we or our families get healthy when the systems around us are sick—abusive by their very structures? What do we do when, for all our efforts to live from our souls, we face systems every day that pressure us to react addictively? What sense does it make to throw ourselves into personal or family recovery but leave abusive systems as they are?

We can't recover alone. Society's systems must come with us. But neither we nor our social systems can recover without a fundamental paradigm shift.

TIME FOR "NORMAL SCIENCE" OR "EXTRAORDINARY SCIENCE"?

The control-paradigm response to addiction. Not surprisingly, established systems—and the people who identify with them—don't agree. Social systems have built-in mechanisms for maintaining the established order, from experts to executive orders to threats of violence. Systems neutralize change by convincing their adherents that we're in the "normal-science" stage: "After millennia of building civilization by using power-over policies, who are you to question it?" "If it was good enough for your parents, it's good enough for you and your children."

On this analysis, the problem isn't with our systems but with a few bad people. To make our systems work, we're told, we simply have to fix or get rid of the bad people. Political elections are an orgy of normal-science thinking: if we just elect the right people, everything will be okay. All we have to do is figure out how to make the jerks and deadbeats stop drinking, smoking, taking drugs, robbing, murdering, or stealing.

Yet one group controlling others, even with good intentions, isn't the solution; it's the problem. It's a control-paradigm response, based on a power-over premise, namely, that whatever the problem, getting power over it is the solution.

The paradigm that creates addiction can't also heal it, which is why neither lawmakers, administrators, nor prisons have put an end to addictions. The more they exert their power-over muscle, the more addictive society gets.

A paradigm-shift response. It's time for "extraordinary science"—for taking the leap and shifting paradigms. Healing the planet of addiction isn't about making anyone do or stop anything. It's about tackling the root issue, the control-paradigm conspiracy: how our dignity as human beings is denied by social systems designed to do precisely that.

Modern schooling, for example, wasn't designed to develop our minds. As John Taylor Gatto points out, it was designed to teach conformity, obedience to authority, tolerance for performing boring tasks, and other qualities useful in factory life. Schools run like factories, and students in them behave like zombies before they ever set foot on the factory floor. They're well trained as do-what-you're-told, don't-think-for-yourselves workers. Active minds are the bane of a military-model workplace, and schooling makes sure they're unplugged.[17]

To heal the planet of addiction, we have to admit both that systems unplug us from our inner resources and that they do so because our paradigm mandates it. Only then are we paradigm-savvy enough to shift paradigms.

Support from systems thinking. Systems thinking underscores the need to move beyond normal science to extraordinary science—beyond paradigm-applying to paradigm-restructuring. Instead of treating problems as isolated events, systems thinking focuses on how systems work and why. It looks at the deep structures generating behavior and interprets events within larger system dynamics. Until we understand the generative systems—the system of concepts that make up a paradigm—we won't understand the social structures they create.

With a system approach, we no longer see problems in isolation. Instead, we see the systems—outward as well as internalized—generating our problems. Fixing the immediate breakdown not only doesn't get to the source, it also distracts us from the underlying structures. We blame specifics—specific people or circumstances—leaving the systems causing the breakdown unchanged.

Systems thinker and business consultant Peter Senge writes in the management bestseller *The Fifth Discipline*, "The systems perspective tells us that we must look beyond individual mistakes or bad luck to understand important problems. We must look beyond personalities and events. We must look into the underlying structures which shape individual actions." His "first principle of systems thinking" states: "When placed in the same system, people, however different, tend to produce similar results."[18] Powerful systems—from the belief system called a paradigm to the social system called a school, church, business, or profession—cause us to behave addictively. "Structures of which we are unaware hold us prisoner."[19]

Applied to addictions, systems thinking shows that a global explosion of addiction doesn't happen because of a few bad apples, neither are people in pain defective oddities. Global substance addiction into the trillions of dollars is not an anomalous event. There are system causes and, behind them, paradigm causes. Addiction sounds the alarm. We're acting out in our own lives and on each other what it's like to be in systems that are soul-abusive by nature.

CASHING IN A PARADIGM/SYSTEMS PERSPECTIVE

Listening to parts as reflective of the whole. True, it's easy to focus on one facet of our systems—on the achievers or heroes, the "A" students or the business elite—and claim as a result that our systems work. It's easier to think something is wrong with persons than with systems. Yet addicts are part of systems too. Addicts mirror our social systems in ways we can't ignore.

Systems thinking says that each part reflects the whole. Each aspect mirrors the total system from a unique perspective, just as each facet of a crystal mirrors the whole stone in its own way, or each DNA molecule encodes the whole body but doesn't make us all thumbs. If one part is hurting, the entire system is hurting. If a few people are caught in self-destructive patterns—and millions of Americans struggle with some form of substance addiction alone*—then the total system is functioning self-destructively, and we need to know why.

The body provides an example. If we're ingesting toxins, we may not

---

*Statistics are impossible to pin down for many reasons. When, for example, does social use become dependence and addiction? Also, how are statistics obtained? For every person being treated, many more remain unidentified and untreated. John Bradshaw estimates that 50 percent of men and 60 percent of women have an eating disorder (*Bradshaw On: The Family*, Deerfield Beach, FL: Health Communications, 1988, 6), whereas other researchers define the disorder more narrowly. Suffice it to say, if we include all substances—from alcohol, drugs (legal and illegal), and nicotine to food and caffeine—the number of people caught in substance dependence is enormous.

know it at first. But after a while, we start getting symptoms: headaches, nausea, sore joints. If we ignore the pains or dismiss them as random events, the body gets worse. We don't change what's poisoning us.

Inner pain, manifested in addiction, tells us that our social systems and the paradigm behind them are toxic—lethal to our happiness and well-being. They're doing violence to us, our societies, and our planet. If we ignore the pain, then we won't notice the system poisons, and neither we nor our systems can heal.

Everyone is abused. Moreover, the notion that abusive systems work well for some people and not for others is false. A person playing the role of hero in the family system is just as cut off from his or her soul as a person playing the role of scapegoat. Neither the A-student nor the class clown is free to express who he or she is, and both are vulnerable to addictions. Both put roles before souls.

It's no surprise, then, that substance and process addictions are rampant among the so-called heroes of society: the wealthy, celebrities, sports stars, and the powerful. If the system doesn't work for the people for whom it appears to work, then for whom does it work? Who is truly benefited if those "at the top" are in pain and addicted as well?

In other words, abusive systems don't abuse one person and not another. To be in such systems at all is abusive. Controller and controlled, powerful and disempowered, those rewarded and those paying the price are all abused on soul levels.

Systems are not outside us. Yet just when we're ready to march, sue, or tear down some institution, we find out that abusive systems aren't entirely "out there." Unless we shift the governing paradigm—one that we've internalized as our own—then tearing down some external system won't help. We'll create another just like it, only we'll be the ones in charge.

The well-documented pattern of victims identifying with their abusers—and later becoming abusers themselves—illustrates this out-there/in-here mirroring. We defend the paradigms that abuse us because we internalize them. We believe our world would collapse without the "order" that a control paradigm imposes.

Even as our world is collapsing under this order, though, we don't name the internalized belief structures as the cause of the collapse. Their order is all we know. The Titanic is invincible, even as we're sinking.

Peter Senge explains: "The nature of structure in human systems is sub-tle because *we* are part of the structure. This means that we often have the power to alter structures within which we are operating. However, more often than not, we do not perceive that power. In fact, we usually don't see the structures at play much at all. Rather, *we just find ourselves feeling compelled to act in certain ways.*"[20]

Is it human nature or our paradigms? "Feeling compelled to act in cer-tain ways" is a perfect description of addiction. Humanity seems compelled to act self-destructively both personally and globally.

Some say this is just human nature. We're greedy and selfish, and that's all. But what if our self-destructive habits stem not from our nature but from the paradigm that shapes us and our social systems? What if the channels we're flowing in make us self-destruct?

If so, then the very fact that we behave self-destructively means that the paradigm and its systems don't fit us. If they did, we'd thrive. Instead, we go crazy. We start mutilating ourselves, as wild animals do when they're caught in traps—only the traps we're caught in are paradigm-created.

When caged animals behave self-destructively, we don't assume that it reflects their real nature—how they behave in their right habitat. So too, the fact that we're mutilating ourselves and our world may not be an expression of who we are but of who we don't want to be. We can't stand who we've become, but we see no way out.

THE PERSONAL PARADIGM SHIFT GOES PUBLIC

Changing paradigms changes everything. The fact that the control para-digm draws its power from our shared commitment to it gives us the lever-age we need to make a paradigm shift, since we can withdraw our commitment at any time. Because we're part of our social systems, every shift we make precipitates shifts in the systems around us. They can't stay the same.

Mahatma Gandhi's approach to ending British rule in India illustrates the power of shifting our paradigm commitment. Leading the Indian inde-pendence movement in the 1920s, 1930s, and 1940s, Gandhi argued that several thousand British couldn't enslave several million Indians if the

Indians didn't accept British control. The Indians allowed the British to rule them by accepting their model of domination. Once they refused to accept this paradigm, the British had to leave.

By embarking on a paradigm shift, we engage in the most powerful level of transformation. Senge writes: "Learning to see the structures within which we operate begins a process of freeing ourselves from previously unseen forces and ultimately mastering the ability to work with them and change them."[21]

How do we make a paradigm shift in our social systems? Through the same process that we make a paradigm shift within ourselves.

1. Tracing social pain back to its paradigm origins. As with personal recovery, system recovery begins with acknowledging the pain that systems generate and tracing this pain back to its control-paradigm origins. Until we acknowledge this pain, we won't name abusive systems as abusive. We'll think they're okay and something must be wrong with us.

Example: pain in education. Take the educational system again, since that's a system we all share. It's not uncommon for adults in successful careers to have recurring nightmares about taking tests. Many find no joy in reading. Whereas hungry babies would rather learn than eat, by the time they reach high-school age, their innate joy of learning is gone. Students blank out on tests because the stress and fear are so great. Most can't wait to get out of school, and once they do, they swear never to get near a book again. On the job, people avoid learning new things, because they find the learning experience so intimidating.

How about the pain of those paid to inflict grade-fear on young minds? Realizing that students' performance improves when the pressure of grades is off, most teachers dislike grading students. Many have lost their jobs when they refused to grade on the bell curve.* The late W. Edwards Deming, the

---

*Alfie Kohn has brilliantly analyzed the problem of externalized rewards in his books *No Contest: The Case Against Competition* (New York: Houghton Mifflin, 1992) and *Punished by Rewards: The Trouble with Gold Stars, Incentive Plans, A's, Praise, and Other Bribes* (New York: Houghton Mifflin, 1993). He discusses studies that show the ineffectiveness of grades and other rewards in *No Contest*, pp. 31–32, 47–50, 51–53, 107–8, and in *Punished by Rewards*, pp. 39, 42–45, 56, 58, 64–65, 70–73, 144–45, 150–51. See also specific arguments against grading, pp. 200–10.

guru and grandfather of "total quality management philosophy," was "unalterably opposed to grades being given to children in school, and in his classes at New York University, he did not grade his students. He believed that any time you introduce competition between people, you automatically diminish cooperation."[22]

Example: pain at work. Deming's views on education followed his views on business. Business methods, he said, abuse people out of their intrinsic joy of work—the joy of doing something with others that society values. Like schools, prevailing models of management destroy our natural inclination to learn and be of service. "Deming said that management grinds that intrinsic motivation out of people with rankings, ratings, personnel appraisals, bonuses, merit pay, and anything else that sets up a competition. Over a lifetime of playground games, school grades, and adult rewards and punishments, extrinsic motivation destroys intrinsic motivation, Deming said, and it is wrong."[23]

Rafael Aguayo, a student of Deming's, wrote in *Dr. Deming, The American Who Taught the Japanese About Quality*: "Deming stated unequivocally that merit reviews, by whatever name…are the single most destructive force in American management today"[24] —a theme Alfie Kohn explores in depth in his excellent book *Punished by Rewards*.

In other words, soul-destructive forces are built into at least two of the systems we and our children cope with daily—school and work. We need to acknowledge the pain we experience just from being in these systems. Otherwise, we excuse the systems, while blaming ourselves and our children for not thriving in them.

Just as naming personal pain is the first step in personal recovery, so naming pain-making social systems and the paradigm behind them is the first step in social transformation.

2. Spiritual awakening. As with individual recovery, system-wide paradigm shifts move from pain to spiritual awakening. Awakening to who we are through micro recovery, we gain a new vision of who and what we can be together. Shifting to a paradigm that puts soul-connectedness at the center, we tune in to the soul-nurturing character of relationships and design our systems to honor or at least not violate this fundamental quality.

On a soul-grounded paradigm, every relationship has a quality of sacredness, and every social system—whether government, school, work, or church—presents an opportunity to serve our souls' journey. When our inner aliveness is allowed to resonate with the aliveness in others—that is, when our social systems don't shut it down—we create communities founded on reverence for life, soul, freedom, and individuality.

Spiritual traditions typically teach the sacredness of community based on values of soul respect: the Sangha in Buddhism, the Umma in Islam, or the Church in Christianity, for example. Deep in spiritual traditions is the idea that living beings come together for more than mere efficiency. Communities have a spiritual meaning, because they have the potential to facilitate our inward evolution.*

Every relationship, therefore, is sacred and deserves respect, whether it involves exchanging knowledge (education), goods and services (businesses and professions), responsibilities (governments), or spiritual support (religious institutions). Exchanging energies to enrich our lives is the guiding purpose of social systems.

Myths often teach a soul-honoring approach to human interaction by having the hero—usually royalty, in this context, a symbol of the governing paradigm—meet an angel or a good fairy, often disguised as a beggar. If the hero reacts with respect, he's blessed with angelic powers. However, if he abuses the other from a one-up position—as the prince does in *Beauty and the Beast*—he's cursed: the prince turns into a beast. His inward paradigm is no longer invisible; it's reflected in his outward form.

Waking up to the spiritual purpose of social systems and envisioning social structures built on this model represent a major paradigm shift. The control paradigm, of course, says it can't be done. Nonetheless, if every person is worthy of honor and respect, if every person is sacred and carries hidden treasures, then we need a paradigm that enables us to tap our souls' treasures and to let them flow through our lives together. Why shouldn't we be able to do this?

---

*Of course, since the control paradigm has pervaded most cultures on the planet at least for 6,000 years by Riane Eisler's estimate (see the following footnote), communities— even if they start with high spiritual ideals—can turn dysfunctional and oppressive fast. Nonetheless, the ideal of putting soul values first is there, offering us an alternative to soul-devaluing control-paradigm systems.

3. Creativity. Pulling off a paradigm shift of this magnitude takes creativity, though, and plenty of it. Fortunately, according to spiritual teachings, Judaism especially, our spiritual nature is profoundly creative. We're not lacking in this department. The creative process symbolized by the Bible's seven days of creation is the nature of the universe. Because we're part of the universe, it's our nature as well. We're creative in our bones, and we get destructive only when our innate creativity gets squashed.

Honoring our souls connects us with immense creative powers—so powerful, in fact, that control systems are petrified of us. They want our creative energies harnessed for their use. We're capable of making power-over social structures obsolete in no time, which is why a control paradigm conspires through social systems to keep us ignorant of our powers.

The only thing that prevents us from exercising our creative potential to restructure our systems is our lingering commitment to the control paradigm and our acceptance of its "you're powerless" verdict on us. Thanks to decades of programming, we're scared that the control paradigm may be right: maybe things would be worse if we each followed our souls. Maybe our souls are worthless troublemakers.

And maybe rain falls up. But can a soul-honoring paradigm do worse than bring the planet to the edge of annihilation? What's more, cross-cultural history offers many examples of cultures running successfully on soul-honoring models, including Native societies from all over the world—what Riane Eisler calls "partnership" cultures.* It's possible to both keep our souls and have social order.

The moment our paradigm commitment starts to shift, we become a force for transformation. We tap our inner resources for system shifting—or system busting. Ideas start rolling, and we get busy redrawing the blueprint that shapes our lives together.

Creativity narrowed by control-paradigm structures. By contrast, the control paradigm narrows creativity to the "official," normal-science channels. We can't be creative together when we're not free to express ourselves.

---

*See Riane Eisler, *The Chalice and the Blade* (San Francisco: HarperSanFrancisco, 1988), Robert Lawlor, *Voices of the First Day* (Rochester, VT: Inner Traditions, 1991), and Peter Gold, *Navajo and Tibetan Sacred Wisdom: The Circle of the Spirit* (Rochester, VT: Inner Traditions, 1994).

Yet answers to business, family, and world problems lie precisely in expressing parts of ourselves that social systems haven't allowed us to express. We're more than our roles, more than our images. We have more to offer the systems than they allow us to give.

If we can't be honest with our "superiors," for example, or candidly tell them our views, the creative options within a system are narrowed by the system's control of who can say what to whom. Systems cut themselves off from system-degraded, "inferior" groups—e.g., workers, secretaries, assistants, janitors—though they're a source of knowledge and creativity that our systems desperately need.

In industry, for example, managers and engineers aren't supposed to compromise their authority by taking seriously the ideas of technicians, much less workers. Knowledge and decisions flow down, not up. Yet workers and technicians—people on the front lines of production and sales—are the ones who know what's successful and what isn't. Their knowledge and experiences are valuable resources, no matter how much top-down systems ignore them.

Exercising our paradigm-shifting powers. Stepping outside the control paradigm's hierarchies and divisions, we break through the barriers that cut us off from each other, so we can exchange knowledge freely. We reclaim the real treasures of earth—ourselves and our communities—and we use these treasures to call a new humanity into being. We free ourselves to create worlds we never imagined.

In other words, what's true for shifting paradigms in our lives personally is also true for shifting the paradigms behind our social systems. Both shifts involve confronting pain and tracing it to its paradigm source. Both involve a spiritual awakening—the reintroduction of values that the control paradigm excluded. And both involve creativity. We're creative about carving new, soul-friendly niches in our personal lives. And we're creative in designing soul-friendly, earth-friendly social structures—the very things that the control paradigm claims are impossible.

At the center of both shifts is the paradigm issue—an old paradigm that's in crisis and a new paradigm that's gradually coming into focus.

Paradigm anatomy 101

What makes up a paradigm? Shifting paradigms, as Senge observes, initiates change at the most powerful, generative level, since our mental models set the pattern for everything else. If paradigms are the key to transformation, what makes up a paradigm? To smoke out a paradigm, what are we looking for?

For the sake of simplicity, we've boiled down a paradigm's constituents to four elements:

    a. *Assumptions* are what we take for granted and assume to be true, the premises from which everything else follows. Do we assume, for example, that control is our top priority or that our souls are? Both are assumptions. We're free to choose.

    b. *Strategies* include the theories, concepts, rules, roles, and methods that put our assumptions into practice. An assumption that says control is everything spawns strategies that tell us how to get control and keep it. An assumption that puts soul at the center gives rise to strategies that respect the inner creative powers of all human beings and help us develop those powers.

    c. *Responses* show the everyday face of a paradigm through our habits, reactions, social structures, and patterns of behavior. Whatever happens, we respond from one paradigm or another, even if we don't sit down and analyze it first. To some people, for instance, every interaction is a chance to prove who's better, smarter, more successful, more important, wealthier, even more "spiritually advanced." That's a control-paradigm response. To others, every interaction is a chance to learn and evolve in mutually supportive ways.

    d. *Goals* are how paradigms guide our actions. A control-paradigm goal might be to establish a military model of social order, for example, or to establish ourselves in a superior position. Soul-based paradigms, by contrast, give us goals that have to do with inward evolution.

Integral systems. These four elements work together as one seamless process. Analyzing them separately only helps us understand what's going on. In practice, all the elements are present with every thought or action, and they play off each other to make up our working paradigm.

That's why it helps to know the elements. When assumptions change, strategies, responses, and goals shift too. If certain strategies aren't working, we need to go back and question our paradigm's assumptions, responses, and goals. If we arrive at goals different from those we intended—if we aimed at being Mother Teresa and ended up Leona Helmsley, for instance, we'd need to check our assumptions, strategies, and responses to find out what the heck happened.

Partial shifts don't cut it. Because paradigms are integral—they're connected like a body and function that way—shifting one aspect calls for whole-paradigm shifts. We can't pick and choose which bits are convenient to change and which aren't.

Managers can't ask for new responses from production teams, for instance, but hang on to old assumptions, strategies, and goals. It won't work. If the paradigm governing the business doesn't shift—if power-over assumptions and profit-for-a-few goals hang on—strategies and responses won't budge either, no matter how many consultants and training programs pass through the company. Paradigm shifts can't be faked. If it's not a total shift, it's not a shift at all. It's just the old model dressed up with new language or gimmicks.

The same holds for paradigm shifts in families, schools, and governments. Parents, teachers, and public servants can't talk empowerment and at the same time keep their authoritarian attitudes. If the *goal* is a soul-nurturing, egalitarian system, then *power-over assumptions* (e.g., parents, teachers, and experts must always be right and obeyed), *dominating strategies* (e.g., abuse is "for your own good," grading systems motivate, and power plays work), and *control responses* (e.g., react to "unruly" children by breaking their wills or respond to business and political problems by encroaching on rights) must change as well.

THE THREEFOLD RHYTHM OF SHIFTING PARADIGMS

How do we shift paradigms? Through the threefold process of recovery: (1) by confronting pain, (2) waking up to our souls, and (3) reclaiming our innate creative powers. Through this process, we withdraw our commitment to a paradigm that's not working and start evolving another. To our assumptions, strategies, responses, and goals, we ask the following questions:

1. *Where are we, and where are we going?* What are our social systems' assumptions, strategies, responses, and goals, and where do they lead? What kind of worlds do they create? Here's where pain comes up, as we confront abusive social structures. We take stock of what's going on—and the paradigm reasons for it.

2. *How do we get from here to there?* What process takes us, for instance, from a control to a soul-centered paradigm or from a power-over to a mutual-support model? Spiritual awakening. We wake up to who we are and to what our systems can be, and this new awareness gives us the courage that transformation—micro and macro—requires.

3. *How can we make the shift and go for change?* In the third phase, we withdraw our commitment to the old model and put it behind transformation. As Captain Picard says on *Star Trek, The Next Generation*, "Make it so." We no longer tolerate the abuse that goes with "life as usual." Instead, we demand soul-honoring paradigms and work to restructure ourselves, our relationships, and our social systems accordingly.

That's a tall order. How do we pull it off? By reclaiming our innate creativity. Since everything involves participation with some paradigm or another, everything we think and do is open to "creative transformation," as Confucian scholar Tu Wei-ming calls it—a process he considers "ceaseless."[25]

FOUR BY THREE EQUALS ANCIENT STEPS OF TRANSFORMATION

A twelvefold path of shifting paradigms. Combining these two categories—the four elements of paradigms on one side and the threefold dynamics of paradigm shifting on the other—we get a twelvefold path for transformation that starts at a paradigm level and percolates down to transform everything else, us included.

A twelvefold path and recovery have been linked before, and AA's Twelve Steps provide a well-tested model for confronting a paradigm in crisis and embarking on a paradigm shift. A big piece of what we're doing in this book is exploring how the wisdom and experience gained from personal recovery applies to the paradigm shift we face in our social systems.

However, there's more to a twelvefold journey than meets the eye. It has an ancient history—and a meaning in archetypal consciousness that relates precisely to what a paradigm shift is all about. The Buddha's twelvefold chain of causation, for example, identifies the addictive process on both micro and macro levels, showing how we get trapped in paradigms that have ignorance at their root.

Western spiritual traditions also use twelve as a number-symbol of what gives rise to a spiritually founded community. In addition to all the twelves in astrology (twelve signs, twelve houses), there are the twelve tribes of Israel (each representing different qualities), the twelve Babylonian gods, the ideal twelve-tribe constitution in Plato's *Laws*, the twelve divine councilors of Odin, the twelve primordial deities of Greece, the twelve adventuring knights of King Arthur, the twelve disciples of Jesus, the twelve gates of the new Jerusalem in *Revelation*, guarded by twelve angels, with twenty-four elders (12 x 2) sitting before the throne, and 144,000 people (12 x 12,000) whose names were sealed—and that doesn't count the Eastern twelves.

"The 12-sided foundation plan of civilized order." In *Twelve-Tribe Nations and the Science of Enchanting the Landscape*, John Michell and Christine Rhone explore the relation between twelvefold cycles and social order. As they see it, enchantment is the missing quality in modern life. In earlier cultures, enchantment threw a mantle of meaning over society that wove everyone into a unity.

From their study of myths, symbols, and spiritual traditions, Michell and Rhone claim that twelvefold orders are, archetypally speaking, how this meaning and enchantment emerge in community life. The idea behind "the 12-sided foundation plan of civilized order" is "to create and maintain a perfectly balanced human order in harmony with the heavenly order, where life is experienced on a high level of spiritual intensity."[26]

As symbols, "twelves" speak to the central issue that the control paradigm raises: What creates order in society? What's the best foundation for building social systems? Is control—who owns what, and who dominates whom—the cement that binds us together? Or are reverence for life and respect for the human soul and spirit the foundations of civilized order?

The Iroquois Peace Confederacy. These core questions arose in the 1500s among the Native Americans of the Northeast when tribal warfare was decimating the population. No tribe trusted another, and all were engaged in one-up/one-down lethal conquests. Entire families were wiped out in battles for domination.

The historic Hiawatha lived during this period and saw his wife and children brutally slaughtered. Once idealistic, Hiawatha became a cynical, brokenhearted hermit who terrorized, killed, and ate anyone passing near his cave in the woods.

To say the least, the Northeast Nations experienced their paradigm in crisis.

Out of this intense social trauma arose The Great Peacemaker, Deganawidah of the Hurons, who is rightfully the great-grandfather of democratic ideals on the planet, at least in known history. The Greek democracies fell far short of what Deganawidah both envisioned and implemented. He abolished slavery and gave everyone the vote, including women, children, and babies. Since babies are too young to vote, their mothers voted on their behalf, giving many women twice the voting power of men. Government representatives had to serve the people, commit to the public good, and answer to the public welfare for seven generations to come.

Spiritual values were the warp and woof of this remarkable social innovation. Deganawidah's paradigm for social order honored soul and life, and every rule, policy, and practice reflected this priority in values. The form of government he introduced was called The Great Peace, resulting in the League of Five Nations (eventually Six Nations), later known as the Iroquois Confederacy.

Benjamin Franklin worked with the Iroquois Confederacy as a diplomat and studied its government. Raised on the control paradigm, the classically trained Europeans involved in framing the Constitution were suspicious of democracies. It was the Iroquois Confederacy's ability to thrive for centuries that convinced Franklin and others to push for democracy as part of the Noble Experiment that became the American Republic. Even then, the American Constitution offered nowhere near the egalitarian participation that Deganawidah's government did three centuries earlier.[27]

The Twelve Cycles of Truth. To ground democratic government in spiritual principles, Deganawidah gave teachings that expressed his soul-honoring paradigm. Among these teachings is the "Twelve Cycles of Truth," which Jamie Sams summarizes in her *Sacred Path Cards* book: "Learning the truth, honoring the truth, accepting the truth, observing the truth, hearing the truth, presenting the truth, loving the truth, serving the truth, living the truth, working the truth, walking the truth, and being grateful for the truth."[28]

We've chosen this twelvefold path to focus the steps of a paradigm shift because of its proven track record. Like the Twelve Steps of AA, the Twelve Cycles of Truth guided personal transformation. But they also guided the shift away from the same control-and-dominate paradigm in social systems that we now face.

The Twelve Cycles brought the Northeast Nations back from the brink of annihilation. They helped the people recover from community-destroying wars. They fostered social institutions that respected all forms of life. And they wove together a harmonious social fabric for centuries—until, of course, some power-and-greed addicted Europeans forcefully unraveled it.

What they did once, the Twelve Cycles of Truth may do again—though their challenge today is even greater. Power-over systems are ravaging on a global scale. Fortunately, we're identifying the paradigm that causes the ravaging. And we're acknowledging—after years of denial, idealizing, avoiding, and looking the other way—that we don't like ravaging. We don't like the systems that do it or the paradigm that causes it.

What we don't like, we can conspire to change.

Notes to Introduction

1. John Moyne and Coleman Barks, trans., *Say I Am You* (Athens, GA: Maypop Books, 1994), 101.
2. Anne Wilson Schaef, *When Society Becomes an Addict* (San Francisco: HarperSanFrancisco, 1987), 18–19.
3. Schaef, *When Society Becomes an Addict*, 4.
4. John Taylor Gatto, *Dumbing Us Down: The Hidden Curriculum of Compulsory Schooling* (Philadelphia: New Society Publishers, 1992), xii.
5. Donna Boundy, *When Money Is the Drug: The Compulsion for Credit, Cash, and Chronic Debt* (San Francisco: HarperSanFrancisco, 1993), 57.
6. Thomas S. Kuhn, *The Structure of Scientific Revolutions*, 2d ed. (Chicago: University of Chicago Press, 1970), 83.
7. John Romer, *Testament* (New York: Henry Holt, 1988), 203, 205.
8. Hal Zina Bennett, ed., *Larry Dossey in Conversation with Michael Toms* (Lower Lake, CA: Aslan Publishing/New Dimensions Books, 1994), 48.
9. Robert Jay Lifton, *The Nazi Doctors: Medical Killing and the Psychology of Genocide* (New York: Basic Books/HarperCollins, 1986), 106.
10. Na'im Akbar, *The Community of Self*, rev. ed. (Jersey City, NJ: New Mind Productions, 1985), 18.
11. Charles L. Whitfield, *Co-Dependence: Healing the Human Condition* (Deerfield Beach, FL: Health Communications, 1991), 3.
12. Mel B., *New Wine: The Spiritual Roots of the Twelve Step Miracle* (Center City, MN: Hazelden, 1991), 12.
13. Irwin Hyman, *Reading, Writing, and the Hickory Stick: The Appalling Story of Physical and Psychological Abuse in American Schools* (Lexington, MA: Lexington Books, 1990), 199.
14. Alice Miller, *For Your Own Good* (New York: Noonday/Farrar, Straus, Giroux, 1983), 226–31.
15. Charles Reich, *Opposing the System* (New York: Crown Publishers, 1995), 37.
16. Willis Harman and John Hormann, *Creative Work: The Constructive Role of Business in a Transforming Society* (Indianapolis: Knowledge Systems, 1990), 36–37.
17. Gatto, *Dumbing Us Down*, 1–33.
18. Peter Senge, *The Fifth Discipline: The Art and Practice of the Learning Organization* (New York: Doubleday/Currency, 1990), 42–43.
19. Senge, *Fifth Discipline*, 94.
20. Senge, *Fifth Discipline*, 44.
21. Senge, *Fifth Discipline*, 94.
22. Lloyd Dobyns and Clare Crawford-Mason, *Quality or Else: The Revolution in World Business* (New York: Houghton Mifflin, 1991), 60.
23. Dobyns and Crawford-Mason, *Quality or Else*, 62.
24. Rafael Aguayo, *Dr. Deming: The American Who Taught the Japanese About Quality* (New York: Simon and Schuster, 1990), 11.
25. Tu Wei-ming, *Confucian Thought: Selfhood as Creative Transformation* (Albany, NY: State University of New York Press, 1985), 8.

26. John Michell and Christine Rhone, *Twelve-Tribe Nations and the Science of Enchanting the Landscape* (Grand Rapids, MI: Phanes Press, 1991), 16–17.
27. Scott Peterson, *Native American Prophecies: Examining the History, Wisdom and Startling Predictions of Visionary Native Americans* (New York: Paragon House, 1990), 62–89.
28. Jamie Sams, *Sacred Path Cards: The Discovery of Self Through Native Teachings* (New York: HarperCollins, 1990), 156.

CHAPTER 1

Pain and the Power of
Shifting Assumptions

Learning the truth
First of the Twelve Cycles of Truth,
the Iroquois Peace Confederacy Tradition

The minute I'm disappointed, I feel encouraged.
When I'm ruined, I'm healed.
When I'm quiet and solid as the ground, then I talk
the low tones of thunder for everyone.
Rumi[1]

GOING FOR THE GOLD

What do we assume about our social systems, and what do we take for granted about our place in them? When we ask questions like these, we're serious about finding out what makes our systems' paradigm tick—and we can encounter some fairly nasty stuff. Confronting where we are and how we got here can sink us in muck up to our necks.

So before we get going, the upside: recovery happens because there's gold in us and in society, and this gold wants to be free of muck. The control paradigm that pervades our systems seems to eclipse all else. Yet confronting this paradigm is how a paradigm shift begins. We find out that we're more than the traumatized person we've become, and we start exploring paradigms that reveal the gems of the universe that human beings and human societies ultimately are. Rumi said:

A True Human Being is never what he or she
appears to be. Rub your eyes,
and look again.*

Some human beings no bigger than a water trough
scooped out of a log are greater glories
than the universe full of stars.[2]

You already have the precious mixture
that will make you well. Use it.[3]

In other words, the story we're telling has a happy ending—or it can have, if we go for it.

That said, how do things work around here? What assumptions about ourselves, our systems, and the world has the control paradigm drummed into us?

Confronting pain-making assumptions

Assuming misery as usual. Unfortunately, misery: we assume it's part of life. We try not to make a big deal out of it—stiff upper lip and all that. Yet it's not uncommon to dread getting up in the morning and to walk around stressed out or in a low-grade depression. Young and old, yuppie and un-employed alike take drugs just to make it through the day, while both we and the helping professions assume that what's wrong is our own inability to cope.

Maybe so, but the systems around us—not only family but also school, business, religious, media, and professional—never get equal scrutiny. We're shored up chemically just so we can get knocked around by systems that have soul-knocking built into their structures. Life under a control paradigm is miserable, and as long as the control paradigm stays in place, it's fair to assume that misery is what we'll experience.

Example: Competition. Take a misery-making assumption that's embed-ded in most social systems: competition. We assume that competing against each other is the best way to get the best out of us.

---

*Coleman Barks, trans., *Delicious Laughter: Rambunctious Teaching Stories from the Mathnawi of Jelaluddin Rumi* (Athens, GA: Maypop Books, 1990), 65. We say "Rumi said" because he spoke all his poems; his students wrote down what he said.

From a control-paradigm perspective, it's also a potent way to get us to play by the rules. If rewards (high grades, degrees, jobs, promotions, honors, or pay raises) go to those best at playing by control-paradigm rules—and low or failing grades, unemployment, or minimum wages go to the rest—then we have incentives to play along: the old carrot-and-stick idea.

The cost of accepting the competition assumption. Competition has side effects, though. It leads to one-upping/one-downing, which leads to humiliation for the one-down, which leads to insecurity for the one-up since we never know who's down next, which leads to stress, because no one likes being one-down, which zaps self-esteem since only when we're up do we "make the grade," which leads to self-blame when we don't win the "up" position, which leads to anger or frustration or aggression, because self-hate isn't fun, which leads to heart attacks and cancer if stress and self-hate get stuffed inside, or to business-as-usual and crime if it spills over outside, which then leads to the evening news—and God knows where that leads.

But despite suspicions that competition isn't getting the best out of us— never mind the mountain of studies that show how destructive it is to both the human psyche and group dynamics*—we still don't challenge it. Competition remains a core assumption of our social systems. We see it on nature shows, plus we were brought up with it—"Why can't you be as good or as smart as that one? Why aren't you on the dean's list or first string?"— so we assume it's universal, not something we can alter. It's just the way things are: classic normal-science thinking.

Until we take the leap into extraordinary science and question the assumption that competition must be a fact of life, we accept competition as inescapable, no matter how miserable it makes us. Competition may not capture Joseph Campbell's notion of "Follow your bliss," we tell ourselves, but at least it keeps us in line. We're the cattle, and competition is the prod.

We pay the price. Buying the competition assumption, we further assume that we're the ones who need improvement. We end up paying the price of our culturally shared commitment to this assumption. If there's nothing

---

*As we mentioned in the introduction, Alfie Kohn's *No Contest: The Case Against Competition* provides an excellent overview of the research on the subject of competition.

wrong with competition, there must be something wrong with us when we don't win. We simply have to learn how to compete better, even if it breaks up friendships, drives wedges in families, and makes us sick to our stomachs with stress.

To gain experience for what we assume to be life in the "real world," we invent competitive games—from Monopoly to football—and then use images from those games to flog ourselves into working harder. "Business is like baseball," or "Our work here is about winning," or "Remember what Vince Lombardi said!"—as if reality should conform to the assumptions behind our games. We forget that games are our inventions and that Vince Lombardi was a football coach, not God.

"Hard work brings rewards." When we try to fit into the control paradigm's version of business, for instance, do we get competition's promised rewards? More likely, we slip into workaholism, as Diane Fassel describes in her excellent book *Working Ourselves to Death*, hoping that, if we work hard enough, rewards will come our way. But no matter how hard we work, the rewards—at least for most people—are few and far between. Pulitzer Prize–winning journalists Donald Barlett and James Steele contrast the situation of conscientious and hard-working Rosalind Webb, who lost her job when Bonwit Teller closed in Philadelphia, with that of those who move millions of dollars with a phone call:

> Rosalind Webb, like millions of Americans, is snared in an economic shift in the United States in which the middle class is being squeezed and the ranks of the working poor are growing, while new jobs paying up to $500 an hour are being created for a select group of professionals—lawyers, accountants, bankers, investment advisers, brokers, and management specialists.[4]

Do the members of this select group work harder than Rosalind Webb and so deserve their stratospheric salaries? Are they doing brain surgery, high-energy physics, a day's work in a classroom, or something as physically taxing as collecting other people's garbage in all weather? Concerning the everyday chores of the $500-an-hour elites, Barlett and Steele observe:

> They get paid to talk for a few minutes on the telephone. They get paid to pack files. They get paid to unpack files. They get paid to pick up their

mail. They get paid to sort their mail. They get paid to schedule conferences. They get paid to attend conferences. They get paid to keep a list of
the conferences. They get paid to keep track of the way they spend their
time. They get paid to fill out expense reports. And they get paid to eliminate the jobs of people who work for two weeks to earn what they charge
for one hour.[5]

Japanese economist Hiroshi Takeuchi summarizes the situation, "Those
who work the hardest get the least."[6]

Working hard on ourselves. But still we keep working. To perform our
best, we even throw ourselves into self-help and motivational programs—
there's the cattle prod again. We get our navel-gazing and self-improvement
compulsions honestly. Our systems' message to us is clear: "We systems
aren't lacking; you people are." "There's nothing wrong with the family,
school, church or business; what's your problem?"

To suggest that systems share responsibility for the pain we feel whenever we're in them—people break into cold sweats and rashes just thinking
about school or work—elicits the familiar rebuke: "That's right, blame your
problems on the system!"

Vintage methods of enforcement. Until we question our assumptions,
they come get us and with a vengeance. They scare us into compliance with
the control paradigm's demands—demands that, in control-paradigm
worlds, have teeth: "Would you like to eat or starve, sleep in a bed or in a
box on the street?"

Competition sends children a message not unlike the one sent by Senator
Joseph McCarthy during his 1950–1954 Senate subcommittee investigations
into "un-American activities" to expose supposed Communists and
Communist sympathizers. Whether or not McCarthy set out to do something good, he ended up creating a witch hunt that destroyed hundreds of
people's lives and careers. Though McCarthy's tactics were condemned by
the Senate in 1954, the Hollywood blacklist continued to bar people from
work until 1970.

The message was vintage control paradigm, with a pedigree that goes
back at least to the Inquisition, which terrified Europeans from the thir-
teenth to the nineteenth centuries: The ruling paradigm tolerates no dissent.
If any dissent from the authority position is suspected, we must confess our

mistake of dissenting. Plus, we should win the good graces of the authorities at others' expense, even if that means destroying their lives. The test of our loyalty to authorities is our willingness to betray our friends, to sacrifice their happiness and success in order to secure our own.

That's what children are asked to do every day. They're supposed to win, to be on top; they're not supposed to look into the faces of those they beat, whether in the classroom or on the "playing" field. Any success they have is rigged to entail another's defeat. Bell-curve grading, as Alfie Kohn observes, poses "a version of artificial scarcity in which my chance of receiving an A is reduced by your getting one."[7] Those are the rules of the control-paradigm game. If we dissent from those rules, we're the next losers.

Given this culture-wide training, it's puzzling that we're surprised or shocked when individuals behave exactly as they've been trained. When the corporate raiders of the eighties and nineties took billions from solvent companies, leaving the companies insolvent and their employees jobless, they were following the culture's formula for success. They embraced the competition assumption fully and lived it without hesitation.

Assumptions are powerful. They call the shots by defining both our social systems and our relation to them: how they work and how we work in them.

Shifting assumptions

Assuming that misery is a message. Shifting paradigms begins with acknowledging exactly what's going on: what our systems' core assumptions are, where these assumptions take us, and how we feel about living in the social systems they create day in, day out.

The last part—how we feel living in our systems—is how we nail down the other two. It's not easy to identify paradigm assumptions, but we do know how social systems make us feel. When family, school, professional, business, and religious systems bombard us with soul-abusive messages— that we're never quite good enough, for instance, or that our worth is conditional on obedience, conformity, and winning—we can't write off how those systems make us feel as if it's just our problem.

Soul pain is feedback.

A message that we need. It's feedback we need to understand the premises shaping our personal experiences. Naming how social systems make us feel doesn't mean we abdicate our responsibility for ourselves; it means we take responsibility for naming what's going on, for "learning the truth" about the forces shaping our lives.

Otherwise, soul-violating forces still operate and we still feel them, but we misidentify the source of our pain. We figure we're in pain because we're no good. We didn't measure up. Since that's a bit hard to stomach, we project pain outward on others for relief. Spouses, children, employees, animal companions, even human nature in general become the focal point of our pain and anger, as if they're the source.

In *For Your Own Good*, Alice Miller shows how child-rearing and schooling methods that we assume are "for our own good" aren't. They're good for control-paradigm systems to break our will—preferably by age three—and to gain control over our lives from the inside out. She quotes a 1748 instructional essay on child-rearing:

> It is quite natural for the child's soul to want to have a will of its own, and things that are not done correctly in the first two years will be difficult to rectify thereafter. One of the advantages of these early years is that then force and compulsion can be used....If their wills can be broken at this time, they will never remember afterwards that they had a will, and for this very reason the severity that is required will not have any serious consequences.[8]

What are the emotional consequences? One young African American woman struggling with depression related to us that because she was dyslexic in school—she often wrote her numerals and letters backwards, for which she was regularly beaten—the teacher told her that she was stupid and refused to teach her at all, giving her model cars to play with instead. Presumably the severity of this punishment would "not have any serious consequences."

If paradigms tell us they're creating social systems for our own good but they're not, we need to know this. Whenever we and our systems labor under an abusive paradigm, some part of us feels it, and we need to listen to that part. The real irresponsibility in such a situation is to look the other way—to ignore assumptions that, when translated into social institutions, lead straight to abuse.

A message that our systems need. Soul pain is feedback our systems also need. We're not alone in feeling battered. To survive in a culture dominated by a paradigm of external control, we all go through the motions of obeying, conforming, competing, and getting ahead, while inwardly we're out to lunch.

Yet how can we give our systems our best when we're numb inside? All they get from us is a robotic shell, and like robots, we continue in the same obedience-to-abusive systems that shocked everyone at the Nuremberg trials after World War II. As good robots, we stick to our programming. We don't merely obey abusive social systems; we embrace, endorse, and defend them. Control-paradigm assumptions take over our minds.

The Nazi doctors and ideologues, for example, assumed that competition is the natural order, that some win and some lose, that some are better fitted to survive and some are inferior and should be selectively eliminated. Like wolves helping to keep the caribou herd healthy by killing the weak, the Nazi soldiers assumed they were improving the health of the human species by systematically killing Jews, Gypsies, and anti-Nazi Christians. As "inferior specimens," they were expendable. The purity of the race was at stake.[9]

Not that today's robots shock us any less. It's now come to light that the American government has experimented for decades on citizens without their knowledge or consent. From 1932 to 1972, for example, the U.S. Public Health Service ran the Tuskegee Syphilis Project, which involved selecting 430 African American men (mostly poor) from rural Macon County, Alabama, with syphilis and then refusing them medical treatment— or pretending to treat them and really doing nothing—in order to study their symptoms and death rates.*

Just in case anyone thinks that being a member of a majority makes a person immune from such treatment, a 1977 Senate subcommittee found that the government was experimenting on all of us by the 1940s:

- The Army, for instance, blanketed 239 populated areas with bacteria between 1949 and 1969, including areas of Alaska and Hawaii, St. Louis, San Francisco, Washington, D.C. (interesting choice), Key West and Panama City in Florida, Washington National Airport, the Pennsylvania Turnpike, and the New York City subway system.

---

*We saw this on a television documentary and discovered later that it was based on James H. Jones's book, *Bad Blood* (New York: Free Press/Simon and Schuster, 1993).

- Between 1944 and 1975, 60,000 soldiers were subjected to chemical weapons tests, including gas chamber and skin tests.
- Under the infamous MKULTRA program, approved in 1953 by CIA Director Allen Dulles, the CIA administered LSD to individuals without their consent, using eighty organizations to do it. The General Accounting Office found that the records of most participants had been lost or destroyed.
- Between 1945 and 1962, 210,000 people were used in radiation experiments. In one test, 26,000 people occupied trenches, bunkers, and armored vehicles from 2,500 to 55,000 yards from ground zero. In another, five individuals were located directly below a high-altitude nuclear test.*

As reported in *Good Medicine*, put out by the Physicians Committee for Responsible Medicine, experimenting on humans is only the tip of the iceberg. Twenty million chimpanzees, cats, dogs, and rabbits are used every year in laboratories, and the tests are anything but humane. What's more, they're unnecessary. The National Anti-Vivisection Society outlines the many alternatives to animal testing now available, such as cloned skin, cell and organ cultures, "gas chromatography and mass spectrometry, which are used in the molecular analysis of bodily fluids, computer-aided drug design, computer simulation and imaging techniques, mathematical modeling, and non-invasive scanning technologies (MRI and CAT scans)."[10]

Nazi Germany evidently has no corner on atrocities. Why should it, when the same control paradigm came over here with European immigrants? If we train people to distrust their inner truth and instead to give authorities unquestioning obedience, what do we expect? We're deprived of the inner touchstone that yells "Stop!" when we're intimidated into supporting insanity.

---

*See Leonard Cole's *Clouds of Secrecy: The Army's Germ Warfare Tests over Populated Areas* (Lanham, MD: University Press of America, 1989), Harvey Weinstein's investigation of the MKULTRA LSD experiments on citizens in *Psychiatry and the CIA: Victims of Mind Control* (Washington, DC: American Psychiatric Press, 1990), DEA agent Michael Levine's exposing the CIA's collusion in smuggling drugs into the United States in *The Big White Lie: The CIA and the Cocaine/Crack Epidemic* (New York: Thunder's Mouth Press, 1993), and "U.S. Government Human Experiments: The Story Gets Uglier," *Good Medicine* Physicians Committee for Responsible Medicine (Summer 1995): 8–10.

Tuning out the message. The downside here is not that our cultural paradigm needs work. As long as we're evolving, we'll always be asking our paradigm to come up to speed with our souls' growth. The bummer is that we're constipating this natural development by ignoring obvious, under-our-noses pain.

Once again, we discount pain's messages because of control-paradigm assumptions. We assume that: (1) misery is a given in life, therefore the fact that we're miserable says nothing about the prevailing paradigm, (2) systems are okay as long as they maintain top-down order, and (3) if anything is wrong, it must be our fault. Since we have enough problems without our own pain giving evidence that we're a failure, we try to ignore it. In doing so, we ignore feedback that both we and our systems need.

Unheeded, pain messages keep upping their volume.

CLAIMING OUR POWER

Acknowledging misery's message empowers. Acknowledging paradigm-created pain isn't defeat. It's where recovery—a paradigm shift—starts. We connect with something real in us, and that reality link gives us the power to demand reality of ourselves, our systems, and our paradigm.

Rather than assuming that misery is our lot in life, we assume that pain conveys valid information about the paradigm we've internalized from our social systems. Instead of looking the other way, we square with how we feel in systems and stay grounded there. As we do, we trigger an inner shift. We question control-paradigm assumptions and begin to explore alternatives.

By shifting assumptions, we reclaim the one thing that's always in our power: our inward lives. Instead of assuming that our inner voice is untrustworthy—the official, authoritarian message to us—we assume that our inner voice is a sure guide in helping us learn the truth.

This new assumption allows us to confront our pain in systems and to value this pain as an ally in healing both us and our systems. Investigating new assumptions, we end our tacit agreement to idealize our systems and to stay in denial about the toll they take on us. We do the unthinkable and name what's going on.

The power of naming where we are. The call to name addictions as addictions, pain as pain, system craziness as system craziness, and the control paradigm as soul-violating is, according to wisdom teachings, the wake-up call from our souls. Whether it's Plato or Muhammad, the Buddha or Gandhi, philosophers of the soul claim that the soul's journey begins with an honest awareness of the suffering we feel.

If our lives have become afflicted, the most healing thing we can do is face our afflictedness. Pain is there for a reason. It tells us what works and what doesn't, what fits our souls and what abuses them. Pain says we're caught in paradigms that are hurting us, and something has to change.

Micro recovery teaches this method as well: not to avoid pain but to go into it and to come out the other side more whole because we're more aware. That's why AA's Twelve Steps begin with admitting the pain of addiction: that "we were powerless over alcohol—that our lives had become unmanageable." (We would add nicotine, drugs, money making, money spending, power, relationships, sex, work, gambling, or whatever the addiction to the list of things over which we're powerless.) The point is that, we come out of denial about the pain we feel from living under a soul-violating paradigm.

Facing our suffering—manifested as addiction—we heed its wisdom. Our emotions and bodies are no dummies. When they're abused, they register the abuse. If something is wrong, they say so, and both we and our systems need to listen.

Learning the truth about where we are is a new assumption. It's new to assume that soul pain isn't to be anesthetized or written off as personal failure so that we can get on with robot life as usual.

NORMAL SCIENCE: JUSTIFYING MISERY

Assumptions that defend the old order. Listening to pain isn't what abusive systems invite, however. Control-paradigm systems maintain control precisely by ignoring pain. They defend their workings by dismissing the suffering they impose. To them, suffering is just an unfortunate side effect of life.

If we're to succeed in control-paradigm systems, we also learn to look the other way on pain—our own or someone else's. The truth of pain is a non-truth. The control paradigm has no category for it, since control is all that matters. Human pain is deemed irrelevant to maintaining power. It's unfortunate, but not an issue.

The slavery of Africans, for instance, was—to the control-minded—an unfortunate but necessary evil, just as economic slavery around the world is today. The genocide of Native Peoples is merely the unavoidable course of progress. Oil spills are simply the cost of driving cars, animal testing is the sad fee paid for cosmetics and defense, while war industries are the price of peace. (Logic isn't the selling point here.)

That mega-wealthy multinationals pay diddly to workers who live in cardboard shacks without running water is simply the wages of a free global market. Never mind that, unlike his robber-baron competitors, when Milton Hershey built a sugar cane factory in Cuba early in this century, he built lovely, spacious, modern homes for the workers, like the ones he built for those working at his chocolate factory in Hershey, Pennsylvania. He modeled an alternative paradigm for doing business decades ago, but control-paradigm CEOs paid no attention.

Control-paradigm systems get away with their crimes against humanity and keep our commitment because they've taught us to follow their lead and ignore pain as well. When we were children and cried, we were told to stop crying—that nothing was wrong with us. We had little choice but to buy pain-dismissive assumptions: humiliating children is for their own good, Ds and Fs give students incentives to do better, unemployment is necessary to the economy, while fear of failure makes us "hungry" on the job, ready to do anything to succeed.

All these ways of dismissing pain are assumptions, not truths. They're assumptions that abusive systems use to remain unaccountable for the pain they inflict.

Assuming systems and problems are separate. Nor are these the only assumptions in the paradigm-defense arsenal. The control paradigm thwarts change by putting itself on a pedestal, out of reach. We assume that if the control paradigm is behind all our social systems, then the control paradigm must be successful. After all, it's built this huge structure of institutions—that must be some kind of achievement.

We assume further that problems are random and isolated; that they arise from outside the system and don't reflect social systems themselves; that problems are *not* system-created, certainly not paradigm-created. Paradigms and the systems that go with them are always innocent; it's the people who screw up—or maybe the random acts of nature that throw us a curve.

When a cyclone hit Bangladesh on April 30, 1991, for example, most damage occurred where three rivers—the Ganges, Brahmaputra, and Meghna—converged to form a huge delta. Massive summer floods later occurred in eastern and southeastern China. The media blamed the floods on changes in the weather, some even calling it an act of God. Few journalists mentioned the decimation of Tibetan forests by China's occupying army. Because the major rivers of Asia have their origins in Tibet, destroying Tibet's forests destroyed the natural watershed of Asia. Water poured off the mountains with no trees to stop it. The natural water management system of the continent was sold with the $54 billion worth of lumber that China "harvested" from Tibet between 1950 and 1980 (which continues to this day). The floods were therefore neither a random act of nature nor an act of God; they were an act of China's communist government ravaging invaded territory, but few in the official media noticed.*

Given assumptions that explain away problems in ways that save the paradigm and its systems, we put our energies into coping with specific problems, tackling them one by one—the reactive mode. It never occurs to us to investigate system causes, much less paradigm ones.

Caught in such system-blind, paradigm-blinded patterns, we go from crisis to crisis. We obey the no-talk rule: if we ignore pain long enough, it'll go away. We won't have to disturb the prevailing order with our suffering.

EXTRAORDINARY SCIENCE: "LEARNING THE TRUTH"

Naming the system sources of pain. Recovery allied to philosophy drops a bomb on these assumptions. Recognizing pain as pain and exposing the worldviews and systems that create pain foments revolution—a paradigm shift. We and our systems aren't separate, and our problems aren't unrelated to how social systems work. We internalize their structures and act out their dynamics. We're moving pictures of what's going on around us, walking

---

*Petra K. Kelly, *The Anguish of Tibet*, eds. Gert Bastian and Pat Aiello (Berkeley, CA: Parallax Press, 1991), 225. See also Elmar R. Reiter's chapter, "Tibetan Deforestation and Possible Climate Effects," 217–21.

libraries of what it means to live in our systems.

If we're caught in self-destructive patterns, we can bet our systems are too. That's where we got our habits in the first place. We mirror our systems in our bodies, psyches, relationships, families, and lives. Like butterflies and snail-darters, we collect system toxins inside us, until they do us in.

If we sit around wondering what we did wrong, we don't pass along the warning signals. We gum up the transformation process by trying to be stoic and cope. But the longer we deny what's happening to us as a result of being in our systems, the closer both we and our systems are to death.

Recovery sounds the alarm: we're bound by a mental model—one that's culturally endorsed, promoted, and defended—whose primary agenda is not our health or happiness but our controllability. It's time to learn the truth about what's going on.

To do this, though, we have to go outside normal-science thinking and move into extraordinary science. In the extraordinary-science phase, all our assumptions go on the table for questioning.

THE PRICE OF NOT CONFRONTING PAIN-MAKERS

Social systems in crisis. If we don't learn the truth about what's behind our pain, we and our systems go from bad to worse. When we don't take the inward initiative to confront suffering and the paradigm that creates it, outward events act out our pain. We're dragged to a point where pain can no longer be ignored.

Big business, banking, and Congress. In *When Money Is the Drug*, Donna Boundy describes how "money dysfunction" during the 1970s and 1980s created economic pain on a massive scale. Aided by the federal government, "corporations went on an unprecedented spending spree, assuming massive debt, selling assets, and failing to produce new capital, to the point where, collectively, American corporations now have more debt than net worth, and many businesses are foundering."[11]

How bad does pain have to get? The banking scandal that closed sixty-nine Ohio savings and loans and swamped investment firms in Florida, for instance, could have been avoided. After $2 million had been lost, the bank's officers could have admitted they were in over their heads—that the bank was in pain and its losses had become unmanageable. But as Donald Maggin recounts in *Builders, Bankers, Knaves, and Thieves*, it took an additional $288-million loss, criminal charges, two suicides, a fatal heart attack, and the vanishing savings of countless depositors before banking officials admitted where they were financially.

Any time during the eighties, Congress, the capitol of denial, could have blown the whistle on the mushrooming savings and loan fiasco—of which this was just one case—and prevented billions of dollars from being speculated away. Representative Henry Gonzalez of Texas, described by journalist William Greider in *Who Will Tell the People?* as an "inner directed man," was yelling about the dangers of bank deregulation as early as 1982, but his warnings fell on deaf ears. By refusing to confront a banking system out of control—made unmanageable by their own legislation—Congress refused to face the money addiction devouring both Congress and banks.

Poverty and race. Another sign of social systems in crisis is the distribution of jobs and justice among races. Donna Boundy points out that between 1973 and 1990, "African-American families lost a staggering 48 percent of their real income, compared with young white families, which lost an average of 22 percent."[12] In the 1960s, African Americans were discriminated against, but most black men had jobs, even though the jobs were minimum wage. Today, almost half of young male African Americans in cities are unemployed. Out of work, they get caught in drugs or gangs. On any given day, over half a million are in jail and prison. As legal critics observe, poverty, among other things, diminishes our access to "due process."*

Gandhi called poverty the worst form of violence. Until we name poverty as violence, we're powerless to stop it. As long as we assume it's inevitable, we'll never ask where all the wealth went. Where did all the money from all those savings and loans go, for instance? The Cayman Islands? Liechtenstein? Switzerland? And in whose names?

Instead of asking these relevant questions, we keep putting people in jail—prisons are now big business, while investment advisors continue to

---

The American Almanac: Statistical Abstract of the United States, 1995–1996 (Austin, TX: The Reference Press, 1995), chart 658, p. 420, shows unemployment figures (which are higher city by city); chart 353, p. 219, shows incarceration statistics: African Americans in prison number 427,700; in jail 195,200; on parole 301,600; and on probation 857,100; giving a total of 1,781,600.

counsel the public not to invest in inner cities. We don't ask: What core paradigm assumptions about race, human worth, and economic reality get acted out in our social systems to create this violence?

Education. How about the school system? Among the poor, illiteracy and innumeracy are rampant. But even privileged medical students forget up to 90 percent of what they're taught in the first two years of intense lectures and testing. One doctor from Eastern Europe, a personal friend of ours now administering a hospital in Ukraine, was shocked at how little American students know after medical school. He observed that the American system produces doctors who can take tests and write lab reports but who know virtually nothing about healing people.

In *Quantum Learning*, Bobbi DePorter observes that educators—following the work of psychologist Howard Gardner—identify many "higher intelligences" or "ways of knowing" that include linguistic, mathematical, visual/spatial, kinesthetic/bodily, musical, interpersonal, intrapersonal, and intuitive—but that educators resist developing any but a few of these in students.*

Now educators identify more than forty ways that students learn, yet schools continue to function as if only three or four of these exist. As we all discovered growing up, exercising interpersonal skills in the classroom—talking—brings swift punishment. That's one major skill lost to the learning process. As cooperative learning studies indicate, children discussing class material among themselves accelerates both learning and creativity.[13]

Stuck in the teacher-to-student control model, however, schools replace our multifaceted intellects with memorized facts and our creative powers with obedience to authorities. "Don't think—regurgitate" is the message. From our full range of learning styles, we're trained to ignore most and use only a few.

To change the school system, we must first admit that our schools aren't educating us—that, as John Gatto says, they're "dumbing us down." Only then will we begin to question the assumptions that make modern schooling a disaster for both students and teachers.[14]

---

*Bobbi DePorter and Mike Hernacki, *Quantum Learning* (New York: Dell, 1992), 30–31, referring to Howard Gardner's theory of multiple intelligences in his 1983 work *Frames of Mind.*

Ecology. Then there's the environment. We all know the litany: Thousands of species of plants and animals have become extinct. Millions of acres of rainforests have burned. The air and water are so polluted that we have filters on everything. So why don't things change?

Assuming that the earth is a place to be owned and controlled—exploited and polluted—creates industrial systems that function on the planet as a progressive fatal disease. Already human babies near the Mexican border are being born without brains, a condition known as *anencephaly*, at near-epidemic rates.[15] Assumptions create the corporate mind-set that creates the disasters. Until we acknowledge biosphere-pain and the assumptions that cause it, we won't make a paradigm shift. We'll go on fiddling reactively. "If we just had a better law..."

It's not just a few jerks. Somewhere along the line we have to admit not only that we have problems—we do that watching the news—but more, that our systems and the paradigm behind them bear responsibility. Global ills can't be blamed on a few jerks—the "lone assassin" dodge. Pain is caused by how our systems "think" and operate, and how we think and operate when we're in them. Once we admit this, we have to name the paradigm assumptions that turn otherwise well-intentioned social systems into factories of personal and planetary pain-making.

FROM THE CONTROL ASSUMPTION TO INSATIABILITY

Born into the control assumption. Behind all the assumptions of the control paradigm lies the central one: the control assumption. As long as we commit to the control paradigm, we assume that control is everything: it's power, success, safety, and security; it's good child-rearing, good management, and good government; it's future security, prestige, and predictable relationships. During the East Coast blizzard of 1996, at the height of the storm with gale-force winds, snow falling so fast that visibility disappeared, roads closed in many states, and emergencies declared everywhere, our local newscaster announced, "We're on top of the situation." The more control we have, the better things turn out. With control, society runs like clockwork, and we all do what we're supposed to do—what our systems expect.

As with the other assumptions, we get this one honestly. Caught in the storms and volleys of growing up, we found peace only when we were in control of our surroundings, even if the only times we felt this was when we were in our own bedroom. Being in control as adults still means seeking a haven from assault. It gives us a respite from being vulnerable to those who not only have power over us but regularly abuse it.

Control isn't everything; it's the only thing. What's more, the control assumption is culturally reinforced. From the day we're born, we find it's best to be in control. Even if we suspect that we're slipping, the last thing to do is admit it. Cover, fake it, do anything to keep the on-top image. The impression of being in control is what counts. It's what parents want, teachers demand, bosses reward, clergy preach, and voters elect.

We then carry this assumption everywhere, and our systems show it. Governments, for example, do anything to perpetuate the impression of being on top. Social order, they claim, is at stake. If, as a growing number of books and television programs suggest, alien beings are visiting the planet, some even abducting humans for medical experiments, governments likely will care first about maintaining their control image. It's the Exxon Valdez oil spill assumption: never mind the problem, just preserve the control image. Don't admit you're in over your head.

This isn't a new assumption—or apparently a new problem. In the ninth century, Emperor Charlemagne (a well-meaning monarch but a textbook case of control addiction) heard that spaceships were whizzing around, causing weather disturbances and health problems. His solution was to issue an imperial edict forbidding them to fly over his territories.[16] He may have been out of his league, but that was no reason to give up control or at least the appearance of it.

Whether it's the ninth century or the present, whether it's over foreign regimes or children, the weather or our bodies, aliens or spouses, control is the solution. With control, we're golden.

Control techniques—using drugs, money, position, deal-making, power, force, obligations, scheming, surveillance, or manipulation to get what we want—become second nature. From boardrooms to bedrooms, nonprofits to corporations, churches to crime rings, city halls to the White House, control dramas play out. The driving questions are not "How can we best do our job?" but "Who controls whom?" and "How much money did *you* get in *your* budget?"

Control leads to insatiability. But the control assumption doesn't bring the order it promises, since no amount of control is ever enough. The quest for control becomes insatiable. No one gives in to being controlled without a fight, while circumstances are even more resistant. We need more control—and more and more—to keep our edge, fighting all the way.

Insatiability in medicine. For instance, physician Larry Dossey claims that the assumption that doctors should be in control of their clients medically is a source of pain for doctors. It makes them unreceptive to alternative healing modalities, it puts them under enormous pressure to "make" people heal, and it leads to high rates of drug addiction, alcoholism, and divorce among doctors. The assumption that being a doctor means having complete and exclusive power over other people's physical health doesn't work, since not all solutions come from drugs or surgery. Believing that doctors should be omnipotent not only makes them insatiable about power—as Dossey says, they have "a need for power," and "they want to keep everything to themselves"—but also causes them pain: "The level of pain for the average M.D. in this culture is enormous!"[17]

It causes us pain as well. Dependence on high-tech chemical solutions to all our health problems has turned our bodies into flasks of drugs blending in lethal combinations. A former high-level executive with a Ph.D. in chemistry took a drug prescribed by his doctor for stress and to lower his blood pressure. But this drug had side effects, which included gout, a condition he'd never had before. The doctor prescribed a second drug, which caused bleeding stomach ulcers. Our friend lost half the blood in his body and nearly died in the hospital—all for a condition that a change in diet and regular meditation ended up alleviating. The doctor's quest for perfect chemical control of our friend's body backfired.

Insatiability in government regulations. In the quest for perfect social control, governments suffocate us with burgeoning laws, regulations, restrictions, funding procedures, rules and prohibitions, authorizations, enforcement and punishment agencies. Whatever goes wrong, control by legislation is supposed to solve it.

Thanks to decades of this policy in government, small businesses find themselves swamped with bureaucratic paperwork as they try to follow all the rules and regulations, while big businesses hire corporate lawyers to dance rings around any legislation anyone thinks up to stop them.

Insatiability in corporate media control. But not all efforts at social control come from government. Corporations take a strong interest in controlling public discourse—and are insatiable about achieving control, insofar as they're not bothered by their violations of the First Amendment. In November 1995, for instance, CBS pressured the investigative program *60 Minutes* into canceling a segment critical of the tobacco industry, presumably because CBS was about to merge with electronics giant Westinghouse, chaired by Lawrence Tisch who also heads the nation's fourth largest tobacco company, Lorillard. Because the testimony of the doctor critical of the tobacco industry was later leaked to the media, CBS decided to reverse its decision, and the program aired February 4, 1996. But the issue of corporate control of the media remains. In an editorial in *The Nation*, Peter Eisner wrote:

> Maintaining an unprecedented degree of day-to-day control over the news is high on today's corporate agenda. The CBS case and that of Hazel O'Leary, caught paying corporate consultants to "evaluate" journalists, suggest the many forms such "management" can take: dossiers on reporters; "nondisclosure" agreements with executives designed to intimidate whistleblowers; ever more imaginative and costly lawsuits to frighten news executives and their budget-minded bosses....together, they are the beginnings of a newly integrated structure for the control and limitation of news-gathering.[18]

Control worlds don't work. The seventeenth-century social philosopher Thomas Hobbes described control worlds as culminating in a war of each against all, each entity trying to maximize his or her share. Buying the assumption himself, the only solution Hobbes saw was intervention by a "Leviathan," an all-powerful dictator. But we've tried that solution more than once. With a Hitler or Stalin—who spared nothing in the quest for absolute control—pain goes through the roof, and social order goes out the window.

In case we're unconvinced about the futility of the control method, the effects of insatiability come out in society. In the post–World War II arms escalation, for instance, no amount of military might proved satisfying. The more firepower we commanded, the more we needed. After decades of a foreign policy obsessed with military control, we're faced with mind-boggling debt levels, covert criminal operations at home and abroad in the name of intelligence gathering, past decades of mutually assured destruction (MAD) defense systems, and future decades of space-age weaponry against—whom? All the while, real life-and-death issues go unaddressed: pollution, squandering natural resources, poverty, unemployment, health care, public safety, education, even topsoil erosion (growing crops without ancient volcano droppings doesn't work).

Government by control creates a government in chaos. Taoist sage Lao Tzu predicted this long ago: "Too obvious a growth in laws and regulations, and too many criminals emerge."[19] The control assumption creates worlds out of control.

STRUGGLING WITH THE CONTROL ASSUMPTION

Assumptions are powerful, for better or worse. They're like axioms in geometry—everything flows from them. Assumptions mark off the field and tell us what game to play.

Questioning assumptions has the power to change the game.

That's scary. Our problems may be frightening but, so far at least, changing the paradigm game seems scarier. It's more threatening than all the personal, social, and global ills combined because it threatens the control structure. Rethinking our core paradigm assumptions means changing social systems from the ground up—and with them, the lines of power.

Autonomy vs. the control model. What's our alternative to the control assumption, though? It's true that having some say in our lives isn't a bad idea. It's certainly better than being jerked around by the next authority figure we meet. It's also a big step out of feeling helpless. ("Hi, how are you today?" "I'm a pawn of circumstances, thanks. How are you?")

Exploring the right balance between personal autonomy and community needs is an old debate, and every culture faces it. Having some control over our lives is a basic human right. But that's precisely what the control paradigm has little concept of or respect for. Control regimes—whether patriarchal or matriarchal families, dictatorships, or religious hierarchies—assume that personal autonomy is a threat, not a right.

The control paradigm can't therefore defend itself by claiming the alternative is for us to abdicate all control over our lives—as if the only alternative to the control paradigm is our being utterly helpless. Our autonomy is what the control paradigm strives to take from us in the first place. The paradigm isn't about guaranteeing human autonomy but about invading it, so that our energies are put at the disposal of authoritarian systems.

By violating our basic rights, the control paradigm deranges our sense of what's appropriately within our control and what isn't. When little children in school aren't allowed to go to the bathroom except on breaks and wet themselves as a result, their basic rights over their bodies are violated. The message is that they don't decide when they have to go to the bathroom; authorities and their schedules do. Long term, the message is that our rights over our own bodies are conditional. If the government decides to have a war, it can forcibly round up all the male bodies of a certain age and mutilate and kill them.

More control doesn't protect us. To protect ourselves from the onslaught of control-paradigm violations, we get compulsive about controlling what's going on around us. And we have good reason. In control-paradigm worlds, the atmosphere is definitely predatory.

South Carolinians in Moore County, for instance, thought they had some measure of control over their economic lives when, during the 1960s and 1970s, they attracted large manufacturers such as Proctor Silex by offering tax breaks and ready labor. They even stretched to keep their control when Proctor Silex needed new sewer and water hook-ups to expand their plant. Moore County floated a $5.5 million municipal bond to finance these facilities, even though nearby residents lived without running water. Imagine Moore County's shock when in 1990 Proctor Silex packed up and moved to Mexico, leaving in its wake, as David Korten reports, "800 unemployed Moore County workers, drums of buried toxic waste, and the public debts that the county had incurred to finance public facilities in the company's behalf."[20]

If Moore County residents had exercised more clout, would the outcome have changed? Perhaps, but is more control a solution? Do contests for greater control protect us? One of the lessons of the corporate takeovers of the eighties is that, no matter how big we are—and who in those days would top RJR Nabisco?—there's always someone bigger with an appetite.

Playing the control game better doesn't work either. Control, it seems, isn't the answer. For one thing, if we suffer when others attempt to control us, then it's likely that others suffer when we attempt to control them. Suffering is not a good foundation for social order. It doesn't make our relationships safer.

Moreover, complete control is unattainable. Expecting ourselves to achieve it is too much of a good thing. It's not true to the human condition. Rumi said:

> In complete control, pretending control,
> with dignified authority, we are charlatans.
> Or maybe just a goat's hair brush in a painter's hand.
> We have no idea what we are.[21]

Nor can we restore personal autonomy that way. As long as we buy the control paradigm, our autonomy will be invaded by its demands—and we'll catch ourselves invading the autonomy of others. We'll invade our children's autonomy, for instance, as our parents and teachers invaded ours. Control-paradigm child-rearing leads each generation to violate the next.

In other words, playing the control game more forcefully or effectively doesn't restore our human rights. Learning the truth about the control paradigm does. It triggers a shift—an assumption shift—that's in our power to make. We take responsibility for what's ours to control: our mental models. In this new game, who's one-up isn't the issue; learning the truth is.

Making the invisible visible. From a control perspective, learning the truth without prepackaging it is unthinkable. How can we question assumptions—change the game—without first ensuring that our control remains intact? Yet that's Recovery 101. Until we analyze them, paradigm assumptions remain invisible. We figure we're just doing the usual: What paradigm? As Peter Senge says, "Structures of which we are unaware hold us prisoner."

To shift paradigms, we have to make the unseen structures visible, whether they're "out there" in social systems or ones we've internalized.

Until we do, pain-making systems continue. Their power persists as long as they remain hidden. Wilson Bryan Key, a pioneer in exposing subliminals in advertising, for instance, discovered that people who didn't believe in subliminals or didn't think they were affected were the ones most influenced.[22] It's the invisible stuff—the stuff we take for granted—that traps us. Our not noticing, not admitting, and not naming the unseen structures is how authoritarian systems get away with abuse.

Once exposed, the paradigm's days are numbered.

SHIFTING ASSUMPTIONS: THE FOOL'S LEAP

The Fool: an antidote for control. In mythology, the Fool is the one who, more than anyone, can learn the truth and admit it because the Fool is the soul of noncontrol. In medieval and Renaissance courts, no one had less power than the Fool. But that very powerlessness freed the Fool to speak the truth when no one else could, as Shakespeare shows in *King Lear*. In that sense, the Fool had more power than the king.

As a universal archetype, the Fool in us sees the absurdity of control-addicted, pain-making systems and so has no qualms about taking the leap into the unknown. Because the Fool can say what's what when everyone else is too afraid, only the Fool can name pain and its cause.

As in the old courts, our Fool doesn't care about defending the prevailing paradigm but about exposing hidden assumptions. Fools are paradigm-savvy, since juxtaposing different paradigm perspectives is how Fools both amuse and enlighten. The Fool makes us question our assumptions, even everyday ones.

One of our favorite Fools is Nasrudin, a classic character in the Sufi tradition, about whom stories are still being invented. In one story, Nasrudin goes to a bank with a check to cash. The teller asks him if he can identify himself. Nasrudin whips out a mirror and peers into it: "Yep, that's me."[23]

Another story, this time from Zen literature, illustrates how juxtaposing different perspectives makes us reflect on our paradigm's assumptions:

> Tanzan [a famous Zen monk] and Ekido were once traveling together down a muddy road. A heavy rain was still falling.
>
> Coming around a bend, they met a lovely girl in a silk kimono and sash, unable to cross the intersection.
>
> "Come on, girl," said Tanzan at once. Lifting her in his arms, he carried her over the mud.
>
> Ekido did not speak again until that night when they reached a lodging temple. Then he no longer could restrain himself. "We monks don't go near females," he told Tanzan, "especially not young and lovely ones. It is dangerous. Why did you do that?"
>
> "I left the girl there," said Tanzan. "Are you still carrying her?"[24]

Fools: Extraordinary scientists. In Kuhn's language, our inner Fool is an extraordinary scientist through and through. That's why the Fool is often depicted as ready to step off a cliff. It's an image of giving ourselves over to learning the truth, without making truth conform to our models. We throw ourselves onto reality and let truth emerge.

To show how important learning the truth is, the Fool archetype both begins and ends the hero's journey, as in the Tarot's major-arcana archetypes. The Fool is free to evolve, to go wherever the journey leads: no control assumptions obscuring where we are now, no control assumptions constricting where our path may lead. For the Fool—as for the Native American and African Tricksters—shifting paradigms isn't scary; it's fun. It's what keeps us on our toes and full of life.

John Patrick Shanley's film *Joe vs. the Volcano*, with Meg Ryan and Tom Hanks, is a wonderful meditation on the power of the Fool consciousness to name soul pain and to get us going on a paradigm shift. This theme runs through the movie, but when Joe and Patricia are about to leap into a volcano, Patricia delivers a classic Fool's line: "Joe, nobody knows anything. We'll take this leap, and we'll see. We'll jump, and we'll see. That's life." True to the Fool archetype, that leap saves their lives.

In his "Bloodstream Sermon," the fifth-century Zen Buddhist master Bodhidharma said much the same: "Once you stop clinging and let things be, you'll be free, even of birth and death. You'll transform every-thing….And you'll be at peace wherever you are."[25]

Assumptions about the universe. Fools and Tricksters can take the leap where control folks can't because they assume something different about the universe. Fools don't see the universe as hostile, always ready to take us down. If they did, they'd flee to the control assumption like everyone else. In a hostile world, we can't ever rest or let go, because that's just when bad things happen—or so we fear.

Fools and Tricksters, by contrast, assume that the universe is an inter-connected whole that's ultimately benevolent. This assumption makes it safe to take risks—safe to let go and trust that reality works with us, even if we step off the cliff. The Fool in us takes the big s—ity words to heart: we mean, of course, *synchronicity, serendipity,* and *spontaneity.*

In other words, the Fool assumes that the most meaningful things come out of the blue and turn our lives in directions we never dreamed possible. Western religions call it "grace." Granted, it takes a Fool consciousness to live by grace (they didn't tell us that in the Bible), but without this consciousness, we miss gifts that can't be controlled into existence. Love, for example, is a free gift; we can't force someone to love us.

No fools, they. Not that Fools are complete idiots. They know that the control paradigm can make the world dangerous. But Fools and Tricksters don't assume that the control paradigm has the last word on reality, neither do they assume that we must commit to it or roll over and play dead before it. As long as they're willing to take the leap into extraordinary science, they don't get stuck in paradigms that make life dangerous. Instead, they're light on their feet and "wiser than serpents."

Following the Fool's wisdom, we make a paradigm shift away from the control model, and we don't live the negative Fool archetype of repeatedly giving ourselves over to systems that chew us up and spit us out. Once or twice is sufficient to get our attention and convince our inner Fool that it's time to take the leap.

Assumptions about human beings. As to the Fool's assumptions about human nature, Fools don't assume that human beings are competitive, selfish, and greedy by nature, as Hobbes did and the control paradigm does. Native American Tricksters have great fun showing how silly greed and arrogance are—they're just not human ways of being. Try as we may, we can't make them work. One story, "Coyote and Wasichu," told at Grass Mountain, Rosebud Indian Reservation, South Dakota, makes the point:

> There was a white man [*wasichu*] who was such a sharp trader that nobody ever got the better of him. Or so people said, until one day a man told this *wasichu:* "There's somebody who can outcheat you anytime, anywhere."
>
> "That's not possible," said the *wasichu.* "I've had a trading post for many years, and I've cheated all the Indians around here."
>
> "Even so, Coyote can beat you in any deal."
>
> "Let's see whether he can. Where is Coyote?"
>
> "Over there, that tricky-looking guy."
>
> "Okay, all right, I'll try him."
>
> The *wasichu* trader went over to Coyote. "Hey, let's see you outsmart me."

"I'm sorry," said Coyote, "I'd like to help you out, but I can't do it without my cheating medicine."

"Cheating medicine, hah! Go get it."

"I live miles from here and I'm on foot. But if you'd lend me your fast horse?"

"Well, all right, you can borrow it. Go on home and get your cheating medicine!"

"Well, friend, I'm a poor rider. Your horse is afraid of me, and I'm afraid of him. Lend me your clothes; then your horse will think that I am you."

"Well, all right. Here are my clothes; now you can ride him. Go get that medicine. I'm sure I can beat it!"

So Coyote rode off with the *wasichu's* fast horse and his fine clothes while the *wasichu* stood there bare-assed.[26]

Taoist philosophy concurs. A controlling, domineering attitude is the greatest unwisdom, because it violates our natural capacities. Like the Fool, the Taoist sage feels no urge to force people into particular roles. They assume instead the power of "actionless action":

I take no action and the people are transformed of themselves;
I prefer stillness and the people are rectified of themselves;
I am not meddlesome and the people prosper of themselves;
I am free from desire and the people of themselves become simple like the
    uncarved block [their original nature].[27]

When we're neither being controlled nor trying to control others, our innate wholeness emerges.

FLEXING OUR ASSUMPTION-SHIFTING POWERS

The tools of transformation. All these assumptions—about misery, competition, social systems, problems, control, the nature of the universe, and human nature—serve as axioms for us and our societies. They define the starting point of our paradigm, which in turn provides the channels that our lives flow in. Paradigm assumptions set up the games we play. They call our systems into being and define how they operate and how we operate in them. Assumptions hold awesome power over us—that is, until we use our inner power to question them.

Shifting assumptions is the stuff of change. It carries a force that terrifies control systems, because it's where transformation starts. Recovery lets our paradigm-shifting powers out of the cage, so we can flex our inward muscles.

Assuming that we're supposed to be in control, for instance, is one premise. Realizing that this doesn't work is another. Shifting from one to the other gets our wheels turning. We're on our way to new models.

What's within our power. Tapping our power to change our mental models—shift paradigms—is an ancient wisdom path. Epictetus, a Roman philosopher living in the first to second centuries C.E., started his teaching by sorting out what's in our power and what's not. Born a slave and crippled in one leg by his master, Epictetus knew what was and wasn't in his power. Using this knowledge, he became one of the most respected teachers in the classical world.

Beyond our power, Epictetus said, are things such as our birth and upbringing, our race and gender, what other people think and do, the weather, laws of nature, and ultimately the laws of the whole.

Within our power is our inward awareness—our assumptions and ideas, our beliefs, desires, goals, and expectations—all the mind tools that make up our inward operating system, our paradigm. In other words, within our power is everything that shapes the way we look at the world and live in it. According to Epictetus, that's our greatest power—a power that's ours no matter what.

That's also the most interesting part, because that's what we can change.

Using what's in our power—or not. The trouble is, Epictetus explained, our real powers lie unused, while we struggle to control things that aren't ours to control. We get insatiable almost immediately—trying harder and harder to control things we can't while neglecting to do what we can. Working to maintain power over people and events, we don't use the power we have to change our inward models. It's a formula for disaster—real powerlessness.

In Zen Mind, Beginner's Mind, the late Zen master Shunryu Suzuki put it this way: "When we have our body and mind in order, everything else will exist in the right place, in the right way. But usually, without being aware of it, we try to change something other than ourselves, we try to order things outside us. But it is impossible to organize things if you yourself are not in order."[28]

Why do we get so confused about what's in our power?

For one thing, we don't see our inward life as being powerful. Our assumptions have become part of us, so they're functionally invisible (there's that invisible element again). We've picked up our assumptions from television, friends, teachers, and family and then taken them on as our own. Our paradigm is just who we are. What power is there in that?

Also, fiddling with our inward make-up seems scary. Outward systems have conditioned us not to trust what's within; we dare not tamper with their programming of us. We're afraid we'll lose our place in systems if we start challenging what we've internalized from them.

But most of all, we don't use this power because control-minded systems tell us not to: it's not adult to change. Experts and authorities don't change their minds, much less their entire inward operating system. Change implies that we didn't know what we were doing in the first place, and that's not something control-conscious societies encourage. If we've "arrived," we know how to do things, we're sure about it, and we stick to it. Shift paradigms? No way.

Open to evolution. But these are old traps, ones a wise Fool won't fall for. Along with Epictetus, Fools know that the same invisible dimension that, in Senge's words, "holds us prisoner" can be our way to freedom and strength: inward change—shifting paradigms—is the ticket.

According to spiritual teachings, change is what we're here to do. It's all around us. The pre-Socratic philosopher Heraclitus said we can't step into the same river twice, because the river never stays the same. Currents shift, and different water flows through. The Buddha and Lao Tzu, who lived roughly at the same time as Heraclitus, said much the same: reality is an ongoing process.

For that matter, so are we. Learning change is learning the truth of who we are. Even our bodies, which seem constant, are constantly changing. As physician Deepak Chopra says, we get new stomachs every few days, new hearts and livers every few months, new bones every few years. Why shouldn't our inner lives be as free and fluid as our cells?

Change doesn't mean we've failed; it means reality is doing its thing with us, and we're moving with it. We're currents in reality's fluid process, and we're simply acting from our nature in response to what is.

By opening our assumptions to change, we open ourselves to transformation. We don't necessarily know what's coming next; we simply refuse to be locked into assumptions that turn our systems into pain-makers and ourselves into addicts. We start flexing our inward muscles to use our greatest power: our capacity to evolve.

PARADIGM SHIFTS RIPPLING OUT

Change on a roll. As we question our assumptions, our systems are in for a surprise. Inward change percolates outward. When we shift our paradigm commitment, our systems feel the impact. Just as a stone thrown into a lake sends ripples over the entire surface, we find ourselves creating—even demanding—new worlds.

How does this ripple effect work?

To start, instead of spinning our wheels trying to maximize control "out there," we investigate the invisible control programming that we carry within. Rather than trying to "control" pain away, mostly by ignoring it, we begin to allow ourselves to feel it, to pay attention to its message, and to go on the journey of transformation that soul pain asks us to take.

Shifting our assumptions, we start altering our decisions. Whereas control assumptions limit what friends we'll have, what person we'll marry, what education we'll pursue, or what job we'll seek, abandoning the control paradigm expands our options. We let other factors enter into the process besides "How does this affect my position in the control hierarchy?"—factors such as "Does this bring happiness or meaning?" "Does it offer opportunities for being creative?" "Is this something I'd love doing?"

Our shift in assumptions ripples farther out to our relationships. We don't assume that we must control relationships in order for them to "work." Putting aside the roles designed to preserve the chain of control, we begin interacting person to person, soul to soul.

As we move away from the control paradigm ourselves and in our relationships, we change what we'll tolerate in our social systems. Knowing how deadly the control game is, we spot it in schools, businesses, churches, communities, and governments. The notion that power-over muscling is just business as usual, government as usual, or education as usual doesn't sway us. We know it's deadly.

Changes reverberating in consciousness. That's not all. If the Fool is right—not to mention spiritual teachings, quantum physics, and ecological science—we live in an interconnected universe. It's not just the systems closest to us that our assumption shifts affect. A Chinese proverb states: "Cut a blade of grass and you shake the universe."

Physicists such as Fred Alan Wolf, John Wheeler, and David Bohm have said as much. At the deepest levels of atoms and energy, everything is woven together "without seam or rent." That being so, "in here" changes spark changes "out there," even if we don't see them. The invisible has its impact, only this time on the side of world change.

Those who study consciousness—whether Buddhists, biologists, or neurophysiologists—often suggest that consciousness operates through interconnecting fields that embrace all things: earth and animals, plants and humans, stars and galaxies, and possibly other dimensions. When something moves within these consciousness fields, the totality feels it. Even slight shifts send out pattern-changing vibrations.

Morphogenetic fields. Biologist Rupert Sheldrake calls these unseen patterns "morphogenetic fields." *Morphic* means "form," while *genetic* means "generative" or "creative." Combined, the term points to invisible fields that generate the forms we experience. That's exactly what paradigms do.

The idea of consciousness fields creating forms is really a simple concept. For example, the paradigm we bring to businesses, families, schools, relationships, and religious institutions is a morphogenetic field, and it generates the forms of businesses, families, and so forth that we have. As long as we use a particular morphogenetic field (a given paradigm), we bring into existence certain types of businesses, families, schools, and relationships.

If, for example, we bring a control paradigm to education, we create a system devoted to conformity. Students learn to do what they're told, and they're told to be normal, act normally, and think normally. If, by contrast, we bring a creativity paradigm to education, we create a system devoted to...well, learning. Students wrestle with ideas, which challenge them both to express themselves and to contribute to the community. The paradigm determines the form of the system.

When the paradigm or invisible field shifts, we all sense it, even though we're physically unconnected. Sheldrake calls this "morphic resonance." It's as if we're all on-line with the same consciousness database. When we forge new models of relationships, self-worth, or business, suddenly our databank gets richer. New models spontaneously come up on our screens. We all start tapping into the new forms and using them without even being told that they're there.

Simultaneous learning. This isn't how we usually think social change happens. Assuming quantitative models, we assume change occurs only when a majority of people read about it in the paper and agree. Polls then tell us what's changing.

But that's not what Sheldrake finds—not only among humans but among blue tits as well. (That's a bird, not a body part of a blue alien on *Star Trek*, but we digress....) When only a few birds discovered a new trick for getting food—specifically, stealing milk from milk bottles—blue tits all over England started pulling the same trick. Even blue tits in Holland joined in, though few of the birds had been in physical contact with each other.[29]

People encounter the same phenomenon in animal training. A few chimpanzees in Australia may take six months to learn a word. But once they learn the word, other chimps around the world learn the same word in less time, though they've had no contact with the learned primates. Somehow, in the chimp field of consciousness, the word is there and others pick up on it.*

This consciousness-connectedness is suggested by the "hundredth monkey" idea, derived from a case of monkeys learning to wash sand off sweet potatoes: "When a certain critical number achieves an awareness, this new awareness may be communicated mind to mind,...so that this awareness is picked up by almost everyone."[30] All of a sudden, monkeys everywhere started washing their sand-covered food, even on isolated islands.

Sports analysts observe the phenomenon as well. Before a record is broken—lifting five hundred pounds or running a four-minute mile—no one seems able to do the feat. But after one person breaks the record, suddenly

---

*Actually, we can't cite the source for this, but we seem to remember seeing it on television. Rupert Sheldrake explores this issue—"the transmission of learning by morphic resonance"—extensively in *The Presence of the Past*, especially pp. 173–81, and though he does mention the anecdotal evidence of dog and horse trainers, falconers, cattle ranchers, and dairy farmers, the main species he discusses is rats. Rats are a noble and much maligned species, but we thought you'd rather hear about chimps.

many athletes do that and better. Once a resistance point is broken, the door opens, and others sail through.

In other words, when there's a breakthrough in consciousness, we all feel it. When one of us takes a leap into extraordinary science, we're all more able to make a leap as well. When one of us breaks a paradigm commitment, we're all less bound to it.

The power of recovery. That's a long way of saying that the progress each of us makes in learning the truth has consciousness-changing, paradigm-changing, system-changing, and ultimately world-changing effects. As we each go forward in questioning assumptions and confronting where we are, neither our paradigms nor the systems created by them can stay the same. By admitting how certain assumptions disempower us in our personal experience, we break their spell everywhere. What looks like a few people acknowledging that they're in pain turns out to be a breakthrough for humanity—what we as a species will tolerate.

Far from disempowering us, then, learning the truth, admitting pain, and questioning assumptions gives us the courage to take the leap and go on the journey—and to bring our systems along with us.

When we leap, what next? If our assumptions need to shift, how do we do it? How do we evolve our assumptions in the directions we want to go?

Notes to Chapter 1

1. John Moyne and Coleman Barks, trans., *Open Secret: Versions of Rumi* (Putney, VT: Threshold Books, 1984), 16.
2. Coleman Barks, trans., *One-Handed Basket Weaving: Poems on the Theme of Work from the Mathnawi* (Athens, GA: Maypop Books, 1991), 116.
3. Coleman Barks, trans., *Feeling the Shoulder of the Lion: Poems and Teaching Stories from the Mathnawi* (Putney, VT: Threshold Books, 1991), 88.
4. Donald Barlett and James Steele, *America: What Went Wrong?* (Kansas City, MO: Andrews and McMeel, 1992), 67.
5. Barlett and Steele, *America: What Went Wrong?*, 69.
6. Qtd. in Kevin Phillips, *The Politics of Rich and Poor: Wealth and the American Electorate in the Reagan Aftermath* (New York: Random House, 1990), 219.
7. Alfie Kohn, *No Contest: The Case Against Competition* (New York: Houghton Mifflin, 1992), 198.
8. Alice Miller, *For Your Own Good* (New York: Noonday Press/Farrar, Straus, Giroux, 1983), 13.
9. Robert Jay Lifton, *The Nazi Doctors* (New York: Basic Books/HarperCollins, 1986), 22–44.
10. *Credible Answers for a Cruelty-Free World*, a publication by The National Anti-Vivisection Society (53 W. Jackson Boulevard, Suite 1552, Chicago, IL 60604).
11. Donna Boundy, *When Money Is the Drug: The Compulsion for Credit, Cash, and Chronic Debt* (San Francisco: HarperSanFrancisco, 1993), 78–79.
12. Boundy, *When Money Is the Drug*, 78.
13. Alfie Kohn, *Punished by Rewards* (New York: Houghton Mifflin, 1993), 54, 214–16, 223, 246.
14. John Taylor Gatto, *Dumbing Us Down: The Hidden Curriculum of Compulsory Schooling* (Philadelphia: New Society, 1992), 8–9, 19, 100.
15. Elizabeth Kadetsky, "International News," *Ms.* (January/February 1994), 12.
16. William Bramley, *The Gods of Eden* (San Jose: Dahlin Family Press, 1990), 13.
17. Hal Zina Bennett, ed. *Larry Dossey in Conversation with Michael Toms* (Lower Lake, CA: Aslan Publishing, 1994), 70–71.
18. Peter Eisner, "Editorial: Tobacco's Chokehold," *The Nation*, 4 December 1995.
19. Lao Tzu, *Tao Te Ching*, LVI (The Tao of Power), trans. R. L. Wing (Garden City, NY: Dolphin/Doubleday, 1986), 57.
20. David Korten, *When Corporations Rule the World* (West Hartford, CT: Kumarian Press, and San Francisco: Berrett-Koehler, 1995), 128–29.
21. John Moyne and Coleman Barks, trans., *Unseen Rain: Quatrains of Rumi* (Putney, VT: Threshold Books, 1986), 79.
22. Wilson Bryan Key, *The Age of Manipulation: The Con in Confidence, the Sin in Sincere* (New York: Henry Holt, 1989), 37.
23. Idries Shah, ed., *The Subtleties of the Inimitable Mulla Nasrudin* (New York: E. P. Dutton & Co., 1973), 154.
24. Nyogen Senzaki and Paul Reps, trans., *Zen Flesh, Zen Bones: A Collection of Zen and Pre-Zen Writings* (New York: Anchor Books/Doubleday, 1961), 18.

25. Red Pine, trans., *The Zen Teaching of Bodhidharma* (Berkeley, CA: North Point Press, 1987), 41.
26. Richard Erdoes and Alfonso Ortiz, eds., *American Indian Myths and Legends* (New York: Pantheon, 1984), 342.
27. Lao Tzu, *Tao Te Ching*, LVII, trans., D. C. Lau (New York: Penguin Classics, 1963), 118.
28. Shunryu Suzuki, *Zen Mind, Beginner's Mind*, ed. Trudy Dixon (New York: John Weatherhill Inc., 1970), 27.
29. Rupert Sheldrake, *The Presence of the Past: Morphic Resonance and the Habits of Nature* (Rochester, VT: Park Street Press, 1988, 1995), 177–80.
30. Ken Keyes, *The Hundredth Monkey: And Other Paradigms of the Paranormal* (Coos Bay, OR: Vision Books, 1981), 17.

CHAPTER 2

Power in Whole-Minded Shifts

Honoring the truth
Second of the Twelve Cycles of Truth,
the Iroquois Peace Confederacy Tradition

Something opens our wings. Something
makes boredom and hurt disappear.
Someone fills the cup in front of us:
We taste only sacredness.
Rumi[1]

Once we're aware that we need to shift the assumptions behind our social systems, how do we set the process in motion? We're lugging around an army of assumptions that aren't doing us or our systems any good, yet for some reason we can't get the army to budge. Why? What's keeping us from changing on the deep, paradigm levels that have the greatest power to turn us in new directions?

MAY THE FORCE BE WITH US

Assuming a force for wholeness. It's not because reality forbids the change. If anything, reality manifests a force for evolution. Otherwise, why would there be evolution at all? Even the most die-hard Darwinians, for instance, admit that it's statistically impossible for a brain such as ours to evolve by random mutation within a few million years. The odds are phenomenal against that degree of complexity appearing by chance in such an evolutionarily short period of time.

When it comes to our psyches, we experience a similar force for evolving wholeness. Why, for example, do we receive dreams that spur our inner growth? Why does happiness consistently elude us, if our self-esteem has been zapped? The fact that we become self-destructive both personally and culturally when our inner lives are fractured suggests that our souls want wholeness or they want out. Soulless living appears not to be an option, not a tolerable one anyway.

Those in the healing professions depend on this force for wholeness. It's innate to living beings, though it eludes science. Medicine can make the conditions right for healing, but it can't make healing happen. Doctors can't make bones knit, for instance, nor can therapists make emotional wounds mend. That's something our bodies and psyches do on their own.

The wholeness principle. This has led many healers, transformers, and change agents to assume a force for wholeness that operates on all levels—personal to cultural, cellular to global. They call it the "wholeness principle," a power that moves us toward unity. As Anna Lemkow explores in her book *The Wholeness Principle*, something causes our physical, mental, emotional, and social systems to strive for unity and to work to restore wholeness when it's been violated.

What is that something? The wholeness principle seems to be a dynamic in our lives that urges us to integrate all aspects of who we are and what we do. Whereas the control paradigm fragments, the wholeness principle unifies (one reason that the control paradigm can't ultimately work). Transpersonal psychologist Frances Vaughan writes, "wholeness implies a harmonious integration of physical, emotional, mental, and spiritual aspects of well-being as well as social responsibility."[2]

This unification or integration seems to be the force behind healing. Deepak Chopra writes: "Healing is nothing other than the restoration of the memory of wholeness."[3] Integration and unity live in our bones, as Chopra says, "literally." Why shouldn't this force operate to bring about psychological and social healing as well? After all, we're talking about wholeness. If wholeness is a universal principle, pieces of our lives can't opt out.

The "holomovement": Unfolding and enfolding. Why is there a force for wholeness? Presumably because wholeness is the nature of reality. Reality, as physicist and holistic philosopher David Bohm suggested, is "an undivided, unbroken wholeness" that isn't static but has its own dynamics. Bohm called it the "holomovement." In *Wholeness and the Implicate Order*, he wrote: "In my scientific and philosophical work, my main concern has been with understanding the nature of reality in general and of consciousness in particular as a coherent whole, which is never static or complete, but which is in an unending process of movement and unfoldment."[4] What we experience as the world of incredible diversity is actually the holomovement unfolding in time and space, both as consciousness and as matter, with wholeness embedded in each part. Wholeness is written in our bones. It's our cosmic DNA, the universal life code.

As a result, we can't cut and carve this wholeness without running into trouble. Our essence is to be whole and to move with the holomovement. Split us into pieces, and we start trying to rediscover our wholeness—the first step of which is to acknowledge how painful it is to be broken. That's the force for wholeness at work.

This view of reality as fundamentally whole was pioneered by Jan Christiaan Smuts in his 1926 book *Holism and Evolution* (yes, the same General Smuts who, as field marshal and prime minister of South Africa, faced off against Gandhi, and who later became his good friend). Smuts conceived "a Holistic Universe," which gave wholeness to everything from matter to human personality to evolution. In fact, he referred to evolution as "the gradual development and stratification of progressive series of wholes, stretching from the inorganic beginnings to the highest levels of spiritual creation."[5]

It's behind our spiritual journey. But this hierarchy of wholes—what the late comprehensive thinker Arthur Koestler called the "holarchy"[6]—isn't static. It's the integrating force which, on consciousness levels, urges our spiritual growth. In Bohm's terms, the holomovement not only unfolds its order into time-space diversity but also enfolds diversity back into its original wholeness. We experience that enfolding as our inner evolution.

As we enfold back into the holomovement, we find we've never left it. We and the whole of reality exist in an unbroken relationship. That's another way of expressing what many spiritual traditions teach: that the soul, inner self, or "Atman" (the Hindu term) is one with the Whole, God, the

Tao, Brahman, or Being, just as a wave exists in an unbroken relationship with the ocean (an ancient metaphysical image).

Because of this unbroken relationship, our inner whole-connectedness is always there to help us reclaim our wholeness. Psychosynthesis counselor Molly Young Brown writes that our soul or "Higher Self" "transcends our personality, our situation in life, our roles, our gender." But this doesn't make our souls remote or above our everyday needs:

> Self is present no matter how confused, in pain, lost, or broken we may feel. Its energy is available for guidance and support as we make our way through our lives, in these bodies, with these personalities, within whatever situations we find ourselves. I believe "Self" is akin to the "Higher Power" that is the source of healing for recovering alcoholics and others in Twelve Step programs of recovery.[7]

REAL INCENTIVES TO SHIFT

Shifting assumptions as our response to reality. Given these assumptions about wholeness and our relation to it, shifting paradigms is actually our response to something deeper. We confront paradigms that violate our wholeness because on some level reality pushes us to do so.

In the end, the holomovement is greater than our control-paradigm systems. Trying to reduce us and our worlds to something compartmentalized and controllable isn't all that successful. Or, in biblical terms, "God is bigger than the rule of tyrants"—the gist of Isaiah's famous fortieth chapter.

Philosopher Danah Zohar and psychiatrist Ian Marshall put this in practical terms. In the really real world, doing everything for power, influence, or control doesn't work as well as we're supposed to think it does. Being sensitive to our environment and listening to what it's telling us may be much more effective. In *The Quantum Society*, they write: "Quantum holism may be telling us that power relations are not the only, or perhaps even the most effective, way that people and events can be linked in society. The politician or the manager who tries to 'influence' or 'control' events may be less effective than one who can be sensitive to the spontaneous emergence of social or political 'trends.'"[8]

If one set of assumptions cuts us off from our wholeness and another doesn't, it makes sense to shift. Our innate link to wholeness requires it.

Shifting assumptions doesn't depend, therefore, on our strength of will, or even on our wanting or not wanting to buck the established control-order. A power beyond us makes us react against systems that wage war on our reality. It's not being rebellious or willful to resent assaults on who we are. It's being moved by the wholeness principle to seek paradigms that honor our inner lives.

The wholeness principle won't be denied by us. Learning the truth by admitting pain (chapter 1) brings the change process into the open. But the wholeness principle was operating long before.

The force for wholeness was already at work, for example, when addictive habits started ruining our health and relationships. Our innate wholeness wouldn't let us be both soul-traumatized and okay. Before that, the wholeness principle was at work to expose soul-fracturing assumptions by giving us addictions. Addictions express our pain when systems say to our face or to our wallets: "You're nobody, you're not worth beans, and until you conform and move up in the system, you don't exist except as an object of exploitation and abuse."

It's hard not to warm up to such an endearing message. But as much as we try to get along with control-paradigm systems, we couldn't have them abuse us repeatedly and not react. When we tried to squelch our rage and "do our duty," the wholeness principle made sure it all came out in addictions.

The wholeness principle even made our system-induced diseases progressive. We had to face our situation, or we'd die. Wholeness wouldn't be denied.

It won't be denied by society either. But the same assumption that holds for personal change holds for social change as well. The same force for wholeness that operates on us individually operates on society.

And it can be as much of a nuisance. As in personal life, the wholeness principle can put our social structures through hell if that's what it takes to expose pain-making assumptions. The realization that we either shift paradigms or go belly up doesn't come easily.

For example, the wholeness principle operates when corporate raiders bring down entire industries. Seeing this, we're not so quick to buy the assumption that economies need greed to be healthy. Greed is a win/lose,

I-have/you-don't premise—the opposite of wholeness in economic exchange. Because greed is compulsive, insatiable, and destructive, it's not good business sense; it's addiction. To recover our business systems, we have to understand that greed is addiction and that it'll wipe us out if we don't give it up. One compelling way to learn this is to live through greed's fury.

The robber barons: Discovering what we don't want. The force for wholeness operates, therefore, when bottom-line thinking destroys communities and the earth. Making decisions only to maximize profits is addict-think, born directly from the control paradigm. It's fear driven, blind to wider consequences, designed to concentrate wealth and power, and definitely mood altering.

Since the post–Civil War rise of corporations, power-and-money-addicted men drove themselves to control markets and multiply their wealth far beyond what they could ever spend, even at cost to their own health and happiness. Their fear-driven and ruthlessly competitive mentalities have been widely documented. Matthew Josephson's *The Robber Barons* and the countless biographies of the turn of the century "wealthy and powerful" show how these people thought and where it took them.

But money and power addiction didn't stop with the old robber barons. Profit addiction achieves new levels in corporations, where blindness to consequences is an art form. Russell Mokhiber in *Corporate Crime and Violence* writes that "corporations kill 28,000 people and seriously injure 130,000 every year by selling dangerous and defective products. On the job, over 100,000 employees die annually owing to workplace exposure to toxins and other hazards." As Paul Hawken notes, that doesn't count "the Ford Pinto, Bhopal, the Dalkon Shield, Exxon Valdez, Love Canal, et al."[9]

The fact that economic textbooks teach bottom-lining doesn't change the results. Appealing to the sanctity of the bottom line doesn't make the air and water less polluted, for instance, nor does it stop Washington Beltway consultants and lobbyists from using public taxes to multiply private profits. The pervasiveness of bottom-line thinking doesn't make it less of an addiction either. If something is an addiction, it's destructive, and the wholeness principle exposes it as such.

"Let all the poisons hatch out." In the televised version of Robert Graves' *I Claudius*, the aged emperor Claudius, surrounded by those plotting against his life, says, "Let all the poisons that lurk in the mud hatch out." In paradigm-shift terms: "Let soul-violating assumptions—and the addictions we get from them—expose themselves for what they are, so that we can name them as destructive and rid ourselves of them." The wholeness principle makes poison assumptions hatch out.

What else could we expect? Wholeness-violating premises don't work. They fragment and isolate, which means they offer no sustainability. Further, control-paradigm assumptions lack the coordinating intelligence of whole systems, which means they create systems that function as cancers: they don't know when to stop, even when they're killing their host.

By assuming that it's okay for a part to dominate the whole—for a few people to control the lives of millions—control systems shut out whole system information, which means they're blind to the toll they take on the people and systems around them. But their blindness doesn't save them. One way or another, a power beyond us makes us face this toll, even when we'd rather not rock the boat. Either we change our premises or we suffer.

Prophecies for this age. That's more or less the choice that seers have prophesied for the present age. Heavy-duty prophecies about our current period exist in many religions—prophecies that make sense in a paradigm-shift context. No matter what calendar ancient peoples used (Native American, Buddhist, Zoroastrian, Hindu, Christian, or Jewish) prophets saw the next few decades as bringing massive, planetwide upheaval.

But the predictions aren't only ancient or made by the visionary few. In the seventies and eighties, psychologist Helen Wambach and her colleague Chet Snow, who documented their research in *Mass Dreams of the Future*, discovered similar predictions of global trauma emerging from the everyday folks they hypno-progressed into the future.

What did these college students, truck drivers, lawyers, and doctors see? From a paradigm-shift perspective, they foresaw destructive models reaching their zenith in personal, social, and earth crises. To put it another way, they saw the wholeness principle spurring transformation by exposing abusive systems for what they are. Just as the body brings dead cells to the surface to expel them, the force for wholeness brings deadening patterns to the surface so we can shake them off and come alive again.

The downside is that the enlivening process can be traumatic. Like a limb that's gone to sleep, the waking up can hurt. The upside is that the wholeness principle intervenes on mass addictions as well as personal ones. Our systems can't deny the mandate for wholeness any more than we can. The longer they try, the worse things get.

In fact, how quickly we respond—how bad crises get before we act—is the question. Here prophecies stop. That control systems culminate in crises is predictable. How we respond isn't.

The good news is that the Native Americans who have begun to talk publicly about their sacred prophecies say that the consciousness on earth is changing so quickly that the worst-case scenarios probably won't happen. The wholeness principle has our attention, we're acknowledging pain, and we're tracing pain to its system and paradigm sources. That's enough for global healing to begin.

The force for wholeness. The first assumption, then, concerning how we shift paradigms is that we're brought to a shift-or-suffer crisis because of a power greater than us but central to reality.

It's the same assumption expressed in the second of AA's Twelve Steps, which summarizes the reflections of AA's founders on their own change experiences: we "Came to believe that a Power greater than ourselves could restore us to sanity." As with doctors, AA's founders realized they couldn't make recovery happen; they had to assume a force for wholeness that urges recovery in spite of the insanity of addiction.

True, the wholeness force can shake us up. Because of it, we can't harbor assumptions that violate our innate wholeness and not have trouble. Our assumptions and those of our systems will surface. Either we evolve beyond them, or we go through hell.

If there were no wholeness principle, we'd take hell in stride. Soul-fracturing assumptions would create a norm we'd be happy to accept. No voice in us would object. The fact that whole-violating assumptions create micro and macro system collapse, however, suggests that something's amiss. We can't fly in the face of the integrity of individuals, communities, societies, and the planet and expect everyone to thrive.

We can't, for example, have schools where students aren't allowed to think, businesses where employees can't be creative, governments where public servants can't serve the public, or churches where people aren't free spiritually—and be healthy. Fracturing assumptions—as the control, power-over, and competition assumptions are—don't create worlds that work; they create worlds in pain.

The wholeness principle makes this awareness inescapable.

ASSUMPTIONS THAT BLOCK PARADIGM SHIFTS

So what's the problem? If the wholeness principle is at work, what's stopping us from chucking pain-making assumptions? Why are we still bound by premises that make us suffer? "How long, O Lord, how long?"

The "why?" and "how long?" don't have to do with the wholeness principle but with assumptions that clog its workings.

Doctors assume that healing occurs most rapidly when conditions are right for it. Though they can't force healing, they can remove obstacles to the process. As therapists Richard Carlson and Benjamin Shield write in *Healers on Healing*, "Wholeness or health is our natural state. The nature of healing involves removing the obstructions to this natural state and bringing individuals into alignment with themselves and their world."[10]

If something obstructs our innate wholeness, though we're capable of healing, we won't heal. In paradigm shifts, micro or macro, that's where philosophy doctors come in—and we're each our own best doctor. Our philosophical task is to uncover the obstacles: assumptions that put a wall between us and the force for wholeness.

Assuming the norm is good. For instance, a powerful assumption that blocks paradigm shifts is the assumption that the norm is good and that we should all conform to it. Change is useful, we assume, only if it brings us in line with the social standard, whatever that's perceived to be.

For decades this was the premise of therapy: people are healthy when they've adjusted to the social norm, whether it's having a *Leave It to Beaver* nuclear family or working a job just for money.

But what if the norm is unhealthy? Is there such a thing as a healthy Nazi, for instance? Yet Nazi-like obedience to authorities is the norm expected of us in compulsory schooling as well as in many corporations, governments, and churches. It's also been considered normal to smoke and sunbathe, as well as to have low self-esteem and to die of decrepitude.

Assuming that the norm is good makes us exchange our own values for something that's collectively sick. Rumi said, "If you follow the ways in which you have been trained, which you may have inherited, for no other reason than this, you are illogical."[11]

Questioning the norm and its power over us, Deepak Chopra writes, "According to the ancient Indian philosophy of ayurveda, one of the reasons people grow old, age and die is that they see other people growing old, aging and dying.... I'd like to persuade you that seeing is not believing, that it is just a superstition, a superstition of materialism."[12]

But most important, assuming the norm is good denies our uniqueness. Even our dysfunctions are unique to us, in that they're our own souls' ways of coping with abuse. Instead of denying them, we need to listen to their special message. Why should we give up who we uniquely are for something everybody else presumably is? (Whether everybody really is monolithically "normal" is another question.)

Assuming system norms. The same norm-is-good assumption blocks change in systems. Systems grow healthier as their internal diversity increases, because then they respond to challenges with greater flexibility. Nonetheless, our assumptions about social systems discourage diversity.

Families, schools, businesses, churches, and governments work out a norm that we take for granted. We assume a set of roles and then limit ourselves to those few differences: e.g., parent/child, boss/employee, expert/student, all variations of authority/underling. We act out the roles and perpetuate the behavior patterns. From our full range of talents and creativity, run-of-the-mill controller/controlled roles are all systems get from us.

Even when we all experience the norm as unsatisfying and realize that our systems are impoverished by it, we still tolerate it. Our paradigm says the system norm is good, or at least not so bad as to warrant change. Whenever change—new diversity—pops up on the horizon, we rally to neutralize it and to reestablish systems-as-usual. To borrow an image from Arthur Koestler, whenever a new idea appears, the "normal scientists" of our social systems grab their Neanderthal clubs, run out of their caves, and beat it to death.

Maintaining system equilibrium. In systems language, assuming that the norm is good reflects the tendency in systems to maintain homeostasis—stability and equilibrium—by offsetting outside influences. Systems perpetuate stable states, because that's what we ask them to do. We expect social systems to lend some predictable order to our lives.

But when order becomes a straitjacket, we have to weigh the benefits of a predictable order against the price we're paying: narrowing our possibilities, ignoring our talents, and suppressing our pain.

Assuming the norm is good isn't good at that point. The assumption keeps us from responding to the force for wholeness and moving into extraordinary science. As long as we defend the system norm, we won't seek paradigms that honor the truth and bring out the best in us and in our societies. A norm-is-good assumption blocks a paradigm shift.

Vine Deloria Jr., a Native American writer and professor of history, law, religious studies, and political science at the University of Colorado, shows how the norm operates in academia to shut out new perspectives and narrow the range of officially acceptable academic discourse:

> Many subjects, no matter how interesting, are simply prohibited because they call into question long-standing beliefs. Prestigious personalities can determine what is published and what is not. Journals do not reflect science or human knowledge; they represent the subjects that are not prohibited in polite discussion by a few established personalities in the larger intellectual world.[13]

The control assumption revisited. The norm-is-good assumption is actually a front for a far greater obstacle to wholeness change. Maintaining a norm maintains control. Most parents appeal to the norm, as do many teachers, administrators, managers, and ministers, to get us to fall in line. What's healthy for us or our systems isn't the issue; control by enforcing conformity is. For the sake of fitting the norm, we marry the right person, take the right job, go broke buying the right house(s) and car(s), have the right number and gender of children, even the right breed and pedigree of "pets."*

The same control assumption that gets in the way of learning the truth, therefore, gets in the way of shifting paradigms, since a shift threatens control structures.

---

*"Pets" have owners, which means they're property; "animal companions" have human companions, which means they're friends. (Just what you needed—another politically incorrect term that will make you subject to the Politically Incorrect Police if you use it.)

Assuming reason controls change. This isn't a shocking revelation. But the control assumption takes many guises. One in particular gives it an innocuous, even seductive form: change is allowed as long as we're in control of the process, and—here's the seductive bit—we're in control through our minds. We assume faith in the rational management of change, and the norm is assumed to be the product of this rational process.

In other words, we assume that change is good when our reason directs it, and we assume that reason has given us the norm we have. The accumulated unresolved traumas of generations pass as their accumulated wisdom. Thinking becomes our way of securing power over change—of containing it within the existing paradigm.

In personal life, the norm tells us what we need to do, and our minds make it happen. When problems arise, we expect our heads to solve them so that our place in the control hierarchy remains intact. We're not looking for the wholeness principle to intervene and restructure our entire operating system. "Thanks but no thanks! We've got it all figured out."

We apply the same assumption to social problems. When crises arise, we put the "best minds" together to figure out what to do. We create "think tanks" to tell us which social bandage to apply. Though problems emerge from a paradigm-created context, the paradigm behind problems doesn't come under scrutiny. Instead, we want problems "fixed" so we can get back to systems-as-usual. Trained in control-paradigm institutions, the "best minds" fall back on the same power-over paradigm that caused the problems. Deloria pulls no punches about the process that creates our culture's "best minds":

> While graduate school education does provide further training in one's chosen field, its primary purpose is to ensure that people wishing to become scholars and scientists are rendered socially acceptable to people already entrenched in the respective professions.
>
> Originally, graduate theses were supposed to be creative and original scholarly work which advances knowledge of the world in some significant way. In recent decades this requirement has lapsed completely, and in order to receive an advanced degree today a student need only demonstrate to the committee that he or she will not embarrass the sponsoring professors by being outspoken or taking radical positions that would disrupt the discipline. Rarely do M.A. theses or Ph.D. dissertations contribute anything to our knowledge.[14]

THE INSANITY OF HALF A BRAIN

"Yes" to the left brain. The assumption that we use reason to control change draws on one mind power in particular: left-brain thinking. That's the side of our brains that's good at carrying out orders and staying within limits, because it's primarily a filter.

Given paradigm-defined parameters, our analytic powers sort and eliminate, filter and exclude. Left brains process input so that the prevailing paradigm looks irrefutable. When the control assumption marks off a field, the left brain jumps into action. Its job is to establish dominance and eliminate whatever jeopardizes the reigning position. Proof and success are gauged by the degree to which we gain control, whether it's over a natural phenomenon, a child, an employee, or a business market.

With our minds under orders from the control assumption, analytic, statistical, quantitative, rational, and empirical methods prevail because they're good at giving us a sense of control. We make tests, conduct surveys, collect data, count profits, and measure progress. "Just the facts, please," as if facts, statistics, tests, data, or piles of money have significance on their own—as if there's no paradigm involved with interpreting what all these things mean.

That's not so. "Millions of Americans ate eggs today" is a fact, but what is it a fact about? What is its significance? Are we interested in chicken farmer profits, cholesterol levels, protein consumption, damage to the environment, or cruelty to chickens?

Tests mean something relative to a theory, and facts are collected to support a hypothesis. Another hypothesis could collect a different set of facts, as often happens in the history of science—and now in political life as well. One paradigm or another interprets what's going on, and the data fit that interpretation.

Example: control by intelligence agencies. Social change is currently controlled by "information politics"—using information to establish one political interest in a power-over position. It's a classic example of the control assumption using left-brain thinking to "manage" change.

One obvious example of control-by-information is, of course, intelligence agencies. In their justly famous book *The CIA and the Cult of Intelligence*, former CIA agent Victor Marchetti and State Department intelligence analyst John Marks write that the CIA "is intent upon conducting

the foreign affairs of the U.S. government without the awareness or participation of the people." To what end? Using "covert and usually illegal
means," the CIA "seeks largely to advance America's self-appointed role as
the dominant arbiter of social, economic, and political change in the awakening regions of Asia, Africa, and Latin America."[15]

And we all know what a blessing this has been to the people of those
regions—their democratically elected leaders deposed or assassinated, pup-
pet dictators with secret police and torture chambers instituted, reigns of
terror in which citizens disappear overnight, economies toppled when
national currencies are devalued on the international market, crushing debts
to the World Bank incurred by a ruling elite who take the money for themselves, labor unions destroyed, media controlled, natural resources stolen
and ravaged, land used as a dumping ground for industrial toxic waste generated on the opposite side of the globe—the usual stuff.

Example: Corporate information politics. Back at home, information
politics is very much alive and well, though its methods are cleaned up to
look scientific. In *Who Will Tell the People?*, William Greider exposes
Washington's "K Street" consultants, who hire scientists to come up with
figures to support whatever position their corporate clients need to verify,
prove, or document. Left brains are for hire to the highest corporate bidder—hired to convince Congress that whatever the monied interests want is
also objectively good. Then it's sold to all of us.

David Korten points out that public relations employees outnumber
actual news reporters by a growing gap of 40,000 and that "a 1990 study
found that almost 40 percent of the news content in a typical U.S. newspaper
originates from public-relations press releases, story memos, and suggestions....The distinction between advertising space and news space grows less
distinct with each passing day."[16]

Using reason to gain political advantage, though, makes a sham of reason. "Information is never neutral."[17] On any issue, "scientific opinion" splits
along lines that reflect the interests of those who pay the scientists. PR firms
refer to Gibson's Law: "For every Ph.D., there is an equal and opposite
Ph.D."[18] Greider asks: "If the experts' opinions on...basic question[s] can be
defined by where they work, who can say what is rational or irrational?"[19]
Scientists are now as distrusted by the public as lawyers, he says, because
their minds are bought.

With society's left brains controlled by the monied elite, a "shadow government" emerges that functions as a "mock democracy." All the facts are there—and paid for. Change is controlled by reason, and reason is controlled by power-over assumptions.

By putting ideas in the background and "facts" center stage, change is easily orchestrated—or blocked. If an idea doesn't fit the view-holding-power, there's plenty of left-brain-generated ammunition to blow it out of the water.

"No" to the right brain. For this control-paradigm use of reason to work, we have to assume that: (1) it's rational to go with the facts and studies, (2) it's emotional to side with values, and (3) rational is good, and emotional is bad.

Greider writes: "In the masculine culture of management, 'emotion' is assigned a position of weakness, whereas 'facts' are hard and potent. The reality, of course, is that the ability to define what is or isn't 'rational' is itself laden with political self-interest, whether the definition comes from a corporate lobbyist or from a federal agency. One way or another, information is loaded."[20]

Clearly, when control assumptions prevail, intuition, creativity, and feelings, as well as aesthetic, ethical, moral, and spiritual values aren't invited into the change process. Values are too subversive, too threatening. They have a nasty habit of introducing perspectives that redraw the game and invite whole-minded paradigm shifts.

The right brain—the home of holistic perceptions and values—isn't a good partner for the control assumption because it doesn't take kindly to being controlled. It's open to transcending limits, which means it doesn't stay in the narrow confines that control systems require. The right brain is the side of us that's most attuned to the wholeness principle and most ready to respond to it.

Psychologist Carl Jung regarded intuition not as something contrary to reason but as something outside the province of reason. For the control-minded, to invite intuition into the process is the same as courting the end of the world as we know it.

And they're right.

Example: Whole-minded shifts in business. Working from the right brain's emphasis on whole systems, for instance, someone like W. Edwards Deming—who marshalled left-brain statistics for support—could call for the restructuring of business management from the top down, including a change in everything from core philosophies to pay ratios.

But as Deming discovered, American CEOs wouldn't listen until their backs were to the wall, and even then they fell short of real change. To dodge the paradigm shift that Deming deemed necessary, many managers reduced Total Quality Management to techniques and slogans—and annoying ones at that. One TQM bank we observed through the eyes of employees seemed like something out of *The Stepford Wives*. Toward the end of his life, Deming railed at how his call for a philosophy shift had been buried by American managers justifying "business as usual" with TQM bells and whistles.

For bottom liners, nowhere is there clearer evidence of the lack of paradigm shifts than in the trend of corporate salaries. In a now-famous section of *The Politics of Rich and Poor*, Kevin Phillips writes: "In 1979 CEOs made twenty-nine times the income of the average manufacturing worker. By 1985 the multiple was forty. By 1988, *Business Week* said the total compensation of the average CEO in its annual survey had risen to ninety-three times the earnings of the average factory worker, prompting the magazine to editorialize that 'executive pay is growing out of all proportion to increases in what many other people make—from the worker on the plant floor to the teacher in the classroom.'"[21] It doesn't seem as if CEOs have learned a thing from Deming, whose battle cry has always been: "Optimize the system." Treat it as an interconnected whole. Or, as Thomas Paine argued over two centuries ago, don't cram all the body's blood into one toe.

If CEOs were listening to the side of their minds that thinks in wholes, they wouldn't take stratospheric salaries. They'd realize that such massive cash drains are devastating to business systems—and demoralizing to the people who do the work, produce the goods, and yet can barely make ends meet.

But the CEOs' assumptions about change blocks this awareness. As consultant Alan Weiss—who's worked with many CEOs of blue chip companies—writes, these executives "haven't the slightest intention of changing." They "got where they are precisely because they have rigidly controlled everything in sight, including, but not limited to, the lunch menu."[22] They're not yielding an inch of the control-mindedness that they believe got them to where they are.

"No" to philosophy. Neither is questioning our basic premises welcome in the change process. We can see why the question—"Which paradigm is calling our worlds into being?"—may not be on the tip of the tongue. Philosophy, like Socrates, is unwelcome in dominator worlds.

But how about inquiring into the values that govern our systems? How about looking at the behind-the-scenes beliefs that shape every organizational chart, rule, procedure, and memo? What ideas lie behind schools, businesses, and governments as we know them? *Paradigm* and *philosophy* may be ten-dollar words, but *ideas*, *values*, and *beliefs* are home-grown, garden variety. They're the stuff of change.

"No" to change. No, we're told, that's all too vague—which is to say right-brain questions leave the door too open to change. When the control assumption dominates how we use our minds, we go only where our left brains take us—with instruments and data, facts and figures. That's how the assumption controls change and, if it's threatening, guarantees no change. The best ideas get buried under a pile of "inconclusive studies."

The consequences can be tragic.

Example: AIDS. For instance, Randy Shilts's book about AIDS *And The Band Played On* showed that the early researchers who suspected the danger of AIDS and how it was transmitted weren't able to convince the medical or political establishments to act rapidly to contain its spread. They couldn't produce ironclad evidence that their theories were correct, though the evidence was highly suggestive. Bottom-line concerns were more compelling than the value of public health—or intuition in scientific research. A dogmatic commitment to left-brain authority and money allowed San Francisco bath houses to stay open and hospitals not to test their blood supplies. Left braining and bottom lining proved to be a progressive, fatal disease for thousands, perhaps millions.

THINKING ADDICTION

Thinking addiction. The more we observe the use of "rational" thinking by the control paradigm, the more it resembles addiction. It's not a healthy use of our minds, since our minds are more than computers.

Limiting ourselves to left-brain calculating for control, we abuse our minds by making them one-sided. The rational attacks the intuitive, though the two work best as partners. A craving for control takes over our thought processes, leaving our minds the objects of a dangerous addiction: thinking addiction.*

Assuming that we gain power by thinking creates addicts. We want power, and thinking becomes the way to get it. We use our left brains not for problem solving but to maximize power-over, whether it's in Washington politics or family dynamics, professional angling or religious one-upping. Nothing is too small or too great to control by mental gaming, from our health to foreign countries, Congress to the family dog.

In personal life, we go into our heads and don't come out. We worry and plan nonstop. Busy running mind laps, we close ourselves off from the wholeness principle and filter out its messages. If one does come through, we ignore it, especially if it's not "positive," i.e., "rah-rah" for the control game. Our left-brain, stay-on-top programming blocks any counter awareness—any awareness suggesting that maybe the control paradigm isn't working.

System questions go unasked. When we go into our social systems, the requirement for entering is that we adopt their assumptions about the control use of the mind. We catch their disease, or we're not allowed in. So we dutifully worry about lines of authority, where we are in them, and how to advance our position.

"Optimizing systems," to use Deming's phrase, isn't a priority. What's healthy for us or for the system as a whole isn't on the official agenda.

With everyone focused on turf wars, system questions go unasked. Change doesn't happen, and the lack of wholeness-change catches up with us. It's like fault lines in the earth: frequent little slips can move the earth without a huge quake. But if something blocks smooth slippage, we're in for "The Big One."

Looking at our social systems, we're in for something. For all our left braining, we're in a worse fix than the human species has ever been. Used

---

*We first heard about thinking addiction listening to one of Anne Wilson Schaef's tapes, and bells went off for us. It describes exactly what we've experienced in both academic and religious institutions, and we know from our colleagues that we're not alone.

one-sidedly for control, our minds operate blindly—whole blind, paradigm blind, planet blind. We make successful control moves but destroy our health and happiness.

For instance, ten million chemicals have been synthesized by chemists in industry and universities. Of these ten million new substances introduced on the planet, fewer than 50,000 have been tested for toxicity to humans, animals, and the environment. The inventory of the Toxic Substances Control Act (TSCA) includes 74,000 entries of highly toxic substances: more than 50 percent lack toxicity data on them at all and less than 6 percent have experimental ecotoxicological and environmental fate data. In spite of the fact that we don't know the impact of these chemicals on us and the environment, over 5,000 new chemicals are being synthesized every year.*

Our minds have been busy, no question, but what have they created? They've given us power, but what kind? They've created systems with awesome resources at their command, but where are these systems taking us?

The longer we labor under the control assumption, the longer we avoid facing the real crisis: that control thinking can't save us; it too is a progressive, fatal disease.

Cut off in the control booth. Why is control-paradigm thinking such a trap?

Trap reason number one: Using our minds for control gives us a sense of security, albeit a false one. We create an empire and sit on top. Then we make sure nothing changes so that our security isn't threatened. We lock ourselves in the control booth and don't come out.

The last thing we want to do, if security by control is our agenda, is to use our minds for learning, developing our character, or evolving. Self-transcendence is unthinkable. Rather, we shut down the side of us that's good at these things. Stuck in the control booth of our left brains, we don't allow the wholeness principle to work its magic of personal, system, and paradigm transformation.

---

*We draw on the research of Dr. Subhash C. Basak, a biochemist and mathematical chemist who works at the Natural Resources Research Institute of the University of Minnesota, Duluth, and who does toxicity studies for the EPA. He has over twenty publications on the subject of toxic chemicals. Data on the TSCA comes from C. M. Aver, M. Zeeman, J. V. Nabholz, and R. G. Clements, *1994 SAR-The U.S. Regulatory Perspective, SAR and QSAR in Environmental Research*, 29–38.

Trap reason number two: As blocks go, the control-by-reason assumption is a doozy, because it's culturally reinforced. The control booth door has big locks on it. Thinking addiction is the most acceptable and ingrained of all addictions, even more than work. While we know the stress of work can kill us, we assume that thinking is a savior, and reason is the king of thinking. We count it among the treasures of human evolution—and in a whole and balanced context, we should.

But using reason to gain control warps it and us. All our reasoning powers get channeled into the service of addiction. When we use our minds to make up for what we've lost in our souls, we lose both.

Trap reason number three: Caught in the addictive cycle, our left brains can't help us break out of addiction. They're too engaged in the addictive process themselves—too sure that the next mind gymnastic will do the trick: if only our minds could give us that extra power-over edge, everything would turn out all right.

Given the power of both addiction and our left brains, that's scary. Combine the two, and we're lucky things aren't worse.

OPENING OURSELVES AND OUR SYSTEMS TO WHOLENESS CHANGE

The control assumption is a formidable block. If we're going to evolve, we have to get past it. But how?

Honoring the truth. Simple: by assuming that we're more than our assumptions. That's the beginning of spiritual awakening. We open ourselves to the wholeness that we are and that reality is.

Specifically, we're more than the grasping creatures that control assumptions turn us into, and our minds are more than our left brains. Reality is more than our paradigms represent, and wholeness-change is more than we can control. That's the truth of wholeness.

In the tradition of the Iroquois Peace Confederacy, we honor the truth by honoring the "more" and by not funneling it through narrowing assumptions. Once we learn the truth about the control paradigm, we honor the truth by not rationalizing away what we've learned or twisting it so that we don't have to shift paradigms.

By contrast, filtering out whatever doesn't fit our paradigm scheme dishonors truth. It puts our assumptions above truth, when the relation should be reversed. We can't deny reality and make systems work. Reality won't go away. The more our systems get out of synch with the reality around them, the more they produce inner and outer chaos.

That's why Deganawidah founded the Great Peace not only on learning the truth but on honoring it as well—letting truth be what it is and not distorting it to serve control agendas.

As the wholeness principle spurs us to shift our assumptions, we honor the truth by allowing it to do its transforming work unhindered. We can't control where wholeness change takes us, otherwise it becomes another contrivance. In his article "The Mystery of Wholeness," physician Richard Moss writes: "True healing…is never fully on our terms. Any original and wholehearted response to life carries the capacity to shift the energy of consciousness, and the result is transformation of one degree or another. "[23]

Making control worlds obsolete. Whatever happens, neither we nor our societies will look like the control-defined past. Evolution's course is wide open. We can't accurately predict from past control-paradigm worlds what our future whole-minded possibilities may be.

Who, for example, worries about cornering the market on buggy whips these days? Perhaps we'll soon feel the same irrelevancy about who corners the oil market—or any market, for that matter. Who controls which resources just won't make sense as we assume the role of earth steward rather than earth owner.

Neither will who's richest be of interest when we assume that economies are systems of exchange for mutual benefit. They exist to serve all of us, not just a few. Human beings are treasures themselves. Social systems can't afford not to value us. They need our knowledge and creativity as much as we need their support.

As systems honor our worth—and we honor it ourselves—we don't feel driven to establish ourselves in power-over positions. Playing control games takes energy and can consume entire lives. John D. Rockefeller confessed that he never had a good night's sleep after he got his fortune. Control games become boring and irrelevant the more we assume that our worth has nothing to do with who's up and who's down, who has power over whom, or who has the most money. To John D.'s great-grandson Michael Rockefeller, for instance, the life of a New York business magnate seemed empty, so he pursued the life of an anthropologist, photographer, and artist among the Asmat of New Guinea, even though it cost him his life. He knew the dangers, but in spite of them he chose a life that was meaningful to him.

Within our reach. The upshot of all this is that moving with wholeness-change is entirely within our reach. It's doable. We're each linked to the whole and encoded with wholeness, even though this seems remote from what we've become under control-paradigm systems.

The inscription under the All-Seeing Eye in *The Thief of Baghdad* reads: "What you seek is within your reach." The thief saw the All-Seeing Eye jewel suspended far above him in the Temple of Truth, apparently unreachable. But the distance was just an illusion created by his ordinary assumptions about space. Once he put aside his assumptions and reached up, "the most precious thing in all the world" settled into his hand.

Right-brain receiving. How can we, like the thief, access our wholeness? By assuming that we possess the powers we do. The right brain is the side of us that experiences wholes—patterns, relationships, ideas, values. It's the side of us that yearns for wholeness. It's also the side that's intuitive, imaginative, artistic, spiritual, compassionate, wise, and creative.

Whereas our left brains critique and eliminate information, our right brains perceive connectedness. Whereas our left brains organize what we already know, our intuitive, learning powers look beyond what's currently in our heads.

As a result, our right brains tap levels of consciousness that our left brains—under control-paradigm programming at least—filter out. That's why our intuitive powers are the ones first touched by the wholeness principle. We sense the force for wholeness at work before we can rationally explain why.

Naturalist Lyall Watson described whole-connected knowing as something that's universal and that cuts across species: "Speaking once again as a biologist, I am aware at times of a kind of consciousness that is timeless, unlimited by space or by the confines of my own identity; in which I perceive things very clearly, and am able to acquire information almost by a process of osmosis. I find myself, in this state, with knowledge that comes directly from being part of something very much larger, a global ecology of mind."[24]

Reintegrating the mind. Yet this powerfully whole-connected side of us remains undeveloped, even ridiculed as "unscientific." Very little in traditional schooling supports right-brain training, nor are intuitive powers welcome on the job. One group of managers who experimented with intuition in decision making at a Fortune 500 company were told to stop or be fired, even though their intuitive-based decisions had a track record equal to ones made by traditional analytic methods.

Though the side of us that lives and breathes wholeness has been virtually turned off—relegated to the domain of fortune tellers and superstition—we're finally waking up to the value of our right-brain powers and to the price of shutting ourselves and our social systems off from them. How do we reclaim them?

To start, we can assume it's possible to survive outside the control booth. A Hindu teaching compares the control mind to a drunken monkey that continually grabs goodies but then tosses them away. Meditation or contemplation quiets the monkey long enough for our minds to flex our whole-sensing abilities. In left-brain/right-brain language—and it is just a language since our brains aren't entirely split in their functions—contemplative disciplines liberate the left brain from the narrow role of doing the control paradigm's bidding.

The *Upanishads*, among the most sacred texts in Hindu philosophies, describe the path of going beyond the control mind: "Even as fire without fuel finds peace in its resting-place, when thoughts become silence the soul finds peace in its own source....When the mind is silent,...then it can enter into a world which is far beyond the mind: the highest End."[25]

Reclaiming reason. By nesting our rational skills within our intuitive powers, we reclaim "reason" as Plato and Rumi understood it. Reason is more than moving facts around to gain the upper hand. In fact, that's not reason at all; it's just control-paradigm manipulation.

For Rumi, reason unites revelation with understanding, intuition with practical knowing, love with intellect, whole-knowing with here-acting. True reason is whole minded. Annemarie Schimmel, a Rumi scholar, explains: "Reason, or intellect...should be grounded in the Universal Intellect....In fact [Universal Intellect] illuminates the horizons, while partial reason 'blackens the books of action,' because it may lead to unlawful acts."[26]

In that, Rumi agreed with Plato, who used myths, jokes, puns, dialogues, and stories to explore the nature of reality. Platonic reason was a whole-brain activity. Reason wasn't to be used for selfish or control ends.

Claiming true reason means responding to the wholeness principle with our whole-sensing mind. We keep our analytic powers wedded to our intuitive, feeling, whole-connected powers. The *Maitri Upanishad* puts it simply: "The mind should be kept in the heart as long as it has not reached the Highest End. This is wisdom, and this is liberation."[27]

Reconnecting with the force for wholeness. By shifting our assumptions about change and the role our minds have in it, we open ourselves to the wholeness principle and its power to transform us. This assumption-shift invites change in both ourselves and our social systems. Both need whole-guided reason. Both have been hurt by the one-sided control use of the mind. Both have had wholeness-change blocked. And both are ready to break out of the control cage and claim what's within their reach.

Poised for a shift, how do we go for it?

NOTES TO CHAPTER 2

1. John Moyne and Coleman Barks, trans., *Unseen Rain: Quatrains of Rumi* (Putney, VT: Threshold Books, 1986), 56. Also in Coleman Barks with John Moyne, A. J. Arberry, and Reynold Nicholson, trans., *The Essential Rumi* (San Francisco: HarperSanFrancisco, 1995), 280.
2. Roger Walsh and Frances Vaughan, eds., *Paths Beyond Ego: The Transpersonal Vision* (New York: Tarcher/Putnam, 1993), 162.
3. *Noetic Sciences Review* (Winter 1993), no. 28, 20.
4. David Bohm, *Wholeness and the Implicate Order* (London: Ark Books/Routledge and Kegan Paul, 1980, 1983), ix.
5. Jan Christiaan Smuts, *Holism and Evolution* (New York: Viking, 1926, 1961), v.
6. Arthur Koestler, *Janus: A Summing Up* (New York: Random House, 1978), 23–56.
7. Molly Young Brown, *Growing Whole* (Center City, MN: Hazelden, 1993), 41.
8. Danah Zohar and Ian Marshall, *The Quantum Society: Mind, Physics and a New Social Vision* (New York: William Morrow, 1994), 63.
9. Mokhiber and the Harris poll are quoted in Paul Hawken, *The Ecology of Commerce* (New York: HarperBusiness, 1993), 118.
10. Richard Carlson and Benjamin Shield, eds., *Healers on Healing* (Los Angeles: Jeremy Tarcher, 1989), 33.
11. Idries Shah, *The Sufis* (New York: Doubleday; 1964, Anchor/Doubleday, 1990), 135.
12. *Noetic Sciences Review* (Winter 1993), no. 28, 17.
13. Vine Deloria Jr., *Red Earth, White Lies: Native Americans and the Myth of Scientific Fact* (New York: Scribner, 1995), 43.
14. Deloria, *Red Earth, White Lies*, 53–54.
15. Victor Marchetti and John Marks, *The CIA and the Cult of Intelligence* (New York: Dell/Laurel, 1984), 3, 4.
16. David Korten, *When Corporations Rule the World* (West Hartford, CT: Kumarian and San Francisco: Berrett-Koehler, 1995), 146.
17. William Greider, *Who Will Tell the People?* (New York: Simon and Schuster, 1992), 46.
18. Robert Proctor, *Cancer Wars: How Politics Shapes What We Know and Don't Know About Cancer* (New York: Basic Books, 1995), 10.
19. Greider, *Who Will Tell the People*, 56.
20. Greider, *Who Will Tell the People*, 54.
21. Kevin P. Phillips, *The Politics of Rich and Poor* (New York: Random House, 1990), 179–80.
22. Alan Weiss, *Our Emperors Have No Clothes* (Franklin Lakes, NJ: Career Press, 1995), 6.
23. Richard Moss, "The Mystery of Wholeness," in Carlson and Shield, eds., *Healers on Healing*, 40.
24. Lyall Watson, *Beyond Supernature* (New York: Bantam, 1988), 267.
25. Juan Mascaro, trans., *The Upanishads* (New York: Penguin Classics, 1965), 102–3.
26. Annemarie Schimmel, *I Am Wind, You Are Fire: The Life and Work of Rumi* (Boston: Shambhala Publications, 1992), 108.
27. Mascaro, *The Upanishads*, 103.

≈≈≈
CHAPTER 3

Power in Shifting the Context

Accepting the truth
Third of the Twelve Cycles of Truth,
the Iroquois Peace Confederacy Tradition

You have read about the inspired spring.

Drink from there. Be companions with those
whose lips are wet with that water.

Others, even though they may be your father
or your mother, they're your enemies.
Leave, before they kill you!

The pathless path opens
whenever you genuinely say,

There is no Reality but God.
There is only God.
Rumi[1]

CONTEXTS ARE CHANGE-SHAPERS

Total change. Shifting paradigms means transformation, whether it's micro or macro, transforming individuals or the globe. If we change paradigms, things won't be the same with a few minor adjustments; we won't have power-over types standing over us who are just a bit nicer. With a paradigm shift, everything is different, because the structures that channel our energies change. Whereas control assumptions trap us in no-win patterns, a paradigm shift changes both the patterns and the assumptions behind them.

Total change is in fact what we experience in personal recovery. Recovery doesn't let us continue with pain-making assumptions minus the painful results. It doesn't, for example, take away binges without changing our assumptions about self-worth. We lose both binges and self-hate.

The same holds for recovering our social systems. We can't take away pollution or white-collar crime without changing what we assume business and politics are all about. Recovery doesn't patch up our worlds without making us rethink our core operating system. Paradigm shifts are thorough-going. We're restructured inside and out, in symptom and cause, part and whole, because total transformation is the mandate of wholeness.

Context: Room to change. Our role in the shift process is to give wholeness space to work, so its effects can be total. Though the wholeness principle urges us to claim our potential, if our life's context is limited to a sandbox, we won't be able to claim much. That is, if we limit ourselves to fixed ideas about how things should be, we don't leave much room for wholeness to do its thing.

Rumi said it's like trying to contain the ocean in a water jug; either the ocean won't fit or the jug breaks. The water inside the jug has the potential to move with the ocean, but it can't realize this potential as long as it's confined in clay.

Context, in fact, turns out to be the key to making a paradigm shift. For the wholeness principle to transform us, our context has to be flexible enough to allow this to happen. If we're Newtonian scientists faced with Einstein's relativity theories, for instance, we have to expand our assumptions about physics before we can grasp what Einstein's theories propose. Like Einstein, we have to imagine traveling on a beam of light and how this might change our assumptions about the physical universe.

Example: Contexts for physical health. Closer to home, if our behavior patterns are making us sick, our ability to heal depends on restructuring how we live. We need a context that supports physical health. If we keep the old habits, doctors can drug, cut, and patch us as much as our insurance will cover, but we won't get well. We'll go from sickness to sickness.

For instance, many people now live from antibiotic to antibiotic. As soon as they stop taking antibiotics, they get sick again. A physician told a friend of ours that she'd been on so many different antibiotics and for so long that essentially she didn't have much of an immune system left. She'd get whatever bug came along. Through antibiotics, we've become addicted to maintaining the appearance of health, while internally we're severely compromising it.

Healing depends on our assuming new patterns, so that health can emerge. We need a context that includes fresh air and walks, good sleep, good nutrition, not to mention a sense of meaning and purpose, peace of mind, self-worth, and joy in relationships, whether it's with people, animals, nature, or ideas. We also need medicine that strengthens rather than weakens our immune systems—in other words, a different concept of medicine than the current "go in and zap the little buggers." More than the buggers get zapped. A context that doesn't include these essentials can't create health.

Example: School system contexts. What is true regarding context in medical treatment is also true for our social systems. Systems won't change as long as their contexts remain fixed. For instance, as long as lower schools prepare for high schools, high schools prepare for colleges, and colleges prepare for rat-race jobs in power-over systems, education won't change. The context shaping schools won't invite systems that develop our manifold learning styles or tap the full range of our intelligence. Instead, the context will continue to create systems that select an elite to rise to the top, while persuading everyone else to believe that they're not that smart and aren't capable of much but taking orders. The system of bell-curve grading does just that—and will continue to do so as long as the context that defines education stays the same.

Fields form things. In other words, contexts make wholeness change possible—or not. Contexts define the space we live in, because they're generative. Like a matrix or womb, they provide a fertile environment—either fertile for addictions and conflicts or fertile for health and evolution. What we experience depends on what context we assume: what's our playing field and what's the game?

By defining a space, contexts hatch worlds; they give rise to certain forms and not others. The context of a rainforest, for instance, provides fertile ground for orchids but not fields of daisies. The context of authoritarian management provides fertile ground for sucking up but not individual initiative. The context of external reward-driven systems provides fertile ground for soul loss but not soul-connectedness. The context of secret-riddled groups—families, businesses, churches, or governments—provides fertile ground for pretending, denying problems, forming factions according to who knows what, and manipulating, but not for dealing with issues openly or achieving real intimacy or partnership.

Einstein was right: objects don't generate fields so much as fields generate objects. In *The Dancing Wu Li Masters*, Gary Zukav explains, "According to quantum field theory, fields alone are real. *They* are the substance of the universe and not 'matter'. Matter (particles) is simply the momentary manifestations of interacting fields which, intangible and insubstantial as they are, are the only real things in the universe."[2]

Just as matter distills from energy fields, we distill our lives from social fields. Social fields, in turn, distill their forms from idea fields—paradigms.

Contexts shape change. By generating certain forms and not others, paradigm contexts are change-shapers. They define not only the way things are but also the possibilities for change, allowing some things to happen and not others.

Captain Picard's command, "Make it so!" on *Star Trek: The Next Generation* assumed a context—the starship *Enterprise*, the crew, Starfleet rules, and the knowledge that wove them all together—and this twenty-fourth-century context made change possible, change that we'd consider impossible. He assumed the power of that context to come together in a dynamic, creative way: "Engage!"

Without the context to support him, however much the captain may have wanted something to happen, it wouldn't. He had to know which context he was working in, and he had to assume its presence when it was time for action.

What's more, if the context wasn't up to a needed change, Picard had to alter the context, usually by extending the crew's knowledge and creativity.

Example: Profits and biodiversity. That's how we hope contexts will work for us. But there's a downside to how contexts shape change. A context designed to control growth in order to maximize profits can, for instance, undo millennia of evolution. That's what's happening in global agriculture with the "green revolution" and the introduction of so-called miracle hybrid seeds. These seeds seem miraculous only under ideal conditions, which means with plenty of irrigation, chemical fertilizers, and pesticides. Without these conditions, miracle hybrids tend to have lower yields than indigenous seeds which, used over millennia, have adapted to the climate, combined in ways that preserve the soil's fertility, developed resistance to drought, pests, and diseases, and evolved to thrive without synthetic chemicals.

The main miracle about new seeds comes in the profits for the corporations that hold patents on them. "Many of the biggest seed companies are now owned by corporations like Monsanto and Ciba-Geigy, which make the very chemicals their seeds require" (what a coincidence).* When corporations are able to maneuver farmers here and around the world into becoming dependent on the hybrids, their profits are ensured.

Since chemical fertilizers and pesticides alter the soil conditions in which indigenous seeds thrived, farmers discover that it's not always easy to go back to them. Not only bad bugs but good ones have been destroyed.† Farmers' choices of what to plant the next year are limited to the crop options specified by the chemical manufacturers. Their fields are hooked.

In addition, hybrid seeds, like mules, are nonreproducing. That is, many hybrids do not reproduce "true" seeds unless farmers use open pollination, which often has to be done by hand—the sort of thing indigenous seeds do naturally. Every year farmers must purchase new seeds. Farmers who do reproduce usable hybrid seeds are increasingly forbidden by patent law to use the next-generation hybrids unless they pay royalties to the corporations that own the patents on that variety. David Korten writes, "Through the ages, farmers have saved seed from one harvest to plant their next crop. Under existing U.S. patent law, a farmer who saves and replants the offspring of a patented seed is in violation of patent law."[3]

---

*Martin Teitel, "Endangered Dinner," *Sierra Magazine*, January/February 1996, 12. Teitel's book *Rain Forest in Your Kitchen: The Hidden Connection Between Extinction and Your Supermarket* (Island Press, 1992), is an excellent source on this subject.

†After all, 90 percent of all insects are beneficial, and of the remaining destructive species, 800 of them have become resistant to one or more insecticides. So what's the point of pesticides? They only kill off dinner for birds and reduce the butterfly population. See David A. Birk, "Preserving Our Natural State-Integrated Pest Management ABCs," *Audubon Journal*, Delaware Audubon Society, January–February 1996, 1. Birk is the horticultural supervisor and integrated pest management coordinator for Winterthur Gardens in Greenville, Delaware.

Saving seed from harvest and using it to plant next year's crop is how seeds "learn" and adapt to regional conditions. To make this ancient practice illegal is to make evolution and adaptation illegal—to guarantee that seeds will never naturally adapt to the fields they grow in and must be artificially adapted with chemicals.

Controlling, patenting, and owning the earth's genetic resources—from microorganisms to plants and animals, excluding only genetically engineered humans—means that indigenous varieties threaten the monopoly sought for patented hybrids. The loss of biodiversity on the planet is no accident. Indigenous or "heirloom seeds" are disappearing, pushed out by hybrids. Indian scientist Vandana Shiva warns about the loss of food varieties all over the world—varieties which are nutritionally superior and environmentally safer, since they're not chemical-fertilizer/pesticide junkies. Since 1900, for instance, over 6,000 varieties of apples (that's 86 percent of all apple types the earth has ever seen) have become extinct,[4] and apples aren't alone. In *Staying Alive: Women, Ecology, and Development*, Shiva writes:

> The implications of the centralised control of genetic resources is best illustrated by the case of rice, the staple food for most of Asia....Over the last half century, India has probably grown over 30,000 different varieties of rice. With the green revolution, this genetic diversity is fast being eroded, as uniform populations of hybrids are introduced from IRRI [The International Rice Research Institute set up in 1959 by the Rockefeller and Ford Foundations].[5]

Thanks to the context defined by chemical corporations, even our crops are now substance-addicted. Biological diversity—and the special adaptation of certain varieties to certain regions—developed over millennia is disappearing, and agricultural sustainability is compromised by a context that's concerned only with maximizing profits. Shiva writes, "A corporate assessment is that at the turn of the century only five multinationals will survive as integrated seed and chemical corporations. Scientists accept that in the future, goals of biotechnology research will be for profit not for public interest."[6]

Context power. That's the power of contexts. Contexts can change us or prevent us from changing—or change us in damaging directions. If we seek personal, social, or global transformation, our field has to shift too. Like Captain Picard, we need to restructure our current context if it isn't up to change—or if it's changing us in unhealthy, even life-threatening directions. Transformation depends on how ready we are to redraw the field.

There's no more powerful way to do this than to go back to the paradigm level. Shifting our assumptions means shifting our paradigm and with it, the context that creates our world.

CAUGHT BETWEEN OURSELVES AND OUR SYSTEMS

The context dilemma. But shifting our context is a daunting proposition. How can we draw our field to include soul values when the social systems around us exclude them? We face what seems to be an insoluble dilemma.

Losing our souls. On one hand, if we accept current social systems as our life's context—as we must to survive in society—we risk being cut off from ourselves and what we consider meaningful, just, or right. Control-paradigm families, schools, churches, and jobs leave little room for soul values. In fact, they demand that we surrender our souls in order to do their bidding. We adapt to systems; they don't adapt to us.

In the academic community, for instance, as Shiva writes, "No more will the separation of science and profits work as a patriarchal fiction because the universities, the modern intellectual 'commons,' are being totally 'corporatised' and privatised. Companies are buying up scientists and entire departments and programmes with multimillion-dollar, multi-year contracts."[7] They're not buying these university departments so that professors can work in the public interest or listen to their souls as to what's best.

Losing our livelihood. On the other hand, if we make soul values our life's context, we don't fit into systems that require soul surrender as the condition for drawing a paycheck. We don't get the job, the grant, the contract, the promotion. We try to keep our souls intact, but it may mean, as it does for a friend of ours with professional training in community development, driving an oil truck for a living.

There's the dilemma: Which context do we accept? Which shapes us and gives our lives form? If we accept society's context, we may move up in social systems but at the cost of our ideals, dreams, and values. Our inner life gets socked in the stomach. If, however, we accept our inner truth as the context for making our life's decisions, we may go hungry. The stomach gets it either way.

Soul-sick social systems. The society-vs.-our-souls dilemma makes us soul sick, and it makes society sick as well. We get caught in a deadly cycle. We're trained to be soul sick so that we can fit into a soul-sick society, which means we perpetuate soul-sick patterns, which causes the next generation to grow up soul sick as well.

Fortunately, we're at a crossroads. Soul sickness is proving deadly both to us and to the planet.

That's because soul sickness doesn't generate social systems that work. We're not healthy in them, and our systems aren't healthy either. Schools aren't educating—not in the sense of "drawing out" the whole person. In Japan, as we saw on one television documentary, children study most of their waking hours. Driven by fierce competition, Japanese students graduating from high school know more than American students graduating from college. Yet the suicide rate among Japanese students is high, and addictive behavior epidemic. Even where authoritarian, competition-driven schooling seems successful in turning the human brain into a computer, it fails the whole person.

Nor is education the only sick system. Economies aren't prospering; they're bloating the rich. Governments aren't serving the common good; they're serving special interests. Religious hierarchies aren't championing freedom, justice, and spiritual awakening; they're justifying ecclesiastical hierarchies and church doctrines.

Our social systems are behaving like mind-control cults. It's only a difference in time between Jim Jones's followers drinking cyanide and our ingesting toxic air, water, food, and drugs, not to mention tolerating a lethal oil-based transportation system whose death rate beats the average war.* Our culture is as mind controlled as any cult member by a paradigm that's making us both destructive and tolerant of destruction. We blame each other

---

*The American Almanac: Statistical Abstract of the United States, 1995–1996 (Austin, TX: The Reference Press, 1995), chart no. 133, p. 99, indicates that in the three years of 1990, 1991, and 1992, motor vehicle accidents killed roughly 500,000 Americans. Roughly 50,000 Americans died in Vietnam between 1952 and 1992 (see chart no. 568, p. 365). Roughly 300,000 Americans died in World War II between Dec. 7, 1941 and 1945 (Britannica Macropaedia, 15th ed., vol. 21, p. 799). The wars stop; the killings on the highways don't. Why isn't there the same public concern for stopping highway killings as there was for ending U.S. involvement in Vietnam?

or maybe the human species but not the paradigm.

When a paradigm context stifles transformation, the wholeness principle goes on operating. But we experience it as exposing the consequences of not-wholeness—of what it's like to live in a jug. Yet the very failure of control-paradigm systems should alert us: "This is the wake-up call," Malcolm X said, "Let us know who we are."

The dilemma is unacceptable. The good news is that we don't have to choose between ourselves and our systems. The dilemma is a false one, since paradigm transformation engages both us and our societies.

Denying our souls can't be an option. That only creates worlds peopled by defensive shells running into each other—zombielike bumper cars.

But neither can we opt out of our systems. They're all around us. We can't squeak through untouched by the systems around us. Even retirees depend on social systems. Their pension funds depend on wise financial management, their safety depends on reliable local government, while their social security and medical coverage depend on efficient national government (uh oh…).

Systems won't go away. When they're working well, they function invisibly, but when they're malfunctioning, they're constantly in our faces.

Giving up on our systems—tolerating them until either we escape or they crumble—is what creates the dilemma. It forces a no-win polarity by not applying to systems the same whole-making assumptions we apply to ourselves.

"Accepting the truth"—the third Cycle of Truth—is the only practical course, but it's not a course we go alone. We have to accept the truth of what both we and our systems are and can be. This begins with taking stock of the contexts we've been raised to assume: How have they affected us? And which paradigm created them?

CONTEXTS WE'VE BEEN RAISED TO ASSUME

Born and raised in contexts. Contexts are no strangers to us; we were born into them, and we took them for granted without thinking twice.

Families. First it was families. From birth, we turned our lives over to the care of parents and siblings, whose mental and emotional worlds became our playing field. Families provided the mirroring context from which our identities emerged. Self-images distilled out of the ways they treated us, and habits formed in response to their needs.

That's why it's hard to be objective about families. Until we go through the process of sorting out our original family dynamics, we can't tell where they end and we begin. Our self-awareness distilled out of theirs.

Social systems. But families aren't the only contexts that shape us. We've distilled personal patterns from schools and the media, and we've adopted roles modeled on TV or by friends and colleagues. Social contexts shape us as much as family contexts do.

Irwin Hyman, for instance—whose book *Reading, Writing, and the Hickory Stick* documents ongoing physical and emotional abuse in schools—discovered that children raised in nonabusive homes take on the characteristics of abused children if they even witness physical or emotional abuse, much less receive it, at school. Seeing other pupils beaten or humiliated by teachers, they internalize self-abusive attitudes and may later marry partners who physically or emotionally abuse them, though such patterns were never modeled at home.

Paradigm contexts. Social systems, in turn, get shaped by contexts as well. Behind families and social systems are beliefs and worldviews—once again, paradigms. We can't take two steps without running into them. Each person, institution, and subculture has a story about who they are and why, and these meaning contexts shape behavior. Paradigms underlie every thought, feeling, and action, as well as every rule, policy, goal, and plan of implementation. Some open us to creativity, others don't. Some create warring factions; others create mutually supportive communities.

The control paradigm: ranking differences. Specifically, the control-paradigm context creates systems in which relationships are unequal: one side exerts superior status over another. It's a question of who gains the upper hand first.

How differences get ranked defines all interactions. Every exchange turns into a form of one-upping/one-downing. Every difference becomes an opportunity to elevate one side by putting the other down, of getting ahead at someone else's expense.

Being raised in this paradigm atmosphere, we find it hard to envision systems without ranking mechanisms. Our first thought in a relationship is "Where do I stand? Who's one-up between the two of us? Who has more power, wealth, knowledge, cleverness, or status?"

When we encounter differences, we immediately try to figure out which are superior and which inferior. The paradigm context allows no room for both as equals. There's little hope for equality among genders, races, religions, or nations as long as this paradigm provides the context shaping our social systems.

A connectedness paradigm: Valuing differences. By contrast, a paradigm of connectedness views relationships as celebrating unique talents—talents that come together for mutually beneficial growth. Instead of ranking differences, we value them, appreciating how differences blend to create something greater than any one of them, like varied stones in a mosaic or instruments in an orchestra.

Instead of putting people down for what they don't have, a connectedness paradigm looks for what's special about each person or group. Then it designs systems around that specialness. Instead of juxtaposing differences in a competitive contest, the model finds ways for needs, talents, knowledge, and visions to complement each other. A connectedness paradigm accepts our differences as the treasures they are and then allows the treasures to enrich and diversify our social systems.

Accepting the truth of differences, therefore, means learning from differences and using them to evolve. The very differences that a control paradigm treats as obstacles become the key to creating truly successful support systems.

The control paradigm at school. In schools, for instance, the ranking context rewards children who excel in mathematical and verbal skills by putting them one-up over children with intuitive, artistic, interpersonal, intrapersonal, musical, or kinesthetic learning talents—the different intelligences identified by Howard Gardner in *Frames of Mind.** The math- and

---

*Since this book appeared, Gardner's work has been revolutionizing education, suggesting (1) that educational systems grow from an understanding of how our minds operate, and (2) that our minds learn through a rich multiplicity of media and methods.

verbal-oriented students master the material, while students oriented to other learning styles don't.

In the process, everyone learns one-up/one-down ranking, though no teacher ever needs to give a lecture on it. The paradigm permeates the school structure, so much so that students are relieved when classmates fail, because any failure makes them look good by comparison. Get-ahead-by-putting-down-the-competition becomes the context—the fertile ground—for success.

A connectedness paradigm and learning. By contrast, a paradigm that values differences leads to cooperative learning. Students use their unique blend of learning styles to help themselves and others learn, so that everyone masters the material. Students learn faster, more easily, and with less stress. In place of threats to their self-esteem in the form of low grades, cooperative learning affirms and enhances each student's unique aptitude. Students leave the school system with their innate joy of learning intact.

In both cases, the school system springs from the paradigm context.

CONTROL-PARADIGM RULES

Paradigms speak through rules. We're swimming in contexts and have been since day one. Behind individuals are family contexts, behind families are social system contexts, and behind all of them are paradigm contexts. Paradigms turn out to be the deep-structure contexts that shape both us and our systems.

Yet paradigms have powerful cloaking devices; they hide themselves well. Instead of coming right out and saying, "All people are unequal and will be treated unequally in power-over systems dominated by the strongest, richest, or most aggressive," the control paradigm does its change shaping through rules.

Rules draw the paradigm context. They tell us what it means to live within the playing field. We know the rules and obey them. If asked, we may be hard pressed to verbalize them, but we can spot in a minute someone who isn't following them.

Insofar as we take the rules for granted, paradigms become invisible. We don't think about the messages behind the rules. We just accept the rules as necessary to running our systems. In the case of schools, for instance, we assume that grades and competition are necessary to motivate students, not realizing how much control-paradigm baggage comes with these rules.

Not that all rules are bad. Ideally, rules help us channel our energies. They make paradigms down-home and practical. As Zen master Shunryu Suzuki explained in outlining rules for meditation: "The purpose of these rules is not to make everyone the same, but to allow each to express his own self most fully."[8] In any context, that's what we hope rules will do.

Control-paradigm rules. But rules are only as good as the paradigms behind them. Not all paradigms are committed to each person "expressing his own self most fully." If the paradigm centers around control, its rules carry out the dominate-and-control agenda.

Pervasive as the control paradigm is, we encounter its injunctions whether we're in families, schools, churches, or professions: Follow experts and obey authorities. Ignore feelings. Fit the norm. Put on the right face. Deny that problems are problems. Never make or admit mistakes. Lie to get what you want, or lie to protect the authorities. Support the official view. Be what others expect. Don't trust your inner voice. Value outward achievements over inward needs. Place doing over being. Above all, be serious; don't joke around or have fun—unless it's at someone else's expense.

Power-over rules in families. Psychologists Robert Subby and John Friel study the family versions of these control-paradigm rules. For family harmony, parents are expected to maintain authority: Don't discuss problems, and don't show feelings. Have ready answers. Stay in control. Assume children are up to no good—and hard of hearing. Don't hesitate to use force, humiliation, or intimidation. Don't encourage self-confidence. Keep them scared and on their toes. Drive them constantly, and up your expectations. Don't indulge them with praise or pamper them with sympathy. Assume that children's reasons are either not legitimate or not important. And never deviate from the rules. Family life would disintegrate, and children would become addicts.[9]

As it turns out, such rules are precisely what turn bright and healthy children into addicts. Why?

The rules are designed to break our soul-connectedness, so that we fit into the controlled context. The corresponding rules for children train them to be underlings, responsive to external authorities and cut off from their inner lives: Don't get angry or upset. Don't express emotions, especially unpleasant ones. Don't make noise. Don't cause trouble. Do what you're told without question. Don't argue. Obey your elders and betters. Please authorities. Be seen and not heard. Do it better next time. Win and excel. Above all, be perfect.

These rules assume a controller/controlled context for family life. Change in the family dynamics as well as change within family members is limited by this water jug. Not much ocean flows through.

Power-over rules in societies. Because almost everyone in our culture has experienced these rules in some form or another—we've all, for instance, been children—it's no wonder that the same rules that create soul-violating families create soul-violating societies. The power-over paradigm instilled in us at home goes with us to school and work, creating a control-paradigm context that's not hard to recognize.

In *The Adult Children of Alcoholics Syndrome*, for instance, Wayne Kritsberg cites four rules that operate in addictive families[10]—rules that are easily recognizable in businesses, churches, schools, nonprofits, and governments as well.

1. The rule of rigidity. The first rule, the rule of rigidity, maintains the balance of power by avoiding change. In families, this means adhering to family rules and roles, so that the family control structure stays in place.

As family systems writer John Bradshaw points out, all of us as children had to play some role in our original families: "Surrogate Spouse," "Little Parent," "Mascot," "Saint and Hero," or "Scapegoat." "I've capitalized these roles," he writes, "to show that they are rigid. They result from the needs of the system, not from anyone's individual choice.... As a role becomes more and more rigid, the family system closes more and more into a frozen trance-like state. Once this freezing occurs, the family is stuck. And the more each one tries to help by playing his role, the more the family stays the same."[11]

Social systems exhibit the same rigidity. Rules and roles are sacrosanct, no matter how silly or unnecessary. History is full of such silliness in the rigidity of class structures, for instance. How many Einsteins born to parents without money or status ended up shoveling manure instead of using their minds to benefit their culture? In rigid class-bound societies, mobility across class lines is perceived as a threat to the power structure. Even those at the bottom feel threatened, since they're on the verge of being bumped out.

Or consider the rigidity of schools: we don't question the classroom structure despite its obvious relation to factory life at the turn of the century. Henry Ford and his ilk wanted workers who could tolerate sitting silently in rows, doing boring and repetitive tasks, obeying authorities mindlessly, all in an atmosphere of distrust and constant surveillance. And educators complied. Nowadays, most parents, teachers, and administrators just accept that this is the way it's always been done, so we must keep doing it that way. The system and its rules and roles stay frozen.

The same is true for the top-down power structures of organizations. Though challenged by companies such as Gore in Delaware—and unpopular among feminist writers—military-style patriarchies sit atop organizations with stonelike rigidity. Complaining about the autocratic attitudes of the director of a public horticultural garden, for instance, one employee nonetheless concluded, "Well, I guess at times like this we need a captain of this ship." However, the employee failed to notice that he didn't work on a ship, it didn't need a captain, and they weren't going to war. Emergencies and day-to-day operations are not identical. Nonetheless, following the control-paradigm rule of rigidity, the employee's role and that of the autocrat couldn't be challenged, no matter how mad it made him.

To his credit, he was at least willing to verbalize his dissatisfaction, which is more than occurs in many systems. And this leads to the second rule.

2. The rule of silence. According to this rule, we're not allowed to voice what's happening. Family members are discouraged from airing feelings or expressing honestly how they're experiencing the family dynamics. "For example," John Bradshaw writes, "in the White family Dad is an alcoholic. He gets drunk and can't go to work the next day. Mom calls in sick for him. The children don't ask questions and pretend to believe that Dad is sick."[12]

In social systems, we don't question how things are done, nor do we speak our truth about how we're being treated—a lesson we learn in school when we watch abuse in the name of education and are expected to ignore it.

In first grade, for example, I had a teacher who regularly hit students with a long wooden pointer when they answered incorrectly, not to mention her yelling at and humiliating students. Some children wet their pants with fear and were further beaten. One of my classmates was so traumatized she had trouble reading as late as fifth grade, when I left the school and lost touch with her. (I learned to read because my mother taught me phonics at home.) Although such "teaching methods" are not uncommon even today, students in my class nonetheless complained to their parents, and parents complained to the principal, which resulted in official visits to the classroom, when the teacher would behave like Saint Pedagogue. Afterwards, it was clear from her behavior that she knew who had talked, and she was that much harder on everyone. We all learned it was easier not to complain—not to say what was really going on in the first grade.

As long as we agree to be part of a system, we don't talk about problems, even blatantly obvious ones, from the boss being an addict to toxic wastes being illegally dumped to fellow employees being treated unjustly. We don't say what we think or feel. We certainly don't blow the whistle on the abuse of power or position.

Instead, if we have an opinion, we wait to find out whether it accords with the teacher's, boss's, company policy, or conventional wisdom. If it does, we voice it; if it doesn't, we either keep quiet or switch our views fast. If we violate this rule, we risk being kicked out. Because the stakes are high, we most likely don't allow our concerns to reach conscious awareness, which is the next rule.

3. The rule of denial. This rule teaches us to deny that problems are system problems, much less paradigm problems. When problems surface, we convince ourselves that nothing is wrong with the family system; it's just this circumstance or that person—the Scapegoat—that's fouling things up. As in Bradshaw's example of the White family, the worse things get, the more we tell each other that our family is fine. Or to paraphrase Bart on an episode of *The Simpsons*, "Nothing happened, and I didn't do it." Everything is okay.

Social systems operate by the same rule. We're expected to be loyal to our church, employer, or institution—and criticism means that we're disloyal. Being loyal means staying in denial about how our systems work. Instead of naming harmful messages embedded in rules, we blame this person or that decision. Then we settle for Band-Aid changes that don't address the crisis-makers built into our systems—put there by the control model and the context created through its rules.

Using denial of job stress as an example, Barbara Brandt writes in *Whole Life Economics*, "Many people need to deny that their jobs are stressful for economic as well as emotional reasons. In this age of disappearing jobs, both women and men lucky enough to have paid work may feel they have no recourse except to put up with demeaning or stressful jobs—until they end up with stress disorders or have accidents and have to go on disability." But denying stresses doesn't make them go away. "As the extent and costs of job-related stress have become ever more painfully apparent, a new form of denial has recently become popular: blaming the worker. Familiar responses to job stress today include programs in stress-management or relaxation techniques...."[13] Change the person; don't imagine that there could be something wrong with the system.

Denying even to ourselves that there's a system problem, we try to survive inside the group—which leads to the last rule.

4. The rule of isolation. This rule tells us to keep to the group; don't trust outsiders. Only those who share the same narrow context will understand. Control-paradigm families operate on we-they, insider-outsider divisions. Those outside the family can't be trusted. Within the family, secrets and factions build, creating more we-they divisiveness.

Control-paradigm social systems manifest the same insider-outsider dynamics, determined by who has access to what information. Insiders know the biggest secrets. Before long, though, factions spring up among the insiders, creating internal wars. Isolation becomes intense among the in-group. Insiders don't trust each other, and no one feels appreciated. In control-paradigm families, loneliness runs deep. In control-paradigm social systems, isolation is every bit as profound.

Isolation is also the way control systems deal with those who break the rule and interact with outsiders. A famous case is composer Johann Sebastian Bach's imprisonment by his employer, Duke Wilhelm Ernst of Weimar. Bach had done the unthinkable: he accepted a job from a friend of the duke's nephew, to whom the duke was not speaking and so no one in his court was allowed to either. Bach had broken the rule of isolation, and so he himself was isolated, being imprisoned from November 6 to December 2 of 1717, when he was "freed from arrest with notice of his unfavorable discharge."[14] When European nobles couldn't enforce isolation any other way, they resorted to dungeons.

These four rules draw a playing field where the control paradigm gets acted out both through specific actions, such as Bach's imprisonment, and through the structures of systems, such as the class structure that put Bach's genius under the thumb of a control addict. According to the paradigm, the "foundation plan of civilized order" is for one person or group to dominate others, and every rule, structure, institution, and policy generated from this paradigm context conveys this message.

The legacy of the power-over paradigm. The history of the control paradigm coincides with the rise of patriarchy, which anthropologist Riane Eisler dates to 4000 B.C.E. in her book *The Chalice and the Blade*. In patriarchies, the senior male has absolute authority over the family, just as kings command subjects. Women and children become property, often valued less than livestock. Human rights aren't rights but privileges granted by the ruling authority—when he's in a good mood.

During the first century C.E., several emperors worked hard to make the Roman Empire as absolute a patriarchy as they could. The thorn in their side was the universally famous teacher, healer, and social reformer Apollonius of Tyana, all biographies of whom except one have mysteriously disappeared over the centuries.

Typical of Apollonius's annoying activities was saving a town called Aspendus whose citizens were starving, "for the rich men had shut up all the corn and were holding it up for export from the country." In his usual no-nonsense style, Apollonius told the merchants, whom he was sparing from a mob that was about to lynch them: "The earth is mother of us all, for she is just; but you, because you are unjust have pretended that she is your mother alone; and if you do not stop, I will not permit you to remain upon her."[15]

What Apollonius and the Aspendians faced still happens. Inheriting the control model, we continue to tolerate it as the context for forming rules and setting up social systems. One anecdote we came across illustrates the power of the patriarchy as of 1991:

> In Utah a young woman who went to the state Driver's License Division after her divorce to change the name on her license back to her maiden name was told that she would need her former husband's permission. The woman, who claimed no prior feminist leanings, found the rule so biased

that she filed suit, claiming discrimination against divorced women. A Utah court and a federal appeals court rejected her claim.*

Women in power-over systems. Women remain far from experiencing equal respect. In businesses, for example, women still don't receive equal pay for equal work. Having male equipment in America brings an extra 15–60 percent in salaries. Of all age groups, men make 31 percent more than women; among those over twenty-five years or older, men make 37 percent more than women.[16] That's one set of statistics. The January 1994 issue of *Working Woman* estimates that women "still earn just 70.6 cents for every dollar a man makes."[17] By that calculation, men make on average 42 percent more than women.

Whatever the figure, it's high, and it varies job to job. *Working Woman* cites the case of "female orthopedic surgeons and women in financial-services sales, who pull in less than 55 percent of what the men earn." Male executives, administrators, and managers make on average 47 percent more than their female colleagues, while male operators, fabricators, and laborers make on average 38 percent more than their female counterparts (1994 figures). Husbands generally make 46 percent more than their working wives (1990 figures).[18]

At home, the work of women becomes invisible. As Barbara Brandt notes, "If a woman cooks and cleans in a man's home as a paid domestic servant, she is counted as part of the economy because her paid work is included in society's key economic measure, the gross domestic product (GDP). However, if a man marries his maid, she no longer gets paid for her housework in his home, and her contribution to the GDP is suddenly eliminated from the official statistics."[19]

Work at home, though, especially when children or entertaining business associates are involved, is far more demanding than maid service. The hours are round the clock; it's hard physically and emotionally; it requires both specialized and wide-ranging skills and talents, including nutritional and medical knowledge; it often involves split-second responses to crises; and it demands considerable management ability. How much is this worth? Divorce lawyer Michael Minton used several standard economic measures to develop "a model through which he estimated that the average value of a

---

*We found this in that radical feminist publication, the *1992 Britannica Book of the Year* (Chicago: Encyclopedia Britannica, 1992), 463.

homemaker's services came to about $40,000 per year (in 1983)—and he has won many settlements using this model."[20] In *Outrageous Acts and Everyday Rebellions*, Gloria Steinem writes, "If all the productive work of human maintenance that women do in the home were valued at its replacement cost, the gross national product of the United States would go up by 26 percent."[21]

As a further legacy of patriarchal attitudes, even beating women and children is a "domestic problem" in many states—a civil offense but not a crime such as assault. These ownership attitudes reflect the archaic practice of collecting dowries as "wife insurance": if the wife turned out to be a dud as a possession, at least the husband would have her stuff.

Employees in power-over systems. But marital slavery is just the beginning. The control paradigm says that employees are also property. Their time, minds, bodies, and energies are owned by their employers. As long as they receive a paycheck, they forfeit rights granted them by the Constitution and the Bill of Rights.

Thanks to the rules of silence and denial, for instance, free speech and freedom of thought are the first rights to go. Few employees dare cross their superiors without risking their jobs or at least their promotions and raises.

Even the right to life is abrogated under a corporate model. Today, in poverty-stricken countries where big corporations go to avoid environmental regulations and labor laws, employees must either tolerate dangerous and toxic working conditions or lose their jobs. When people get so ill that they can't work, they're fired and new people are brought in. It's the corporate version of genocide to indigenous peoples.

In *Healing the Shame That Binds You*, John Bradshaw writes: "Society itself is…a sick family system built on the rules of the poisonous pedagogy." He adds the historical note that, "These rules come from the time of Kings. They are non-democratic and are based on a kind of master-slave inequality." The results? "Such rules allow no place for vitality, spontaneity, inner freedom, inner independence and critical judgment."[22]

BAD-NEWS CONTEXTS DAY TO DAY

Rules aren't the only way we experience a paradigm context, though. To borrow the image of a tree, paradigms are the root context, rules are the branches context, while the act/react worlds we live in day to day are the leaves-and-fruit context. According to the tree, the fruit can be sweet or bitter, fresh or rotten.

As our immediate context, the details, dramas, and routines of our lives become all-absorbing. They're so in-our-faces that it's hard to see, first, that they're paradigm-created, and second, that we can change them. We've internalized the paradigm's apparatus so thoroughly that we can't distinguish between the paradigm's rules and our own character. By force of habit, we assume they're identical.

Context-created roles. Living under control-paradigm rules, for instance, we slip into roles—roles distilled from our immediate social context. We identify with the roles: parent or child, authority or dependent, go-getter or victim, boss or employee. The roles are familiar; we think they're us. They may not be great, but without them, we fear we'd be treated like nobody.

And that's a real fear. Control-paradigm contexts convey that message: who we are is unacceptable; we need external trappings to be somebody. We're paid for the roles we play, not for connecting with our inner powers.

As Sharon Wegscheider-Cruse found in her now-classic studies, family roles are more predictable than we'd guess.* One member typically becomes the problem person who drives everyone crazy—dramatizing outwardly the family's inward conflict—and every family has one. To compensate, someone else becomes the superachiever to save the family image. Another person becomes the caregiver to pick up the pieces. Other family members become the lost soul who watches from the sidelines, the scapegoat who gets the blame, or the comic who uses humor to divert attention from pain.

The same roles appear within other social systems. Some groups play the role of problem people, the troublemakers who act out the pain generated by the system. We love to be mad at these people, even hate, imprison, and kill them. It gives us a socially acceptable outlet for pent-up anger.

Other types find their niche in caregiving: listening to everyone's problems or doing social work. They patch, bandage, and drug clients and then send them back into the same structures that wounded them. As a result, they unwittingly cover for an abusive system, so that system ills don't come

---

*Sharon Wegscheider-Cruse, *Another Chance: Hope and Health for the Alcoholic Family*, 2d ed. (Palo Alto: Science and Behavior Books, 1989). This book outlines her pioneering work as well as that of Virginia Satir in family structures and the roles they produce.

to a crisis—professional enabling on behalf of control-paradigm systems.

Others become the superachievers and heroes, the ones we point to as proof of society's success. We venerate these people and would love to be them, which is yet another way of underscoring the system message that we're unworthy as we are, that we don't measure up, and that outward recognition is the true measure of our life's worth.

The soul cost and social cost of roles. In *Bradshaw On: The Family*, John Bradshaw explains how damaging role-fixedness is. Caught in roles, we stay in the water jug. We do what role dynamics require of us, even at cost to our development. Long after we leave our family of origin, for instance, we continue to reproduce original-family roles in our lives. Even when we want to change, we find ourselves unable to do so. Or we change briefly, only to fall back to old patterns.

Social roles are equally resistant to change. Long after legislation passes to end injustices, for instance, abusive practices persist. Legal slavery ended over a hundred years ago, and women have had the vote for decades, but the roles of slave and underling persist. If we're the wrong race (nonwhite), gender (nonmale), age group (nonproductive years), or species (nonhuman), we have neither rights nor respect. Our place is on the receiving end of whatever control structures do to us. If it's good, the one-down role tells us to fawn with gratitude; if it's bad, the role tells us to put up and shut up.

Instead of expanding soul expression, roles narrow it. When we get stuck in roles, we suppress sides of ourselves that don't fit the script. Heroes can't be afraid, caregivers can't receive care, and problem people can't be responsible. On the job, we put aside our creativity to be the efficient administrator, our morality to be the successful deal maker, our sensitivities to be the tough executive, or our dreams to be the mover and shaker. The role context tells us what we can and can't express.

Trained to put role contexts first. That we put roles first, though, is no accident. We're trained to do this.

If family training didn't get the message across, schools seal the lesson. We create a persona—a mask—that enables us to survive the trauma of schooling. First we learn to suppress our intuition, initiative, independent thought, joy, and cooperation. In their place, the classroom structure rewards military-style obedience, fear-and-insecurity motivation in the pursuit of external rewards, analytic rationality, machinelike memorization, aggression against peers (competition), and dependence on idealized authorities. By putting our school role first, we get A's.

For what? To fit in what sort of context? D. Bob Gowin in his book *Educating* describes school life as "routine, boring, and life-defeating," and as being "readily associated with humiliation and aggression."[23] While Gowin identifies schooling with "violence," Sufi sage Hazrat Inayat Khan associates it with death. In the *Spiritual Dimensions of Psychology*, he writes: "It is a great fault of learning today that the [feeling] side is kept apart, which is the most important side. It is like wanting a person to come not with his life but as a corpse; as if in order to educate a person the life should be taken out of him, and he should be turned from a living person into a dead one."[24]

We'd think Hitler designed the system, but recovery researcher Alice Miller discovered that Hitler attended schools generated from the same control model. Miller is less kind to Western education than Gowin or even Khan. She says: "Our whole system of raising and educating children provides the power-hungry with a ready-made railway network they can use to reach the destination of their choice. They need only push the buttons that parents and educators have already installed."[25] Obedience to roles—using them as our life's context—provides the mechanism.

Abusing ourselves with control-paradigm tapes. Even our most personal thoughts distill out of the control-paradigm context. We develop attitudes that correspond with the control-paradigm messages we've heard and the rules we've had to follow.

For instance, we develop a story about the "real world" as a dog-eat-dog struggle—a story that not only reflects what we've experienced but also reproduces the world it describes. The rules are simple. In any situation, assume a zero-sum, survival of the fittest, win-lose game. Then react. And survive. Even better, win by beating someone else. "If you don't look out for Number One, no one else will." Such rules sound like the formula for a bad B-movie—where's the MST 3K crowd* when you need them?—but it passes

---

*"MST 3K" stands for *Mystery Science Theater 3000*. If you don't know this television program, it's hard to capture what's made it such a hit. Essentially, one human and two robots sit and make fun of dreadful movies. Once you see it, though, watching movies is never quite the same again.

as a common worldview, even as the way to success.

So, too, with the story of the universe as an unpredictable, meaningless, hostile place—one where we can be wiped out from one moment to the next. The story inspires fear, which makes us contract within a world we consider safe. We avoid intimate relationships because we might be hurt or lose them, and we don't want to risk rejection. Before we know it, we create a fear-filled world, which convinces us that our personal paradigm must be right.

What we're doing is abusing ourselves with assumptions about our life's context—assumptions we've derived from living in system contexts created by the control paradigm. We no longer need messages from without to undermine our worth and intimidate us into conformity. Our personal thought-context becomes our primary abuser. It incorporates all the messages sent by power-over systems, and these messages create a context that leaves no room for growth. As Brenda Schaeffer writes in *Is It Love or Is It Addiction?*, "To deny oneself growth is personal abuse."[26] The soul-violating messages aren't "out there" anymore; we take them to heart with a personal paradigm that keeps us bottled in a jug.

Jug-dependent no more. In short, the contexts we've turned our will and lives over to have trapped us in no-win, pain-filled patterns. We're caught, and our societies are caught along with us.

Context-bound, we find transformation an uphill struggle, if not impossible. The contexts won't allow it. As long as we assume them, wholeness change won't happen. Or if it does, it comes by making contexts burst in crises.

A less traumatic path is to expand the context—to take the plunge and redraw the field. This calls for creativity, courage, and a conviction that there's more to reality than life in a jug, no matter how outwardly successful the jug makes us.

ACCEPTING THE TRUTH OF WHOLENESS AS OUR CONTEXT

Expanding the context to the whole. The contexts we've assumed and the rules we've obeyed aren't our only options. We can envision other contexts with more soul-nurturing rules. In fact, we can go the whole nine yards and assume an ultimate context, that of ultimate reality—the ocean beyond the jug.

Spiritual teachings may differ on what this ultimate context is and on the rules that express it, but they all agree that it comes first among our assumptions about what's really going on. Ultimate reality—whether it's called Being, the Tao, God, the Absolute, the One, the Whole, Nature, the Creator, or Bohm's concept of the holomovement—is the ultimate context. Rumi said:

> The whole world lives within a safeguarding: fish
> inside waves, birds held in the sky, the elephant,
> the wolf, the lion as he hunts, the dragon, the ant,
> the waiting snake, even the ground, the air,
> water, every spark floating up from the fire,
> all subsist, exist, in God. Nothing
> is ever alone for a single moment.
>
> All giving comes from There, no matter who
> you think you put your open hand out
> toward, it's That which gives.[27]

The whole context spurs evolution. Spiritual traditions even agree that their rules consistently nurture spiritual evolution. As an infinite field, reality's ultimate context continually invites us to transcend limits—fixed contexts—and to experience our lives from a wider perspective. That's what Apollonius did with the corn merchants. They looked at their lives from the narrow context of making money for themselves, even if it meant starving fellow townspeople. He made them look at their lives from the expanded context of co-inhabitants of earth, the mother of all. (It didn't hurt that he also pointed out to them the expanded context of furious townspeople who now knew where they lived.)

By constantly inviting us to push past rigid rules and roles, the whole context is life affirming in a way that no other context can be. No matter how fixed or ingrained the social system—no matter how narrow, rigid, and deadening it may have become—the whole context affirms life by encouraging evolution and self-transcendence in spite of it.

Seeking a whole-context perspective on truth. Assuming all this, we can't accept the truth of our existence without accepting the truth as the whole context reveals it. Partial contexts skew the truth. What's omitted from the picture becomes a powerful tool of manipulation, as people are fooled into acting on pieces of truth without access to the whole story.

True, we may not ever be able to know what the whole truth is—we'd have to be the whole ourselves to do it—but that's no reason not to seek it. Otherwise, we get trapped in narrow contexts, as Marley did in Charles Dickens's *A Christmas Carol*. Only when he died did he realize, as his ghost told Scrooge, that his business context had been far too small: "Mankind was my business. The common welfare way my business; charity, mercy, forbearance, and benevolence were, all, my business. The dealings of my trade were but a drop of water in the comprehensive ocean of my business!"

Accepting the truth means seeking the whole truth, which we do as we expand our context without end. AA's Third Step moves us in this direction. It involves a decision "to turn our will and our lives over to the care of God *as we understand [God]*." The Step's effectiveness doesn't lie in adopting fixed notions about God; fixed concepts block change. The change power of this Step lies in the conscious act of expanding the paradigm context—of opening to All That Is—so that transformation can occur. And it does occur.

"A transformation *will* take place." Accepting a higher, ultimate, whole context—however we conceive of it—precipitates transformation. Expanding the context gets our creative, self-transcending juices flowing. We no longer accept jug-bound worlds as absolute.

By opening our paradigm context, we give the wholeness principle room to work. In his article "The Mystery of Wholeness," physician Richard Moss writes: "True healing means drawing the circle of our being larger and becoming more inclusive…. In this sense, healing is not for the sick alone, but for all humankind."[28]

"Drawing the circle of our being larger" brings transformation. This happens not only in healing but in personal and cultural transformation as well. Historically, whenever cultures interact outside the control paradigm—even for a short time—they change. When Renaissance artists and philosophers rediscovered Greek and Roman classics, for instance, Western culture took a huge leap forward. When Muslims interacted peacefully with Christians in pre-fifteenth-century Spain, both cultures developed new spiritual, artistic, and architectural forms. When Apollonius carried Buddhist teachings from India to Egypt, the Nile mystics widened their spiritual perspective.

Edgar Mitchell, the sixth astronaut to walk on the moon and the founder of the Institute of Noetic Sciences, states that transformation "is what happens when humans perceive a larger, more all-encompassing reality than they previously held." When that happens, "a transformation will take place."[29]

Expanding our personal context. Perceiving a larger, more encompassing reality may come from something as simple as taking a walk or as profound as a near-death experience. Traveling is an ancient way of confronting new worlds, as is interacting with people. Perceiving new realities may also come from being with animals, who have a calming, healing effect on humans. Animals elicit responses from comatose patients, for instance, that humans can't. Animals invite us into their worlds and give us windows on a different experience, even a different dimension.

Perceiving "a larger, more all-encompassing reality than [we] previously held" can also come from going within. Study and reflection open us to the worlds of the mind and soul. Contemplation and meditation take us on inner journeys.

Therapy and recovery paths open us to worlds of feeling that we've suppressed. We accept the truth of the soul traumas we've experienced from living in control-paradigm contexts and allow ourselves to grieve soul loss. In other words, we allow into our context feelings that the control paradigm shut out.

However we go about expanding our context, something in us wants us re-embedded in wholeness—our original home—and this quest for wholeness leads us to accept the truth that the whole is our ultimate context. Control-paradigm contexts—socially sanctioned jugs—are not ultimate. Their narrow contexts cannot reveal the truth of who we are; therefore, we cannot accept their "truth" as ours.

Re-embedding social systems in wholeness. By accepting whole-context truth, we once again foment revolution. Expanding our personal paradigm context, we demand that our systems come along and respect our new playing field. Our expanded awareness operates as the "larger circle" that transforms them: we become the larger, more encompassing reality for our systems.

In doing this, we change whose context shapes whom. Instead of our personal context being shaped by control-paradigm social systems—their rules, roles, structures, and norms—our whole-oriented paradigm becomes the context that shapes them. Government, work, church, and school forms distill out of our vision, ideas, and values. We reclaim our systems as our creations—created to serve us—and we change them to reflect our evolving needs.

In such a context, power-over systems don't have to be destroyed; they wither for lack of feeding. When the paradigm generating power-over energies isn't there to fuel power-play dramas, people simply walk out from under the old-paradigm norm.

Sketching whole-based contexts

Rules that support personal transformation. Rules sketch what it may mean to accept a context of whole-connectedness and "draw the circle of our being larger." And these rules aren't unfamiliar: "To thine own self be true...." Listen to your inner voice. Follow your soul. Let spiritual growth—character, soul, and true-self issues—set your priorities. Pursue the quest for meaning. Seek your life's purpose. Learn, honor, and accept the truth of your feelings as emissaries from your soul. Feel your connectedness to all that is and honor those connections. Don't conform to outward pressures but allow transformation to operate from the inside out. Or as Paul put it, "Don't let the world around you squeeze you into its own mold, but let God re-mold your minds from within."[30] Tibetan Buddhists say, "Follow wisdom and compassion—and use skillful means."

These rules open us to self-transcendence, because they attune us to our inner experience of whole-connectedness. If we accept the truth of how the whole touches us through our inner lives, there's no way we'll ever be stuck in a jug. The ocean flowing through us just won't allow it.

Rules that support social transformation. Rules that support social transformation aren't unfamiliar either. In fact, spiritual teachings agree on one basic rule: the Golden Rule. If we do to others what we'd like done to ourselves—or don't do what we wouldn't like done to us—we create a context that's fertile ground for ongoing social transformation.

To a friend who doubted that nonviolence could be attained by the masses, Gandhi replied: "We find the general work of mankind is being carried on from day to day by the mass of people acting in harmony as if by instinct. If they were instinctively violent, the world would end in no time. They remain peaceful...."[31]

Some core understanding of mutual fair treatment is born in us and lives on in our interactions, sometimes more, sometimes less, otherwise "the world would end in no time." Reciprocity is the fabric of healthy social systems. When we're each guided by this rule, we go into relationships with our soul-connectedness honored and come away with it intact.

Rules that don't. By contrast, whenever social systems disregard the Golden Rule, they become oppressive. It becomes okay to do to others what we wouldn't like done to ourselves, as long as we're in a position to get away with it. The assumption, for example, that "earth is the mother of us all, for she is just" gets displaced by an assumption that earth should be owned by a few, depending on who's most ruthless about grabbing it.

Social systems that violate reciprocity don't, however, ultimately work. Oppressive rules cause social systems to slide into collapse, and for two good reasons.

First, oppressive social systems ignore their greatest resource: human knowledge and creativity. Because we're each linked to the whole, we each have access to untold powers. Social systems need our creative powers to cope with change, but when oppressive rules dominate, neither we nor our systems have access to them.

Second, oppressive systems generate mountains of suffering that sooner or later erupt in crisis. The conquerors end up controlling a ravaged world where they're hated. What security is there in that? What prize?

Open to who we are beyond roles. With rules that support transformation by expanding the context, we start exploring the wider territory and who we're allowed to become in it. "Lost" dimensions of our souls return, and powers emerge that roles shut out. We don't have to limit ourselves to being a parent, breadwinner, caregiver, expert, or employee. Neither do we have to become what we believe some parent, teacher, or religious official would want.

People who've had near-death experiences (NDEs), for instance, often report a liberating self-awareness when they leave their bodies and hear themselves declared dead. Psychiatrist, physician, and philosopher Raymond Moody reports:

> One NDEer described this stage as being "a time when you are not the wife of your husband, you are not the parent of your children, you are not the

child of your parents. You are totally and completely you." Another woman said she felt like she was going through a "cutting of ribbons," like the freedom given to a balloon when its strings are cut. It is at this point that fear turns to bliss, as well as understanding.[32]

But we don't have to wait until we die to experience this "larger circle of our being." Instead of accepting a paradigm that narrows us to something controllable, we can accept the truth that we're more than personalities bound by roles, obligations, guilts, and regrets, more even than creatures of time, space, and societies. We're whole-endowed beings. Moving with the ocean, we find our whole nature emerging.

BREAKING THE JUG WITH "MORE"

Opening to the "more." How we experience transformation—whether as jugs breaking apart or as wholeness emerging—depends on our readiness to redraw the field. Not that we have to settle on "the one, right context." We simply need assumptions that keep our paradigm context open and expanding, so that transformation can occur.

Spiritual teachings offer such an approach with the premise that there's "more" going on than appears on the surface. A spiritual perspective assumes deeper dimensions of meaning everywhere—of ourselves, others, events, society, history, nature, the earth, or God. Assuming the "more to life" keeps us open to the "more" and out of jugs.

More to God. For instance, a strong tradition in mystical teachings is negative theology. Negative theology isn't pessimistic or anti-God. It assumes that the whole surpasses our concepts about it. Whatever label we put on reality, Reality itself is more. The infinite context can't be captured by finite concepts. We can't put God inside any belief system, Jewish or Christian, Hindu or Muslim. What these religions teach about God provides direction, but the reality of Reality is more—as the teachings themselves affirm.

More to us. This assumption applies to us as well. Whatever labels we put on ourselves, we're more. Whatever roles we take on or stages we go through, we're more. No matter how we define ourselves, our reality is greater, and this "more to us" unfolds as the paradigm context we assume makes room for it. Assuming the more, we don't lock each other inside family, educa-

tional, social, economic, racial, gender, or other limited contexts; we give the
more a chance to emerge.

More to social systems. Assuming the more to everything, we open our social
systems to being more than they are. Schools don't exhaust the possibilities
of learning. Economies don't exhaust the possibilities of prosperity.
Newspapers, magazines, and television programs don't exhaust the possibilities of communicating knowledge and ideas. Current medical and pharma-
ceutical industries don't exhaust the possibilities of nurturing health.
Religions don't exhaust the possibilities of exploring spiritual growth.
Social-action groups don't exhaust the possibilities of social change, nor do
governments run by the monied elite exhaust the possibilities of furthering
the public good.

When we draw the circle larger to include the more, a transformation
will take place.

Surrendering to transformation. The flip side of expanding the paradigm
context is surrendering power-over contexts—letting go of the jug.

Surrender is a big issue in personal recovery. It's not abdicating our will
and with it our responsibility. It's opening our life's context by letting go of
the tightness—the bottled-in-a-jug-ness—that we've been trained to
impose.

Surrender means, for example, letting go of rigid roles. It means not getting stuck in control games. It means letting go of restrictive assumptions
(e.g., competition, misery, or control) built into our social systems, so that
the more we are and the more our systems can be have a chance to emerge.

C. S. Lewis said he learned the meaning of surrender when he learned
how to dive. At some point in the dive, he explained, we give ourselves over
to the forces of gravity. In wholeness change, surrender is like that. We give
ourselves over to the wholeness principle and how it breaks open our context.

From assumptions to strategies. When the field expands, we're called to
expand our assumptions. Generative as fields are, the new field calls them
into being.

As we shift our assumptions, though, we find our strategies shifting as
well—the next three chapters.

Notes to Chapter 3

1. Coleman Barks, trans., *One-Handed Basket Weaving—Poems on the Theme of Work* (Athens, GA: Maypop Books, 1991), 54.
2. Gary Zukav, *The Dancing Wu Li Masters: An Overview of the New Physics* (New York: William Morrow and Company, 1979), 219.
3. David Korten, *When Corporations Rule the World* (West Hartford, CT: Kumarian Press and San Francisco, CA: Berrett-Koehler Publishers, 1995), 180.
4. Martin Teitel, "Endangered Dinner," *Sierra Magazine* (January/Feruary 1996), 12.
5. Vandana Shiva, *Staying Alive: Women, Ecology, and Development* (London: Zed Books, 1988), 131.
6. Shiva, *Staying Alive*, 136.
7. Shiva, *Staying Alive*, 136.
8. Shunryu Suzuki, *Zen Mind, Beginner's Mind* (New York: John Weatherhill Inc., 1970), 27.
9. Robert Subby and John Friel, "Co-Dependence: A Paradoxical Dependency" in *Co-Dependency: An Emerging Issue* (Deerfield Beach, FL: Health Communications, 1984), 32.
10. Wayne Kritsberg, *The Adult Children of Alcoholics Syndrome* (New York: Bantam edition, 1988), 15–24.
11. John Bradshaw, *Bradshaw On: The Family: A Revolutionary Way of Self-Discovery* (Deerfield Beach, FL: Health Communications, 1988), 32.
12. Bradshaw, *Bradshaw On: The Family*, 29.
13. Barbara Brandt, *Whole Life Economics: Revaluing Daily Life* (Philadelphia: New Society Publishers, 1995), 30.
14. Hannsdieter Wohlfarth, *Johann Sebastian Bach* (Philadelphia: Fortress Press, 1966), 65.
15. Philostratus, *The Life of Apollonius of Tyana* (Cambridge: Loeb Classical Library, Harvard University Press, 1989), 41–43.
16. These statistics are calculated from *The American Almanac: Statistical Abstract of the United States 1995–1996* (Austin, TX: The Reference Press, 1995), chart no. 677: "Full-Time Wage and Salary Workers—Number and Earnings 1983–1994," 433.
17. Diane Harris, "Does Your Pay Measure Up?" *Working Woman* (January 1994), 26.
18. Calculated from *The American Almanac: Statistical Abstract of the United States 1995–1996*, Chart No. 677: "Full-Time Wage and Salary Workers—Number and Earnings 1983–1994," 433.
19. Brandt, *Whole Life Economics*, 17.
20. Brandt, *Whole Life Economics*, 19–20.
21. Gloria Steinem, *Outrageous Acts and Everyday Rebellions* (New York: Henry Holt, 1983), 183.
22. John Bradshaw, *Healing the Shame That Binds You* (Deerfield Beach, FL: Health Communications, 1988), 67.
23. D. Bob Gowin, *Educating* (Ithaca, NY: Cornell University Press, 1981), 14.
24. Hazrat Inayat Khan, *Spiritual Dimensions of Psychology* (New Lebanon, NY: Omega Uniform Edition, 1988), 7.

25. Alice Miller, *Thou Shalt Not Be Aware: Society's Betrayal of the Child* (New York: Farrar Strauss Giroux, 1984), 20.
26. Brenda Schaeffer, *Is It Love Or Is It Addiction?* (San Francisco: Harper/Hazelden, 1987), 43.
27. Coleman Barks, trans., *Delicious Laughter: Rambunctious Teaching Stories from the Mathnawi* (Athens, GA: Maypop Books, 1990), 50.
28. Richard Carlson and Benjamin Shield, eds., *Healers on Healing* (Los Angeles: Jeremy Tarcher, 1989), 36.
29. *The New Leaders*, May/June 1992, 3.
30. Romans 12:2, trans. J. B. Phillips, *Letters to Young Churches* (New York: Macmillan Co., 1954), 28.
31. Louis Fischer, ed., *The Essential Gandhi* (New York: Vintage, Random House, 1962), 201.
32. Raymond Moody, *The Light Beyond* (New York: Bantam Books, 1988), 7.

CHAPTER 4

Self-Knowledge:
Knowing Our Paradigm Filters

Observing the truth
Fourth of the Twelve Cycles of Truth,
the Iroquois Peace Confederacy Tradition

Days are sieves to filter spirit,
reveal impurities, and too,
show the light of some who throw
their own shining into the universe.
Rumi[1]

HOW DO WE FORM PARADIGMS?

Thanks but no thanks. What's the first strategy for shifting our personal and shared paradigms? Finding out what strategy has been forming the paradigm we have.

The control paradigm didn't take shape around our soul needs; it shaped *us* around its agenda. The paradigm was imposed from without for the purpose of taking charge of what's within. No wonder it harms us. Our meaning and purpose in life—our souls' longings—have never been factors for the control paradigm; we exist solely as objects to be controlled.

Schools, for instance, did not develop from an understanding of the human mind: from studying conditions most conducive to learning or developing human creativity. Industrialists designed the modern school system to produce punctual, do-what-you're-told, detail-memorizing, external-rewards-driven, sit-in-rows, factory workers.

To shift paradigms big-time, we have to shift the strategy of how we get paradigms. Whenever they're imposed from without, they wage war on our inner lives, because our inner experience isn't part of the paradigm-forming process. What else do we expect?

If we want a paradigm that's soul-honoring, we have to take the lead and demand that our existence be affirmed. This isn't being selfish; it's being true to where we are—true to our existence as part of the social reality.

Then, to any paradigm that blusters in to take over our minds and souls—to remake us in its image—we can say "Thanks, but no thanks!" We're not exchanging one external control paradigm for another; our strategy for forming paradigms starts with our deepening self-awareness.

Soul-honoring paradigms start with us. To deepen our self-awareness, though, we have to be soul-connected. We can't demand of our paradigms an awareness that we ourselves lack. If soul sensitivity is what our paradigm needs, we're the ones to give it.

Otherwise, we're easy prey for new-and-improved, imposed-from-without paradigms, appearing as the latest motivational, religious, educational, or psychological program guaranteed to turn us into the best fill-in-the-blank, assuming that anything is better than who we are.

For a true strategy shift, we have to make soul awareness central to the paradigm-forming process. That's the revolutionary shift that Socrates introduced 2,400 years ago. He said all knowledge is remembering from our deep soul-knowing. Instead of looking outside ourselves for a paradigm that models truth, we look within.

The shift that Socrates proposed has been long in coming, though—and for a reason. Given our multimillennia history in control-paradigm social systems, soul awareness is hard to come by. Our experience of ourselves is paradigm-conditioned, paradigm-shaped, colored, and packaged. We've been molded to fit into control-paradigm societies. We're their puzzle pieces, cut to match their paradigm-defined needs.

As long as we keep providing a perfect match—dovetailing with the paradigm-cut pieces around us—our paradigm won't change, nor will we be able to connect with more of our souls than the control paradigm allows. Our social roles are all that control-paradigm institutions recognize of us. For that matter, they dominate what we experience of ourselves. Because our souls have been classified as threats (willful children, troublemakers, sinners, uncooperative employees, and general nuisances), they've been erased from the picture. Our souls remain offstage, functionally invisible.

The journey of self-knowledge. Shifting paradigms starts with getting our souls back on stage, front and center. Do the stamped-out puzzle pieces exhaust our identity? How much of what we're living is our souls' finding a meaningful outlet through social systems, and how much is doing what's expected for money, acceptance, family expectation, or some other exteriorly motivated, not-our-souls reason? Are we living our souls' passion? Do we even feel soul passion, or has it been pushed down below where we have access to it? What's it take for us to regain access?

The journey of self-knowledge explores these questions. We "observe the truth" of who we are—not to judge ourselves but rather to understand our souls' processes and to connect with our individuality beneath the roles.

To this end, we need to observe the dance we've been doing with our social systems. Insofar as we got cookie-cuttered by social systems, the control paradigm designed the shapes. Self-knowledge is the process of sorting out what's us, what's cookie-cuttered, and what's raw edges in between.

THROUGH THE HALL OF MIRRORS TO WHERE WE ARE

Society's hall of mirrors. The sorting out isn't easy. When we enter social systems, we walk into a hall of mirrors. Images surround us and patterns repeat as far as the eye can see. But who's projecting the images? What's really us? We move a finger, and a thousand fingers move the same way. Seeing all those fingers wiggling, we wiggle ours again.

But after decades of personal wiggling and millennia of social wiggling, we can't recall who wiggled first. The paradigm patterns seem "out there," but who's creating them? Are we initiating the patterns or following them? Do we really want to spend our lives pursuing money and status, for instance, or have we been convinced by the control paradigm that we must? Are we the ones standing before the mirror, or are we the thousand images in the glass?

Who's reflecting whom?

We reflect systems. For the first twenty to thirty years of life, we adapt to our systems to find some place in them. We mirror what goes on in families, schools, workplaces, churches, and the media—and we do it without thinking.

Reproducing paradigm patterns in our lives, we become the thousand images echoing society's worldview. After our social systems induct us into the power-over, ranking paradigm, we carry it not only into every social exchange but even into how we feel about ourselves. We feel less than human if we're out of work, for instance, and more than human if we're a CEO of a multinational corporation.

Tapping soul memories. Once we've proven our social-system package-ability, though, we begin to reflect on the process. We start asking who we are beyond the roles. Sometimes it takes personal crises to trigger this self-reflection; other times we just feel bored. We've done the expected and mirrored the dutiful. Is that all we came here for?

We start imagining the unimaginable—for instance, that it may be better to be unemployed and soul-searching than making fistfuls of money polluting the earth. Unemployed, we may not be drawing a paycheck, but at least we're not making other people's lives hell in Mexico or Indonesia or causing global damage for generations to come. Which is closer to being soul-connected?

Connecting with how we feel about the social-packaging process, we tap soul memories reminding us that the image in the mirror isn't all there is. With the third Cycle of Truth to build on, we explore wider meanings than the ones our social systems provide.

Systems reflect us. As we expand our identity beyond the roles we've mirrored, we lay the groundwork for a strategy shift. Reconnecting with who we are, we demand that systems change to reflect our nature—to mirror us.

This switch in who-reflects-whom is actually more accurate to what's going on in the big picture. Systems aren't out there; they're us—all of us. They act out our paradigms on a collective stage. All the paradigm apparatus—ideas, values, perceptions, and qualities—that we take into social systems make our systems function as they do. It's our image—our shared paradigm and stage of development—that's reflected in society's mirror. Society has no absolute nature apart from what we together give it.

Example: We help create the super-wealthy. We may not be the ones making billions at others' expense, for instance, but as long as we regard the super-wealthy as super-successful, the cream of society, we endorse their methods. Our only argument is that we'd rather be the ones with the billions. With this attitude—one straight out of control-paradigm conditioning—we unwittingly contribute to their robbery, because we don't view their strategies *as* robbing; we call John D. Rockefeller's usually unethical, sometimes illegal methods "shrewd business" or corporate raiders who may pull a million dollars an hour "being in the right place at the right time." "If they can get away with it," we say, "more power to them"—and, oddly enough, more power does go to them.

We create the super-wealthy elite as much as they create themselves, because we share the attitudes that provide fertile ground for their strategies to thrive. A control paradigm states that societies work best when the few dominate the many. The few and the many are necessary for the model to work, and each participates in creating the other.

Example: We support the diamond monopoly. As Arthur Epstein exposes in *The Rise and Fall of Diamonds*, we-the-many dutifully purchase diamonds at every romantic milestone, paying thousands for one of the most abundant gems on the planet. The high price of diamonds—mined by virtual slave labor in South Africa and cut by child workers in India paid pennies per jewel—is a result of a public relations coup by the few, in fact, by two mega-wealthy families. We buyers believe this common stone is rare, because the company controlling the world supply says it is, contrary to common geological knowledge. Wherever there's carbon, there are diamonds. We accept the slogan that "a diamond is forever"—a slogan crafted to discourage the trade-in of old diamonds, because that would glut the market. Without our purchases of this overpriced stone and our acceptance of an overhyped sentiment, the Oppenheimer/DeBeers global monopoly of diamonds would collapse.

Social systems don't exist without us. They have no life apart from our collective involvement. Social systems are our creations—not only in the past but minute by minute now.

What we create we can also change. Systems live on our paradigm-packaged energies. If we withdraw those energies and give them new paradigm channels, the patterns must change.

Not using our power. However, as long as we tolerate the strategy of having a paradigm imposed on us—as long as we act as if we're the thousand reflections in the mirror—though we have the power to initiate a new paradigm, we don't exercise it. Instead of flexing our paradigm-shifting powers, we project back onto society's mirror what's already there.

Mesmerized by the images and seeing them multiplied by the millions, we conclude that there's no other way to be: "We have no choice but to behave thus to survive." "We must accept the hard realities of the control-and-dominate model." Ignorant of our power, we follow the patterns, and the thousand reflected images don't change.

That's our situation, personally, culturally, and globally.

Knowing what's happening breaks the mesmerism. Immediately, we're more soul aware, because we name the de-souling dance for what it is. Deep memories begin to stir, and the next control type who expects us to fall in line had better watch out. We're not accepting any paradigm that fails to resonate with the truth we've observed.

SELF-KNOWLEDGE: A FORCE FOR TRANSFORMATION

Knowing we're not the images. By forcing a shift in how we form our paradigms, self-knowledge is revolutionary by nature. The more we're connected to our own individuality, the less we're mesmerized by the thousand reflected images. Though we may not know clearly who we are, at least we know we're more than how the control paradigm packages us. Even that first movement of self-awareness gives us the strength not to yield our paradigm-choosing powers. We stand our ground in front of the mirror.

Then the journey of self-knowledge begins: Who are we? Where are we in our inner growth? What patterns are we living? Did they arise from us or the mirror?

What's doable. Self-knowledge comes first among paradigm-shifting strategies, not only because systems are us—and therefore how soul-connected we are determines what kind of energies we put into our systems—but also because self-knowledge is doable. We can't change cultural paradigms overnight; it's a process. We can, however, observe the truth of who we are and let our paradigms grow from the truth of self-awareness.

Granted, self-knowledge is a process as well; it's ongoing because we're evolving. It is not particularly "sweetness and light," especially when we consider how much we've conformed to a control-paradigm role, how it didn't fit, and how our dis-ease in ill-fitting roles got projected onto or acted out on others.

Self-knowledge does, however, give us the option to build our paradigms on the deeper truth we gain, and this shift in paradigm strategy revolutionizes relationships, families, schools, religious institutions, businesses, professions, and governments.

Self-awareness: The key to transformation. To show how self-knowledge works its transforming powers, we can look at how it works in healing, which involves mini- or sometimes maxi-paradigm shifts. Sickness or depression is a crisis in our personal operating system. Healing moves us to new levels of awareness: body awareness, relationship awareness, life-purpose awareness, our-role-in-systems awareness, or our-connectedness-to-the-whole awareness.

Healers appeal to our powers of awareness. They give us the option to make whatever shift is needed. In this sense, healing is not about fixing us or returning us to normal. True to ancient healing concepts, healing is transformation. We go back to our origins in whole-connectedness—back to creation time, dream time, or soul-knowing time—and reemerge a new being.

Lynn Andrews, trained as a Native American medicine woman, says that self-awareness is the key to healing: "A healer does not really heal; a healer can only present a mirror. You can never really help anyone; you can only help people to see themselves.... What I essentially do is to look at them as they are and give them an image of that. If the image is true, and they can see it, they can learn from it and decide if they want to change."[2]

Good healing therapists, whatever their specific form of practice, don't impose opinions or judgments (their own paradigms) on clients. Rather, they provide a mirror for clients to see themselves and to grow from their expanding self-awareness. They facilitate "observing the truth" of who the client is and evolving his or her personal paradigm on that basis.

For example, therapists help clients observe the pain they've experienced, so they can deal with it straight-on. Since joy, meaning, and peace of mind don't usually lead to malignant tumors or chronic ailments, illness often signifies some unresolved inner conflict—caused or suppressed by control-paradigm conditioning. Becoming more aware of our inner processing lets these conflicts come to the surface where we can deal with them. At the same time, becoming more self-aware precipitates a paradigm shift: we no longer operate from a model that requires us to suppress our inner experience.

Reflecting on the healing process, osteopath John E. Upledger writes: "The secret something that is shared by all effective healing methods [is] the process of leading the patient to an honest and truthful self-discovery. This self-discovery is required for the initiation and continuation of self-healing; for it is only through self-healing—in contrast to curing—that patients can experience both permanent recovery and spiritual growth.... The closer our perception of self approaches the truth, the deeper our capacity for self-healing becomes. When there is a very close correspondence between self-image and truth, our self-healing power may be virtually unlimited."[3]

Social systems as healing mirrors. Because social systems reflect us, they have the potential to serve not as mirrored illusions but as mirroring healers: they show us who we are and what paradigm we're living.

Looking into society's mirror is like looking into the mirror of personal experiences. The processes we observe are our processes. Sometimes that's heartening, other times it's painful.

Whichever way, social systems can catalyze transformation. Not that they "fix" us with social programs. Patching symptoms isn't transforming. Rather, by mirroring us, shared systems turn us back on our inner resources. We make a strategy shift that puts self-knowledge at the center of not only personal but also social, cultural, and global change.

Given the need for self-knowledge and its transforming, paradigm-shifting powers, how do we cultivate it?

INNER OBSERVATION

Inner observation. Self-knowledge begins with "inner observation," as Tibetan Buddhist Tarthang Tulku calls it. We become mindful of our thoughts, feelings, and actions. We notice ourselves in different contexts, and we witness how we create, screen, and digest experiences.

Some things we open ourselves to, like a good laugh or going on vacation, while other things we avoid, like going to the dentist or doing taxes. Some things feel comfortable, like playing a familiar role or believing what we've always believed, while other things seem threatening, like changing careers, exploring foreign ideas, or expressing new sides of ourselves.

Through inner observation, we observe what's going on—again, not to judge ourselves but to gain clarity about who we are and what we're experiencing.

"You can practice inner observation wherever you are, whatever you are doing," Tulku writes, "by being aware of each thought and the feelings that accompany it. You can be sensitive to how your actions affect your thoughts, your body, and your senses. As you do this, you reopen the channel between your body and mind, and gain a greater awareness of who you are; you become familiar with the quality of your inner being. Your body and mind begin to support one another, lending a vital quality to all your efforts. You enter into a living, dynamic process of learning about yourself, and the self-knowledge you gain enhances all that you do."[4]

Listening to our bodies. Tulku includes body awareness as a vital channel for observing the truth of who we are. Our bodies are living, knowing systems. They manifest a soul awareness that doesn't lie.

One of the few Westerners to embrace this idea early in the twentieth century was psychologist Wilhelm Reich. His research led him to assert, as writer Sherry Suib Cohen explains, "that the body reflected one's state of mind and that one's state of mind reflected the physical condition of one's body. If you are angry, frightened, or depressed, he reasoned, you 'carry' your body in the depressed attitude. The body is always vulnerable to a threat from within, and emotional disturbances reflect themselves in physical manifestations."[5]

We may deny our dreams, we may stuff our rage at how authoritarian systems treat us, and we may dig in our heels and refuse to change, but our bodies register this denial, stuffing, and rigidity as soul-destructive—a policy which our bodies then carry out. They register how we feel and act it out in our cells, so we can observe the processes we're living.

In Western medicine, because of the prevailing mechanistic view, we treat our bodies as dumb machines. We move in with surgery and drugs to make them do what we want, bypassing strategies that support the body's capacity to solve its own problems, learn, and regenerate itself. The communication is one-way—until we get really sick. Dr. Rachel Naomi Remen calls illness "a Western form of meditation,"[6] because only then are we forced to do the inner observation that transformation requires.

Body-knowing. Eastern philosophies, by contrast, take a preventive approach. They emphasize body-sensitivity through such disciplines as meditation, yoga, and massage. For them, the body is a friend and wise messenger, receiving information on many levels. Our bodies encode a vital awareness that's often more attuned to the force for wholeness than our conscious minds. Instead of discounting this body-knowing, Eastern philosophies honor it as valuable input.

And why not? Our bodies know us better than we know ourselves. They've registered all the thoughts and feelings we've had since conception. They know the trauma and abuse. They can tell what makes us feel alive and what deadens us, what rings true in our bones and what makes us uneasy.

They also sense when we're in trouble, and they're good at intervention. They can put us in bed for as long as we need—not because there's something wrong with us, but because there's something right with us. Attuned to our souls, our bodies want bigger lives for us than we'll allow for ourselves.

For example, they're not happy about us plugging away at jobs we hate or staying in destructive relationships. They don't want us to settle for passionless lives. Instead of allowing us to persist in soul-denying patterns, they figure we're here for a soul-expanding purpose so they give us time off to get on with it.

Listening to our shared bodies. Native and Aboriginal traditions apply this same strategy to society and the environment, viewing them as our shared bodies. These whole-oriented traditions embrace the notion of society as a mirroring healer. They respect our communal bodies, care for them, and don't ignore their messages. What we do to our shared systems, we do to ourselves, since our actions come back to us through the worlds we create.

The contempt we show for the poor and weak, for instance, exposes our self-loathing for our own weak and powerless side. Our psyches block what we're afraid to face. Yet like the body, society talks back. Oppressed people don't stuff it forever. They hold demonstrations, riots, and sometimes revolutions—not for the heck of it, but, like the body, to alert us to pain in the system.

Our treatment of animals is another mirroring image of where we are collectively. How we treat creatures who don't happen to carry Uzzies marks our humanity. If our paradigm says it's okay to abuse life forms less armed than ourselves—as the control paradigm does[7]—then we'll beat up not only on animals and the environment but also on other people and nations, as well as on our own children, and they'll grow up to do the same. We pass on to the next generation the strategy "Might makes abuse right."

Listening to what's going on in our bodies, society, and the environment is as much a part of inner observation as observing our private thoughts and feelings. We discover the paradigms we're embodying together and how our private strategies contribute to our public worlds.

Inner observation isn't, therefore, solitary navel-gazing. It's observing how we filter what's coming in, what's going out, and how it all adds up as our lived, operating awareness.

OBSERVING OUR PARADIGM FILTERS

We, the paradigm filters. Observing how we filter experience deepens self-knowledge, since filtering turns out to be central both to who we are and to how paradigms shape us. Filtering is a good image for what's going on. It's also a good way to discuss how paradigms operate in our lives. By filtering life through one paradigm or another, we become paradigm filters in action, agreeing to filter life through certain categories.

Not that this is strange. Filtering is a normal human function. That's how we work, as do all life forms. On a physical level, for instance, our ears filter out radio waves, while our eyes filter out x rays and gamma rays. Light, sound, and other energy frequencies are all around us, but we can't afford to receive all of them. We'd get overwhelmed. We pick and choose according to our needs and receiving equipment.

Our personalities do the same. Through the screens composed of our egos, minds, senses, belief systems, emotional structures, and personal histories, we filter consciousness. From the entire universe of possibilities, we narrow the field, until we find a life that's manageable. We process infinite reality through the grid that is us.

Paradigms package our filtering apparatus and supervise its use. Therefore, paradigms aren't things we carry in our heads; they're structures we live. Paradigm filters fuse with us and we with them. That's why shifting paradigms requires self-knowledge. It means shifting the filtering structures we've come to embody.

Screening out and letting through. Filters do two things: their grids screen out, and they let through. Thanks to our paradigm filters, we're not this but that.

For instance, we screen out and let through differently if we're men than if we're women, if we're authorities than if we're underlings, if we're of European descent than if we're Native Americans or of African or Asian descent. As Deborah Tannen discusses in her books *That's Not What I Meant* and *You Just Don't Understand*, cultural (that is, patriarchal, control paradigm) gender filters lead men to screen out conversation skills that build intimacy but let through skills that take charge and show who's one-up; women tend to do the reverse.

Between the two filter functions—(1) screening out and (2) letting through—our filters do more of the first than the second. They exclude more than they allow into our experience. This isn't good or bad; it's how we live, and everyone filters the totality differently. In fact, the more diverse filters are from person to person, the more we have access to the totality through each other.

1. Screening out. We need filters so we don't get overloaded by sensory and consciousness input, and we need intelligent filters—filters guided by some paradigm that's smart about what to screen out. We'd go nuts trying to process all the physical stimuli that comes our way, and the same holds for thoughts and feelings.

Thought filtering keeps us focused amid all the emotions, perceptions, and images filling the mind waves. Minds aren't the separate and isolated boxes we once took them for. They're more like receivers in a vast, interconnected field of consciousness. All sorts of thought energies float our way that we could pick up and often do without realizing it. We need to sift the consciousness energies, so we can focus on what's most helpful to us—what's ours to digest.

On an episode of *Star Trek: The Next Generation*, for instance, a visiting Betazoid—empathic human-type—who registered the thoughts and emotions of everyone around him could barely function. Because he hadn't learned how to filter the mind-field, the onslaught of feelings swirling around the starship *Enterprise* was more than he could handle. It was like listening to a thousand radio stations blaring at once.

That's less science fiction than we might think. To get around, we've had to screen out input on many levels—inner, outer, physical, emotional, conceptual, social, ordinary, and nonordinary. The totality is there, it affects us, and we each have access to it. We simply can't pay attention to all of it at once and still function.

2. Letting through—what? The question is, what do we let through? What should we focus on, and what should we relegate to the status of background noise? Our paradigm decides.

Take the authentic self. For surviving in a family or a job, our souls don't seem as relevant as the outward persona we devise to cope with work and family demands. We screen out inward processes to make a place for ourselves in the outward world. Instead of letting our real self through, we let through the expected reactions.

It wasn't originally our desire to filter out our souls, though. Our paradigm filters mirror those of society—as they must, at least to some extent, for us to survive in social systems. Since we live in a society that's externally oriented, our paradigm filters let through what increases outward success—things like retaining facts, getting the better side of a deal, or being efficient, productive, and obedient to authorities. Less success-oriented values—ecological health, human freedom and dignity, inner growth, compassion, social and economic justice, the quality of life, or aesthetics—get screened out.

As a society, we're not particularly proud of this filtering priority. It's just that our shared paradigm says we have no choice: outward demands take precedence.

Claiming our filter options. But choice is precisely what's at stake—choice of paradigms, choice of filters, choice of worlds. If we don't realize that we function as filters, we believe that we're experiencing life the way it is and must be: our only option. We accept personal, professional, economic, political, religious, and educational worlds "as is"—not realizing that alternative worlds could evolve from different paradigm filters.

In other words, filter-blind, paradigm-blind strategies keep us locked in puzzle-piece patterns by making us believe we have no choice. Strategies that don't first observe the truth of how we function as filters make our filtering powers invisible. We stay in denial about the fact that where we are isn't where we have to be.

By contrast, a strategy that begins with self-knowledge blows our options wide open. We observe the truth of how we filter our lives and how shifting paradigms could change our filtering processes.

EVALUATING OUR FILTERS

Taking stock of our filters. Addictions and crises send signals that our paradigm-defined screening priorities are askew. We're screening out dimensions that give our lives meaning, while letting through expectations and demands that consume us, devouring humanity and the earth as well.

First, when we screen out our soul-self, we use filters that block what we most need. Without our souls, we spend our days filtering out spirit in search of "the good life." We become the perfect puzzle pieces—worn-out, soulless shells.

Second, when we not only screen out what we need but also let through what abuses us, we're doubly hit. In place of our souls, soul-violating filters muscle in to ravage our self-worth. For instance, profit-only, get-ahead filters take over, and we believe we must live them to survive. Instead of protecting us, though, outward-measuring filters drive us to work more, do more, make more, impress more, succeed more, be more. Who we are is never good enough.

When we take these filters into our social systems, we and they become insatiable, as the titles of best-selling exposé books on business suggest: *Den of Thieves*, *House of Cards*, *Dirty Money*, *Merchants of Debt*, and *The Bankruptcy of America*. No amount of success is ever enough because nothing is ever enough to take the place of our souls. Our systems take on the features of the classic addict: insecure, driven, bound to an insane and self-defeating logic, rigid and dogmatic, polarized in thought and relationships, control-obsessed, riddled with secrets and hidden agendas, and dependent on externals—all of which adds up to systems caught in a "progressive, fatal disease."

When our filters neither let through what we need nor shield us from what's abusive, it's time to take stock of our filters. We need to rethink which we want to live. As AA's Fourth Step puts it, we make "a searching and fearless moral inventory of ourselves."

The yardstick of transformation. The moral part of "making a moral inventory" raises the practical issue: Which paradigm filters are good for us and which aren't? Not any set of filters will do, since each paradigm filters reality differently. Hitler's world wasn't Gandhi's. Observing the truth of how we're filtering things isn't an academic exercise. We observe not only the filters we have but also where they take us—what kind of world they create—so we can decide if we really want to live there.

But how do we know a good paradigm from a bad one? It'd be nice to sort this out before we find ourselves up to our necks in crises. How do we detect filters that create nightmare worlds? What yardstick do we use?

In recovery, as in spiritual teachings, the yardstick is transformation. Whatever moves us toward wholeness—soul-aliveness for us or justice, peace, and freedom for our societies—is good; whatever puts us back into addictive, abusive, soul-denying, disease modes is bad. Good and bad are measured by spiritual growth—our awakening to wholeness.

A yardstick that moves with us. Since transformation is a process, spiritual evolution's yardstick is dynamic. What's good or bad isn't fixed. A paradigm that supports growth at one time may hinder it at another. The measure of what's good or not changes as we evolve.

Take a chick's start in life. Is its shell good or bad? An embryo depends on the shell to filter out the world—its mother's feet and feathers, for instance—but to let in oxygen and warmth. Without the shell, the chick would die. At that stage, the shell is good; it serves the chick's growth.

But as the chick grows, the shell becomes a danger. If the chick can't break the shell at the right moment, it'll suffocate. A filter that once saved the embryo's life can now threaten it. It's not a good filter anymore, not because the shell became evil, but because the chick grew beyond it.

So, too, paradigm filters that serve a child's development won't do for an adult. Children need parents' love, and they more or less choose filters that win it. When we grow to adults, however, those same filters get in the way.

Pleasing people out of insecurity costs us our self-esteem, and obeying authorities without question can land us in jail.

Self-knowledge investigates which paradigm filters saved us in the past but hinder us now, using inner development as the yardstick.

EVOLVING OUR PARADIGM FILTERS

We can't make choices about our filters, though, until we know (a) what filters we're living, (b) how we got them, and (c) what we can do to change them, so that (d) our awareness of filters expands our options and helps us decide (e) which filters most serve our transformation.

(a) What paradigm filters are we living? Like glasses on our face, we don't see our filters; we see through them. The more we use them, the more they become us. We don't realize they're there. That's why self-knowledge is a lifelong strategy: coaxing paradigm filters out into the open isn't easy.

Example: lying. Marlo Morgan, a Missouri chiropractor, got a lesson in filters from some Australian Aborigines. Having worked with indigent Aborigines in the city, she received an invitation for what she thought would be an afternoon's award luncheon. Instead, she found herself being driven deep into the Australian outback for a three-month "walkabout"—an amazing experience which she describes in *Mutant Message Downunder*.

As she traveled with the tribespeople on foot, she realized everyone was communicating, but no one was talking. They explained that it was easier for them to converse mind to mind, telepathically, and that the reason white folks—"Mutants"—don't do it is that they tell too many lies.

As Ooota, the one tribal member who spoke English, put it, "The reason that the Real People can use telepathy is because above all they never tell a lie, not a small fabrication, not a partial truth, nor any gross unreal statement. No lies at all, so they have nothing to hide. They are a group of people who are not afraid to have their minds open to receive and are willing to give one another information."[8]

True, we may not want to walk down the street and know what everyone is thinking, but is lying a good strategy for filtering our exchanges? This is a control-paradigm filter if ever there was one: by lying, we control what people think. Shackled with secrets, we interact with others not heart to heart but lie to lie. Lying is so bound up with addictive behavior that it's one of Anne Wilson Schaef's definitions: "Addiction is anything we're tempted to lie about."

All sorts of motives keep the lying filter in place. Sometimes we think the others couldn't handle the truth, or we couldn't handle their knowing it. If they knew the truth, perhaps they'd think less of us. Other times we suspect that if we knew the truth, *we* couldn't handle it, so we're happy to play along, even when things don't add up. We buy the official government, church, corporate, financial, or school line—even when our gut says something is very wrong—because we don't want to believe that the institutional pillars of society are as rotten as we suspect. Like Samson, if we bring these pillars down, we might get destroyed with them. So we buy the official lies.

But our souls need truth to grow, and so do our social institutions. We depend on reality's feedback to learn and develop. Observing the truth openly together empowers each of us to act on it and to be real with each other.

Institutionalized lying. Nonetheless, soul growth is threatening to control systems because it demands that systems evolve with us. Control-paradigm systems prefer static puzzle pieces over continually evolving beings, so they reward those who use official filters to fragment, rearrange, manipulate, and generally obscure the truth. If employees, citizens, congregations, consumers, or students don't know the whole truth, they'll react according to the official telling of it. "We the people" stay where control systems put us, manipulated by half-truths.

To keep control hierarchies in place, systems not only encourage lying but require it. In *The Addictive Organization,* Anne Wilson Schaef and co-author Diane Fassel report, "We have interviewed many executives who have been told that if they did not learn to be dishonest, they would never 'make it' in the company.… Dishonesty has so become the norm that we all expect not to be able to believe what we are told in advertising, product guarantees, construction bids, or in business in general."[9]

The example of lying illustrates how hard it is to spot paradigm filters—and how important it is to do precisely that. As pervasive as lying is in our society, we'd probably never list it as one of our culturally shared filters, despite many books drawing our attention to the subject: e.g., Sissela Bok's

Lying and Secrets, Adrienne Rich's *Lies, Secrets, and Silence*, Harriet Lerner's *The Dance of Deception*, and John Bradshaw's *Family Secrets*. Yet how many other unnoticed filters do we live that have the same soul-deadening effect?

Knowing the filters we live is what self-awareness, system-awareness, and transformation require. One way to bring our filters to the surface is to investigate their origin: Where did we get our filters? How did we come by them?

(b) How we got our filters. Filters aren't our personal inventions. We took them on from the systems around us. We put on glasses designed for us before we had a chance to see whether or not we liked how they made things look, ourselves included.

Scientists call these filters "precognitive commitments"—mind filters that form from birth or even before. Deepak Chopra recounts studies of fish raised in a tank with a glass partition in the middle. Cognitively committed to living in only half the tank, adult fish won't venture farther even when the partition is removed. The same happens to gnats raised in a jar. Except for a few pioneers, the gnats won't fly out even when the lid is off.

Tarthang Tulku summarizes the process:

> Our obstacles to inner freedom are usually formed during childhood. As children we know how we feel about things, and we seldom hesitate to make our feelings known. But pressure from family and friends leads us to adopt the more narrow views and patterns that conform to what people expect. When our natural ideas and feelings are discouraged, we grow out of touch with our senses, and the flow of communication between our bodies and minds is inhibited; we no longer know what we truly feel. As the patterns of suppression grow stronger and more fixed, our opportunities for self-expression diminish. We become so used to conforming, that as we grow older we let these patterns rule our lives; we become strangers to ourselves.[10]

"Dependent arising." Tulku is keenly aware of this process not because he just read Bradshaw but because of the 2,500-year-old Buddhist teaching of "dependent arising": everything flows from conditions that came before it; nothing stands as a separate entity; nothing comes to be what it is on its own. We can't understand who we are apart from the processes that gave rise to us.

The same process of one stage arising from what came before applies to social systems, each of which has a history. Education, for example, wasn't always structured into the institutions we have now. As we mentioned, turn-of-the-century industrialists wanted our current system to prepare "the masses" for factory life. Stimulating minds wasn't a priority.

Accordingly, educational systems teach a high tolerance for boredom and routine work (class material), a dependence on external motivation (grades), and a habit of fear-driven behavior (10 percent of every class must get Fs). Those children who aren't able to cope with the boredom, stress, and humiliation get labelled as either having learning disabilities (and it's not yet clear how many disabilities are system-caused)* or unruly personalities, which usually legitimizes forced drugging: take Ritalin or get out of the classroom. Nineteenth-century ecologist and scholar Ellen Swallow, reflecting on schooling, wrote in 1881 that, "Children are always eager to *do something....* It is cruelty to children to keep five-year-olds sitting still gazing into vacancy even for one hour at a time. We have little idea of the torture we thus inflict."[11]

So what do we do about these soul-abusive filters?

(c) Changing filters. Can we change the filtering processes that abuse us, or are we permanently stuck with them? Can we ever free ourselves of the precognitive commitments that make us "strangers to ourselves"?

The paradox of change. Buddhist reasoning says we can, precisely because of dependent arising. According to this view, everything affects everything else, and the process continues without end. We'd be permanently damaged by past experiences and stuck with one set of filters *if we stopped changing.*

Since all forms are impermanent—all things are in flux—no past influences can be permanent. No precognitive commitment, no filter, is ever fixed. New influences offer new filters and make us rethink those we have. As a result, we're never the same. We're in flux too.

One Buddhist text states: "The being of a past moment of thought has lived, but does not live, nor will it live. The being of a future moment of thought will live, but has not lived, nor does it live. The being of the present

---

*See, for instance, books by Thomas Hartmann, *Attention Deficit Disorder: A Different Perception* (Grass Valley, CA: Underwood, 1993), Lynn Weiss's *Attention Deficit Disorder in Adults* (Dallas: Taylor, 1991), and Edward Hallowell and John Ratey's *Driven to Distraction* (New York: Pantheon, 1994).

moment of thought does live, but has not lived, nor will it live."[12]

That's the paradox of change. We're shaped by both what came before and what is totally new now. Being mindful of the process lifts the weight of the past. We experience the past not as we did originally but from where we are today. We see the past through our evolving filters. Its imprint changes as we change, and we change because reality is dynamic. Our context for experiencing the past doesn't stay fixed; it evolves with us.

That's why the past can be reframed. Like the chick pecking through its shell, we outgrow precognitive commitments. Every time we go through the past, we rethink the filters it gave us. As we do, we dislodge filter after filter, until our overall paradigm for filtering shifts.

NDEs: seeing how we got our filters and reframing them. Near-death experiences (NDEs) illustrate how powerful reframing the past can be for evolving our filters, since NDEs often include a life review. In *Heading Toward Omega*, for example, Kenneth Ring presents Barbara Harris's account of her life review, in which she saw how her filters arose from childhood experiences. The NDE helped her evolve beyond those filters by giving her a new awareness of her filtering possibilities:

> I was that child again…I was picking up all the physical sensations of my mother hitting me again, yet at the same time, besides my feelings, I understood her feelings and I understood my father in the hallway…. I was saying "no wonder." No wonder you are the way you are, you know? Look at what's being done to you at such a young age….
>
> And then it was like I moved through, on to where I am now…. It was like I was understanding how insecure I was and how inferior I felt because nobody had put their arms around me and given me a sense of value. Now this was my adult, my real adult observer. Then I was able to see my whole life unwinding from that perspective of this poor, neurotic little girl who was, you know, not really coming from the same place all the other little kids were coming from…. I was watching this whole childhood unfold and realizing that my head was in the wrong place and I was able to refocus so that I had a better understanding of all the rejection I had felt. All that rejection was in my own head. It wasn't everybody else rejecting me. Everyone else was just coming from their own problems and hangups. All of that stuff that had been layered on me was because my vision of what was going on was really screwed up….

It was like the most healing therapy there could be.... It was the kind of a thing where I just wasn't the victim anymore; we had all been victims...the structure was becoming stronger and stronger of us victimizing each other and it seemed like I was able to just very objectively observe it.... We were just establishing more and more walls....

What I was really sensing was that I had layers and layers and layers of this stuff. Like the domino effect, the sudden realization from the beginning was just going through and everything was shifting. Like each electron was jumping into another orbit. It was like a healing. It was going right through me. And I was sensing this entire evolvement of my lifetime through my feelings, and wherever I wanted to, I could sort of zoom in on different huge events in my life maybe I felt were good or bad—but there was no good or bad, just me reexperiencing stuff....

The whole overall effect was that I had relived my life with a much healthier attitude that had healed me. And by the time I got to the end I had the first sense of wanting to live, of wanting to turn around and struggle again in that bed.[13]

A shared NDE. Our social systems are having their own version of a near-death experience. We're doing as a society what Barbara did for herself: observing our paradigm filters, finding out how we got them, and deciding what they mean for us now.

It's not pretty. Social filters say, for instance, that it's okay for groups to behave in ways that individuals cannot. Systems play by their own rules: if a group or institution says wrong is right, that's the way it is.

A government can decimate people if it wants their land or enslave them if it wants their labor, but when individuals do this, it's murder, theft, kidnapping, or torture. Queen Elizabeth I hired "privateers" to loot Spanish ships, but when individuals did it, it was "piracy" punishable by death. Our own Congress even exempted itself for decades from laws it passed for everyone else.

Schools develop policies to humiliate students, beginning with swallowing John Locke's tabula rasa concept—that students are stupid and useless until teachers fill their heads with facts—and extending to ridicule and beatings, as Irwin Hyman documents in *Reading, Writing, and the Hickory Stick*. But if individuals regularly belittled and beat each other, no one would call it education; quite the contrary, they'd be arrested for harrassment and assault.

Churches insult people publicly and call it redemption. In our neighborhood (and many others, we hear), well-intentioned people turn up on our front porch to tell us that if our spirituality doesn't match theirs, we're going to hell, and they have plenty of institutional backing to say so. As Vine Deloria Jr. points out in *Custer Died for Your Sins*, many churches worked to destroy the American Indian way of life in the name of saving souls for God, and missionary policies sometimes made government landgrabbing look friendly by comparison. But could individuals make friends doing this stuff?

When banks charge the skies in loan interest but pay a pittance on savings, they say it's smart finance. If an individual did that, we'd call the person a loan shark. When banks attach "service charges" to accounts—which in the old days was considered a sign of incompetence, revealing that the company couldn't invest all that money wisely enough to make a decent profit—but give no better service, they tell us it's necessary to do business. But if some individual charged us a service fee to spend our money in his shop and then gave us the same service we got before we paid the fee, we'd think the guy was a shyster.

A collective NDE may be just what we need to observe, evaluate, and evolve our systems' paradigm filters—to apply to systems the same yardstick that we apply to ourselves. The trick is avoiding a collective DE.

How can filter-awareness bring more filter evolution with less trauma?

(d) Filter-awareness expands our options. Not all paradigm filters are a pain in the neck. We need filters, just as we need a good paradigm to orchestrate them. From the infinite sea of connections, filters focus our energies and give us direction.

On one hand, that's great. Using filters, we develop certain sides of ourselves to the fullest. For several hundred years, for example, we've been developing our scientific, rational, efficient, analytic abilities—and we have the technology, scientific information, and efficiency experts to prove it.

On the other hand, that's just one side of us. If we identify exclusively with one set of filters, we push other sides of ourselves into the background and don't develop our potential. We need filters that open us to the full dimensions of who we are—and keep opening us.

Rediscovering our potential. As we become more aware of our paradigm filters, we distinguish between ourselves and them, and so leave ourselves open to evolve beyond any given set. Observing our filters gives us a strategy for rediscovering dimensions of ourselves that current filters—however much they've helped us—have screened out.

Within us are healers, advisors, seekers, artists, messengers, creators, dreamers, lovers, fools, seers, players—all waiting to be expressed. Carol Pearson's *Awakening the Heroes Within*, for example, shows the power and universality of these archetypes. Our nature is far richer than any one set of filters can cash in.

Both for ourselves and our systems, we need filters that help us tap our richness. The only limit to our expression comes from the range of filters we're willing to try.

Rediscovering society's potential. Our social systems hold every bit the same promise, because they're composed of all of us. So far, though, we've shackled them with filters that say domination is efficient, exploitation is necessary, work is misery, conformity is social adjustment, fear is prudent, and soul abuse is good for social order.

But such filters—pitting our systems against our souls, societies against individuals—aren't our only options. Different paradigm filters create different social systems, as they have throughout history. From the study of comparative cultures, it's clear that societies can just as readily choose openness, creativity, trust, freedom, dignity, integrity, and equality and let these filters guide social systems.

With different filters, we discover social possibilities that current control-and-dominate filters claim couldn't exist. By changing our system's filters, we rediscover what our lives together can be.

(e) Which filters most serve transformation? Ultimately, self-knowledge leads us to ask these questions: Out of the infinite possibilities of life, which do we want to explore? Which paradigm filters do we choose to do our selecting for us?

True, we may choose to explore the worlds created by fragmentation, fear, mutual distrust, and an addictive drive for money, power, and control. It's been our national and international experience to find out what such worlds look like. We see them every night on the news and struggle with them every day.

But we don't have to go this route; other filters create alternative worlds.

We don't have to learn the most painful of ways by using filters that maximize soul suffering. Transformation can be a path of joy, liberation, and creativity, but we need filters that don't screen out this soul-expansive experience.

Dolores Krieger, a pioneer in therapeutic touch and a professor at New York University, sees this filter-questioning strategy as central to transformation, whether it's personal, system, or global: "A common recognition among healers is that there are multiple realities, reflecting the multifold states of consciousness at our command. Which reality we relate to depends largely on the predominant facet of consciousness [the filters] through which we choose to perceive our interactions with the universe."[14]

Inviting transformation through filter-awareness shows us where we are, where we're going, and our options for going somewhere else. The strategy gets us off to a good start with paradigm-shifting methods, but it needs follow-through since old-paradigm filters don't yield without a fight.

Notes to Chapter 4

1. John Moyne and Coleman Barks, trans., *Unseen Rain: Quatrains of Rumi* (Putney, VT: Threshold Books, 1986), 4.
2. Richard Carlson and Benjamin Shield, eds., *Healers on Healing* (Los Angeles: Jeremy P. Tarcher, 1989), 43–44.
3. Carlson and Shield, eds., *Healers on Healing*, 67, 70.
4. Tarthang Tulku, *Skillful Means: Gentle Ways to Successful Work* (Berkeley, CA: Dharma Publishing, 1978), 5–6.
5. Sherry Suib Cohen, *The Magic of Touch* (New York: Harper, 1987), 93.
6. Carlson and Shield, eds., *Healers on Healing*, 79.
7. Peter Singer, *Animal Liberation* (New York: Avon, 1975).
8. Marlo Morgan, *Mutant Message Downunder* (Lees Summit, MO: MM Company, 1991), 63–64.
9. Anne Wilson Schaef and Diane Fassel, *The Addictive Organization* (San Francisco: Harper & Row, 1990), 63–64.
10. Tulku, *Skillful Means*, 5.
11. Carolyn Hunt, *The Life of Ellen H. Richards* (Boston: Whitcomb and Barrows, 1912), 173.
12. Henry C. Warren, trans., *Visuddhi-Magga*, VIII (Columbia, MO: Motilal Banarsidass, 1989).
13. Kenneth Ring, *Heading Toward Omega: In Search of the Meaning of the Near-Death Experience* (New York: William Morrow, 1984), 105–7.
14. Carlson and Shield, eds., *Healers on Healing*, 124.

CHAPTER 5

Self-Disclosure:
Breaking Through Paradigm Defenses

Hearing the truth
Fifth of the Twelve Cycles of Truth,
the Iroquois Peace Confederacy Tradition

I honor those who try
to rid themselves of any lying,
who empty the self
and have only clear being there.
Rumi[1]

FROM PARADIGM FILTERS TO PARADIGM COVERS

Covering soul loss. Self-knowledge observes the paradigms we use to filter consciousnesss and focus our energies. But self-knowledge also observes the price we pay for filtering reality as we do. To focus on some energies, other energies get blocked. That's natural and necessary, even a good idea.

What's not such a good idea is to decide that soul energies are the ones we need to block. Yet that's exactly what happens. To fit into a control-paradigm family, school, church, peer group, workplace, or profession, we factor out our inner self. Coping with the shame, humiliation, and trauma implanted by control-paradigm institutions takes precedence—and drives our souls into hiding; our inner being can endure only so much trampling.

When paradigm filters obscure our inner self to create an outer self that does the coping, the gap left inside grows into a chasm. Wang Yang-ming, the sixteenth-century neo-Confucian teacher, put it succinctly: "With the true self, one lives; without it, one dies."[2]

At first we ignore soul loss. When that doesn't work, we keep problems a secret and pretend everything is okay. Since we're not sure what's wrong, we cover to get by. We devise stories—which we then live out—to shore up the outward image, while we search for something to fill the inner void.

Seeking without for what can only be found within, though, is the formula for compulsive behavior, since no amount of outward compensating can compensate. We don't feel connected with what's meaningful. Life seems empty, which, without our souls' aliveness, it is.

Are we our filters? The trouble intensifies when we forget the gold we are and instead identify with our paradigm filters. We believe that to expose our filters is to expose ourselves; worse, to lose our filters is to lose ourselves. Our filters are how we've survived. We fuse with them, believing they're all we've got.

Hindu philosophy describes our personality filters as vehicles for our souls. They give us the tools to learn and evolve, but they have the same status as the cars we purchase and resell after we're done with them. Our paradigm-packaged, space-time-race-gender-culture personalities are vehicles, not who we are in our core.

Yet, given the traumas of coming into this world, we-our-souls forget this teensy distinction and come to identify with we-our-filters—the mask part of us that bears a name and carries a personal history filled with abuse and defenses. It's as if we identify with our armor rather than with the living person that the armor protects.

In this light, the rigidity that makes paradigm shifts traumatic turns out to be a fear reaction—fear of the emptiness and vulnerability we'd face if we didn't have paradigm filters to fill in and protect us. Treating our inner lives as having little value—a strategy we've acquired from control systems—we build our paradigm's filters into forts of invulnerability.

ACCEPTABLE CLOAKING DEVICES

The best way to make our paradigm armor invulnerable is to make it invisible. The cloaking shield of invisibility is the most potent defense, as

Klingon, Romulan, and American defense engineers know. What can't be seen or detected can't be shot down. Invisible, our paradigms avoid the risk of attack. We hide our paradigm's filtering processes under acceptable cloaking devices—and many such covers will do the trick.

Staying within a group. For example, one way to make paradigm filters invisible is to surround ourselves with people who share our set. We align ourselves with groups that take the same paradigm for granted. Surrounded by filter-familiars, ours blend in. Paradigm filters stay invisible: "What filters?" "What paradigm?"

As long as we remain within the group, our paradigm filters are safe. No one questions them, since everyone shares the agenda of keeping them unchanged. When paradigm issues do surface, it's to reinforce how successful and right the group's paradigm is. The official lines get repeated and the catchphrases and shibboleths echoed. To speak the language of a given paradigm isn't to do paradigm reflection but to identify with a group whose strategy is to keep the paradigm in place. Those who question it are soon out.

Small wonder cliques permeate paradigm-rigid societies—with each group accusing the others of being cultish. The more researchers studied the religious cults that shocked everyone in the seventies, the more the paradigm dynamics—or more accurately, paradigm dogmatics—resembled what goes on in mainline churches, corporations, schools, universities, governments, labor unions, and nonprofits. The strategy of keeping filters invisible under the cover of a group-shared paradigm turns out to be not aberrational behavior but the required norm.

When groups support growth. Not that the support of a group-shared paradigm is all bad. If we're shifting to a new paradigm and letting go of damaging filters, group support is exactly what we need. Transitions of this magnitude aren't easy. We're on new ground—and usually in systems that work hard to keep us as we were.

We also need the support of a group-shared paradigm if we're exploring its full potential, as happens in scientific, therapeutic, creative, artistic, and spiritual communities. Working with people of like mind takes us forward by leaps and bounds. As we work with others synergetically, developments emerge greater than any one person could produce.

We also need support if we're restructuring social systems, since we're bucking the collective commitment to a particular paradigm. Social change takes heavy lifting—more than one person can do alone. Gandhi needed the Indian people to join in his strategy of nonviolent noncooperation with British rule, a major paradigm shift, for his efforts to have effect.

Whether group involvement supports filter evolution or filter fixedness, therefore, is a matter of paradigm development: what phase are we in? As with the chick and eggshell, what supports paradigm evolution at one stage may stifle it at another. It all depends on where we are—and how relatedness to a group either supports or hinders our paradigm-evolving process.

Compartmentalized. Another way to keep paradigms invisible is to split our lives into compartments and to design paradigm filters for each box. We divide our lives into love relationships, family, school, work, social circles, and church. We divide our businesses into labor, management, staff, and customers. We divide our governments into powerful, celebrated leaders and powerless, nameless citizens, into liberals, conservatives, and radicals on both ends, or into clout-carrying PACs (political action committees) and the cloutless masses. We divide our professions into experts and clients, doctors and patients, know-it-alls and know-nothings, perfect ones and sickies. We divide our minds into reason and emotions, money making and family values. We divide our culture into sciences and humanities—and within each a dizzying number of specialized fields. And we divide reality into spirit and matter, mind and body, positive and negative, God and humanity, inner and outer, spirituality and "the real world."

By splitting our world into separate pieces, we protect the paradigm filters we use for each bit. Soul has nothing to do with economies. Spirituality has no relation to government. In a fixed area, certain paradigm filters apply, and we don't mix them with filters we use for another box. That way, we never have to ask how it all adds up; it just doesn't. No one expects it to.

We don't ask, for example, whether the values we use at work are the values we'd like our children to live at home. If we're management, we can't be bothered with the filters of labor. If we're scientists, we don't have much time for the humanities. If we're doctors, we pay little heed to the self-healing powers of clients. Or if we adhere to one religion or political faction, we don't want to hear about the views of another.

By putting walls between our filters, we protect our overall filter arrangement. We avoid filter comparisons, which invariably bring our paradigm out into the open and subject it to revision. As we mentioned in chapter 3, some of the greatest leaps in knowledge and art—cultural paradigms—occurred when two or more societies interacted. Box-category thinking, valuable as it is for developing specialized knowledge, prevents this fertile exchange. It forbids us even to attempt to integrate our filters with wider contexts, which paradigm evolution demands. There's no overall paradigm, we tell ourselves, which means our cultural paradigm stays offstage, invisible.

Open and objective. Another way to keep paradigms hidden is to appear to be filter-free, as if we have no paradigm, no filters—and no covers for them either. For decades, scientists hid their filters behind claims of objectivity: they weren't using filters; they were unbiased observers. Only when physicist Werner Heisenberg's "uncertainty principle" suggested that scientists' perspectives influence and even determine what they observe did scientists begin to acknowledge their filters and examine how they affected their findings.

Being "open" and "skeptical" are other ways of hiding paradigms we're not keen to question. Not that open-mindedness is the prime evil plaguing the globe. Rather, sometimes claiming to be open is used as a strategy to make us appear paradigm-free, which guarantees that neither we nor anyone else has a chance to look at our filters. By appearing to be oh-so big-minded, we keep our paradigm close to the chest and off-limits.

No matter how open we are, we're not without paradigm equipment, nor is that desirable. As long as we have bodies, minds, and a space-time awareness, we have filters. And as long as we live in control-paradigm systems, we have defenses. We need them for protection.

Suffocating. The trouble is, our paradigm covers work so effectively that they obscure our paradigm's filters not only from others but from ourselves as well. If we're to evolve, we need to know what paradigm we're using, so we can change it. Defensive covers block this awareness.

How far will we go, though, to protect our paradigm? What cost are we willing to pay to keep it in place? Would we rather die than change it? That's the danger. Like a chick trapped inside a shell it can't break, we can suffocate inside an outgrown paradigm—and in the groups that share it, especially if they've raised us, paid our salaries, or promised love, security, prestige, meaning, and salvation as long as we stay committed to them. Taking our chances and pecking through doesn't sound attractive, even though we suspect the shell is what's smothering us. The more afraid we get, the more fervently we try to make life in the shell work.

And why should pecking through sound attractive? Being inside the shell is what we know. We've learned how to adjust. Like the chick, we haven't a clue about life outside. Our filters have shielded us. It's hard to imagine that they may now be killing us.

Shifting paradigms is scary. No wonder our strategies for keeping paradigms in place are more developed than our strategies for changing them.

System covers

System filters. The same paradigm-protective dynamics occur in systems. Like individuals, systems need paradigms to do their jobs. Paradigms organize a shared activity, whether it's education, spiritual pursuits, doing business, or running a town or nation. They coordinate the energies of everyone involved by giving them an overall view—a framework of ideas, concepts, and values. This framework then translates into specifics: methods, policies, roles, strategies, structures, and goals. The paradigm has a track record of working, at least by paradigm-defined standards.

When they're serving us well, for instance, paradigm filters of religion screen out separateness and intolerance, so we can see our lives whole and connected; business filters screen out greed, so we can manage our human household wisely (the original meaning of *economy*); school filters screen out fears of inadequacy, so we can tap the treasures of our minds; and government filters screen out power-grabbing and exploitation, so we can build a just, fair, and free world together.

Off-limits and invisible. Somehow, though, our social paradigm filters aren't working this way. To paraphrase from Paul's letter to the Romans, they're filtering out what they should let through and letting through what they should filter out.

Yet getting at our systems' filtering paradigm and changing it is no small task.

System filters, orchestrated by the control paradigm, have their own ways of staying off-limits. Many of the most soul-damaging control filters—

such as the win-lose competition filter that dominates school and business, or the power-over filter that creates heavy-handed hierarchies in families, religions, the military, law enforcement agencies, and corporations—go unquestioned, even by otherwise change-oriented people. We take the filters and the paradigm behind them for granted. We'll fire people and hire new ones, spend money by the billions, conduct studies and form committees, yet not question the core paradigm creating our social structures.

Changing actors in bad plays won't make the plays better; we have to rewrite the scripts. But that's hard to do when the scripts are functionally invisible. How do the cloaking devices become so effective?

As with personal paradigms, system paradigms enjoy invisibility as their best defense against change. Systems use many covers to hide their paradigm filters, but one strategy beats all for blocking filter-awareness: taboos.

SILENCED BY TABOOS

Societies' most potent cloaking devices for its paradigm are its taboos: the questions we dare not raise, the things we dare not do, and the ways we dare not think. Obeying taboos, we pretend that aspects of our lives don't exist. Problems aren't problems, and obvious sources of trouble remain off-limits; we never speak of them. We let our systems throw walls of silence around us, so neither we nor they are threatened by hearing the truth about what we're experiencing.

Taboos about sex. From the Puritans' version of Christianity, for example, we inherit taboos about sex. As H. L. Mencken observed, puritanism is "the haunting fear that someone, somewhere, may be happy." Because we're not as committed to perpetuating puritanism as we were several hundred years ago, we're examining and changing these taboos.

For instance, even talking about sex (yes, we almost didn't write this section, because there's a taboo about that too) makes people uncomfortable, but the taboos go way beyond that. Everyone knows that sex is pleasurable, but no one's supposed to experience it (except Mae West and Marilyn Monroe). Men are supposed to have sex only to satisfy their "drives," while women are only supposed to do it to have children. Neither is really allowed to feel the pleasure of the experience (good women don't enjoy it, and real men don't have feelings).

Gender-specific taboos even invade our most private practices, though many of these are being changed: men aren't supposed to get involved in intimacies (cuddling and all that); women aren't supposed to be on top; men aren't supposed to touch each other except for athletic slaps; women aren't supposed to initiate sexual activity; neither men nor women are supposed to touch themselves, except for bathing, and you'd better be quick about that.

Significantly for a patriarchal society, more taboos exist for women than for men. Women aren't supposed to have more than one partner, for example, even if they're not married, while the opposite is encouraged in men, even if they are. Older men may team up with younger women, but older women aren't supposed to go for younger men. It's more okay for men to talk about sex—especially using specific language or slang—than it is for women.

And everyone who has a sexual experience is programmed to experience guilt and shame afterwards.

That's the control paradigm in force—and invisible. We're too absorbed in fulfilling gender roles or feeling guilty to reflect on the paradigm that sets us up to feel these things. We think it's us, and taboos keep it that way. They make us controllable.

Taboos about feelings. Another paradigm-protective taboo makes our feelings off-limits in social systems. In family systems, for instance, we learn to stifle "unacceptable" feelings and feel guilty for having them. In school systems, we learn to get tough and hide how we feel, whether it's fear of tests, shame in competition, or joy in learning. Blasé cool is the way to survive school, with emotions tucked safely away. At work and in professions, feelings have no place. The most professional-looking expert is the one most "in control" of his or her emotions, therefore apparently least emotionally involved. Even the words *emotion* and *emotional* have negative connotations. To say someone is being emotional more or less discredits what the person says.

Factoring out our emotions is convenient for control-paradigm systems. If we're cut off from how we feel when we're being dominated or shamed, we'll tolerate it more readily. And we'll learn to disregard the pain we feel when we witness control-system abuse to others. We'll flee into our heads, where the control paradigm feeds us with rationalizations, judgments, and ultimata—"Things must be done this way, or chaos follows."

Science taboos. From science, we've inherited a host of taboos about what's real and what's not, what we can talk about "intelligently" and what's superstitious or pseudoscience. In general, the rule is this: If you can measure something, manipulate it, predict its functionings, and then replicate it—i.e., control the outcome of experiments on it—it's scientific and real; if not, it's imagination or illusion.

We accept this approach to science because it gives us some measure of control over our environment. Yet there's the rub. The strategy reduces knowledge to control. We think that knowing something means being able to control it—control-paradigm epistemology. Given the authority we grant science, we don't question this strategy, even though it discounts mountains of observed but nonreproducible—therefore "anecdotal"—evidence.

Science taboos: Their wider impact. But defining knowledge in terms of control raises questions. To take some practical ones first, what kind of control does control science give us? Control-paradigm science inevitably disregards wider contexts, because wider contexts aren't easily controlled. To gain control, scientists eliminate variables and constrict the field. In fact, early in their schooling, scientists learn to think in narrowly focused ways and to disregard broader contexts. The most defensible Ph.D. thesis is the most specialized one.

When we act on control knowledge, as we do in devising technologies, we act on highly focused information—information that has eliminated broader-context considerations. Using narrowed control-think to create all our modern goodies, we find ourselves faced with wider-context messes. Yes, aspirin can help with heart disease, but it can also cause bleeding stomach ulcers. Yes, combustion engines move us around, but they pollute like crazy. Yes, we can invent super-poisons for pesticides, but we end up ingesting the stuff, while mutant bugs use it for seasoning.

As long as the immediate control objective is achieved, though, control-paradigm science doesn't worry about the larger impact. No wonder we're stuck with radioactive toxic waste that has a half-life of several million years and traveling clouds of acid rain that kill forests. As we discovered on a trip to eastern Canada, seeing trees—entire forests—sick and dying from the top down can ruin your whole vacation.

It's no good using the dodge that science operates apart from technology—that the endeavor of science is unrelated to its technical, commercial applications. Who funds scientific research in universities? Who decides which projects receive grants and which don't? It's not the Good Fairy—or science in the public interest. If the same money went into researching alternative energy sources, for instance, as gushes into developing new oil fields, new uses for petroleum by-products, or subsidies for nuclear power, our economy wouldn't be fossil-fuel dependent, our environment wouldn't be choking with petroleum fumes and discarded plastics, and our knowledge of energy wouldn't be stalled with burning things—caveman science.

Thanks to taboos protecting control science, though, we buy the dodge. Science is a pure intellectual activity, unaffected by economic or political forces, and we're the Easter Bunny. Fantasy for fantasy, ours is less dangerous.

Science taboos: Ethics and values. The taboos that insulate control science from its impact on society also hide its values. The directions that science and technology take involve decisions based on values—control values. Nonetheless, taboos place science above ethics. In other words, control-science taboos hide its decision-making processes and the values that guide them.

These values and decisions affect the course of science. The fact that some scientific research gets screened out while other research receives both funding and publication is attributed to the natural course of scientific development, as if there's no paradigm-based filtering going on.

Our experience in several universities showed us exactly what Vine Deloria Jr. described earlier: the "experts" who dominate the field also dominate the direction and limits of research. They give their positions at conferences, where reputations may be made or broken, and they edit the journals. If someone steps outside the experts' prevailing paradigm, the step had better not be too great—or his or her reputation and publishing career (a "must" for tenure) is at stake.

Even more telling, though, is the funding of research by industry. Because the college and the science department as well as the researcher get money, there's an unspoken but real incentive to present projects that support the agenda of work being done in various industries. Historian of science Robert Proctor documents this process in *Cancer Wars: How Politics Shapes What We Can and Can't Know about Cancer*. Proctor details how combinations of industrial, academic, and political interests influence—even control—what should otherwise be open scientific research to save lives.

Science taboos: Accepted practices. Control-science decisions affect not only the direction of research but also how knowledge is applied. As long as some practice is labelled "scientific," we're hesitant to ask whether it's wise or cruel. The status of "accepted scientific opinion" is often enough to put a theory along with its applications beyond moral question.

Example: Babies and birth. Accepted scientific opinion has long held, for instance, that babies have primitively developed nervous systems and can't register pain. Accordingly, doctors routinely perform painful tests and surgery on screaming infants without anesthesia. "They're just screaming to exercise their lungs," we're supposed to believe, not because needles are going into them all over—and fresh out of that warm, safe, mostly needle-free womb.

Through hypnosis we now know the pain and anger such "scientific" practices produced. If we walked up to someone on the street and lopped off a body part, we'd land in jail. If an obstetrician does it to a baby boy—again without anesthesia—he gets paid. What message does this send to baby boys about the world they're entering? How safe and protected are they going to feel when this experience meets them right off the bat?

In *Babies Remember Birth*—a fascinating book exploring the consciousness that babies bring into the world—psychologist and hypnotherapist David Chamberlain discovered that babies are most annoyed at being treated like objects to be poked and prodded rather than as intelligent, conscious beings. Chamberlain writes:

> A ringing declaration of infant intelligence ends the report [of the birth experience], as Deborah compares her knowledge with that of the hospital staff. Saying that she was more aware of being a mind than a person, she speaks of feeling intelligent and explains why. She decided she was more intelligent than those caring for her, because she knew the real situation *inside* while they seemed to know only the outside. She was also superior in being able to receive their messages while they were unable to receive hers....

In Deborah's own words:

I felt I knew a lot—I really did. I thought I was pretty intelligent. I never thought about being a person, just a mind. I thought I was an intelligent mind....

They seemed to ignore me. They were doing things to me—to the *outside* of me. But they acted like that's all there was. When I tried to tell them things, they just wouldn't listen, like that noise [her crying] wasn't really anything. It didn't sound too impressive, but it was all I had.

I just really felt like I was more intelligent than they were.*

Science taboos: Philosophy and consciousness. But consciousness, certainly infant consciousness, has no place in the official worldview of science, and taboos keep it that way. Taboos hide how control-paradigm science affects our overall philosophy. Because of taboos, we don't ask whether physical observation, quantification, and control under laboratory conditions are adequate for understanding the universe, including ourselves—or babies.

Yet questions persist: If we can't measure or control something, does that mean we can't know it? Does it give us grounds to act as if it doesn't exist? Even if we seem to control something, do we know all there is to know about it?

By making noncontrollable aspects of life off-limits—outside the domain of scientific inquiry—the taboos of science ignore many realities, but most of all, consciousness. Only when scientists figure out a way to reduce consciousness to observable, measurable, and controllable behavior are they allowed to study it. By that time, though, what they study is boring and sheds no light on the complexities that conscious beings face. We have to wonder why we buy a paradigm of knowledge that's incapable of dealing with the most significant aspect of human life.

Consciousness isn't exactly peripheral to us. Yet the dominant paradigm of knowledge places consciousness research off-limits. Intuition, inner advisors, synchronicity, spiritual seeking, the quest for meaning, healing, transformation, near-death experiences, soul work, mythic consciousness, microcosm/macrocosm connectedness and the symbol systems, such as astrology or the *I Ching*, that explore it are all called hokum and nonsense.

---

*David Chamberlain, *Babies Remember Birth* (New York: Ballantine Books, 1988), 157. We are sorry that this book is currently out of print.

No self-respecting scientist would be caught dead investigating them, certainly not if he or she taught at a university and were up for tenure.

Science taboos: The nonordinary. One of the most powerful ways taboos shut down open inquiry is to ridicule those who step outside official scientific opinion. If something doesn't fit control-paradigm science, the phenomenon is dismissed as nonexistent, and the people who persist in speaking about it are dismissed as crackpots.

By the late 1940s, for instance, flying saucers were made off-limits, and anyone who discussed them was called a nut. This taboo persisted even after a front-page article of *The Wall Street Journal*[2] reported that 3.7 million Americans—one in fifty—may have been abducted by alien beings for genetic experimentation. This study wasn't carried out by the scientific establishment but by the Fund for UFO Research, which hired the Roper polling organization.

As far as the scientific establishment is concerned, no matter how traumatic this experience may be, these millions of abductees have to deal with it in silence. If they talk, they're classed with a "lunatic fringe" and may even lose their jobs and standing in communities. Something has been happening to nearly four million Americans—more than have AIDS—but discussing the experience has remained taboo because of the paradigm of science.

The UFO taboo is a biggie, since the introduction of off-planet civilizations could trigger the rethinking of our paradigm in toto, from religion to medicine, science to government, psychology to history. And it raises tough questions. How, for example, do we trust beings we know nothing about? How do we know if they're telling us the truth? Heck, we can't even tell when our own "officials" are telling the truth. How might our species' self-image change if we aren't top on the knowledge, science, and technology ladder—or aren't top on the food chain? It's easier to say we're alone in the universe than to open the door to this kind of paradigm questioning.

These are a few of the taboos of science—taboos that protect the dominant paradigm we use to gain knowledge.

Taboos at work. Back at the daily planet, work life is fraught with taboos—and for the clear purpose of keeping the control paradigm invisible and unchanged. Employees dare not speak out when their company acts illegally, exploits the community, or damages the environment. Neither may they

discuss ways in which the workplace functions abusively. On policy, procedure, scheduling, and operations, people aren't free to speak their minds to
"superiors"—not without risking a lower performance rating, cut in salary,
or loss of job. As Anne Wilson Schaef and Diane Fassel show in *The Addictive
Organization*, to air concerns is to be disloyal.

Yet taboos cripple business effectiveness. The more information flows
freely, the more people base business decisions on a big picture of what's
going on. When taboos shut down this flow of communication, managers
are in the position of a barge captain trying to negotiate the shoals of the
Mississippi with no dials working. It's astonishing how out of touch managers can be with the people they manage. Yet it's logical within a control
paradigm of management: in a control hierarchy, information flows down,
not up. Even when the control model is failing, taboos prevent people from
saying so.

Taboos about addictions and abuse. As the recovery literature documents,
heavy taboos surround addictions and abuse—again, for paradigm-defense
reasons. If we admit that the paradigm behind our social systems is driving
us to self-destructive behavior, we'd be forced to question it. It's easier to
pretend nothing is wrong with our social systems or their paradigm; it's just
a few people who can't cut it. No, addiction is not a global epidemic—or, as
Shakespeare put it, "This is not my nose neither."[4]

Studies indicate that 88 million Americans are chemically dependent or
in a relationship with someone who is, 50 million smoke, 12 million chew
tobacco, and 37 million have a food addiction. One out of every four families suffer from alcohol- or drug-related problems.* That doesn't count people suffering from the emotional trauma of dysfunctional families. Yet
taboos forbid us to deal with these experiences openly or to consider how
they're affecting our adult behavior, from intimacy to parenting to professional conduct to national policy.

In the case of President Lyndon Johnson, for instance, Johnson's mother
wanted him to excel where her husband did not. When young Lyndon got
A's at school, she praised and rewarded him, even by inviting him to sleep in

---

*As we said earlier, it's hard to get statistics. These are as good as anyone's, but the figures
may be much higher. Barbara Yoder, *The Recovery Resource Book* (New York:
Fireside/Simon and Schuster, 1990), 2.

her bed. When he misbehaved or got less than A's, she refused even to acknowledge his presence and would talk about him as if he weren't there— even as if he were dead. The message was clear: if you don't excel, you don't exist.* Decades later, President Johnson couldn't admit that Vietnam was a no-win war, even when his advisors told him. He said he refused to be the first American president to lose a war. His decision reflected not political realities but childhood programming.

Taboos against having problems. In fact, having problems at all is taboo, because it suggests failure—"real men don't have problems," or if they do, they certainly don't talk about them. When we're in systems, we're expected to pretend everything is okay. If problems do arise, they're ours, not the systems', certainly not the paradigm's. Again, if we're in pain as a result of living in systems, something must be wrong with us.

In other words, taboos protect system paradigms, but they don't protect the people within the systems. They don't help us cope with the realities of our lives.

"DEFENSIVE ROUTINES"

"Defensive routines." An excellent analysis of both how paradigm defenses work and how to disarm them comes from two team-learning consultants in business management, Harvard's Chris Argyris and MIT's Peter Senge, who describe "defensive routines" as major obstacles to learning in corporate and business systems. "We trap ourselves, say Argyris and his colleagues, in 'defensive routines' that insulate our mental models [paradigms] from examination."[5] In *The Fifth Discipline*, Peter Senge explains:

> Defensive routines…are entrenched habits we use to protect ourselves
> from the embarrassment and threat that come with exposing our thinking.
> Defensive routines form a sort of protective shell around our deepest
> assumptions, defending us against pain, but also keeping us from learning

---

*We heard this astonishing story about LBJ's childhood in the first of a three-part PBS documentary on Lyndon Johnson. See also Doris Kearns Goodwin, *Lyndon Johnson and the American Dream* (New York: St. Martin's Press, 1991), 25–26; and Robert Dallek, *Lone Star Rising: Lyndon Johnson and His Times, 1908–1960* (New York: Oxford University Press, 1991), 32–34, 36–37.

about the causes of pain. The source of defensive routines, according to Argyris, is...fear of exposing the thinking that lies behind our views.... For most of us, exposing our reasoning is threatening because we are afraid that people will find errors in it. The perceived threat from exposing our thinking starts early in life and, for most of us, is steadily reinforced in school— remember the trauma of being called on and not having the "right answer"—and later in work.[6]

Defensive routines block transformation. Since defensive routines don't let us inside our paradigm's castle, we can't get to the paradigm filters where change is most needed. As a result, defensive routines block learning—and real solutions. "'The paradox,' writes Argyris, 'is that when [defensive routines] succeed in preventing immediate pain, they also prevent us from learning how to reduce what causes the pain in the first place.'"[7] We stay within pain-making structures, trying to avoid the pain those very structures create.

Defensive routines also block communication. We develop rapport when we share which paradigm filters we're using. Our filters don't have to be the same; we just need to know the filters at work in a relationship. Then mutual understanding grows. But when one person hides his or her paradigm, other parties do it too. Defensive routines are contagious. Once defensive postures start, they spread. Up goes the armor.

Trickiest of all, defensive routines are "self-sealing," to use Argyris's term. Not only do they hide paradigms, but they hide their own existence as well—the invisibility trick again. To both hide our paradigm *and* be psychologically correct, we fall back on the openness cover. We want to seem open and candid, so we work hard at *appearing* that way. But this simply pushes paradigm defenses deeper, as we pretend that neither our paradigms nor covers for them exist. If we subjected either to examination, we'd risk having to restructure them—exactly what a paradigm shift requires.

TRAPPED IN OUR OWN DEFENSES

Lies, secrets, and cover-ups. By hiding the paradigm that lies at the root of problems, defensive routines allow situations to get worse. They don't let concerns or confusions surface, even though these may be the key to a breakthrough. Instead of helping us deal with realities, defensive covers divert our energies into preserving masks and images.

By so doing, defensive routines force us to live a lie—not to be honest about what's happening. It's not that we're intentionally dishonest; it's rather that, as long as we're participating in a control system, we're simply not at liberty to speak openly about what we're experiencing.

When taboos forbid us to speak our truth, our lives alone and together get "zippered shut with secrecy," to use journalist Jonathan Vankin's phrase, leaving us vulnerable to "secrecy's chief weapon, propaganda."[8] At home and at work, at school and on the news, we're lobbied into believing the official line that justifies control-paradigm systems. Our family, educational, economic, social, political, and religious institutions are basically fine. All we need to do is get rid of the bad people—lock them up, kill them, or drug them until they fit the norm. Then our systems would work.

But our systems don't work, no matter how many people we drug, lock up, or kill. Instead, a chasm of silence comes between us and system realities. That's not good. "The more taboos there are in the empire," the *Tao Te Ching* says, "the poorer the people."[9] If the recovery movement did nothing more than show how destructive lies, secrets, and covers are, its service would be immeasurable.

In *Healing the Shame That Binds You*, John Bradshaw says, "Families are as sick as their secrets"[10]—a truth that applies to any social system. Defensive covers obstruct our quest to find what's real about ourselves and our systems, while defenses hide our paradigms so well that not even we can get at them. What we can't discuss, we can't change. Or as John Bradshaw puts it, "We cannot heal what we cannot feel."[11]

The toll of the defenses. Whereas lying was one filter among many in the last chapter, it's the one to tackle here. Lying is how we get trapped in our own defenses. Whenever we invent a story to cover, we make matters worse—in many ways.

For one thing, lies obscure self-knowledge. Screening what others know of us, we end up screening what we know of ourselves. Defensive shields come between us and our own reality, as we start believing the half-truths we put out.

Lack of self-knowledge is as devastating for companies, churches, schools, and nations as it is for us personally. Within systems, we need to know where we are—what's working and what isn't, what we're feeling and what others are feeling as well—in order to plan the next step. We can't pretend things are okay if they're not. As we've found with the national debt and the crisis in health care, hidden problems are the most dangerous. They grow in silence, until they're so overwhelming we don't know where to begin to solve them.

Lie defenses are also harmful because they consume our energies, diverting them from where we most need them. Whether we're in business or in a marriage, we need to focus on what's real in the relationship: a real product or service or a real self that's present with the other. Defensive covers make this difficult. Unaware of our filters, we put energy into preserving covers rather than into dealing with real issues. We create a life that's more role than intimacy, more image than substance.

In the Exxon Valdez oil spill, for instance, energies poured into damage control for corporate images but trickled into damage control for Prince William Sound. In the first few critical hours, little energy was spent on actually plugging the leak in the tanker's hull or containing the spill. Salvaging government and oil-conglomerate images by using lies and half-truths took precedence. As with President Johnson's inability to admit that the Vietnam War couldn't be won, the compulsion to maintain an on-top-of-it image eclipsed his ability to cope with reality in a situation that was causing more death and suffering day by day.

Paradigm defenses act like guard dogs at the door of our paradigm's castle. Their assignment is to protect the model-in-charge at all costs. Until we disarm the defenses, we can't get inside. We can't explore our paradigm or what it's doing to us and our systems. The roots of addictive personal behavior and of soul-violating social structures stay off-limits—as does our real being.

"Self-disclosure" cuts through defensive routines

Facing the worst-case scenario makes covers superfluous. Recovery breaks through defenses, and in a simple, straightforward way. We create a space to hear the truth about ourselves, our systems, and the paradigms that shape both.

AA's Fifth Step does this by admitting "to God, to ourselves, and to another human being the exact nature of our wrongs." Admitting wrongs pushes defensive covers way back, because it tackles the worst-case scenario—what we most fear—namely, being exposed for our mistakes.

If it's okay to be wrong, we don't have to hide or cover. Openly admitting the abusive patterns that a paradigm creates—patterns we've participated in and perpetuated ourselves—we no longer need to mount a defense. We can disclose our paradigm filters and get on with evolving them.

With this strategy shift, we're out of the defense business and free to focus on the realities at hand. By facing our worst fears about being exposed, dealing with our paradigm openly, and being up-front about what's happening, we dispense with energy-draining covers and attend to the real job: transformation.

Accessing our paradigm-shifting powers. By so doing, we tap hidden resources of knowledge and growth. Our willingness to confront what's wrong opens us to our paradigm-shifting powers. We see how wrongs get started on a paradigm level, and this insight gets us going on the path of changing paradigms.

Tarthang Tulku explains: "Because our problems are often painful and disturbing, our natural tendency is to try to avoid them; we seek ways to get out of difficult situations, or to go around the obstacles we encounter. But our problems are like clouds: though they appear to disturb the serenity of a clear sky, they contain life-giving moisture that nourishes growth. When we face our problems directly and go through them, we discover new ways of being."[12]

Breaking through defensive routines: self-disclosure. Argyris and Senge agree. The remedy for paradigm covers is self-disclosure: admitting what's bothering us, discussing our defenses, and bringing both our paradigms and their defenses out into the open. As Senge notes, "To retain their power, defensive routines *must remain undiscussable.* Teams stay stuck in their defensive routines only when they pretend that they don't have any defensive routines, that everything is all right, and that they can say 'anything.'"[13]

Self-disclosure breaks the hold that defensive covers have on us. When we admit our defensive habits, they no longer block our growth. Breaking the rule of secrecy and paradigm-protective taboos, we allow our paradigms to surface and our covers to dissipate. Issues start bubbling up that carry us forward in confronting what's really going on. In addition, we have the energy—liberated from the enervating job of maintaining covers—to go forward.

Learning from defensive patterns. With a strategy of self-disclosure, we expose our defenses and find out why they're there. We can't get rid of our protective armor all at once. We have defenses because we need them now, or we needed them in the past, or we think we need them even if we don't. Through self-disclosure, we begin to sort this out. We admit exactly what our defenses are doing for us.

In most cases, identifying defensive covers takes us to the heart of what's obstructing paradigm evolution. We've stumbled on a mother lode of blocked energy and potential awareness. What we're most defensive about is often what we're most quickly outgrowing. However, we may not realize it or perhaps we're not ready to face the consequences of such a shift. Even so, the same defenses that block us can direct us to our deepest insights—the very idea-shifts that we're most primed to make. Again from Senge:

> Defensive routines can become a surprising ally...by providing a signal when learning is not occurring. Most of us know when we are being defensive, even if we cannot fully identify the source or pattern of our defensiveness.... When we are feeling defensive, seeking to avoid an issue, thinking we need to protect someone else or ourselves—these are tangible signals that can be used to reestablish a climate of learning.... Often, the stronger the defensiveness, the more important the issue around which people are defending or protecting their views.[14]

In the body, sore points indicate where physical energy is blocked. In the psyche, defensive covers indicate sore points where soul energy is trapped. In social systems, defensive patterns indicate where human energy is dammed up.

Self-disclosure unbottles the energy. Naming defenses as such and looking behind them to the dynamics of our inner growth loosens blocked awareness and lets this awareness operate as a force for transformation. Core issues surface, and we start working through them.

HEARING THE TRUTH

Commitment to truth. A commitment to self-disclosure is a commitment to hearing the truth, which is by nature transforming. Whereas lies, covers, and taboos limit us to existing paradigm filters, admitting what's going on opens us to learning about reality and to evolving the paradigms we use to move with it. Senge describes this commitment in practice:

> Commitment to the truth…means a relentless willingness to root out the ways we limit or deceive ourselves from seeing what is, and to continually challenge our theories of why things are the way they are. It means continually broadening our awareness, just as the great athlete with extraordinary peripheral vision keeps trying to "see more of the playing field." It also means continually deepening our understanding of the structures underlying current events.[15]

Initiating self-disclosure. When it comes to breaking through paradigm defenses, a strategy of self-disclosure starts with individuals and spreads out. If we're caught in defenses together—if our paradigm filters are so hidden that we can't find out why our systems are behaving abusively—the way to break through the barriers is shared self-disclosure.

To start, we ask ourselves why we're defending our systems as they now function, which relates to why we're part of them in the first place. We admit how we behave when we're in a family or school system, for instance, and how we feel about behaving those ways. Is what we've become by committing to the control paradigm and its systems who we want to be?

In other words, we use a self-disclosing strategy to start with ourselves and to admit how systems mold us. We hear the truth about ourselves in systems and about how the paradigms behind systems lead us to think, feel, and act. That's the beginning—the strategy that gets the momentum of self-disclosure going.

Where else can we start? Accusing others in the name of self-disclosure doesn't work. Charging others with being defensive brings their defenses out in force. By contrast, admitting our feelings, confusions, fears, and defenses breaks the pattern. By relaxing our defensive boundaries, we create space for others to join in and explore what's going on.

Our story is one telling of our systems' story. It's also one telling of a culturally pervasive paradigm. We're a microcosm of the macrocosm. As we share our stories, the system and paradigm no longer remain hidden.

We exchange our stories not to undermine systems but to evolve the paradigms behind them, so that our systems become better servants to human needs. That's why we have social systems in the first place. If we're not functioning happily in systems, systems can't function optimally either. We're like canaries taken down into coal mines; if we're not thriving, our systems can't be either. The more we're honest about how we're experiencing systems—the more we provide the feedback they need—the more our paradigms and systems evolve.

Gandhi: An open experiment with Truth. Gandhi was a master of removing defenses as a strategy for transforming social systems. To start, he used the strategy on himself. Much of his force as a spiritual and political leader came from his commitment to self-disclosure. British spies could learn nothing that he would not openly admit. Even his most personal wrestlings with "brahmacharya," or purifying self-discipline, were made public. He called his life "an experiment with Truth"—an experiment he conducted in the open.

But he also encouraged the Indian people to let down their defenses and to admit their wrongs as well. As Gandhi saw it, self-government is inseparable from self-purification. Otherwise, we're ruled by our shortcomings. Self-purification starts with self-disclosure—admitting exactly what needs correction. Gandhi wrote:

> I have always been loath to hide...the weak points of the community, or to press for its rights without having purged it of its blemishes...I am not interested in freeing India merely from the English yoke. I am bent upon freeing India from any yoke whatsoever.... Hence for me the movement of Swaraj [self-rule] is a movement of self-purification. It is we ourselves with our inertia, apathy and social abuse that more than England or anybody else block our way to freedom. And if we cleanse ourselves of our shortcomings and faults, no power on earth can even for a moment withhold Swaraj from us.[16]

Lincoln: Admitting America's wrongs. Hearing the truth about collective wrongs is liberating. We can't stop soul-violation until we stop defending it. In his famous second inaugural address, for instance, Abraham Lincoln openly admitted the "offence" of "American Slavery" and acknowledged the inevitability of paying the price for such an inhuman, institutionalized evil.

Defending the indefensible, Lincoln reasoned, locks us on the same level as the offense. Withdrawing our defenses, admitting wrongs, and hearing the truth liberates us to move beyond both a soul-violating paradigm and the soul-violating systems it creates.

Lincoln and Gandhi did for their nations what system recovery suggests we do for ours today: face abusive paradigms, name how they build abuse into our social structures, and end the defenses, lies, and cover-ups. With paradigm defenses out in the open, we're free to evaluate the paradigm behind our systems and get on with a paradigm shift.

NOTES TO CHAPTER 5

1. John Moyne and Coleman Barks, trans., *Unseen Rain: Quatrains of Rumi* (Putney, VT: Threshold Books, 1986), 46. Also in Coleman Barks with John Moyne, A. J. Arberry, and Reynold Nicholson, trans., *The Essential Rumi* (San Francisco: HarperSanFrancisco, 1995), 116.
2. Chan Wing-Tsit, trans., *Instructions for Practical Living and Other Neo-Confucian Writings by Wang Yang-ming* (New York: Columbia University Press, 1962), 81.
3. *The Wall Street Journal*, 14 May 1992.
4. *Twelfth Night*, 4.1.
5. Peter Senge, *The Fifth Discipline* (New York: Doubleday/Currency, 1990), 182.
6. Senge, *Fifth Discipline*, 249–50.
7. Senge, *Fifth Discipline*, 254.
8. Jonathan Vankin, *Conspiracies, Cover-ups and Crimes: Political Manipulation and Mind Control in America* (New York: Paragon House Publishers, 1992), 234.
9. Lao Tzu, *Tao Te Ching*, LVII, trans. D. C. Lau (New York: Penguin Classics, 1963), 118.
10. John Bradshaw, *Healing the Shame That Binds You* (Deerfield Beach, FL: Health Communications, 1988), 32.
11. Bradshaw, *Healing the Shame That Binds You*, 32.
12. Tarthang Tulku, *Skillful Means: Gentle Ways to Successful Work* (Berkeley, CA: Dharma Publishing, 1978), 51.
13. Senge, *Fifth Discipline*, 255.
14. Senge, *Fifth Discipline*, 256.
15. Senge, *Fifth Discipline*, 159.
16. Louis Fischer, ed., *The Essential Gandhi: An Anthology of His Writings on His Life, Work and Ideas* (New York: Vintage Books/Random House, 1962), 80, 191, 248.

CHAPTER 6

Self-Acceptance:
Building Systems on Who We Are

Presenting the truth
*Sixth of the Twelve Cycles of Truth,
the Iroquois Peace Confederacy Tradition*

Sloshing kneedeep in fresh riverwater, yet
you keep wanting a drink from other people's waterbags.

Water is everywhere around you, but you only see
barriers that keep you from water.

The horse is beneath the rider's thighs, and still
he asks, *Where's my horse?*
"Right there, under you!"
Yes, this is a horse, but where's the horse?
"Can't you see!"
Yes, I can see, but whoever saw such a horse?

Rumi[1]

HOW CAN WE "MAKE IT SO" AND BE CREATIVE?

We're knee-deep in the dynamics of transformation, and we're shifting paradigms in the direction of greater soul-connectedness.

Strategies of self-awareness (chapter 4) acquaint us with our paradigm filters and how they're distinct from our essence. To evolve a paradigm based on who we are, we need self-knowledge.

Strategies of self-disclosure (chapter 5) relax our paradigm defenses. Self-disclosure makes our paradigm visible, so we can identify the underlying model shaping us and our systems. Until we stop defending a soul-costly paradigm, we're not likely to change it.

Up against the wall. Yet something comes up at this stage to block the process. Sometimes it's something within us that says no. Other times outside forces seem to get in the way. Soul-connectedness is a nice idea, and maybe we can get around to it someday, but it's not practical now. Despite good intentions, we find ourselves and our systems slipping back into the very patterns we need to outgrow.

Whether we call it entropy, the status quo, the drive to maintain equilibrium, inertia, ignorance, fear, or plain old denial, the stonewalling message is the same: "Put things back to the way they were, minus the problems!"

No one comes out and argues against transformation, of course. It just doesn't happen. Things grind on in the old ways—or in new ways that don't change what's soul-damaging. We run into a wall.

Given the wall, how do we "make transformation so"? What strategies get us over the top to a real paradigm shift, one that's soul-worthy?

LEVELS OF CHANGE STRATEGIES

We can be creative about "making change so" on many levels. Strategies work on at least five levels, the first three of which Peter Senge outlines from a systems perspective.[2] Each strategy helps us scale different kinds of walls—and we need all of them.

1. Technique strategies. The most common strategy for changing things operates on the level of specific circumstances—change level one. These walls aren't particularly high; there are just so many of them, and they keep multiplying. The strategy here is to react with techniques adapted to the immediate problem. Whatever's wrong, we fix it, compensate for it, pay for it, or counteract it.

Technique strategies are excellent in emergencies. If we break a bone or lose a job, we need help—on the level of setting bones and figuring out how to pay the bills. If systems are in crisis, such as banks failing or businesses going bankrupt, we need techniques for helping people through the crisis and getting systems up and running again.

But technique strategies don't address the dynamics that lead to crises, which is why we don't stop with them. They're reactive to the problems created by systems. They don't address systems or structures, much less the paradigm behind them.

The best that technique strategies can do is return us to a predetermined state of normal functioning. But again, what if the norm is the problem? If the norm creates soul loss, readapting to the norm returns us to the very dynamics that cause breakdown.

After decades of 1,001 ways to fix, improve, double, or promote whatever, we're a bit weary of fiddling. There's always another crisis around the corner, since we haven't altered the patterns that generate crises. We just keep reacting.

2. Strategies that change patterns of behavior. Which immediate patterns generate crises? Ours do. That's change level two: changing our behavior patterns.

We're the actors in our dramas, and outward events mirror the patterns we set up, follow, and perpetuate. Strategies devoted to preventing crises take a good long look at the patterns we're living. These walls are a bit more formidable, because they make us step back and look at ourselves.

One of the most widely read business books in recent years, Stephen Covey's *Seven Habits of Highly Effective People*, calls for precisely this level-jump from technique strategies to strategies focused on changing behavior patterns. All the techniques in the world won't help us build good relationships, for instance, if we lie, intimidate, and manipulate.

We can't change behavior patterns through techniques alone. Change isn't convincing unless it extends to the level of our character: how we conduct relationships every day. Our ego vehicle has to shift its base.

Covey's habits, for instance, build business relationships on vision, patience, integrity, trust, commitment, respect, mutuality and reciprocity, as well as on continual development and refinement. These qualities can't be faked. Sooner or later our character comes out.

But again, there's a snag. If habits of mutual respect, trust, and integrity are the most effective—and if we feel better about ourselves when we're living them—why don't we?

For a good reason: we're not alone in our systems. It's hard to live patterns of integrity if those around us are living opposite patterns—and making billions doing so. In business jargon, we're swimming with sharks. We keep trying to "do the right thing," but it gets depressing when our competitors threaten to put us out of business by doing things in deceitful, exploitive, or cut-throat ways.

One thing for sure, neither we nor the sharks were born sharks; we started off as humans. Putting people out onto the street unemployed isn't what human beings enjoy doing. Empathy and compassion are natural gifts. So where do shark patterns start?

3. Strategies that change systems, rules, and structures. Behavior patterns come straight from social structures. Change level three: changing social systems.

We dovetail our individual actions with our systems' requirements. If parents, teachers, and bosses want us to please them and they punish us when we don't, we become people-pleasers. We design our character to fit the rules and roles that systems give us.

For instance, humans obviously have the capacity to be ruthlessly competitive when social systems require it. But it's debatable whether humans are innately competitive, since many cultures don't favor competitive behavior and don't suffer its consequences. Cooperation skills are arguably more valuable to human survival.

Nonetheless, modern Western social systems drum competitive patterns into us from the start, equating self-worth with winning and being on top. One of our students recently summed up this training and how it shapes his behavior:

> Within my accounting major, everything functions at a very competitive level. There is no "good for the whole." Everyone in my major is out for themselves. Accounting majors learn that helping someone else succeed is really hurting yourself. This may sound extreme, but this is how it actually is....
>
> My accounting professors stress being at the top of the class. They stress how only a few will get the top grades. This comes down at my level to [mean], "I have to study more than everyone else, know more than everyone else." Somehow this all translates into competition, intense com-

petition. I do believe that everyone working together, especially toward a common goal, results in an overall increased contribution, as opposed to everyone working on their own.

Many times I would have liked to have been able to discuss class material with others in my class. I understand things better when I am able to talk about them with others. But as I have already noted, my major is very competitive and does not allow this. "Why hurt yourself by helping someone else? Why hurt the curve? Why hurt my chances of getting a job by increasing my competitors' credentials…?"

I am really starting to depress myself by realizing how true all of this is.… I also now believe that this competition I am surrounded by and involved with originates not with the students, but at a higher level—the faculty. I do believe that I am better for realizing this and now am facing it honestly.

Other students admit that they're relieved when fellow students fail, because their own chances of getting an A improve. They'd rather not have to succeed at someone else's expense—they feel bad about it—but that's how modern schooling rigs it.

The system creates the behavior patterns.

Our student is right that the competitive drive comes from a higher level; however, it comes from a level higher than the faculty. The source lies in the rules, roles, methods, practices, and structures that dominate modern schooling. These structures remain in place as long and only as long as we all agree to them—not just students, parents, faculty, and administration, but also "we the people," since we all have to live with the products of an educational system whose leading message K through college is "Beat the competition!"

To change patterns of behavior and keep them changed, we need to change the social structures that create them.

No problem, we say. We work to change structures directly. We rewrite rules, expand roles, try new methods, and implement new policies and procedures—and for a time things seem different. Yet the change seems less than convincing. The old approach hangs in the atmosphere, and people find themselves slipping back into old habits, fears, and expectations. Before long, in spite of well-intentioned efforts at structural changes, old system patterns reassert themselves.

4. Strategies that shift paradigms. The breakthrough in changing social systems comes with realizing that social systems are *our* systems. They reflect the paradigm we use to create them. If social systems are failing us, it's time to look at the paradigm behind them, even if it's one that's been in place for millennia: change level four.

Specifically, if a paradigm designs systems that twist us into hungry ghosts of chronic neediness, fear, and insecurity, then the systems lose claim to authority in our lives. A paradigm that makes us slaves to social systems turns the purpose of social systems on its head. By demanding that we serve them, instead of their serving us, control-paradigm systems violate the social contract we have with them, which means they forfeit their claim to legitimacy.

That's the time for revolution—a paradigm shift. Or so the thinkers behind the American Revolution argued.

Their revolutionary idea—if we extend it to family, social, economic, educational, and religious systems—was that the purpose of shared systems is to serve human needs. The purpose isn't to serve only those in power by exploiting everyone else. Social systems do their job when they bring out the best in all of us by challenging us to grow. Any paradigm that argues otherwise is unacceptable.

Example: Two paradigms of business. We often hear, for instance, that the purpose of a business is to make money for the shareholders, but this is a narrow, money-paradigm description. To make money, businesses must contribute products and services that the community values, otherwise no one will pay for what businesses offer. They must also provide a meaningful environment that supports the personal growth of everyone involved, since that's when we do our best. Businesses must serve us, otherwise we want no part of them. If we have economic freedom and a business abuses us, it soon has neither employees nor customers.

Unfortunately, businesses labor under a paradigm that blurs this reality, while pushing the image of business as a win-lose war in the ultimate quest, as economist Thorstein Veblen pointed out, of getting something for nothing. This strategy is successful only when our economic options are limited, i.e., when we have little or no economic choice. Then, we're forced to tolerate business as theft and work as slavery.

What's wrong with this picture isn't the core business idea of exchange for mutual benefit but the paradigm that derails this legitimate purpose and puts business on a track of exploitation and ultimately self-destruction. It's the paradigm, not the essence of business, that must change.

But what gives us the strength to say to a competitive, patriarchal, my-way-or-the-highway paradigm, "You hurt us, you abuse us out of our greatest treasures—our minds and souls—so we won't tolerate you any longer"? Moreover, what guides us in evolving new paradigms, so that we don't end up worse off than we started?

5. Strategies that build on soul-connectedness. Ultimately, who we are gives us the strength to reject soul abuse, wherever it occurs, and guides the paradigm shift. Change level five: soul-connecting.

Our souls are our foundation, the core and touchstone of our existence. To quote Wang Yang-ming again, "With the true self, one lives; without it, one dies."[3]

Fifth-level transformation strategies tackle change by demanding that our paradigm, and therefore also our social structures, answer to us—not to our paradigm-packaged personalities but to our core identity, our souls. Soul values—such as creativity, openness, freedom, individuality, compassion, as well as the traditional Platonic list: truth, love, beauty, wisdom, temperance, courage, and justice—count beyond all else in life. Therefore they must stand at the center of our personal and cultural paradigms.

Making the shift to a soul-centered paradigm suggests a two-pronged approach. On one hand, we ask our paradigms and systems to be responsive to our souls' evolution. On the other, we ask ourselves to be attuned to our "true self"—to the whole being that we are—so we can decide for ourselves whether a paradigm supports our life's processes or not.

THE FIRST PRONG: DIALOGUING WITH PARADIGMS AND SYSTEMS

Checking the fit. To do fifth-level change and bring social structures more in line with their purpose, strategies that "make transformation so" initiate a dialogue between our souls, our paradigm, and our social systems: How present can we be with our souls when we're in social systems? To what extent does our paradigm nurture soul-evolving processes, and in what ways does it shut them down?

In other words, soul-level change-strategies continually check the fit:

Are our souls, paradigm, and social structures pulling together or against each other? Using values essential to inner growth as a checklist, we can get the dialogue going with any paradigm or social system we're considering:

Creativity and learning. Does the paradigm honor the creative process and make room for missteps and false starts, or does it penalize each mistake, throwing our creativity into catalepsy? Does our paradigm affirm our capacities to learn?

Studies show, for example, that we learn best when we're most relaxed. Since learning is the key to business survival—something Peter Senge and many other business consultants have been telling corporations for years—it's critical that we feel free and comfortable about learning. Yet our school and business systems maximize stress. It's hard to relax into the joy of learning when we've been terrorized by the fear of failure since age five. In an information age when lifelong learning is a must, that's crazy—a sure sign of a soul/paradigm misfit.

Noticing this misfit illustrates how we reflect on our paradigm, ask questions of it, and analyze how it functions in our lives. But creativity and learning aren't the only values we can use to check the relation between our paradigm and our souls. We can also ask about the following:

Rhythms of development. Does the paradigm or social system respect that different people work at different rhythms and go through different periods of development? Does it give us space to follow our life's order, which has its own wisdom, or does it put system order above all else?

The fragmentation of subjects and the "crazy sequences" of schooling that John Taylor Gatto criticizes in *Dumbing Us Down* are good examples of putting the conformist interests of an institution above the rhythms of people—to the detriment of both learning and personal development.

Irwin Hyman uses a specific example as his centerpiece in *Reading, Writing, and the Hickory Stick*. In 1983, a senior honors student and member of the all-state band missed a day of classes in order to help a fellow student. For missing the day, she received a beating from an assistant principal/football coach, which caused injuries so severe that the attending physician, horrified, filed child-abuse charges. Not only was the coach exonerated by the court (leaving bruises on a woman's buttocks and causing her menstrual flow to turn into hemorrhaging are within a teacher's legal rights in North

Carolina), but no one noticed that the punishment was designed to assure the institution's totalitarian control over individuals and their life rhythms.*

The message is clear: institutions make us conform to their arbitrary rhythms but make few allowances for ours. This policy follows us through life. If we have a baby, if a family member or close friend dies, if we or someone close to us goes through a personal crisis, or if we struggle with a long-term illness, we're supposed to get ourselves back together ASAP and return to work. We're not paid to have a life. And if having a life interferes with our job performance more than a couple weeks—if, for example, a woman takes off six months to get to know her newborn or even a couple years to give her children a good start in life—she's lucky to get her job back.†

Integrity and trust. Then there's the issue of what kind of person we're "allowed" to be: Does the paradigm or social system allow us our integrity and so foster trust among us? Are we allowed to do the right thing, even if it costs the company money? Can we bring our ideals and compassion to our work?

Or does the paradigm system expect us to do what's "necessary," values be damned? Are we faced with the choice to either become someone we don't like or lose our position? The paradigm's rules and structures can, for instance, pit us against each other, as modern schooling does with grading. Resentments and jealousies get built into the system's methods of supervision, incentives, compensation, and rewards. The man who spat on his $2.1 million monthly bonus check surely had other issues in mind besides $2.1 million.

Worse, we can find ourselves expected to make money at the cost of terrible human suffering and not notice what we're doing. That's the new

---

*Though we've mentioned him earlier, we want to commend Irwin Hyman's courageous work at Temple University's National Center for the Study of Corporal Punishment and Alternatives in the Schools and highly recommend his book *Reading, Writing, and the Hickory Stick* (Lexington, MA: Lexington Books, 1990).

†Thanks to the 1993 "Family and Medical Leave Act," employees, men or women, may take up to twelve weeks off without pay to take care of family needs, such as a new child, but are still guaranteed a comparable job (not necessarily the same job) when they return to work. This is a major breakthrough for families, but it's still a long way from the steady nurturing that children need in their early years and that other cultures now and in the past have given them. Ours is not a culture that puts a priority on raising new generations.

meaning of free trade in the global market. Thanks to the recent international trade agreements, GATT and NAFTA—summarized nicely by the title of an article in *The Nation*, "Global Village or Global Pillage"[4]— American corporations can now build factories in the southern, poorer nations that violate the most basic worker safety laws. The old sweatshops are returning with a vengeance. Who sleeps every night knowing their high salaries are paid for by human suffering?

A close friend of ours knows such a person, a corporate lawyer who specializes in arranging deals between corporations that are moving to poor, southern nations and the foreign governments. When our friend confronted the lawyer with the need to negotiate better working conditions, he got annoyed and asked why he should do that. His response took her by surprise, because she'd known him for years as a good, kind, and decent person. His attitude seemed totally out of character. Yet he's become precisely what the current paradigm of international business requires him to be. If he followed her suggestions and championed a better quality of life for the foreign workers, the American company would probably get a different lawyer, and he couldn't sustain the lifestyle to which he and his family have grown accustomed—which leads us to the next issue:

Principles. What are the paradigm's principles? Are they principles we believe in—ones we're willing to dedicate most of our waking hours to living? If they are, do our systems operate consistently with these principles, or do they talk one game and play another?

Consider, for instance, the principles we bring to business. Businesses are the backbone of our society. Their work dominates our time and energies. And given the work ethic in America, we believe in good work. We feel it's honorable to contribute to the collective welfare through our efforts. We're happy about contributing to systems that enable us and others to earn a good living. This is what good business does. It's based on the principle of exchange for mutual benefit among people who have the freedom to say "No" if their interests aren't being served.

Given these basic economic principles, our business interactions are largely based on trust—trust that products are correctly represented, trust that people will do what they say they'll do, trust that an agreement is being made in good faith, trust that commitment to mutual benefit won't disappear from one day to the next. Years ago when we were arranging to use a college's facilities for a conference, we offered a down payment, and the college coordinator replied: "If we don't trust each other, we shouldn't be doing business together."

But not all business paradigms support these principles, and not all business systems, even if they espouse these principles, follow them. Amitai Etzioni, a writer, founder of the Communitarian political movement, and professor at George Washington University, discovered that "62 percent of the Fortune 500 corporations were involved in one or more 'significant illegalities' in the decade from 1975 to 1984. Almost half of them—42 percent—were identified in two or more episodes of corrupt behavior."[5]

Yet true principles die hard, if they ever do. The executives who make these decisions don't always sleep as well as we may think. In a section of *When Corporations Rule the World* entitled "Pain at the Top," David Korten discusses the toll that the new face of business—massive cutbacks at home and sweatshops being created abroad, all in the name of "efficiency" and "maximizing profits"—is taking on top executives:

> It is a sense that something simply isn't right, that they are leaving their children a deeply troubled world. Many face growing conflicts between their personal values and what their corporate positions demand of them.... As one CEO related to *Fortune*, "You get through firing people the first time around, accepting it as a part of business. The second time I began wondering, 'How many miscarriages is this causing? How many divorces, how many suicides?' I worked harder so that I wouldn't have to think about it."[6]

The toll on these humans-turned-unwilling-Scrooges is both emotional and physical: some lose weight, some gain it, some start smoking, some become extremely nervous and can't look people in the eye, some lose their appetite, some break into spontaneous fits of crying, some can't sleep, while others can't get out of bed.[7]

To have paradigms and systems that serve our souls, we need to ask these questions: Which principles do we want to live by personally, and which do we need to ground our social systems? For our souls to be happy, we need harmony between the two sets—which raises the next issue: Where do we fit in?

Individuality and uniqueness. Does the paradigm call for individuality or conformity? Does it value our uniqueness as what makes social systems strong and flexible, or does it expect us to fall in line and do what we're told? Does the paradigm honor human diversity as the real resource of any social system?

Unfortunately, we have a long history of social systems that demand conformity, so that everyone fits into a predetermined social order. In the temple/state model of ancient Sumer, for instance, kings and priests ruled absolutely through a hierarchy of patriarchal, control-minded institutions. Schools speak volumes about the character of a society, because they turn children into the kind of adults that society expects them to be. In Sumerian schools—which only children of the wealthy could attend, along with the "experts" for each specialized field—"there were monitors in charge of attendance and 'a man in charge of the whip,' who was presumably responsible for discipline."[8]

This same monitor-and-punish model has reemerged in business, churches, schools, even families today. Praised for its "efficiency," this model was originally set up, in the words of religious scholar Burton Mack, "in such a way that everyone knew his or her place in relation to both authority and propriety."[9] The model isn't interested in making room for differences, much less positively valuing them; instead, it's interested in moving people into social boxes and keeping them there. When scholars praise historical examples of totalitarianism for "efficiency," they fail to notice the toll it takes on individuality—a phenomenon Alice Miller finds common among "experts" in patriarchies.

Contrast that with many traditional Native American cultures where individuality is highly respected. "Walking to the beat of a different drummer" poses no crisis for either the person or the society. If anything, differences indicate some special knowledge or awareness that's a gift to the community. Faced with fools, the mentally handicapped, mystics, hermits, psychics, and dreamers, American Indian communities then and now consider themselves enriched, not threatened. Their paradigm is geared to individuality. For instance, flutist R. Carlos Nakai points out that Native American instrument-makers create each flute to fit the hands of an individual musician. They don't expect musicians to conform to one-size-fits-all flutes—which raises the next issue to dialogue about with our paradigms and systems:

Standards. If standards don't mean conformity, what do they mean? What standards does a paradigm give us to decide whether systems are running well or badly?

The control paradigm gives us, of course, the standard of control. Translated into business, for instance, control of profits, control of employees, and control of the market presumably show how successful we are. In families, schools, churches, and political parties, the control standard translates into military standards: discipline, obedience, and loyalty to authorities. The trouble is, control standards aren't working for us. Not only do they give us all the problems we've mentioned, but worse, they aren't much fun.

Fun, in fact, isn't a bad standard to use in dialoguing with social systems: How much fun do we have when we're in them? That's not as frivolous a question as control-paradigm thinking would have us believe. When we're having fun, we're finding meaning and being creative. We relax and laugh more, and, as Norman Cousins pointed out in *The Anatomy of an Illness*, laughter is a potent healer. Consequently, we don't get sick as often, and we tend to give our best to whatever we're doing. Medical costs go down, and performance and creativity go up. How's that for the no-jokes bottom line?

Fun is an anathema to control-paradigm systems, since we can't be ordered to have fun. But fun may well be one of the best touchstones for evaluating schools, workplaces, religious institutions, and governments.

Meaningful whole. The last value we'll consider—and we could consider many more—is that of meaning: Does the paradigm lead us to feel integrated meaningfully with the people and systems around us? Or does it generate social systems that are factionalized, alienating, and misery-and-crisis ridden? How do our paradigm-created systems add up as a whole?

What, for example, are the rewards? If they're monetary, are they concentrating at the top, while the burdens are being carried at the bottom? If they're less tangible, such as being part of a group effort, are each person's insights and contributions taken into fair consideration, even if the person happens to be a child, student, woman, ethnic or racial minority, janitor, or technician?

In *Creative Work*, Willis Harman and John Hormann observe that employees now value intangible rewards more than money: "The traditional motivators for job performance—job security, high pay, and good benefits—

no longer work. Employees want such intangibles as being treated with respect, having work that is personally satisfying, having ample opportunity to learn new skills and to grow personally, having a reasonable amount of autonomy, being recognized for good work."[10]

Korten agrees: "Those who achieve the pinnacles of financial and professional success in America seldom lack for physical comforts. They are learning, however, that no amount of money can buy peace of mind, a strong and loving family, caring friends, and a feeling that one is doing meaningful and important work."[11]

Money isn't enough; we want meaning. We want to feel that we're linked to systems in ways that enrich us and that allow us to enrich others. In other words, we want lives in which we look forward to getting up in the morning.

The most practical way to change. By making our paradigm and its social systems answer to us, we effect change from the most powerful level of transformation. The fear, of course, is that using soul values to guide change is wildly idealistic and won't be practical (who do you suppose started that one...?). In fact, just the opposite is true. Shifting paradigms—and with them our social systems—from the ground of our souls is the most practical approach.

Consider what it means to do the opposite. Sacrificing soul-connectedness for the sake of social order—or the ruling party's concept of it—isn't sustainable. We think we're creating family harmony, school discipline, business efficiency, religious devotion, or political loyalty, but beneath the surface we're creating conflict between our inner dynamics and what social systems require us to become. Like a volcano that's about to blow, a society that builds social order on institutionalized soul denial gets progressively violent rumblings, until it looks as if civilization is coming apart at the seams.

Social order: By brute force or "Soul force"?

Anarchy and chaos? But is a soul-connected society really doable? Can a dialogue between our inner processes and social systems work? We're used to the communication being one-way: from parents to us, teachers to us, clergy to us, employers to us, bureaucrats to us, party officials to us, the media to us.

The one-way communication strategy is based on a control-paradigm assumption, namely, that social order would give way to anarchy if we each expressed our individuality. Society would be pulled apart by conflicting views, and nothing would ever get done—or so the argument goes. The dictator model is the most efficient, especially if we get a benevolent tyrant.

Planted deep in our psyches is a suspicion of democracy, a belief that republics and democracies don't work. Accordingly, most families, schools, religious institutions, and corporations aren't democracies and, it's assumed, can never be so. Governments don't behave much like democracies either. The assumed foundations of social order are power, conformity, and obedience, and the assumed formula for anarchy is individual expression.

If that's so, one-way is how the communication should flow. We need social systems to tell us how to fall in line, and we need them to punish us when we don't. They *should* impose the order. Our job is to obey.

Or "Soul force"? But what if the control paradigm's assumption is wrong, invalidating the one-way communication strategy? What if our souls are, in fact, the one thing our social systems most need to survive?

True, if systems are soul-abusive, our souls don't like it. They want the abuse to stop, and they'll do what it takes to stop it. They'll act out their pain, and they aren't picky about how. The fear that control-paradigm authorities have toward soul-committed individuals isn't unfounded (cf. Nixon's obsessive fear with his enemies lists). They *should* be afraid of our souls if they're abusing us.

But to assume that our souls and society are necessarily at odds isn't warranted. If we assume this, we create systems that suppress our souls to ward off the danger, which our souls rebel against, which creates conflict. The control paradigm creates its own proof by picking a fight with our inner lives.

By contrast, assuming that our souls are the foundation for social order—as Confucius, Lao Tzu, Socrates, and Apollonius of Tyana did—leads to strategies that build social systems on who we are. We're conscious, evolving beings who want lives of meaning. As such, we're in harmony with each other the more we're in harmony with our souls' evolution. We present the truth of who we are as the basis of social systems.

Gandhi argued that "Soul force" is the true alternative to "brute force" in establishing social order. Soul force is the cement of society. When we live who we are—when we're not blasted out inwardly and then stepped on outwardly—order is there on its own. We are society's order.

That's the only real order we have. Order that's imposed from without can't work. It's impossible to enforce. Brute force requires a policing overseer—a "monitor" and "man in charge of the whip"—for every person and relationship. But then who polices the police? Whose notion of order would we be living—or in whose interests?

The second prong: Dialoguing with our souls

To present the truth of Soul force, we need to be present with that truth ourselves. The more we're soul-connected, the more we hold up our end of the dialogue with our paradigms and social systems. For the sake of ourselves and our systems, we have to explore the eternal questions: Who are we, and what processes are we living? How can we connect with our souls' evolution, and how does that present the truth of our relation with All That Is?

Exploring these questions isn't easy, though, because a wall of shame comes between our officially acceptable egos and our inner lives. This shame wall says that the persona we've created to fit in social systems is the cover we need to hide our inner processes, which are inadequate, unworthy, and a nuisance to systems. The outward front is acceptable, but the inward reality is not. Until we confront this wall of shame, we fear our soul-evolving processes and don't allow ourselves to embrace them. We don't trust our inner reality and are hesistant to follow it.

Volumes have been written on shame, but briefly, what's going on?

Shame-blasted

Not brute force but shame force. Shame and guilt—shame for who we are and guilt that we haven't been able to turn ourselves into someone else—are the most potent tools in the control-paradigm arsenal. It doesn't take long for control-paradigm types to notice that brute force doesn't work. Brute force is reactive and requires too much energy. Proactive control strategies focus on controlling our inner lives.

Once we're controlled from within, control becomes invisible and effortless. We-the-controlled believe that the controlling messages we hear in our heads are our own. We don't realize that the control tapes were installed in us by parents and teachers afraid of what happens to people who go into society without the official programming. It's worse than not having your oatmeal.

Families are, as we said, a dress rehearsal for society and designed to be so. Schools are as well. The primary agenda, dictated by a cultural commitment to a control paradigm, is to gain control of a human being from the inside out, and shame is the most efficient way to do it. Instead of energy-intensive brute force, control-paradigm strategies "make it so" with energy-efficient shame force.

Shamed from without. Comparison is a powerful tool of shaming: "Why aren't you as nice and quiet as that child over there?" "Why aren't you on first string?" Shaming through grades is our school system's primary mechanism for motivation and control.

Religious institutions join the act and shame us for not measuring up to their idea of perfection. Being born human is cause enough for shaming: original sin. We're flawed and defective just for having a body, feelings, needs, desires, and a will of our own.

On the job, ranking systems build on the shame categories that families, schools, and religions instill. We're shamed into doing whatever our superiors tell us and shamed out of trusting our own judgment.

As we move around in society, shaming secular systems keep shame going with their own version of original sin. If we don't come from the right race, gender, nationality, social class, or family, we're shamed for who we are by birth.

Not that white males—usually given the role of dominators—aren't shamed as well. Their shaming induction is fierce, as Paul Kivel, cofounder of The Oakland Men's Project, explains in his book *Men's Work*. A shaming campaign begins at birth to make sure boys fit the lean, mean, and hungry mold. They don't feel or cry. As adults, they must be in control at all times. They never have problems, doubts, or fears. They're the authorities. For any question, they have the answer, and for any problem, the solution. They obey the chain of command without question (that's called "courage"), and they don't let intangibles like ethics or ideals interfere with getting ahead (that's called "shrewd business").

Shame gone within: "toxic shame." The barrage of shaming messages starts "out there," but it doesn't stay out there. "Toxic shame," as John Bradshaw calls it, projects outward shaming inward. That's when control strategies get maximally efficient. We no longer need someone else to shame us. The way control-paradigm systems treat us becomes the way we treat ourselves. Their messages become the messages we replay in our heads.

To cope with the shaming, we grow thorny shells to hide our innermost lives, shameful as they must be. In family, school, religious, and work systems, our inner core takes such a shame-blasting that the only part of us we feel safe identifying with are our shells. We pretend the shells are all we are, and if we pretend long enough, we believe it.

Barbara, the woman who had the NDE life review recounted in chapter 4, describes her feeling of shame gone inward:

> My whole life I was acting because I always had the feeling that if people found out who I really was they wouldn't like me, that I was really very bad. I had walked around for thirty-one years hiding the fact that I was bad. Every time I got spanked, I felt I was bad. And the few times something good happened to me, I was aware, "Well, they don't know the real you." So up until that point in my life it was an act, an act to be good so people would know that I was a good person and if I could win everybody over, then I would finally like myself.[12]

However eager we are to communicate with our souls, the wall of shame blocks the exchange. We've listened to our souls before, and we got ridiculed. It happened, and it keeps happening: when we laugh and the control paradigm wants seriousness, when we're idealistic and the control paradigm wants cynicism, when we're curious and the control paradigm wants disbelief, when we're sensitive and the control paradigm wants callousness, or when we're honest and the control paradigm doesn't want to hear it.

So we hide our souls from shaming, until we forget we have them. As Rumi said, we're riding a horse, but somehow we don't recognize it as ours. It's right under us, but somehow we don't see it.

Yet until we do, there's no one home in us to judge whether social systems are serving us well or not. Our fifth-level change powers—change from the deep soul level—lie dormant.

Harnessing Emotions with Shame

The emotion link. Emotions are often how soul processes reopen communication. We feel something, even if we're not sure what. Perhaps emotions are quick to pick up on soul issues because they're associated with the side of the brain that's holistic. They process what's going on within the totality of who we are.

In *Far Journeys*, consciousness researcher Robert Monroe claims that all experiences, even the most intellectual pursuits, are emotion-based. Whatever we do, we have an agenda—what Buddhist scholar Herbert Guenther calls our "project-at-hand"—to which we're emotionally committed. Emotion energizes the activity, linking our inner dynamics with outward life.

This emotion component presents the truth of our inner lives. Describing the Aboriginal "Real People" of Australia, Marlo Morgan writes:

> They believe how you feel emotionally about things is what really registers. It is recorded in every cell of the body, in the core of your personality, in your mind and in your eternal Self.... Action is only the channel whereby the feeling, the intent, is allowed to be expressed and experienced.[13]

In *Heading Toward Omega*, Kenneth Ring gives another NDEer's account of his life review: "What occurred was every emotion I have ever felt in my life.... And my eyes were showing me the basis of how that emotion affected my life."[14]

Blocking the link. Given the power of emotions, it's no wonder that control-paradigm systems work hard to harness them, using the shame emotion to make other emotions controllable. For example, when we're shamed for being idealistic, sentimental, depressed, serious, soft-hearted, silly, concerned about justice, optimistic, pessimistic, exuberant, or (heaven forbid) humanitarian, we feel crushed—ashamed about what's most alive in us.

The effect? For fear of being shamed, we narrow the range of emotions we allow ourselves to experience. Our defensive filters rev up and block whatever emotions call shame down on our heads. From our full emotional spectrum, only a small band gets expressed.

Shamed into social order. Armed with shaming strategies, family heads, employers, political and labor leaders, as well as religious and academic authorities don't have to do much to make us toe the line. A few words, a look, a tone of voice, and we're shamed into compliance. We meet system needs first, instead of attending to our own inward evolution.

In some New York investment banks, for example, the division between senior and junior partners is marked by shaming practices—or so we were told by a friend who ventured into one of the more elite institutions. Junior partners are expected to carry senior partners' briefcases and perform demeaning tasks as part of their initiation into the firm. Like induction into fraternities, this high-brow shaming puts the emotional energies of new partners under the control of "the firm."

Every four years we witness the control-by-shaming process in presidential elections. Quite apart from issues, abilities, and voting records, shame is what really forces candidates out of races. Their lives are searched—though not all lives equally—for some past misstep to cut short their campaigns.

Up and down the political hierarchy, people are shamed into "party unity." As election day approaches, we're expected to accept a party's platform whether we agree with it or not: "My party right or wrong." All the emotion that goes into democratic self-government gets funneled into two narrow channels—channels that shame out of the process the diverse electorate they claim to represent.

Emotion is unpredictable. Emotion is feared by control-paradigm systems because it's unpredictable—an unknown quantity. As long as we're linked to our souls through our emotions, there's a chance that we'll value our souls over control-paradigm systems, challenge authorities, and act from our link to what's alive and soul-sensitive in us. In *For Your Own Good*, Alice Miller shows how control-paradigm family, school, corporate, religious, and political systems make sure this doesn't happen.

PERSONAL AND SYSTEM DEFECTS OF CHARACTER

Styles of hiding shame. What do we do with the shame wall inside? We're programmed to hide it, even from ourselves. The character styles for hiding toxic shame become, as AA's Sixth Step puts it, our "defects of character." Shamed to our limit, we relieve ourselves by passing it on.

In *Healing the Shame That Binds You*, John Bradshaw lists character styles that attempt to offset shame—e.g., becoming perfectionists, striving for power and control, raging, behaving arrogantly, envying, having contempt for those "beneath us," being judgmental, criticizing and blaming, moralizing, meddling, lecturing, patronizing, dominating, being machine-efficient, care-taking, and people-pleasing. Each style for "passing the hot potato," as he puts it, can take many forms. Envy, for example, can be expressed as greed, admiration, disparagement, or self-assertion.[15]

The shamed become the shamers. When we channel shame outwardly, we don't feel it so intensely within. The styles take our minds off shame feelings. Most do this by giving us a "one up, one down" approach to relationships. We climb our way up from shame by shaming others down. The toxically shamed become the habitual shamers.

In 1989, Barbara Bush told what she considered an endearing story about her multimillionaire, president-elect husband. At a private dinner at the Chinese embassy, he amused himself and the Chinese ambassador by tying a dollar bill to a fishing line and waiting for a waiter to fall for the bait. When a waiter tried, George Bush jerked the dollar away and, with the ambassador, burst into laughter.[16]

Contrast Bush's attitude with that of an African tribesman featured on David Maybury-Lewis's documentary *Millennium*. When an impoverished neighbor who'd lost his herd to drought asked for help, the tribesman gave the neighbor livestock to restart his herd, on the philosophy that "A poor man shames us all." It's shameful, the tribesman believes, to be part of a system that lets some people starve while others have plenty.

Whatever relief shaming styles give, they don't remove shame. The paradigm structures that cause shame remain unchallenged, as do the shame walls inside.

Until we face shaming structures within and without, our patterns of reacting to them—our defects of character—aren't budging. Neither are systems in which millionaires watch in amusement as the rest of humanity scrambles for their next dollar.

So what do we do? How do we break through the wall, reconnect with our souls, and, like Prometheus, take their transforming fire back to our social systems?

CONNECTING WITH OUR SOULS TRANSFORMS SYSTEMS

The mystery of soul evolution. Culturally, we're in the throes of exploring these questions. So far, no one knows how to reconnect with our souls after they've been shame-blasted out of us. Psychology has theories and methods, recovery has support groups and programs, self-help has books and seminars, management has consultants, while spirituality has myriad of wisdom teachings.

We need all these and more, because what works for whom remains a mystery. Healing the rift with our inner life is a path of self-discovery, and it's unique to each person each step of the way.

It's no surprise that we're at sea on soul issues either. The industrial society of the last few centuries hasn't put its energies into the dynamics of soul evolution. Combustion engines and plastics, yes. High-tech surgery and drugs, yes. Soul-connecting, no. We're neophytes in understanding the process. One psychiatrist we know says that his years of professional education didn't equip him to help his trauma clients, especially those recovering from ritual abuse, so he turned to Native shamans, as well as alternative and cross-cultural mind-body methods, and found healing wisdom there.

One thing for sure, healing ourselves of shame is the work of a lifetime. Confronting self-shaming tapes is a start. But we must also confront the shaming that continues through the very structure of our social systems. Again, AA's insistence that recovery is a lifelong process doesn't reflect the disease of the addict as much as the disease of a world committed to a soul-shaming paradigm.

With this as a backdrop, we can sketch a process that weaves together personal, system, and paradigm transformation.

1. Recognizing control-shame for what it is. Naming shame as a control strategy is a start. We recognize what shaming is, how it works, why it's there, and when it kicks in—within or without. We're not letting control-paradigm systems off the hook by stuffing shame inside anymore. We're not sacrificing our souls for social order, because then we lose both.

Already this initial awareness of control-shame dynamics diminishes its power. Exposing shaming as a strategy of control loosens its hold on us. We ground ourselves in a clear concept of what's going on.

2. Uncovering shame strategies in our systems. The next challenge is to get specific: to trace shame patterns to social systems and to the paradigm generating them. We uncover the structures that call for shaming and perpetuate them.

What social structures shame us? That's not hard. Racism and sexism, for example, are shaming plain and simple. One group asserts one-upsmanship to cover self-shame. Class distinctions perform the same function. They're institutionalized one-up, one-downing to control who steps up to the money pot and who doesn't. Pulling rank in hierarchies of power and authority keeps us shamed into subordinate roles. The very structure of top-down hierarchies sends a shaming message.

Academic degrees fall in the same category. We forget 80 to 90 percent of what we learn in school. When we go for advanced degrees, we're forced into such specialization that we're unprepared for real-life careers. If such training were truly valuable to society, it would be universally available and we'd be paid to go to school. As it is, degrees—and where we get them—are used to create an elite by shaming the majority out of influential, high-paying positions.

How we treat the environment and nonhuman forms of life is every bit as rooted in control-shame. Whereas ancient cultures experienced all life-forms as diverse but equal partners in a sacred community, today we regard ourselves as the pinnacle of evolution. This one-up status gives us license to destroy life without compunction. We can even drive species to extinction for food, sport, or fashion—or by destroying their habitat.

3. Uncovering control-shame's workings in us. These structures won't stop, though, until we address the shaming going on inside us. We're part of our systems, and we keep them going. Society's "defects of character" won't yield as long as we keep feeding them with shame-packaged energies.

The worse society gets, in fact, the more we're pushed to confront our own shame issues. Here's where our own recovery work comes in, and, given the culture, everyone has some to do. We explore our inner history and dynamics: What experiences trigger toxic shame, and where did the pattern start? How were we shamed and why? What habits have we developed to hide self-shame? What emotions, for instance, have we not allowed ourselves to express?

Exploring our personal shaming is where therapy and recovery programs are invaluable. Thanks to the literature widely available, we can also explore our shame legacy using bibliotherapy as a guide. Working with the recovery programs outlined in books and booklets, we pursue our own healing path. Learning about others' experiences through the literature wakes us up to what's going on and offers insights about what we can do to move with the transformation we're experiencing.

Whatever route we choose, the point is to liberate ourselves from patterns that began with control-paradigm abuse but that we've taken on as our own. One of Rumi's quatrains captures the experience:

> A night full of talking that hurts,
> my worst held-back secrets: Everything
> has to do with loving and not loving.
> This night will pass.
> Then we have work to do.[17]

4. Confronting control-paradigm restrictions. Facing our personal legacies of toxic shame moves us closer to reconnecting with our souls. But we have to confront external restrictions that would throw us back behind shame walls as soon as we step into society. Unless we look at how systems restrict us, we release an ocean of soul energies but get discouraged when they don't flow in the socially approved channels. We'd give up on our souls all over again, believing that following them just won't work.

To present the truth of who we are, we need a life as big as our souls, and neither the control paradigm nor the social, economic, educational, religious, or political systems spawned from it are up to the challenge. We each have to create new niches for ourselves, new systems, new relationships, and, above all, new models. Doing this isn't easy. If we keep measuring ourselves by the old restrictions, we'll think we're failing, when really we're on the cutting edge of cultural change.

What restrictions are we talking about? We're allowed to accept who we are, for instance, if we meet certain outward criteria, such as looking good, making money, marrying the right person, having children, landing the job, achieving the reputation, having the prestigous profession, receiving the largest pension—the usual stuff.

Without connectedness to our souls, though, such successes are empty.

Either we work harder to get affirmation from external sources—we become insatiable about getting approval—or we start looking within.

Yet looking within has its own control-paradigm restrictions. We're allowed to accept ourselves only if we're in the right frame of mind or good according to some notion of how a good person behaves. For instance, if we're angry or jealous—if we feel sad, hassled, frustrated, uncertain, or depressed, or if we have sexual feelings—we're not acceptable. If we're not sufficiently blissful, centered, serene, recovering, or otherwise enlightened, we're back in the shame-based soup.

Identifying restrictions on self-acceptance, we're ready to challenge them.

5. Rebelling against shaming restrictions. Psychoanalyst and social theorist Erik Erikson believes our real identity can't emerge without intense questioning, crisis, and rebellion. To break free of shaming images and restrictions, we need a full-blooded rage about how control-paradigm structures have shamed us, and then we need to challenge the shaming messages for all we're worth.

In *Adult Children*, psychologist John Friel and recovery therapist Linda Friel explain the value of standing on our hind legs and challenging the paradigm structures all around us, most of which are riddled with shame:

> We must question our religious beliefs, the values with which we were raised, career choices that our parents may have overtly or covertly made for us, lifestyle preferences and the like. We may come back to those childhood beliefs after this period of questioning, but we won't be children when we do and we won't be doing it "just because someone told us it was the right way to live or think."…One fact remains: if we don't go through this crisis period of rebellion and questioning, we won't get through the Identity Stage.[18]

In other words, we have to rebel against the notion that outside influences have the last word on who we are—that they have a right to shame us. If some person or system shames us, we have a right to reject the shaming. Their verdict is not ours. We can challenge it and reclaim our right to embrace our own identity.

6. Connecting with our truth. Rebelling against shaming awakens us to our soul's journey. Our soul-self is never really blocked; it just grows subversive about how it makes its presence known. Every emotion is there for a reason that relates to soul issues. Every action is meaningful to the inner quest, even addictive, violent, greedy actions. They're ways of exposing that something is very wrong with the paradigm structures we're living. Either we change the structures—and the paradigm behind them—or this is what we become.

Heeding our souls' messages means accepting the wisdom that we are in our bones. The world's greatest treasure is the treasure we are. Robert Browning's famous poem, "Paracelsus" affirms the strategy of listening to our inner truth and celebrating it:

> Truth is within ourselves; it takes no rise
> From outward things, what'er you may believe.
> There is an inmost centre in us all,
> Where truth abides in fulness;... and to know
> Rather consists in opening out a way
> Whence the imprisoned splendour may escape,
> Than in effecting entry for a light
> Supposed to be without.

"Opening out a way" for our souls to emerge is the issue. Having made the invisible shame wall visible, Tarthang Tulku says that all we have to do is listen to our hearts and minds to liberate what's true in us: "We lead superficial lives only because we choose to ignore the messages from our hearts and minds.... There is no secret to discovering the true quality of our inner nature, for our minds and senses are eager to tell us all about ourselves. All we need to do is listen."[19]

That's what Barbara did after her NDE:

> When I came back from that [NDE],... I had a real feeling of understanding that I was a good person and all I had to do was be me.... Without sounding corny, that was the most important incident of my thirty-nine years and the rebirth of who I am now.... That experience gave me all the tools to struggle through these seven years and get to the feeling now that I'm always here. You know, it took me a long time to recapture that person because everybody around me, I felt, was restricting me from becoming that person because of who they were. So the experience itself gave me the spirituality that I need and the tools that I needed to be who I am now.[20]

7. Taking the transforming fire back to paradigm systems. From soul-connectedness, we take our truth back to our systems and let transformation work its alchemical, lead-to-gold purpose. Not that this is easy. Transitions seldom are.

And not that any of us knows what soul-honoring paradigms or soul-centered social systems look like. Though we have hints from the history of spiritual ideas, we don't know what forms they may take now. Every paradigm that historically facilitated a deeper soul-knowing was adapted to a specific culture, mind-set, and stage of evolution. What was right for the Buddha to teach in India 2,500 years ago needs rethinking now—as the Buddha was the first to acknowledge.

We do, though, have a rough idea of what to avoid—what kind of paradigm zaps us numb. And we have a rough idea of what we want: we're bringing our souls back to the center where they belong. Soul-connected, we find the creativity, imagination, and courage that a personal, cultural, and global paradigm shift require.

Notes to Chapter 6

1. Coleman Barks and John Moyne, trans., *This Longing: Poetry, Teaching Stories, and Letters of Rumi* (Putney, VT: Threshold Books, 1988), 71. Also in Coleman Barks with John Moyne, A. J. Arberry, and Reynold Nicholson, trans., *The Essential Rumi* (San Francisco: HarperSanFrancisco, 1995), 255–56.
2. Peter Senge, *The Fifth Discipline* (New York: Doubleday/Currency, 1990), 52–54.
3. Wing-Tsit Chan, trans., *Instructions for Practical Living and Other Neo-Confucian Writings by Wang Yang-ming* (New York: Columbia University Press, 1962), 81.
4. Jeremy Brecher, "Global Village or Global Pillage," *The Nation*, 6 December 1993, 685.
5. Qtd. in William Greider, *Who Will Tell the People?* (New York: Simon and Schuster, 1992), 352.
6. David Korten, *When Corporations Rule the World* (West Hartford, CT: Kumarian Press, and San Francisco: Berrett-Koehler, 1995), 242–43.
7. Korten, *When Corporations Rule the World*, 243.
8. Samuel Noah Kramer, *History Begins at Sumer* (Philadelphia: University of Pennsylvania Press, 1956, 1994), 5–6.
9. Burton Mack, *Who Wrote the New Testament?* (New York: HarperCollins, 1995), 20.
10. Willis Harman and John Hormann, *Creative Work* (Indianapolis: Knowledge Systems, 1990), 67.
11. Korten, *When Corporations Rule the World*, 243.
12. Kenneth Ring, *Heading Toward Omega* (New York: William Morrow, 1984), 107.
13. Marlo Morgan, *Mutant Message Downunder* (New York: HarperCollins, 1991, 1994), 94.
14. Ring, *Heading Toward Omega*, 71.
15. John Bradshaw, *Healing the Shame That Binds You* (Deerfield Beach, FL: Health Communications, 1988), 88–95.
16. *Time*, 23 January 1989, 24. This incident was also reported in Donnie Radcliffe, *Simply Barbara Bush: A Portrait of America's Candid First Lady* (New York: Warner Books, 1990), 197.
17. John Moyne and Coleman Barks, trans., *Unseen Rain: Quatrains of Rumi* (Putney, VT: Threshold Books, 1986), 18. Also in Coleman Barks with John Moyne, A. J. Arberry, and Reynold Nicholson, trans., *The Essential Rumi* (San Francisco: HarperSanFrancisco, 1995), 50.
18. John Friel and Linda Friel, *Adult Children: The Secrets of Dysfunctional Families* (Deerfield Beach, FL: Health Communications, 1988), 129.
19. Tarthang Tulku, *Skillful Means: Gentle Ways to Successful Work* (Berkeley, CA: Dharma Publishing, 1978), 80.
20. Ring, *Heading Toward Omega*, 107–8.

CHAPTER 7

Dialoguing Our Way to Social Order

Loving the truth
Seventh of the Twelve Cycles of Truth,
the Iroquois Peace Confederacy Tradition

There is a way of breathing
that's a shame and suffocation.

And there's another way of expiring,
a love-breath that lets you open infinitely.

Rumi[1]

THE ART OF DIALOGUE

As a response to the control-paradigm worlds around us, dialogue sends a liberating message. It communicates openness, trust, mutual respect, as well as adventure and shared exploration. Dialogue is "a love-breath that lets you open infinitely." It's a response that invites a paradigm shift in precisely the direction we want to make it, namely, toward soul-honoring interaction.

How does dialogue do this? We talk to each other all the time, but we don't always feel "opened infinitely" as a result.

Discussion vs. dialogue. David Bohm, whose ideas on dialogue follow the Socratic tradition, believed that dialogue is an art that's distinct from ordinary discussion.

Discussion works like Ping-Pong; we toss opinions back and forth to see whose views will win out. It's a competitive game of scoring points: one-up, one-down, argument and rebuttal.

Going back and forth to see which position wins is useful when we need to take action, since by the end one view prevails. We make a decision and go that way.

But discussion has limits. Our options are restricted to the starting positions. Discussion isn't designed to increase but to narrow options. We put them on the table and start knocking them down. Discussion operates on a win-lose model: whose position triumphs?

As useful as discussion is in the thick of action—"Do we turn right or left at the next light?"—it isn't equal to the challenge of exploring a multidimensioned, multioptioned universe. Issues of soul evolution and system transformation have many layers to them. They're not one-dimensional. The value of one perspective doesn't diminish or exclude the value of another.

Neither is there one solution to the challenges we face. The way forward holds many possibilities—no one of which is *the right one*. Each path has many consequences on various levels. Each holds possibilities for learning and growth. The discussion model isn't equipped to explore these possibilities; it's designed to eliminate as many options as possible so only one view remains. As a paradigm-evolving response, discussion is inadequate—and that's on a good day.

Dialogue has a different dynamic. Its purpose isn't to establish a victor or to prove a position but to "love the truth" and pursue it. We let truth be what it is, whether it fits our paradigm agendas or not. And we let our pursuit of the truth spill over our current thought-boundaries, drawing us into areas we haven't considered before. How does a dialogue response do this?

David Bohm mapped out three criteria, three rules of dialogue. These rules can't be imposed from without or faked. If inwardly we're stuck in a one-up, one-down mode—a control-paradigm response—we can try to dialogue all we want; it won't happen. The exercise lapses into Ping-Pong.

Real dialogue grows with soul-connectedness. In paradigm terms, a dialogue response grows from soul-connected assumptions and strategies. The more we're grounded in our soul's worth, the less we try to establish our views in the one-up position. We simply love the truth and want to explore it in the same spirit with others. "The purpose of a dialogue is to go beyond any one individual's understanding. [Bohm states,] 'We are not trying to win in a dialogue. We all win if we are doing it right.'"[2]

Bohm's three criteria facilitate a dialogue response.*

1. Suspending our paradigms. First, since truth is greater than our concepts about it, loving the truth means loving truth more than any one perspective. Even the best paradigm falls short of reality, which is infinite and surpasses our most advanced ideas. We can't both respond in dialogue and be dogmatic about our paradigm. In dialogue, we stay open to exploring our ideas and perceptions from the ground up. Because reality is infinite, there's always room for evolution.

The first criterion for dialogue, then, is that participants must "suspend their assumptions"—"literally to hold them 'as if suspended before us.'"[3] This takes work, because, as we've seen, most paradigm assumptions lie in the shadows where we don't notice them. The more we're aware of what we're assuming and how it affects us, the more we're able to do dialogue, and the more we respond in a way that opens us to a paradigm shift.

Dialogue begins as we put our models on the table for consideration. We don't necessarily have to give them up, since they may be serving us well. A dialogue response doesn't trash what we've assumed so far. It simply keeps our options open, so we can discover the reality lying beyond them. As T. H. Huxley said, "Sit down before fact like a little child, and be prepared to give up every preconceived notion, follow humbly wherever and to whatever abyss Nature leads, or you shall learn nothing."[4]

2. Honoring each other as equals. Whereas the first criterion opens the windows, the second lets the breeze blow through. Dialogue flows when we put up the fewest barriers to it.

This second of Bohm's criteria tackles the control paradigm's response directly, since the most common—and most internalized—barrier to true dialogue is the one-up, one-down model. Whether it's with family, co-workers, friends, or strangers, we're trained to size up where we stand in the pecking order: who's got the superior position?

---

*One of the most concise and easy-to-find explanations of David Bohm's ideas on dialogue can be found in Peter Senge's *The Fifth Discipline: The Art and Practice of the Learning Organization*, chap. 10: "Team Learning," 238–49, from which our quotes come.

Yet knee-jerk ranking responses put barriers between us. We can't have an open dialogue with people who have power over us or whom we perceive as superiors. Neither are we likely to get a meaningful dialogue going if we've got the upper hand. In hierarchies, we're not free to say what we think or feel. When we're one-down on the ladder, we're intimidated; when we're one-up, we're afraid of losing our authority and superior status. Either way, hierarchy concerns override. "Hierarchy is antithetical to dialogue, and it is difficult to escape hierarchy in organizations," Bohm says. "Can those in authority really 'level' with those in subordinate positions?"[5] Can subordinates afford to, either?

But consider the cost: truth isn't heard. "Superiors" don't get the honest feedback they need to make wise decisions, while "inferiors" get frustrated by having their concerns, needs, knowledge, and perceptions ignored. When loving the truth isn't allowed for the sake of preserving the hierarchy, we lose—big time.

Consider the *Challenger* disaster of January 28, 1986. Although many factors went into it, one of the major reasons cited by the Rogers commission investigating the accident was the unwillingness of upper managers to listen to the concerns of the engineers who felt the shuttle program was being rushed and the time being allowed for testing was insufficient. Engineers had been concerned about the possible failure of the seals in the shuttle's solid rocket boosters for two years preceding the accident, reaffirming those concerns even on the night before the launch. Those in charge didn't want to hear feedback that didn't fit their agenda and used their superior status to block it. "In June the Rogers commission released its report on the accident, and one of its strongest recommendations was to tighten the communications gap between shuttle managers and working engineers."[6]

To have dialogue, participants must treat each other as equal partners in the pursuit of truth. As Socrates put it, we work as a team in midwiving the truth that lies hidden in us and in the universe. Responding as colleagues, we support each other and create a space that's safe for exploring the truth— where loving the truth is allowed.

Naturally, the path of evolving awareness raises differences. Responding to each other as equal partners doesn't mean we all must think alike. In fact, without differences, we wouldn't have much to dialogue about. Differences enrich the process. Instead of using differences to divide us, dialogue uses them to expand the possibilities we're able to consider.

Exploring currents of collective thought. Given our socially stratified upbringing, though, this second criterion is often more difficult than the first. A different image of what's going on in dialogue—different from the verbal contest burned on our psyches—may help.

Bohm offers the image of dialogue as a stream and the participants as the banks that hold the water as it passes along. In dialogue, we open ourselves to wider currents of consciousness. Bohm believed all thought is collective at its root. When we do dialogue, we explore the common thought-base, the collective consciousness field. The field itself doesn't have barriers or divisions—it's not parcelled up into egos, for instance—but moves, as physicist Bohm would say, like an electron sea. We each participate in this field and use different channels—paradigm channels—to express this consciousness in our own ways.

Dialogue helps us observe the collective nature of consciousness. It gives us a chance to explore how our thoughts reflect wider paradigm patterns: "You feel that way too? I thought it was just me!" Dialogue carries us beyond the sense of being stuck inside our thoughts or emotions and opens us to their source.

"In dialogue, Bohm contends, a group accesses a larger 'pool of common meaning,' which cannot be accessed individually.... Individuals gain insights that simply could not be achieved individually. 'A new kind of mind begins to come into being which is based on the development of a common meaning.... People are no longer primarily in opposition,... rather they are participating in the pool of common meaning, which is capable of constant development and change.'"[7]

Defending one paradigm or another isn't the focus in dialogue. Broadening our awareness is. The jockeying that goes on in hierarchies through win-lose discussions becomes irrelevant.

3. A genuine spirit of inquiry. Freeing ourselves from internalized ranking, though, is easier said than done. That's why dialogue needs a third criterion: we need to protect the dialogue atmosphere from our own histories of being shamed.

One way to do this is through a facilitator who "holds the context" of dialogue and keeps the space safe for exploration and risk taking. Because dialogue requires that we reveal our deepest and most unofficial thoughts, it makes us vulnerable. And because power-over wounds and habits linger, we need someone to protect the safe space that dialogue requires. One put-down can abort the process. Facilitators keep shaming, one-upsmanship, and official-think at bay. They support the shift from discussion to dialogue by affirming differences and not letting participants become polarized in win-lose contests.

Most of the times when we want to dialogue with friends, family, or co-workers, though, a trained facilitator isn't handy. It's up to us to create a dialogue atmosphere and keep it. That's once again where loving the truth comes in. A genuine spirit of inquiry doesn't keep score or harbor hidden agendas. Rather, it invites a leaderless exchange of ideas that carries us to a deeper awareness—one that we as separate individuals likely wouldn't have explored on our own.

With a genuine spirit of inquiry, we don't care who said what or which direction the dialogue takes. We're not responding through dialogue in order to score points or to come out looking good. We're not out to nail others or railroad our position through either. We're all on the same side in dialogue, pursuing a common quest for understanding.

Advocacy and inquiry balanced. One way of responding that supports a dialogue atmosphere balances advocacy and inquiry.[8] Advocacy presents a position, while inquiry explores it. The more we each do both, the more our responses stay fluid, true to a dialogue context.

When we advocate a paradigm perspective, for instance, we also open our thought processes to inquiry. We explain how we arrived at an assumption, strategy, response, or goal and why, but we also keep the door open to rethinking our positions from the ground up. We reflect on our own paradigm and invite others to do the same. That way, we stay in process and don't get stuck defending one position.

When others present a paradigm perspective, we not only inquire into their processes but also state our assumptions about what they're saying and acknowledge them as assumptions on our part: "What I'm hearing you say is…" Our assumptions may be preventing us from grasping what others truly mean. The real message often lies behind the words and can be the very opposite of what's spoken.

Breathing that opens us. Together, Bohm's three criteria establish dialogue as a way of learning together, rethinking the collective thought-base, and evolving our paradigms for experiencing it. Responding through dialogue supports paradigm evolution, because it connects us with a universe of infinite possibilities. Our current paradigm positions don't turn into "a way of breathing that's a shame and suffocation." Rather, dialogue keeps us flexible and in process—a way of breathing "that lets you open infinitely."

EXAMPLES OF DIALOGUE

Dialogue is proving to be a powerful tool in making the shift from control-paradigm responses to more healing alternatives. The focus is no longer on "who wins?" or "who has more power?" but on "how can we together solve problems in ways that respect the needs and concerns of everyone involved?"

In the Northwest, loggers on one hand and environmentalists on the other have become polarized with lawsuits flying in both directions over the use of old growth forests. But as reported in *Doing Democracy*,* some progress came just over two years ago when parties in conflict began to dialogue their way to mutually acceptable forest management:

> Slowly, very quietly, Jack Shipley, a committed environmentalist, along with Jim Neal, a long-time logger, drew diverse people together. Some, Jack says, "were arch enemies who in the past had only met across a courtroom. But, the more we talked, the more we had in common."
>
> What emerged is the Applegate Partnership—an unlikely mix of environmentalists, loggers, mill owners, federal agency personnel, and other local citizens, that has become a model of collaboration advising the Forest Service and the Bureau of Land Management.
>
> The group seems to have surprised even itself in being able to reach consensus on an experiment that permits limited cutting and may actually improve forest health. What's made possible the Partnership's success, participants tell us, is the time taken to build relationships. "Practice Trust: Them is Us," became the group's slogan.

---

*Doing Democracy (Winter 1995), the newsletter for the Center for Living Democracy, RR#1, Black Fox Road, Brattleboro, VT 05301, 1-800-254-1234. The center was co-founded by Frances Moore Lappé and her husband, Paul Martin Du Bois.

In the early days, the media was barred from meetings, so participants felt freer to get to know each other as individuals, rather than as representatives of a particular organization. At their early meetings, they introduced themselves and their families before identifying their organizations.

Partnership members have learned to go beyond stereotypes in order to really listen. And how! Once, when a contentious issue arose, an industry representative noted than an absent environmentalist was sure to have strong opinions. So she herself proceeded to describe what those views might be.[9]

A similar dialogue between environmentalists and loggers is developing in Minnesota, initiated by Don Arnosti of the Audubon Society and Eric Mayranen, executive director of the Associated Contract Loggers. Together, they have worked out a plan of forest management that would protect Minnesota's "old forests," those with trees more than 120 years old, and their plan is now going into legislation. The *Audubon Activist* reports: "Arnosti and Mayranen have been working together for more than a year to open channels of communication." As elsewhere, Minnesotan loggers and environmentalists have been severely polarized. "'But Don's plan is a start,' Mayranen says. 'We need to keep talking and evolving.' Arnosti is optimistic about recent efforts. 'It's a matter of building trust,' he says. 'This is a hard issue for both sides—but at least we're talking.'"[10]

Such successes have inspired government agencies to encourage dialogue in other regions. But they run into trouble if they try to use dialogue as a cover for the same old control-paradigm responses. For instance, "Steve Huddleston of Bend, Oregon...after nine months of meetings in his AMA [Adaptive Management Area, based on the Applegate model], quit because he believes the Forest Service is dominating the process."[11]

Try as they may, control-paradigm practitioners can't do dialogue. The control agenda comes through, and people aren't fooled. To be convincing, dialogue must be real. But for that, the paradigm must change.

Dialoguing with the unborn child. Examples of dialogue can even be found with some unexpected participants: fetuses and animals, both of whom apparently possess natural dialogue skills.

Perhaps the clearest phone line to the fetus is hypnotherapy. Contrary to Svengali images of mind control presented in the media, hypnotherapy simply facilitates access to deeper levels of awareness. When we access these deeper levels—the alpha brain state in particular—we dive below our everyday masks and have a chance to reflect on our lives from a freer, less role-bound perspective. We relax control-paradigm strictures and open the way for dialogue with the inner side of our lives.

In *Regression Therapy*, Winafred Blake Lucas reports on the use of hypnotherapy to dialogue with the "unborn soul," particularly in cases where pregnancy was unwelcome.[12] When the fetus was engaged in dialogue—i.e., (1) when assumptions about what should happen were suspended, (2) the fetus was approached as an equal partner, and (3) the exchange was conducted with a genuine spirit of inquiry as to what would be best for everyone—the fetus was presented with the emotional, economic, or personal situation of the parents and engaged in the process of deciding what to do. Through dialogue, options were explored, such as being born later to the same or different parents.

In many cases, natural, spontaneous miscarriages followed. Claire Etheridge, one of the contributors to Lucas's compilation, writes:

> The ability of the mother to communicate directly with her unborn child and the corresponding ability of that child to respond in a way that the mother can understand offer a powerful agent for the resolution of ambivalence regarding pregnancy and provide healing if the pregnancy is terminated. Dialogue with the unborn child, whether in thoughts, words, or images, allows the needs of both mother and child to be explored. Spontaneous miscarriages often follow upon such a dialogue where a decision has been reached mutually by neonate and mother that this is not an appropriate time for a child to be born.[13]

Here, dialogue offers a healing alternative to the anything-but-dialogue polarization over the abortion issue. Honoring the concerns of the Right to Life group, the dialogue response treats the fetus as a person from the moment of conception with a right to participate in the decision-making process that affects his or her life. Honoring the concerns of the Pro-Choice group, the dialogue response respects the mother's right to explore options for not having the baby. Simply ordering the fetus to abort—a control response—has no effect. But dialoguing with the fetus so that a mutual understanding develops opens options and supports a healing atmosphere, whatever decision is made or whatever action follows.

Interspecies dialogue. Another remarkable example of dialogue occurs between humans and animals. Gandhi said, "The greatness of a nation and its moral progress can be judged by the way its animals are treated."[14] By that standard, we're in trouble:

- Many animals raised for slaughter live in quarters where they can barely move and end up ingesting their own or others' urine and feces, not to mention the sawdust fed them to increase their poundage.[15]
- Companion animals (pets) are bred indiscriminately, creating millions that go homeless, many of whom end up in laboratories for unnecessary animal testing.*
- Wild animals are either hunted to extinction or go extinct because their habitats have been destroyed.

We respond to animal life these ways because we assume they lack consciousness and are dumb, expendable objects, existing only for our pleasure or needs.

Journalist J. Allen Boone championed a radically different understanding of animals in his classic book *Kinship with All Life*. He recounts how he first learned to dialogue with animals through the efforts of the famous movie dog Strongheart. Through dialogue—(1) suspending assumptions about animals and their abilities, (2) treating them as equals, and (3) joining with them in a genuine spirit of inquiry—Boone discovered from many animal species an amazing source of knowledge, sensitivity, love, and wisdom. Though Native Peoples have valued animals as wise beings and communicated with them for millennia, industrialized cultures are just now learning to appreciate the consciousness of animals.

Boone's work—combined with a growing knowledge of Native cultures—has spawned a generation of animal communicators, whose dialogue with animals produces objective results. In *Animal Talk: Interspecies Telepathic Communication*, Penelope Smith explains how to send thoughts to and

---

*See *The National Anti-Vivisection Society* (53 W. Jackson Boulevard, Suite 1552, Chicago, IL 60604); their publication *Credible Answers for a Cruelty-Free World* outlines the many alternatives to animal testing now available.

receive messages from the family cat, dog, horse, or, believe it or not, rat. (Rats, by the way, tell Smith that humans are oily, dirty, and smell bad. It'd be interesting to get their views on who carried the Black Death to whom.)

Some of the most compelling animal-communication cases come from horse racing. The first one we saw on television involved a horse who refused to run because he hadn't had the vacation he'd been promised. Another concerned a racing champion who wouldn't race because his owner had sold the love of his life, a beautiful mare. In both cases, animal communicators uncovered the roots of the problems and helped the humans and animals work out mutually acceptable solutions.

But interspecies communicators receive all sorts of requests, many similar to the case of Tip, a mixed breed dog, who'd taken to depositing his stools on the living room rug and playing with the litter for the newly acquired cats. Punishment—from yelling to pushing his face in it—failed to stop him. When Smith was called in, Tip told her that "he had observed his person 'playing' in the cat litter, scooping out the poop, and thought this was a great game." He decided to play the same way and as a bonus leave his own signature as a present for his human. "He thought she'd enjoy scooping his poop as much as the cats'. It just didn't compute when she yelled at him for it. She never yelled at the cats. Oh well, he'd ignore it and continue giving her presents, as he was sure she'd be pleased soon."*

For companion animals, such "misunderstandings"—which in this case were easily resolved once each party knew what the other had in mind—can lead to mutilation (declawing cats) or even death (many animals have been "put down" for less).

Built squarely on the rules of dialogue, animal communication is a doorway to new worlds. Contrary to nature show dogma, animals are not control-paradigm beings, rutting and fighting their way to the top. Some are, but

---

*Penelope Smith, *Animal Talk: Interspecies Telepathic Communication* (Point Reyes Station, CA: Pegasus Publications, 1982), 48–49. For more information on dialoguing with animals, see also Penelope Smith, *Animals: Our Return to Wholeness* (Point Reyes, CA: Pegasus Publications, 1993). For anecdotal accounts of animal awareness, see Bill Schul, *Animal Immortality* (New York: Ballantine Books, 1991), *Life Song: In Harmony with All Creation* (Walpole, NH: Stillpoint, 1994), and *The Psychic Power of Animals* (New York: Ballantine Books, 1977). For dialoguing with animals and plants, see Machaelle Small Wright, *Behaving As If the God in All Life Mattered* (Jeffersonton, VA: Perelandra, Ltd., 1983).

most—wild and domesticated—that Smith and other communicators dialogue with are not. Alfie Kohn documents that the widespread idea of animal competition is false and quotes zoologist Marvin Bates, "This competition, this 'struggle,' is a superficial thing, superimposed on an essential mutual dependence. The basic theme in nature is cooperation rather than competition."*

In keeping with this theme, animal communicators find that animals feel both a profound connectedness with and deep concern for the biosphere. Many have delivered "State of the World" addresses to communicators, worrying about what humans are doing to the earth and expressing a wisdom light-years ahead of what today's movers and shakers express.

DIALOGUE AND CONTROL SYSTEMS: NOT EXACTLY SOUL MATES

Dialogue's subversive nature. The same liberating, expansive power that makes dialogue a joy to experience, though, makes it subversive to control systems. Dialogue pushes limits. It searches beyond the barriers of paradigm convention. To engage in dialogue means we're not shut inside one paradigm or married to fixed social structures. Dialogue invites transformation. All bets are off.

But to those committed to perpetuating existing paradigm structures— structures that, for example, treat animals as market commodities or lab statistics in university or government grant programs—dialogue is perceived as a threat, even an act of rebellion. In the movie *Project X*, for instance, the military head-honchos were not the least interested in the discovery that Matthew Broderick's character made: that Virgil, the chimpanzee, could use sign language. Getting congressional funding for lethal radiation experiments on the chimps—unnecessary in today's world—was their sole concern.†

---

*Alfie Kohn, *No Contest* (New York: Houghton Mifflin, 1986), 22. From pp. 19 to 24, Kohn draws from well-known scientists, including Ashley Montagu and Stephen Jay Gould, to show the fallacy of animals as basically competitive. On p. 23, he quotes biologist John Wiens, who, having shown that competition is not ubiquitous among animals, decides that scientists see competition everywhere because it's in their culture. From their cultural paradigm, they read competition into nature.

†We take this film seriously as an example, because a University of Pennsylvania professor specializing in the subject of animal testing told us that the movie's scenario is accurate to what goes on.

To fixed models, dialogue is a threat. If we dialogue with opponents, fetuses, and animals, we're bound to view them differently—not as objects to be controlled but as partners. So, too, for social systems. The more we respond to our institutions with dialogue, the less they and our view of them can remain unchanged. Too many possibilities emerge for us to buy the notion that one way is the only way. Discussions may end in frustrating standoffs, but dialogues inevitably generate options.

Tricks for squelching dialogue. That's why control-paradigm systems distrust dialogue. The outcome can't be controlled. Options arise that the control-minded don't want on the table.

In the popular BBC political satire television series *Yes Minister* and *Yes Prime Minister*—a perfect send-up of the control paradigm in government—the civil servant Sir Humphrey who assisted "the Minister" ("cabinet secretary" in the American system) was skilled at every control-paradigm trick imaginable. Whenever someone called for change, for instance, he used the "three-card trick"; he offered the Minister three options only: one on the extreme right that wouldn't work, one on the extreme left that was no better, and one in the middle that Sir Humphrey wanted the Minister to choose—an option that gave the appearance of change but really kept things just as they were.

Dialogue would be Sir Humphrey's worst nightmare, because he couldn't control where dialogue goes, not if it's the genuine article. But Sir Humphrey gets around, and the three-card trick isn't the only trick Sir Humphreys use to shut down dialogue and control social change.

Factionalizing. Besides the obvious dialogue-excluder of authoritarian hierarchies, one of the most effective ways to eliminate dialogue is to create opposing factions: right/left, conservative/liberal, chauvinists/feminists, black/white, heterosexuals/homosexuals, teachers/students, management/labor, us/them. Once we're sufficiently polarized, we become so preoccupied fighting each other that we don't step back and notice the oppressive structures that turn us all into walking tinderboxes.

Instead of dialoguing to analyze the dynamics that lead to frustration, anger, polarization, and deadlock, we attribute our unhappiness to the opposing faction. Dialogue, which could unite factions in addressing the deeper issues, doesn't happen.

The loyalty block to dialogue. Factions block dialogue other ways as well. Loyalty to a faction means agreeing to assume that the other side is categorically wrong. We're not allowed to agree with opposing groups or to disagree with our own. Being unconditionally loyal is the definition of being a good party member—a good member of the family, church, union, office, profession, or gang. Exploring the reasoning behind all sides isn't welcomed. We maintain the "correct" views—politically, educationally, socially, medically, religiously, and above all, factionally.

For instance, doctors who venture too far into exploring alternative medicine, even with positive results, can find their medical licenses in danger. Until recently, the American Medical Association classed chiropractors with quacks. They still put homeopathy, acupuncture, and herbal treatments in this category, though Samuel Hahnemann, the doctor who founded homeopathy in the West 200 years ago, was so highly respected that a hospital in Philadelphia is named after him. Acupuncture—the practice of which is outlawed in some states—has been tested on millions of people for at least five thousand years, as have herbal remedies. How long have the new potent, mind-altering drugs been tested? Yet to venture outside the surgery and drugging approach that's been dominant only in the last hundred years, doctors risk official censure. Alternative medicine is not the "correct" view; it's not the "informed opinion" among medical schools, journals, and doctors.

Faced with the demand to be loyal to official narrowness, our minds shut down. What's the point of thinking if our thought processes are limited to only a few approved channels? Instead of finding new opportunities to dialogue, we discover that becoming part of social institutions means being told how to think, finding out who it's safe to talk to (if anyone) and who's monitoring our exchanges (besides surveillance cameras and hidden microphones).

Antidialogue schooling. Schools play no small role in creating new generations of no-talk foot soldiers. Not that teachers and administrators are gestapo types—most are genuinely interested in education or they'd be in jobs that pay better. But many fall into the one-way communication pattern: handing down the word.

For example, as a senior and A-student in high school—having been told by my math teacher that female students couldn't grasp calculus and then hearing much the same from my physics teacher—I decided to draw up a program for students to evaluate teachers. I presented the program to the headmaster, including my reasons based on what I'd experienced. The headmaster paused and then asked me if I'd spoken to anyone about the project. I told him I hadn't. He replied that if I did, I would be automatically expelled. Dialogue never happened.

In too many classrooms, not only is free thought not a priority, but worse the ability to explore ideas is scared out of students, replaced by an intense fear of being wrong. Irwin Hyman discovered that many students suffer symptoms not only of high stress but also of post-traumatic stress disorder (PTSD)—as many as half the students in some classes. Even those who are not the object of rebuke are traumatized by seeing others humiliated for wrong answers. Not only are they afraid they may be the ones singled out next, but also they're distressed at what's being done to their friends. Hyman calls this widespread stress pattern EIPTSD: "educator-induced post-traumatic stress disorder."[16]

The symptoms of EIPTSD include personality changes, aggressive and avoidance behaviors, withdrawal, fearful reactions, reexperiencing traumas, memory and concentration problems, sleep disorders, and nervous habits. These patterns are not conducive to dialogue—dialogue doesn't work when people are habitually afraid to talk—and the self-esteem required for dialogue is anything but nurtured in such environments. Yet through taxation, we're legally required to support this systematic muzzling of future generations. We're whole-heartedly committed to true education and would even pay more to support it. However, we don't want to fund a system that turns children into blasted-out, fear-controlled zombies.

The right of transformation. Free speech and assembly—rights acknowledged in the Bill of Rights—are essentially the right to dialogue. Dialogue isn't a frill; it's not an annoying trait worth driving out of us. The right of dialogue is nothing less than the right of transformation.

When genuine dialogue becomes a rarity, and verbal jousting the rule, we can bet that our freedom to evolve is under attack. Whether we're in a family, school, business, church, profession, government, or culture, we find the atmosphere less than conducive to living dialogue's rules: (1) to questioning the official, reigning assumptions, (2) to treating all of those involved as equals, and (3) to being guided by a genuine—open-ended and noncontrolled—spirit of inquiry. Instead, our thought options are closed.

CLOSED SYSTEMS

Closed systems: Preserving the norm. Single individuals don't create a society-wide climate where dialogue has no place. That's the control paradigm's doing. And it uses an effective device for doing it. The control paradigm designs social structures to function as closed systems.

The rules, policies, and structures of closed systems have one purpose: to exclude input—outside, noncontrollable factors—that could initiate system change. To any problem, the first response is to return things to the way they were.

Not that closed social systems are intentionally evil; they're simply designed to maintain the status quo, much as a thermostat maintains a fixed temperature in a house. Maintaining a predetermined order is their mandate, which closed systems carry out through strict rules of control. As long as new energies can be either neutralized or made to conform, things continue on as before. The lines of power are preserved, and control is assured.

Controlling the variables: us. To put it another way, closed systems work to offset variables. That's how they maintain equilibrium. In closed social systems, personal differences are the variables, and roles are the way to offset them.

Because nothing is more variable in marriages than spouses, in families than children, in schools than teachers and students, in businesses than employees, in religions than spiritual seekers, or in society than citizens, closed social systems devise countless techniques for steering us back to role-governed equilibrium, called "family harmony," "school discipline," "business as usual," "religious devotion," or "social order."

The most effective technique for doing this gets us to internalize roles and act them out without question. We meld with the roles, until we *are* the roles. The emperor Constantine was not a person; he was absolute ruler. That's why his dead body sat on the throne rotting for months. People were too afraid to come near it.[17]

Given that dialogue is all about thinking and questioning, no wonder it's not generally welcome. It undermines a powerful tool of control: a control device that reduces our unpredictable nature to predictable boxes and then persuades us that the boxes are who we are—that we're nothing without them.

The control paradigm's claim to legitimacy. The aim of closed systems isn't to shut us down, though, however much that's the effect. Closed systems may behave like the evil "Empire" in *Star Wars*, but those in charge believe that society would collapse without their order-reinforcing, power-concentrating, control-preserving responses.

That's why dictatorships often follow social upheaval; the chaos of transition is used to justify closed-system methods. The greater the chaos, the more absolute rule can be justified. Crafty dictators even welcome a little well-positioned chaos, because it validates their authority. Crack-down methods must be necessary.

CLOSED-SYSTEM MODELS DON'T WORK FOR HUMAN SOCIETIES

But as we're discovering, responding to the need for balance in closed-system ways doesn't work. And for many reasons.

1. Maintaining toxic order. First, if the system equilibrium is toxic, it still gets reinforced. Bad norms are perpetuated, since closed systems run on automatic. They don't have the power of discernment. They don't, for instance, evaluate systems in light of personal needs, human evolution, or planetary health. Their one mandate is to preserve the established order, whatever that equilibrium is.

That's why crazy-making, sick systems keep going long after we recognize that they're hurting us. The system—the family, business, church, or school—takes on a toxic life of its own. Its way of living is the one we've all internalized and come to expect. Fifty-year-old professionals can visit their eighty-year-old parents and feel the same shame they felt when they were five. Or on a cultural level, we know what exploit-and-move-on business attitudes do to the environment, but somehow we're having trouble stopping the pattern.

As long as we use a closed-system response, we keep coming back to the same patterns, even if they're killing us.

2. Putting systems above people. Second, achieving social order through closed-system methods puts systems above people—system needs over personal needs. Systems come first.

That's the message we hear in social systems, namely, preserving systems is more important than nurturing people. "You people—parents or children, teachers or students, bosses or employees, ministers or congregation—are part of us," closed social systems say, "therefore we own you. Who you are is incidental. You must perform the roles we give you in the ways we require. We won't allow you to deviate. If you changed, we'd have to change, and that we won't allow. Social order would collapse."

There are teeth in these assertions too: we conform, or we're out on our ears—tough options. For instance, an acquaintance of ours, now a well-known environmentalist, worked in the 1950s as an executive for one of the world's largest chemical companies. In 1959, feeling that the company was underhiring African Americans, he suggested policy changes to allow for the recruitment of minorities. Not only was his proposal ignored, but because he'd made it, he was refused a promotion and ordered to the company psychiatrist for "emotional instability." (The psychiatrist reported him to be one of the most stable persons in the company, but he still didn't receive the promotion.)

A more alarming example is that of Petra Kelly, German activist and Green Party cofounder who, among her other causes, championed women's rights, the environment, world peace, and freedom for Tibet. Outspoken, intelligent, energetic, and articulate even in print, she was a thorn in many control systems' sides. In autumn 1992, she and her life partner, Gert Bastian, were found dead in their Bonn home. Police quickly concluded that Bastian had shot Kelly, probably at her request, and then killed himself, though the badly decomposed bodies—the two had been dead for weeks when they were discovered—left too few clues. In fact, those closest to the couple don't believe the suicide hypothesis, and the lack of supporting facts would make a Columbo or Poirot sit up and take notice. Aware that closed systems eliminate factors that interfere with their established order, friends believe that Kelly's unrelenting opposition to oppressive social systems, which had already taken a toll on her health, finally cost her her life.[18]

Putting systems first costs all of us. People get chewed up by systems. Sacrificing ourselves for the greater good may be a laudable ideal if the greater is good. But what if it's not?

3. Control is abuse. Third, closed social systems don't work because they keep order through control: force, punishment, and other power-over methods of enforcement. But can social harmony be forced? Is top-down control the way to achieve social order?

Threats and intimidation can't be the fabric of healthy social systems. They do too much violence to our inner lives, costing us our freedom. How healthy can systems be if we're wrecks? When we're deprived of our essential powers as free, creative beings, our social systems reflect our emptiness.

If we do give in to control—children, for instance, don't have much choice—what do we get in return for submission? Not security, as we're led to believe. Being one-down in a control hierarchy isn't a secure place. As people are discovering in all vocations, jobs can disappear overnight—and not because of business loss or poor performance but because of power plays, leveraged buyouts, and worries about next-quarter profits being sufficiently impressive. While corporate profits have soared in the last few years—reflected in the soaring prices of stocks—2.5 million employees of those same profitable corporations have lost their jobs. In 1995 alone, 420,000 U.S. workers received pink slips.*

Deprived of freedom and security yet bound by control systems, we behave like caged animals. Intelligent beings don't do well in cages. While there's no record of dolphins ever attacking humans in the wild, for instance, caged dolphins have occassionally become aggressive. Before long, their immune systems deteriorate, and they die. Chickens do the same, so much so that the agribusiness mass growers cut off their beaks and pump them with antibiotics to keep them minimally alive until slaughter.[19]

Human cages—relationships, schools, jobs, or belief systems—may be less visible, but they're no less closed, and the passive/aggressive, self-destructive behavior we act out on ourselves and others indicates that we fare no better than dolphins or chickens in them.

Peter Grier, "What's Behind the New U.S. Pink-Slip Economy?" *Christian Science Monitor,* 1996, January 4, front page. As with all statistics, however, these depend on who counts what. Allan Sloan's article "The Hit Men" questions such statistics: "Lay off numbers from the Chicago outplacement firm of Challenger, Gray & Christmas, an oft-cited source, are full of holes, as the firm readily admits. They include only publicly announced cuts. I'm not sure what federal job-cut numbers actually measure." (*Newsweek,* 26 February 1996), 45.

Closed-system social order doesn't work, because control is abuse. It can't be the glue that binds us together. To lose ownership of our lives is perhaps the greatest abuse we can endure. Yet that's what our social systems require in the name of social order.

4. Reality isn't closed. A fourth reason closed systems don't bring social order is that reality isn't closed. No matter how much closed systems try to control variables and shut out change, reality won't be shut out. We can't make our social units into islands of no-change, because the greater reality—the context on which our systems depend—is dynamic. That's the Buddhist truth of impermanence: reality as we know it is ever-shifting. It sweeps through our systems and impels change whether we like it or not.

In this century, we've observed closed-system nations. Both the Soviet Union and Communist China tried to create perfectly controlled, closed societies. But it didn't work. On one hand, economic and political realities made it impossible for them to remain isolated. On the other hand, their determination to establish closed-system control exacted a terrible price from their peoples. Individuality, freedom, and creativity had to be crushed. That's the next reason closed social systems don't work.

5. Our spiritual evolution won't be put off. Human beings are every bit as dynamic as reality because we're made up of reality, and we're continually evolving in response to it. We're change processes in our bones. Asian spiritual traditions define humans as profoundly open systems, involved in constant self-transformation.[20]

Just as social systems can't ignore reality's dynamics, so too they can't ignore ours. No matter how hard closed systems try to fit us into boxes, we don't fit. The more systems negate this quality, the more we react as if we're under siege. Our reality as beings-in-process fights back, whether through conflict, addiction, social action, recovery, spiritual awakening—or some combination thereof.

Nor is this bad news. If social systems could make us into static units of conformity, what sort of societies would we create?

6. The awareness gap. A sixth reason closed systems don't work as a model for social order is that closed systems operate blind to the people in them. Social order isn't built on an awareness of what people think and feel but on ignoring human needs and imposing system demands. That's why closed systems are typically out of touch with the real thoughts, feelings, and abilities of their members: they shut the door on this information. It's not deemed relevant to maintaining order.

Because the communication is consistently one-way—from systems and their authorities to us—systems float on a churning sea of they-know-not-what. If the sea is quiet, power structures float on top, seeming to be impregnable fortresses.

But if the sea heaves with discontent—discontent created by control abuse—those same fortresses get tossed like foam. Their ineffectiveness and impracticality appear. For instance, eighteenth-century French aristocratic rule, with a few opulent and many destitute, wasn't social order but a disaster waiting to happen.

7. Too many tragedies, too little order. In the end, closed-system control doesn't work because it creates more tragedies than order. Inwardly, the void left by soul loss drives us to superficiality, apathy, greed, and addictions. Outwardly, we act from pain and unresolved traumas, not from wisdom or what serves social health or global healing.

We all know the personal tragedies. Dysfunctional patterns destroy. If we're murdered, it's likely that it's by someone we know. If we're miserable in a relationship or job but can't seem to change things, our mind-body complex can effect change through disease or accident.

But the tragedies are also collective. The general approach to health care, for instance, is intent on "killing" disease while ignoring what it takes to create health. How healthy can we be when we eat fecal-infested, poison-sprayed food, breathe noxious fumes, drink water laced with toxic chemicals, and sit all day in stress-filled offices? In *Meaning and Medicine*, for instance, physician Larry Dossey devotes a chapter to discussing the fact that most heart attacks occur around nine o'clock Monday mornings, a phenomenon so well known among doctors that it's referred to as the "Black Monday syndrome"—not a subtle message about what work life does to us.* Though we pay with our lives, these deaths are system tragedies.

---

*Larry Dossey, *Meaning and Medicine* (New York: Bantam, 1992), 62–68. Dossey here summarizes the work of Harvard Medical School's Dr. James Muller, who discovered the Black Monday syndrome in many studies and has done much to make it public.

But national ill-health is just one example of closed-system tragedies. In *A Call for Revolution: How Washington Is Strangling America—and How to Stop It*,[21] Martin Gross argues that our government is being dismantled by a closed-system elite of the monied and powerful. Thanks to them, we have taxes that destroy the middle class, a welfare program that keeps people poor, lobbyists who use vast sums of money to advance the interests of multinational corporations, and a Congress that responds to the highest bidder.* Any one of these could have inspired a citizen revolt long since; the American colonists broke with England for less.

For maintaining house temperature, yes. For creating order in human societies, no: closed systems don't work.

DIALOGUING OUR WAY TO SOCIAL BALANCE AND HARMONY

Dialogue, by contrast, is the real source of order in human societies. Exploring our ideas, intuitions, and perceptions together, we evolve social harmony based on shared understanding. Together, we investigate who we are, what's going on, and which paradigms we want to shape our social systems. Order isn't imposed from without; it grows from sharing our inner journeys. Dialogue gives us the awareness we need to make social systems support us and our evolution.

In fact, point for point, dialogue moves us beyond closed-system patterns.

1. Dialogue opens the field. Dialogue isn't interested in maintaining an established equilibrium, so it doesn't lock us in patterns that aren't working. Dialogue elicits new input precisely so that we can evolve the structures shaping our thought and lives.

---

*Gross's *A Call for Revolution* (New York: Ballantine, 1993) and his earlier book *The Government Racket: Washington Waste from A to Z* (New York: Bantam, 1992), represent a crash course in congressional ethics, good companions to such works as Barlett and Steele's *America: What Went Wrong?* to which we've referred earlier. Interestingly, so is writer Marty Kaplan's film *The Distinguished Gentleman*, starring Eddie Murphy. The week before we happened to see this film, we saw an episode of *Frontline* called "The Best Campaign Money Can Buy," a first-rate exposé of PAC money in elections, as the name suggests. Then we saw Kaplan's film and were astonished; there was the same information, fictionalized in an entertaining way.

Because dialogue invites open investigation, nothing is off-limits. No habit or pattern is sacrosanct. In fact, one of the main tasks of dialogue is to help us identify unconscious limits and sacrosanct patterns, so that we can pull them up for conscious reflection. Dialogue operates like a bloodhound on the trail of unfolding meaning, and any mental or emotional walls obstructing this process get exposed.

To this end, David Bohm saw dialogue as revealing the "incoherence in our thought"—the dust-collecting, shadowy places that need light and a brisk breeze to blow through. One of the key patterns of incoherence is when "thought stops tracking reality and 'just goes, like a program'"[22]—a good description of how we're trained to behave in closed systems.

The automatic, programmed response—e.g., the rigid role response—is exactly what dialogue questions. Rigid roles and dialogue don't mix. They're static; dialogue is fluid. They're confining; dialogue is expansive. Dialogue challenges fixed roles—mental, emotional, economic, academic, political, medical, religious, and philosophical—so we can restructure them.

2. Dialogue sorts out what's us and what's unresolved from abusive systems. Whereas closed systems put system needs before people needs, dialogue does the reverse. It goes straight to the people concerns. Right now, the main concern is that we and power-over systems are at odds.

On one hand, our souls have real issues that must be explored. When we're worked up emotionally, our souls are behind it. They want to expose our inner crises, and they'll create the circumstances necessary to get the needed attention.

On the other hand, because we've grown up in power-over systems, we have defensive masks that get in the way of soul reflection. As much as our souls want us to confront inner issues, our social experiences tell us that's a dangerous road. Social systems don't want to hear about our inner processes. They want us to fall in line.

Yet trauma feelings persist. Given our control-minded culture, we've all experienced them. Most of these traumas go unresolved, and they resurface when we least expect them.

Since the traumas originally occurred in a social context, social interactions often trigger trauma-related feelings. Before we know it, we find ourselves using marriages, jobs, or parental roles to replay wounding. Until we make the inner conflicts conscious, we act out our inner turmoil in social experiences, thereby perpetuating painful patterns.

How does dialogue help?

Dialogue takes the lead in restoring wholeness. When therapy is conducted in a nondogmatic, nonauthoritarian, facilitating way—i.e., when it follows Bohm's three rules of dialogue—it uses dialogue to trace soul pain to original traumas, and this dialogue journey catalyzes healing. Once we've put some growing time between us and traumatic experiences, our psyches need to make peace with what happened and evolve. Every time our psyches bring up old pain, that's what they're urging us to do.

Through dialogue, we explore how past experiences affect current responses. We re-experience traumatic feelings, trace them to their sources, and understand how they affect us now. How much is *us* in our responses, and how much is old stuff—our reactions to abuse—coming up to be worked out? Are our souls taking the lead, or are we repeating the very patterns that hurt us?

By putting soul-connectedness first, dialogue builds outer harmony on inner development.

3. Dialogue builds trust in our freedom to evolve. Inner development, though, requires freedom, and freedom is precisely what closed systems deny us. Closed systems suspect soul growth, because it introduces variables that Sir Humphreys can't control.

Dialogue, by contrast, encourages us to trust our inner processes. Whenever our souls assert themselves, they do it for a reason. Following their lead, we may experience uncertainty, but we'll also find ourselves on journeys of discovery we never imagined possible.

It turns out that our souls don't lead us off cliffs or into anarchy. Quite the reverse: we court trouble only when we don't pay attention to what's going on within. Only then do we get trapped inside destructive roles, and we don't know how to contain the destruction.

The more we exercise our freedom to develop, the more we find that security—personally and as a planet—lies in each of us being free to evolve. Respecting the wisdom of our souls, we rely on their guidance about what our next step should be.

4. Dialogue tracks reality. As we evolve, we open ourselves to reality. Dialogue sets our sights on reality in all its dimensions, and then we explore reality on its own mind-stretching, soul-expanding terms. In Shakespeare's view, "There are more things in heaven and earth…than are dreamt of in your philosophy."[23]

That's a fourth reason dialogue succeeds in building social harmony: it tracks reality for what it is, as best we perceive it. Dialogue explores processes exactly as we experience them, so we can discover what works and what doesn't.

For example, we use dialogue to determine whether our self-talk—"you should do this, you shouldn't have done that"—is helpful or abusive, whether punishing children, students, and employees aids creativity or degenerates into violence, or whether partisan politics clarifies issues or makes us tolerate bad policies at home and abroad (as George Washington claimed they would in his farewell address). Dialogue explores what's what and isn't shy about naming things precisely as we perceive them.

Control systems, by contrast, play fast and loose with reality. According to them, what doesn't work—power-over, soul-suppressing methods—does, and what does work—soul-honoring, truth-loving methods—doesn't.

Reality-connected social systems. For Socrates, exploring the difference between reality and what control-minded philosophies tell us about reality is what dialogue is all about. It's also what social systems need to be healthy.

When Socrates was convicted for corrupting the youth, he was allowed to suggest his own sentence. He said that for his philosophical service to Athens, he should be guaranteed an income for the rest of his life. What could be more valuable to a city-state, he argued, than to ground its social systems on the quest for truth, beauty, justice, and the good—on the search for reality?*

Following Socrates' lead by inquiring into our personal reality, we find that beyond survival realities are soul realities: real needs for self-esteem, love, respect, creative expression, meaning, fulfillment, freedom, and evolution—as well as the real need to live in a society that honors our souls. Otherwise, having survival needs met doesn't mean much.

---

*See Plato, *The Apology*, 36b-e. Our favorite translator is R. E. Allen. In vol. I of his translation, *The Dialogues of Plato* (New Haven: Yale University Press, 1984), this part of Socrates' speech falls on pp. 98–99.

Beyond personal realities are wider realities: the reality of other people, of communities and culture, of the biosphere, as well as of consciousness. All these realities must be included to create reality-based social systems.

What's not reality-based are the dysfunctional fantasies used by control systems to keep power structures in place, e.g., money equals freedom, control is security, might makes right, authority is power-over, power-over is success, winning is everything, "you are your role," worth is externally measured, and exploitation is an acceptable method.

Using dialogue to sift reality from fantasy, we make social systems responsive to what works—what's real in ourselves and in the universe.

5. Dialogue links us with our own dynamic reality. The trouble is, we're not always connected to our souls' realities. Given our how-much-you-make-is-what-you're-worth society, it's easy to get swept up in externals.

Yet that's dangerous to social systems. German recovery researcher Alice Miller asked herself how the German people could go along with Hitler. Her conclusion was that the systematic abuse of children by both child-rearing rules and school systems disconnected people from their inner dynamics and made them dependent on external authorities. Once disconnected, they were ripe for mass manipulation.

Dialogue provides a constant check on such tragedies. We explore our inner processes and thereby stay soul-connected. We love the truth that our souls reveal and let that truth take the lead.

Inner truth isn't what we're accustomed to loving, though. From a control-paradigm perspective, we appear inadequate, never quite measuring up or "making the grade," and full of blunders and missed opportunities ("If only I'd kept that Coca-Cola stock back in 1935!").

The truth of who we are is something else entirely. Transformation, self-discovery, seeking meaning and intimacy, evolving through relationships and communities, playing our role in earth changes, and using every conceivable experience to participate in these processes: that's closer to the story of our lives. Dialogue connects us with our real story—our deeper dynamics.

6. Dialogue grounds social harmony on awareness. But how does dialogue establish social order? Soul-connecting is well and good for personal health, but can it create harmony when it's multiplied by millions of people?

Consider an analogy. Our bodies are made up of millions of cells. Each cell is unique, otherwise we'd be an amorphous blob of flesh. Establishing order and harmony among an incredible diversity of cell functions is our bodies' forte. Not only do our bodies coordinate countless cells, but they do it amid change, growth, and new experiences, from dinner to a cut on the hand.

Nor is individuality among cells sacrificed in the process. Quite the opposite: whole-body order suffers when cells "forget" what their individual functions are, as in the case of cancerous cells. When cells don't know what to do with their lives, they multiply randomly without regard to the whole system—they become "corpus raiders."

How does the body create order? The key lies in a constant flow of information—a continual dialogue among cells. Brain researchers such as Candace Pert don't know where the brain ends, since the entire system passes information around in the form of neuropeptides, processes it, and responds to changing conditions. When we're frightened, the body reacts in a split second down to our nerve endings—often before our conscious minds register danger. When there's a foreign body, the immune system knows it and gets rid of it, so that in most cases, we're never even aware of the invader.[24]

Steeped in power-over models, researchers once thought the brain served as a fascist command center. Now they describe the body as an open and omni-directional information flow—the more fluid the information-exchange among cells, the healthier and more resilient the body is. It's only when communication is blocked or overloads that the body breaks down.

Constant dialogue within the body is what enables each cell to do its job effectively. Cells don't get isolated. They respond to the information around them according to their special abilities. Blood cells aren't ordered to return to the heart for re-oxygenation, nor do they do this from fear or coercion. They simply "know" what to do and when.

When social systems work well, they create order in much the same way. They build on a flow of information, so that social harmony grows from mutual awareness. We're aware of our abilities and responsibilities, both to ourselves and to our systems. We know our own needs, and we have a rough and developing idea of the needs of others, of communities, and of the planet. And we trust that awareness flows from the universe back to us as well.

Communities and cultures depend on this awareness-flow to maintain stability amid change. Change is inevitable. But this doesn't mean we have to live in chaos. Through dialogue, we adapt and even use change to develop. We respond to change by creating natural and spontaneous orders.

The deeper the shared awareness, the more social systems thrive. No input goes unvalued, neither do real needs go unmet. When the circle of awareness spots a need, it scans the social system to find ways to meet it. When it spots talents or potentials, it finds ways to nurture them. Information flows freely, without being controlled or blocked. The circle of awareness includes every living being, valuing the knowledge that each embodies.

When awareness oils the social workings, we live in effortless harmony.

This sounds impossible—not even angels could pull it off. But many traditional cultures did, building social order on mutual awareness to a remarkable degree. One glimpse into this way of life comes from Gene Weltfish's 1928–1936 study of the Pawnee, which she reported in *The Lost Universe.*

> [The Pawnee] were a well-disciplined people, maintaining public order under many trying circumstances. Yet they had none of the power mechanisms that we consider essential to a well-ordered life. No orders were ever issued. No assignments for work were ever made nor were over-all plans discussed. There was no code of rules of conduct nor punishment for infraction. There were no commandments nor moralizing proverbs. The only instigator of action was the consenting person.... Whatever social forms existed were carried within the consciousness of the people, not by others who were in a position to make demands....
>
> Time after time I tried to find a case of orders given, and there was none. Gradually I began to realize that democracy is a very personal thing which, like charity, begins at home. Basically it means not being coerced and having no need to coerce anyone else.[25]
>
> There was no prearranged schedule at all as to [who] would take the morning, [who] the evening meal. This was determined on each individual occasion by the inclinations of the principals most directly involved. From our point of view a plan would be made and the people fitted into it—from the Pawnee view, the plan emerged from the feelings of the people. This difference of approach is so basic that I feel impelled to stress it. The Pawnee individual embraced responsibility; he had no inclination to shirk it. In a sense, the rhythm of Pawnee work life was like a ballet, whereas ours is like a prison lockstep: "You must, you must, you must get to work!"[26]

> The Amerindian...preserved an understanding of the individual personality as the keystone of society.... His society is fluid and creative,... rather than inhibiting of the person.[27]

Granted, the size of cultures today demands a concerted effort to create the awareness that global harmony requires. That's where dialogue comes in. Through dialogue, we exchange insights, perspectives, and experiences. We even have all sorts of technologies—telephones, fax machines, e-mail, Internet, satellites—to help us. Until we learn the mind-to-mind communication that Australian Aborigines and other Native Peoples practice, our electronics assist global dialogue. All we need is the commitment to doing it.

When dialogue leads, social order operates not as a straitjacket—which doesn't work anyway—but instead as a consciousness-sea, with its own rhythms and dynamics, out of which new forms grow. In fact, that's the last point.

7. Dialogue keeps social systems evolving. Dialogue works because it keeps social systems up to speed with our development. We don't get locked in social patterns that may have been useful back when, as John Bradshaw puts it, a tiger was growling outside the cave door.

Dialogue does for social transformation—cultural therapy—what AA's Seventh Step does for personal transformation. In Step Seven, we "Humbly asked [God] to remove our shortcomings." We open ourselves to the power of wholeness and let it dissolve whatever breaks us into unconscious fragments. The great Sioux Holy Man, Fools Crow, sang the following song whenever he reflected on himself and sought the help of Wakan-Tanka (the Creator, God) for help and healing:

> Great Ones
> Pity me.
> Help me look honestly at myself.
> Truth is coming.
> It hurts me.
> I am glad.
> You can make me better.[28]

To put it another way, Step Seven draws us out of closed-system patterns by engaging us in a dialogue with God for the purpose of transformation.

Opening to what's greater, we can't stay locked in closed systems.

The same method works for social systems. We dialogue with our systems in the context of what's ultimately real, so that both of us—we and our systems—evolve. Through dialogue, we "access a larger 'pool of common meaning,'" so we can search our ways of being together and dissolve patterns—social shortcomings—we're ready to outgrow.

Using dialogue to create harmony in social systems, we respond to them not as structures that divide us but as opportunities for exploring our connectedness—the next chapter.

NOTES TO CHAPTER 7

1. Coleman Barks, trans., *Birdsong: Rumi* (Athens, GA: Maypop Books, 1993), 57.
2. Peter Senge, *The Fifth Discipline: The Art and Practice of the Learning Organization* (New York: Doubleday/Currency, 1990), 240.
3. Senge, *Fifth Discipline*, 243.
4. Qtd. in Michael Talbot, *The Holographic Universe* (New York: Harper Collins, 1991), 9.
5. Senge, *Fifth Discipline*, 245.
6. 1987 *Britannica Book of the Year* (Chicago: Encyclopedia Britannica, 1987), 343.
7. Senge, *Fifth Discipline*, 240–41.
8. Senge, *Fifth Discipline*, 200–1.
9. *Doing Democracy*, Winter 1995 (Brattleboro, VT: Center for Living Democracy), 1, 8.
10. *Audubon Activist*, June 1995. See also the *Timberjay*, March 7, 1994, and April 18, 1994.
11. *Doing Democracy*, 8.
12. Winafred Blake Lucas, *Regression Therapy: A Handbook for Professionals*, vol. II (Crest Park, CA: Deep Forest Press, 1993), 257–315.
13. Lucas, *Regression Therapy*, 257. See also Clara Riley, (Claire Etheridge), "Transuterine Communication in Problem Pregnancies," *The Journal of Pre- and Perinatal Psychology, Human Sciences Press*, vol. 2, Spring 1987.
14. Qtd. in *In Defense of Animals Magazine* (Spring 1995).
15. John Robbins, *Diet for a New America* (Walpole, NH: Stillpoint Publishing, 1987).
16. "The Aftermath: Educator-Induced Posttraumatic Stress Disorder," in Irwin Hyman, *Reading, Writing, and the Hickory Stick: The Appalling Story of Physical and Psychological Abuse in American Schools* (Lexington, MA: Lexington Books, 1990), 91–105.
17. John Romer, *Testament* (New York: Henry Holt & Company, 1988), 224.
18. Eric Williams, "Last from Petra Kelly," *The Progressive*, January 1993, 26–27; "Environmentalist Petra Kelly's Mysterious Death," *Newsweek*, 2 November 1992; "Petra's Life," *The Nation*, 7 December 1992, 689.
19. Peter Singer, *Animal Liberation* (New York: Avon Books, 1975), 97, 99.
20. Tu Wei Ming, *Confucian Thought: Selfhood as Creative Transformation* (Albany, NY: State University of New York Press, 1985).
21. Martin L. Gross, *A Call for Revolution: How Washington Is Strangling America—and How to Stop It* (New York: Ballantine Books, 1993).
22. Senge, *The Fifth Discipline*, 241.
23. *Hamlet*, 1.5, 1.166.
24. Talbot, *The Holographic Universe*, 112.
25. Gene Weltfish, *The Lost Universe: The Way of Life of the Pawnee* (New York: Ballantine, 1965), 6–8.
26. Weltfish, *Lost Universe*, 18–19.
27. Weltfish, *Lost Universe*, 73.
28. Thomas E. Mails, *Fools Crow: Wisdom and Power* (Tulsa, OK: Council Oaks Books, 1991), 113.

CHAPTER 8

Dialoguing with Our Connectedness

Serving the truth
Eighth of the Twelve Cycles of Truth,
the Iroquois Peace Confederacy Tradition

To the Prophet, everything is soaked in Glory.
To us, things look inert. To Him,
the hill is in motion like the stream.
He hears a subtle conversation between
the clod and the brick. We don't.

Rumi[1]

AWAKENING TO CONNECTEDNESS

Connectedness: we hear it everywhere, from environmentalists, quality control experts, and family-systems counselors to physicists, philosophers, Native Peoples, and mystics. But what does it mean? And what impact does it have on how we respond to experiences?

Sometimes connectedness means *their* toxic waste got into *our* water and made us sick; other times it means networking to find innovative ways to clean up the environment. Sometimes it means we're locked in self-destructive patterns that we've internalized from screwed-up social systems; other times it means social systems register even the slightest changes we make and alter their structures as a result. It may mean that our toes feel pain when a dentist's drill hits a nerve, but it may also mean that our bodies have amazing powers to heal themselves.

In short, connectedness means that we can do harm we never meant to do, but it also means that our capacity to create, spur changes, and help is far greater than we imagine.

Whatever it means, connectedness is a fact of the universe. On that point physicists and mystics, CEOs and Aborigines, doctors and shamans agree. Given this fact, awakening to our connectedness serves the truth. It gives us the awareness we need to respond to the truth of what's going on, whether it's our personal life's truth, the truth of social systems, or the truth of humanity in our current space-time context and stage of evolution.

Dialogue's role. Dialogue is uniquely suited to exploring connectedness, since dialogue is an act of connecting. Through dialogue, we open the thought paths between us and investigate shared consciousness fields. Before we know it, we're exploring the interwoven character of our existence, as the awareness of connectedness dissolves the hard-and-fast walls between us. Where we initially perceived oppositions and differences, we discover unexpected threads of unity.

Responding through dialogue isn't therefore just a handy technique for getting warring factions to get along, though it does that. Dialogue catalyzes a revolution in awareness.

Connectedness in action as us. Right off the bat, the structure of dialogue leads us to question the ordinary sense of being a separate entity walking around in a me-here/you-there mode. The more we explore shared patterns of consciousness, the less we regard our thoughts as stuck inside our heads. Our perceptions and reactions aren't entirely peculiar to us—"just our problem" or "simply our feelings."

For instance, as long as we keep trying to find out what's wrong with African Americans and women that they don't have the same income averages as European American men, we keep the spotlight off social systems that are racist, sexist, and patriarchal. Or, to get nitpicky about it, if we keep trying to find out what's wrong with 99 percent of the earth's population that their assets are one one-hundred-thousandth of what a handful of super-rich have claimed for themselves, we don't look at absurd inequities in the reward structures of our global village—and the exploitation and abuse of power that created those fortunes.

Connectedness doesn't buy the it's-just-their-problem dodge. Homelessness, for instance, doesn't happen because people are lazy. Home equity loans at usurious interest rates, corporate buyouts that result in layoffs, catastrophic illness bills, and insurance companies that use every loophole not to pay are just a few of the system dynamics that have a hand in it.

Seeking a paradigm of connectedness. Connectedness, in fact, summarizes all that we've been considering about social systems and their impact on us. Because of our connectedness to social systems, it's not easy to sort out what's us and what's not. What we've taken to be *our* beliefs, *our* (negative) self-images, *our* fears and traumas, *our* inadequacies, *our* failures and mistakes are really *our responses* to the social systems around us.

Not that we all respond in the same way, not that we lack choice in how we respond, and therefore not that we lack responsibility for the choices we make. Connectedness doesn't mean we become automatons. But systems are part of our choices too.

Not only are we responding to *them*, but also they've communicated to *us* in no uncertain terms how we're expected to respond and what happens to us if we don't do it their way. Systems do their best to define our response options—until we opt to respond differently.

Whoever we are and whatever systems have shaped us, we're connectedness in action. To grasp what's going on and to understand our options for responding differently, we need a paradigm that acknowledges the truth of connectedness and helps us explore it.

Seeking a paradigm of connectedness puts us on the forefront of both spiritual and scientific inquiry.

CONNECTIVITY FROM A BUDDHIST PERSPECTIVE

Connected being. As we reflect on our connectedness, we soon realize that there's no absolute line marking where we end and the world "out there" begins; the demarcation is fuzzier than our skins would have us believe. On many levels, the appearance of division dissolves entirely. This insight lies at the core of many spiritual teachings, Buddhism in particular. One of the best expressions of this understanding comes from the *Avatamsaka Sutra:*

> In the heaven of Indra there is said to be a network of pearls, so arranged that if you look at one you see all the others reflected in it, and if you move

into any part of it, you set off the sound of bells that ring through every part of the network, through every part of reality. In the same way, each person, each object in the world, is not merely itself, but involves every other person and object and, in fact, on one level is every other person and object.*

In this vein, legend has it that when someone asked the Buddha why we should be kind to everyone, he replied, "Because you are everyone."

Activist Joanna Macy cashes in the Buddhist understanding of connectedness through the Buddha's teaching on "dependent arising" or connectedness in action: how one set of conditions gives rise to another set, which gives rise to another set, and so on. In *World as Lover, World as Self*, she explores what this means:

> I used to think that I ended with my skin, that everything within the skin was me and everything outside the skin was not. But now you've read these words, and the concepts they represent are reaching your cortex, so "the process" that is me now extends as far as you.... What I am, as systems theorists have helped me see, is a "flow-through." I am a flow-through of matter, energy, and information, which is transformed in turn by my own experiences and intentions.[2]

We exist because of a matrix of connectivity. Mahayana Buddhism says we have no "own-being," no existence separate from All That Is. Our reality emerges from a ground of connectedness which we never leave. Connectivity is the warp and woof of our being, and without it we'd cease to exist.

Sufis agree. Tales of Rumi's life include many teachings on connectedness. For example: "Once Moulana [Rumi] explained that all members of the entire creation share in the existence of one another—and nothing exists singly and unattached...all are interdependent."[3]

---

*Avatamsaka Sutra, translated as "Flower Garland" or "Flower Ornament Scripture" of the Hua Yen Mahayana school of Buddhism, is longer than the Bible. Thomas Cleary has done the monumental job of translating this sutra into English (Boston: Shambhala Publications, 1993). We originally found this quote in Itzhak Bentov's *A Cosmic Book* (Rochester, VT: Destiny Books, an imprint of Inner Traditions International, 1988), xviii. Bentov, a brilliant thinker in new physics as well as the new science of consciousness, was killed in a 1979 Chicago plane crash. *A Cosmic Book* was finished and copyrighted posthumously by his wife, Mirtala.

"Empty of a separate self means full of everything." Zen Buddhist Thich Nhat Hanh uses the ecosystem to illustrate our connectedness:

> If you are a poet, you will see clearly that there is a cloud floating in this sheet of paper. Without a cloud, there will be no rain; without rain, the trees cannot grow; and without trees, we cannot make paper. The cloud is essential for the paper to exist. If the cloud is not here, the sheet of paper cannot be here either. So we can say that the cloud and the paper *inter-are*. "Interbeing" is a word that is not in the dictionary yet, but if we combine the prefix "inter-" with the verb "to be," we have a new verb, inter-be.... [The paper] cannot just be by itself. It has to inter-be with the sunshine, the cloud, the forest, the logger, the mind, and everything else. It is empty of a separate self. But, empty of a separate self means full of everything.[4]

To use a different analogy, if we don't confine our identity to our bedroom, we can feel at home all over the house or, by extension, all over the world. That's how the Pawnee were raised:

> The Pawnee child was born into a community from the beginning, and he never acquired the notion that he was closed in "within four walls." He was literally trained to feel that the world around him was his home—*kahuraru*, the universe, meaning literally the inside land, and that his house was a small model of it. The infinite cosmos was his constant source of strength and he could safely venture out alone and explore the wide world, even though years should pass before he returned.[5]

SPACE, TIME, AND CONNECTEDNESS

Connectivity from an anthropological view. But spiritual thinkers are no longer the only ones to talk about connectedness. Structural anthropologist Claude Lévi-Strauss saw connectedness as central both to his research and to his personal experience. Professionally, he started the discipline that takes a system/structural approach to understanding human society, called structural anthropology. Personally, he described himself as an intersection, a place where things happen. In his introduction to *Myth and Meaning*, he wrote:

> ...I forget what I have written practically as soon as it is finished.... I don't have the feeling that I write my books. I have the feeling that my books get

written through me and that once they have got across me I feel empty and nothing is left.

You may remember that I have written that myths get thought in man unbeknownst to him. This has been much discussed and even criticized by my English-speaking colleagues, because their feeling is that, from an empirical point of view, it is an utterly meaningless sentence. But for me it describes a lived experience, because it says exactly how I perceive my own relationship to my work. That is, my work gets thought in me unbeknown to me.

I never had, and still do not have, the perception of feeling my personal identity. I appear to myself as the place where something is going on, but there is no "I", no "me." Each of us is a kind of crossroads where things happen.[6]

We are where the universe comes together to create something new—us and our experiences. Since we never cease to be that coming-together process, some new "us" is always emerging.

Connectivity from a philosophical perspective. Philosopher G. W. Leibniz based his entire philosophy on connectedness. We're cosmic connectivity focused in an individual way. If we were to explore every connection that makes up who we are, we'd end up exploring the entire universe. In his *Discourse on Metaphysics*, he explains connectedness (using Alexander the Great as an example):

When we consider the connection of things, we can say that there are at all times in the soul of Alexander vestiges of all that has happened to him and the marks of all that will happen to him, and even traces of all that happens in the universe, although it belongs only to God to recognise them all.

Every substance is like a whole world and like a mirror of God or of all the universe, which each expresses after its own fashion, much as the same town is variously represented according to the different situations of the person who is looking at it.... One can even say that every substance bears in some sort the character of God's infinite wisdom and omnipotence, and imitates him as far as it is capable. For it expresses, albeit confusedly, all that happens in the universe, past, present or future.[7]

It's interesting to note that as a scientific culture, we went with the object-based philosophy of Isaac Newton rather than with Leibniz's philosophy of connectedness. Both men were esteemed scientists of their day, and both, apparently independently, discovered the differential calculus. Whereas Newton developed a science based on the forces surrounding objects, Leibniz developed ideas that laid the foundation for cybernetics and computers. Interestingly, he also studied Chinese philosophy at a time when Christianity wasn't what you'd call open-minded. That's significant for computer technology, because the *I Ching* is based on yin and yang (a binary system) and has eight trigrams combining yin and yang (the base eight used in computers). Scientifically speaking, we'd have had just as good a reason to go with Leibniz's connectedness vision of science, but we didn't. How would our world be different now if we'd spent the last few centuries pondering our connectedness in science rather than our separateness?

Quantum interconnectedness. But truth has a way of coming out, even if it takes a few centuries. Today, the "flow-through," "inter-being," "empty-of-a-separate-self-but-full-of-everything" awareness may not be in line with Newtonian science, but it's a conclusion of quantum physics. The universe as it's now understood isn't broken up into atoms or particles but operates as one undivided whole. Though we all experience the whole process differently, we're all participating in it. Interconnected reality unfolds its patterns, and these different patterns are what we experience as our lives.

Larry Dossey, whose concept of the "nonlocal Mind" explores interconnectedness on the level of consciousness, writes:

> Until recently it would have been scientific heresy to propose...that an invisible connectivity unites all things no matter how disparate. Yet much evidence suggests that the universe must be understood in a new way, a way that defies the strictly local features of reality that have dominated physics since Newton.[8]

One experiment in quantum physics finally convinced scientists that connectedness is a reality to be reckoned with. They discovered that when an electron and a positron annihilate each other, they decay into two photons that travel in opposite directions. The weird thing is that they don't fly off randomly but follow two parallel energy patterns, which stay parallel even as they travel to opposite ends of the universe. The two photons act as if they're in constant contact with each other—as if they're "telepathic twins"—even though there's no physical connection between them. Even at the speed of light, they couldn't send messages back and forth fast enough to keep themselves so perfectly synchronized.

This isn't how a random, atomistic universe ought to behave, but it is how a connected universe might work. It's just that the implied connectedness surpasses what we've yet imagined on a physical level.

As we discussed in chapter 2, physicist David Bohm gave up trying to explain such things within the limits of space, time, and matter and suggested a deeper level of connectivity. The physical and mental worlds, he reasoned, flow from one coherent source, one universal process that encompasses everything—what Bohm called the "holomovement." As a result, they bear its stamp. What we've called "parts" are actually the whole expressed, which means all other "parts" are in some way present—a concept that makes sense of the Buddha's otherwise spacey comment that "you are everyone."

In other words, both a spiritual and a scientific view affirm that a profound connectedness makes our worlds hang together. Interconnectedness isn't tacked on to us once we're here; it's how we got here in the first place. That's not only good spirituality and physics but also good biology (Mom, Dad, and all that). As Einstein put it, the field of connections forms the thing, not vice versa. Interconnections make the universe what it is—and make us who we are.

Everyday connectedness

Connectedness in social systems. This may sound a bit heady, but there's nothing esoteric about connectedness. It's what we experience every day.

In families. Family-systems studies give ample evidence of interconnectedness. If one child is always having tantrums and the other never laughs or cries, how the family functions as a whole produces the behavior. The children can't be "fixed" as separate units—in individual therapy, for instance—since as soon as they return to the family dynamics, the same behavior surfaces. Behavior occurs for reasons, and those reasons lie in how the family is connecting—or not.

Because we grow up not in isolation but within the system dynamics of our original families, we carry these dynamics around. After a few decades of books on family systems and untold hours of therapy, support groups, and tears, we're all finally getting the hang of this.

To take a specific example, when someone marries us, it's a package deal. Our family's history, attitudes, and habits are all present with us, since we've internalized them. Who we've been in the family—the roles we've played and the ways we've been treated—shapes our self-definition, which we then act out in the marriage. With every decision we make and mood we feel, original-family dynamics persist. Only when we make a conscious effort to observe our original-family dynamics and change our relation to them do we start to expand our options beyond them.

In schools. School systems give equally powerful evidence of interconnected being. How teachers feel about students is mirrored in how students feel about themselves. When teachers are told that a so-called average class is exceptional, they treat the students as if they're top performers, and lo and behold, before long they are. But when a class of top students is described to a teacher as the slow group, the A's disappear and the students conform to the teacher's low opinion.

A direct application of teacher-student connectedness is racial and gender stereotyping, which Claude Steele, a professor of social psychology at Stanford University, has been studying. As reported in *Newsweek* magazine:

> Steele argues that when blacks (or any other group) are confronted with a stereotype about their intellectual skills before they take tests, they tend to perform according to the stereotype. Change the expectations, however, and Steele finds that blacks score as high as white students taking the same test....
>
> Blacks aren't the only group that can suffer academically because of stereotypes. Steele and his colleagues found that the scores of female students dropped when they were told that men scored higher on a math test that they were about to take. When not told about the gender differences, women scored about the same as men. Steele's graduate students even saw similar preliminary results when white men were told that Asian-Americans generally performed well on a given standardized test. The scores of the white males subsequently dropped.[9]

In businesses. Businesses manifest the same interconnectedness. The quality of a business and its products reflects the attitudes of those at the top. When Coke bottles appear inside car doors and safety features are slow to become standard, we know something about the mind-set of automakers. Products mirror the company's paradigm.

Employees mirror the company as well. The way sales and service people treat customers mirrors how upper management treats employees, which in turn reflects how upper management is treated by the owners, board, or stockholders. They're all of a piece.

Down-to-earth connectedness. For better or worse, our realities are connected. Even on a molecular level, our bodies are in constant exchange. As Deepak Chopra explains, we breathe in atoms that come from each others' lungs, livers, and who knows what at an after-dinner concert. On mind levels, thinkers from physicist David Bohm and physician Larry Dossey to the Buddha and Fools Crow claim a constant exchange of thought patterns as well. On every level—social, political, economic, environmental—we're linked.

Connectedness is more than a cosmic theory. It's a down-to-earth fact of life.

ISOLATED AND ALONE

The billiard-ball worldview. Culturally, we tend not to look at ourselves this way, though. The ordinary mind-set is still in the Newtonian, mechanistic, separate-objects paradigm. This model of reality depicts the universe as a pile of fragments. Reality works like a pool game with billions of billiard balls knocking against each other. The only connectedness comes from the forces that build up around objects—gravity—which then cause the objects to push and pull at each other.

According to this paradigm, we're objects too, and we're moved around by forces as well. Some come from us (needs, instincts, and drives), while others come from society (family, social, economic, and political pressures). The challenge of life is to survive the push-and-pull: to get our needs met as much as possible by giving in to outside pressures as little as possible. The way to do this is to become a powerful enough object to exert our own force, whether it's force of will, personal charisma, position, political clout, or financial might.

"That's our problem." The bottom line, this philosophy tells us, is that we're on our own. Who we are is what we've made of ourselves. Social systems are "out there" and have no real impact on who we are. If we feel banged and bruised along the way, that's our problem, and we simply need to work harder to fit in or to use systems to our advantage. This is called taking responsibility for our lives. To consider system factors and how they've affected us is to indulge in blaming others for our own inadequacies. We should just grow up, buck up, and make a success of our lives. Others do it; why can't we?

But in spite of the rousing pep talk, adjusting to billiard-ball life is hard. Balls keep flying in every direction, which means we never know what trauma lies ahead. If everything is a matter of chance, our islands of order can be devastated at any moment by outward forces—sickness, death, or some jerk who crosses our path.

Given this philosophy, it's no wonder our worlds are filled with suffering. When our worldview says it's us or them, we act accordingly. We're abused out of our soul-sensitivities and into abusing each other. That's life, we're told.

Isolation. Isolation—the sense that we're separate, selfish interests at each other's throats—is the norm in control-paradigm systems. When we're surrounded by the abuse of power, we feel neither safe nor trusting.

For protection, we don't allow others past our shell, and they don't let us past theirs either. With roles and defenses fixed firmly between us, we don't feel linked to anyone. Two shells bumping into each other doesn't inspire feelings of connectedness. No one, not even family members, ever truly shares our world. We're "home alone."

Connection blind. Nor does the reigning paradigm help us deal with isolation. When "things" are taken as the bottom line, connectedness doesn't count. Only "countables" count. Alone in the universe, we gather things around us to feel secure.

Living in emotional isolation, we've believed we could practice process addictions without counting the cost to others. We're simply trying to make a success of our lives. If, for example, that means cutting corners on quality, safety, or employee benefits, so be it. If it means throwing our weight around to come out looking good, so much the better. If it means using drugs, alcohol, money deals, or power plays to stay on top, it's our choice.

How we cope in the billiard-ball world doesn't affect anyone else. Even if it does, that's not our problem. Connectedness isn't our concern; self-preservation is.

Isolation makes control easy. The isolation that pervades billiard-ball worlds has an interesting side benefit: it makes it easy for closed systems to maintain equilibrium. Isolated parts can be put together in the ways that social systems define. With connectedness controlled, nothing subversive has a chance to start.

Rigid roles serve this isolate-and-control function, but so do social stereotypes—"tracking" in schools; gender, race, and class distinctions; religious sectarianism; political factions; corporate hierarchies; and all the other ways cultures divide people, label them, and then contain them within the labels.

The more we stay inside our social labels, the more social systems control our energies. Our interactions become predictable and uncreative. We don't get out of line. Because we feel isolated, we don't dare.

EGO-SEPARATENESS AND MENTAL HEALTH

Lone-star mental health. Much of the psychological theory and practice that's dominated the twentieth century supports a paradigm of fragmentation by using ego-separateness as a leading criterion of adult mental health. The more we separate ourselves from a context of connectedness and establish a self-definition independent of it, the more we're judged to be psychologically mature.

The theory has even been applied to cultures. Native cultures were regarded as "primitive" and their members psychologically immature, because they didn't operate on the John Wayne, self-against-society model. Their meaning grew from their connectedness, and when they were taken away from it, they died. They couldn't survive when they were put into European culture and treated like lone anthropological specimens—hence their "psychological backwardness."

Different but connected. Not that it isn't important to stand our ground as individuals. Valuing the unique soul-expression we are, speaking our truth whether we're in agreement with others or not, and being able to distinguish what feels right to us from what's imposed externally are all vitally important abilities if we're to step back, rethink, and change our social systems.

But is a *separate* ego necessary to do this? Different doesn't have to mean unconnected. Nor does it have to mean at odds or warring. One person expresses many different qualities, for example, but unless we have a severe case of multiple personalities, we don't see these qualities as being separate or in conflict. Because they're all expressions of one person, they're all connected, even if we're in the process of figuring out how. So, too, our egos may differ—and we assume they will—but they don't need to be separate or disconnected for us to value these differences. In fact, it's through our connectedness that we experience our differences as enriching both to us and to our social systems. (Creating connectedness precisely to explore differences is what the Internet is all about.)

Connecting skills: Weakness and moral immaturity? Traditional psychoanalytic theory, though, doesn't grant comparable value to connected behavior. As Carol Gilligan explained in her landmark book *In a Different Voice*, the sensitivity to connectedness that women are culturally encouraged to develop is judged by male theorists to be morally less advanced than the traditionally masculine talent of standing alone for abstract principles. Valuing connectedness more than separateness is interpreted as moral immaturity.

In other words, the billiard-ball philosophy has defined mental health to accentuate ego separateness and to downplay our connectedness. It's healthy to focus on our differences, it tells us, and unhealthy to attune ourselves to our connectedness.

This is more than a question of masculine or feminine styles, though culturally it tends to play itself out that way. Beyond gender differences lie the questions of reality, culture, and the paradigms we use to shape our responses. Are we most alive to our multifaceted reality when we're asserting separateness and independence, or when we're mindful of our connectedness?

Codependence revisited. The problem with codependents, for instance, isn't that they're too aware of their connectedness in relationships, as is often assumed, but that they're not aware enough. They don't realize that they're connecting in mutually destructive ways. Connectedness isn't the problem; connectedness to addictive, self-destructive roles is.

Not all connectedness is equal. If connectedness to soul-denying systems robs us of happiness, the answer isn't to become islands of ego-independence but to restructure *how* we're connecting.

Because we're never not in systems, we're never truly separate. When we're faced with abusive patterns, ignoring our connectedness by claiming separateness won't help. Given our reality, it's not even possible. The road to freedom lies in redefining ourselves apart from destructive patterns but not apart from any connectedness at all. Instead of downplaying our connectedness, we need to evolve how we respond to it—what we do with it.

RESPONDING TO CONNECTEDNESS: TWO OPTIONS

We can respond to connectedness in two broad ways—that is, from two different paradigms.

We can use connectedness to create closed systems—systems that control connections *within* by minimizing them *without*. That's a closed-system response.

Or we can respond to connectedness by waking up to it, valuing "all our relations" as the Lakota phrase goes, and letting our connectedness continually transform us. That's an open-system response.

Both responses have their pluses and minuses.

THE CLOSED-SYSTEM RESPONSE

The control agenda—again. The plus to the closed-system response is that it increases our immediate, short-term control. By accentuating some connections and ignoring others, we bend connections to suit our purposes.

Focusing on some connections more than others is natural. We can't be conscious of all our connections at once. We pick and choose so we don't get overwhelmed.

But a closed-system response goes beyond this. It tries to control our connectedness by making it fit a pattern and then eliminating connections that don't conform. If a person, event, or piece of information is not controllable, we find ways to exclude, discredit, ignore, or otherwise negate our connection to it.

Good examples of this closed-system response can be found in how the robber barons established their empires in the past or how corporations operate to maximize profits today.

One of the best descriptions of robber-baron responses comes from Daniel Yergin's book *The Prize*—also the name of the PBS series based on the book—which documents the rise of the oil empires. At each step of the way, the response of John D. Rockefeller in particular was to maximize control of the growing industry. He gave competitors a choice: either come under Standard Oil or be driven out of business. Before long, he controlled the drillers, destroyed the independents, dominated the railroads, controlled the refineries, and dictated prices and terms for gas station owners. Every phase of oil production and distribution came under his hegemony. His control of the oil industry became absolute—as close to a closed system as a business can come—leading to court action against his monopoly. He got around the injunction, of course, by breaking up Standard Oil into sister companies, all with interlocking boards.

Today's business magnates use the same closed-system response: create a business system you can control by eliminating any factors that interfere with profit-taking. In *When Corporations Rule the World*, David Korten cites case after case of the devastation that this business response visits on the globe. Nike shoes, for instance, seem as innocent and all-American as companies come. But Korten writes:

> Nike, a major footwear company, refers to itself as a "network firm." This means that it employs 8,000 people in management, design, sales, and promotion and leaves production in the hands of some 75,000 workers hired by independent contractors. Most of the out-sourced production takes place in Indonesia, where a pair of Nikes that sells in the United States or Europe for $73 to $135 is produced for about $5.60 by girls and young women paid as little as fifteen cents an hour. The workers are housed in company barracks, there are no unions, overtime is often mandatory, and if there is a strike, the military may be called to break it up. The $20 million that basketball star Michael Jordan reportedly received in 1992 for promoting Nike shoes exceeded the entire annual payroll of the Indonesian factories that made them.
>
> When asked about the conditions at plants where Nikes are produced, John Woodman, Nike's general manager in Indonesia, gave a classic Stratos-dweller response. Although he knew that there had been labor problems in the six Indonesian factories making Nike shoes, he had no idea what they had been about. Furthermore, he said, "I don't know that I need to know. It's not within our scope to investigate."[10]

By staying disconnected, Woodman takes no responsibility for the fact that his company is profiting from slave-labor conditions. And we're supposed to believe that ignoring our connectedness to systems—the myth of the "self-made man"—makes us more responsible?

Paradigm-inspired responses. "I don't know that I need to know": this defensive response arises from fear. When our paradigm describes reality as competing fragments, disconnectedness becomes our reality. As long as we buy the fragmented model, we're bound to suspect connectedness.

Because philosophies of disconnectedness—atomistic materialism, separate egoism, or dog-eat-dog competition—pervade our culture, closed-system responses are everywhere. They're habitual ways of responding—responses we've come to expect as normal. Whether it's who gets the last word in an argument, who gets control of a market, or who gets away with what, defending separate entities (egos, positions, businesses, religions, or nations) is the challenge, control is the solution, and closed-system responses are the way to get it: "Look out for yourself!" "Intimidate!" "Control their options!" "Assert your authority!" "Show them who's boss!"

Exclusive personal relationships. Closed-system responses also hit home. If we feel insecure in a relationship, the closed-system response is to seal off the relationship, control each other's behavior, and keep each other in positions of neediness. That way, neither party reevaluates the pattern. This is a John D. Rockefeller response to our nearest and dearest.

Friendships and marriages often lapse into closed-system patterns, characterized by possessiveness, jealousy, secretiveness, criticizing those outside the relationship, or polarizing against outsiders. Connectedness with one person means disconnectedness from others.

In fact, the cultural concept of marriage defines it in predominately exclusivist terms. Marriage means you're supposed to love your spouse but not anyone else, and your spouse shouldn't love anyone but you. Each owns the other. Marriage becomes synonymous with exclusivity, inviting all the closed-system responses—possessiveness, suspicion, and the like—as behavior appropriate in a marriage.

The alternative, of course, is not for everyone to fool around randomly with everyone else but to define marriage differently—as an openly committed response to connectedness. Then, rather than treating spouses and partners as possessions, we may be tempted to treat them as persons.

The minus of a closed-system response. Controlling how we connect with each other is, in fact, not only the plus but also the minus of a closed-system response. We gain a measure of control, but we lose our connectedness with all that keeps us alive and evolving.

A perfectly closed system is dead. Nothing changes. Nothing new is allowed to enter, which means nothing disruptive—therefore potentially transformative—is allowed to happen. Living systems must renew themselves, and they require input from without to do it. That's precisely what closed systems don't allow.

Because closed systems shut off sources of regeneration, they run down. As Peter Senge observes, hierarchical, top-down, control-minded corporations are good at taking well-tested ideas to market, but they're not so good at pioneering new ideas. Their habitual ways of responding eliminate what's truly innovative. Hence the average lifespan of a corporation is forty years.[11]

To grow and evolve, human beings, like all living systems, need to breathe in the new. The ideal of a fixed social equilibrium has its appeal on harried days, but we'd all have to be dead to make it work. Closed systems aren't designed for the living but for inert objects, and even then they're artificial. Closed systems don't occur in nature. Larry Dossey sums it up, "living processes embody a trend *away* from equilibrium."[12]

That's the minus: closed systems are impractical for creative, intelligent, changing beings. The quest to create islands of control can't succeed. Our open and evolving nature sabotages the endeavor, no matter how much we'd like to make it work.

Intervention. Whenever we try to be artificially closed, addictions and crises intervene. Humans can't play dead for long. Either we reconnect with our souls, or we kill ourselves with obsessively self-destructive behavior.

That applies to social systems as much as it applies to us. Social sytems that sacrifice our aliveness for their equilibrium can't survive. If we don't demand system change, we soul-die inside the systems. When that happens, how alive can social systems be? How can they keep up with a universe that's constantly changing if those they depend on for new ideas—the collective "yours truly"—are disconnected from their powers to evolve?

Boundaries to the Rescue—and Beyond

When closed-system responses use connectedness to abuse us, it's time to call up the boundaries. We may not be able to change closed systems overnight, but we can find ways to stay soul-connected in spite of them.

Boundaries help us do this. When applied along a spectrum of development, boundaries don't cut us off from our connectedness; they strengthen it by not allowing connectedness to become abusive. Boundaries restrain people from using connectedness for manipulation, which is what gives connectedness a bad name. Once controlling, invasive patterns creep in, connectedness is endangered. Boundaries prevent this along the spectrum of evolution:

1. A protection. First, when our connectedness is being used to abuse us, boundaries come to the rescue. They function like a personal bill of rights: We have a right to exist, to have our needs met, and to have our personal expression of the whole respected. We have a right to be who we are—to know what we know and feel what we feel. We have a right to express our truth beyond our family, social, professional, and religious roles. We have a right to care, to feel our own and others' pain, and not to be shamed into cynicism or indifference. And those rights are just for starters.

The more invasive the system, the more we need to define and assert our boundaries. Having healthy boundaries at this point means knowing how to stop people and systems from walking all over us. How?

To start, boundaries alert us when our rights are being invaded. We stop assuming that it's okay for system authorities to treat us in disrespectful ways—like peons or underlings. We may be slow in catching on to spelling or math, behind in our mortgage payments, or yet another number on the database, but that doesn't make us less worthy of respect. A good, healthy anger tips us off that our human dignity is under siege.

Next, boundaries in the defense mode help us assert our rights, so we can be heard. For cultural dialogue, that's essential. If we don't make our boundaries known, we let those in power go along pretending we're not here, that we don't possess the power we do, or that we don't notice system-endemic abuse. Defining our boundaries and asserting them—whether it's by writing letters, blowing whistles, exchanging views on the Internet, starting alternative social projects, or political activism—we let social systems know when they've pushed us too far.

That's good for both us and social systems. It would have been easier if the peoples of eighteenth-century France, nineteenth-century Russia, or twentieth-century Attica Prison had asserted their boundaries before violent confrontation (though some things are easier said than done). Claiming our boundaries in social systems—even when social systems say we have no right to claim them—serves as an early warning system. It prevents soul pain from building into crises.

Finally, boundaries in the defense mode give us the peace of mind that we live in a safe space, one that can't be invaded by the next bully who comes along, whether it's a person or an institution. We're not at the mercy of abusive systems. We can stand our ground.

2. A matrix or womb for self-development. But boundaries aren't only defensive. Defining our boundaries engages us in inner reflection, which develops our self-definition. Boundaries serve as a matrix or womb in which self-esteem—a deep acceptance of who we are and the processes we're living—grows.

In this context, having healthy boundaries means being able to look at ourselves and appreciate what we perceive. We don't see ourselves with others' eyes, through roles, or through the lens of external standards but through an open self-awareness.

Through this boundary-defining process, we give ourselves permission to be who we are. With boundaries, we can say, "This is who I am, and I accept my own ways of participating in the whole. My boundaries mark the place where the connectedness I'm experiencing is most meaningful and compelling."

3. A window on the whole. Having centered us in who we are, boundaries give us a springboard for being creative in relationships and with society. Aware of our own patterns, we connect with others more mindfully.

As a result, we enter into a dance with society where we don't step on others' toes, and they don't step on ours. We have the inner strength and clarity needed to develop a healthy "social interest," as psychologist Alfred Adler put it. Instead of forming one-sided relationships because we feel inadequate, unworthy, or insatiable, we nurture a two-way flow based on mutual respect. Once we know how to have caring relationships without being swallowed by them, we naturally want to explore our connectedness as it extends out to the universe.

4. Boundaries no longer an issue. As we do, boundaries fade into the background; they're no longer an issue. We're more interested in attuning ourselves to our connectedness, since this awareness serves the truth of who we are. Connectedness is more true to our reality than being separate or isolated.

Letting healthy boundaries slip into the background is different from enmeshment, or sick-connecting. When family members get enmeshed, their boundaries either never were allowed to form properly or became blurred because of stress and trauma. What gets mixed up in the boundary-less soup is unfinished psyche-business: unfulfilled needs, role expectations, corked-up frustrations, grief, anger, and manipulative, self-deceived ways of dealing with all this painful stuff. Enmeshment takes off the bandages to rub two wounds together, so that their separate hurts fuse as one. Of course, nothing can heal that way.

Here, the bandage comes off because we're whole underneath. Boundaries have given us the inner space to grow into who we are. When connecting ceases to be threatening, less of our energy goes into protecting our boundaries and more goes into discovering our true connectedness and responding to the opportunities it offers. "How do differences separate us?" gives way to "how can we use our differences to evolve new and varied expressions of wholeness?"

At this point, it's not our boundaries but our connectedness that protects, nurtures, and expands us. In a connected universe, differences feed growth. We need them to learn and regenerate. When differences aren't under attack, they don't need defending, nor do we need to put others' differences down to feel the worth of our own. Quite the opposite: we embrace differences as enriching our connectedness. Who'd want to live on a planet with several billion clones of oneself?

Psychotherapist Miriam Greenspan writes about the need to move beyond boundary issues to an awareness of connectedness:

> Personally, I have always chafed at the language of boundaries. The imagery of relationships with hard borders between enclosed individuals does not make me feel safe. On the contrary, it brings up feelings of isolation, exclusion, and disconnection. Perhaps the language of boundaries has little emotional appeal for me because as a child of Holocaust survivors, born and raised for four years in a German camp for "displaced persons"

after World War II, I experienced boundaries as the borders that kept my family and thousands of other refugees from entering safer havens. For me, the imagery of interconnection, not separation, feels safe.

Boundaries do not exist in reality; we use the imagery of boundaries to help us understand the relation between self and other....

From the Buddhist point of view, the bounded ego is a profound illusion, and our true nature is, to use Thich Nhat Hanh's term, "interbeing...."

The connection model is safer than the distance model. Healing happens when someone feels seen, heard, held, and empowered, not when one is interpreted, held at a distance, and pathologized. Safe connection and healing in therapy are a matter of breaking through old boundaries—including conventional divisions between self and other, patient and Expert—and embracing a more open system of interconnectedness that rests on respectful compassion.[13]

AN OPEN RESPONSE: EMBRACING CONNECTEDNESS

How might we embrace "a more open system of interconnectedness"?

1. Open to the new. To start, we open ourselves to connectedness as it presents itself. When Native elders, for instance, see a hawk or butterfly, they honor the connection and open themselves to any message it may have for them.

Connectedness opens the window to a new world, one that exists right next to the closed-system world but which we don't allow ourselves to experience. In the new world, connectedness has its own messages that support us on our journey. As oncologist O. Carl Simonton of the Simonton Cancer Center in California writes, "I take the position that everything in the universe is trying to help us regain health and move in that direction.... When we begin to tap inner wisdom, we focus consciously on the help that is available to us everywhere we look."[14]

2. Valuing connectedness. As we listen to connectedness, we respect the messages that come through. When a connection comes into our circle of awareness, we treat it as a friend and teacher.

The closed-system temptation, of course, is to load up every connection with expectations, until the pure connectedness gets lost. We calculate how we can cash in on the connection or make it serve a fixed agenda. If we meet somebody, we wonder, "Is he or she a potential customer? Will he be Mr. Right, or she Ms. Right? Will the person make a good contact, which means we'd better at least smile at any bad jokes?"

Valuing connectedness means valuing the connectedness for its own sake and not for something external to it. Instead of figuring out how to make it serve us, we let the connection be what it is and expand our awareness. Among Native Peoples—what Riane Eisler calls "partnership" societies[15]—each individual is treated as a gift to the group. While children naturally connect to their families and communities as sources of care and wisdom, community members in turn welcome the special gifts that each child brings. Children don't exist primarily to carry on the family name or family business or to fulfill their parents' expectations of them. They exist to be who they are, on the assumption that this itself is the best gift to society.

3. Committed to our connectedness. As we value connectedness, we do what strengthens it and don't do what undermines it. We commit to keeping our connectedness healthy.

Committed to ending abuse. Minimally, we don't abuse those we're connected with—whether family members, employees, other nations, or the earth. More, we commit to ending abuse wherever we can. Control responses impose patterns that aren't natural and come at a price. Committed to healthy connecting, we recognize when control responses interject unhealthy patterns, and we don't tolerate them.

Commitment expressed through values. Next, we nurture "the good, the right, and the true" in the connectedness that's evolving among us. To paraphrase Socrates again, we become midwives to a growing awareness of how a connected world works.

Marriage can illustrate an open-system response to connectedness, namely, to creating loving relationships. There's no formula, but there are basic values of commitment. We commit to being soul-connected ourselves, so that there's someone there for our partners to connect with. Together, we commit to mutual respect, mutual growth, health, happiness, creativity, understanding, and, of course, love.

Committing to connectedness through such values doesn't make relationships static. Quite the reverse, it values connectedness as a matrix for mutual development, which is how relationships stay fun and alive.

Committed to our connectedness with social systems. We then bring the same commitment to connectedness into our social systems. We don't abuse our connectedness with systems by exploiting them for power-over ends.

We don't, for example, abuse the system for generating business capital—the stock exchange—by turning it into a casino stacked in favor of the biggest players. Instead, as many socially responsible investment companies are now doing, we look for ways to bring together venture capital and new ideas, so that businesses prosper, and everyone benefits. We don't leave creative, problem-solving energies unfunded, and we don't let financial resources accumulate in only a few places where only the few have access to them. We express our commitment to our economic connectedness by keeping our financial systems true to their original, life-supporting purpose.

Religious and governmental systems, to take other examples, fall into power-over patterns, but neither has power-over as its original purpose. Committed to keeping them healthy, we hold them accountable to their core reasons for existing. Instead of using religions to divide us, for instance, we look to them to nurture our spiritual growth—and to help us respect the spiritual paths of others.

As to governments, instead of allowing them to slip into illusions of being the masters of humanity, unaccountable to anyone but the monied elite, we demand that they return to their simple mandate of serving the common good. In this country, this means—at the very least—respecting the Bill of Rights and acting once again under the Constitution.*

Committing to our connectedness with social systems means helping systems become more effective in fulfilling their original functions.

4. Awake to expanding contexts. Because no system, no connectedness ever occurs in a vacuum, we're always dealing with factors that go beyond the relationship or system at hand. An open response to connectedness realizes this. Everything participates in patterns of connectedness that extend far beyond it.

At first glance, this makes change seem impossible. To change any system, we'd have to change the entire world, and we assume that's out of the

---

*See Yale Law School's Charles Reich, who in *Opposing the System*, pp. 39–40, 115–16, and 133–37 discusses how "the system" either ignores or flies in the face of the Bill of Rights and the Constitution. Nor is he the only one to have serious concerns.

question. But as we'll see in the next chapter, it's not that unthinkable, not if we think holistically.

For instance, if a bee wants a human to move, she may feel overwhelmed by the size of the beast and the chances of its budging. But a holistic bee isn't daunted. She doesn't try to persuade each cell of the human mass to change position; she just buzzes in the ear, and the big lug is out of there. Whole systems work that way. With incentive, they can move.

OPEN TO RESTRUCTURING

Change, in fact, is what open-system responses are good at inviting. Opening ourselves to the universe of connectedness triggers powerful transformation.

If we're not looking for transformation, that's the minus of an open-system response. We can't both be open to the universe of connectedness and keep our corner of it fixed. Opening ourselves to our connectedness opens us to change we can't always control.

But unforeseen change isn't all bad. Without it, we can't evolve. Organisms that aren't open to being taken apart can't be put back together again in new and more complex ways.

Evolution and dissipative structures. Physician Larry Dossey argues, for example, that we can't be healthy if we eliminate all possibilities of getting sick. Getting sick is how our bodies evolved white blood cells and immune systems. What we call sickness is our bodies' way of responding to challenges. When we recover, we heal into a new being that embodies a new wisdom.

Dossey writes, "It is the quality of fragility, the capacity for being 'shaken up,' that paradoxically is the key to growth. Structures that are insulated from disturbance are protected from change. They are stagnant and never evolve toward a more complex form."[16] As a result, "Health is impossible without disturbances, although we traditionally think it is impossible *with* disturbances."[17]

Nobel Prize–winning chemist Ilya Prigogine discusses this process in his theory of dissipative structures, that is, systems that jump to new levels of complexity after experiencing a shake-up. "Evolution, says dissipative structure theory, is impossible without fragility. Perturbation and susceptibility to dissolution and death are the prices to be paid for the potential for growth and complexity."[18]

By opening us to our connectedness, an open-system response makes us vulnerable to shake-ups, but with that vulnerability comes our ability to evolve. We allow ourselves to be perturbed, our cages to be rattled, and our systems to go into flux. We do this not from masochism but from an intuitive sense that that's how we evolve.

"A central concept of dissipative structures [is that] only through perturbation can the system escape to a higher order of complexity. The key to growth is fragility. While mild disturbances are damped within the system, major ones are not; they have the possibility of stimulating sudden change toward a more complex system."[19]

Dissipating abusive systems. Shaking up systems that aren't working is precisely what addictions do for us. Addictions blow the whistle on the dysfunctionality of control-paradigm systems. The harder we try to keep closed systems from falling apart, the more intense addictive behavior gets.

From the level of behavior alone, this looks as though we're either completely stupid or completely nuts. But people aren't stupid or nuts, not on their own anyway. They're coping with systems that cannot succeed, yet they're not allowed to say so, as Alan Weiss's book *Our Emperors Have No Clothes* suggests. The subtitle of his book is telling: *Incredibly stupid things corporate executives have done while reengineering, restructuring, downsizing, TQM'ing, team-building, and empowering . . . in order to cover their ifs, ands, or "buts."* Of course corporate executives do stupid things. The control paradigm doesn't allow them to identify what's really wrong. They have to be in control, and for that, they'll do anything. Control comes before sanity or good sense.

To not be stupid, we have to let go of the paradigm that's making our systems make us "incredibly stupid." Either we let control-paradigm thinking dissipate, or we resist the evolutionary process, which means things go from bad to worse—stupid to more stupid.

The harm we've done to ourselves and others was part of this process. By acting insanely, we perturbed the systems that trapped us. On some level, we were making the invisible paradigm disease visible, so that the total system—including us—was forced to learn from it.

That's the function of addiction and crises. Like any disease, they "perturb" us and make us "susceptible to dissolution and death" as "the prices to be paid for the potential for growth and complexity." We can't live in abusive systems, the disease tells us. Either we die from the disease, or we "escape to higher orders of complexity"—to healthier connectedness.

Step Eight. Unfortunately, dissolution is traumatic, and we hurt people in the process, including ourselves. The list of harms made in AA's Eighth Step—we "Made a list of all persons we had harmed, and became willing to make amends to them all"—is a list of how we've acted destructively as our way of dissipating structures that we needed to mutate beyond. We intuitively felt it was time for shaking up unhealthy patterns, both within and without, but we weren't sure what to dissipate. Under those circumstances, it's hard not to inflict harm on others, even if it's not our intention to do so. Passing around pain is one way—a hard way—that dissipation occurs.

Step Eight is an open response that embraces the process, perturbation and all. We make a list of what our responses have done to our worlds of connectedness; we document the harms incurred. By so doing, we jump to a new level of awareness. We see ourselves in the wider context of evolving our personal and shared understanding of connectedness.

That's all the disease—the perturbing element—asks us to do. The disease process helps us learn about connectedness. From the measles, our bodies learn how to build a healthy immune system. From addictions, our psyches and social systems learn how to build a humane, soul-honoring way of life.

That's the paradox. The plus of a closed-system response (control) is also its minus (no growth), while the minus of an open-system response (vulnerability to change) is also its plus (we evolve).

Dialoguing with connections

Not that open-system responses don't have challenges. We have to cope with uncertainty and the upheavals that come with change. Once again, though, being mindful of our connectedness helps. Making the shift to higher orders of complexity goes more smoothly when we feel supported.

Here's where our old friend dialogue comes in again. Dialoguing with our connectedness uncovers "the help that is available to us everywhere we look," as Dr. Simonton put it. We turn to our connectedness and talk to it.

Dialoguing with inner worlds. For instance, we're learning to dialogue with our inner child—the child we were and the magical child within us still. We can dialogue with our dreams and the characters in them. We can do a mental dialogue with friends and family members, even when we can't do this face to face. We can dialogue with our fears as well as with our aspirations.

Shamanic traditions suggest we dialogue with our power animals, guides, and teachers, while other spiritual traditions suggest we dialogue with our angels and past lives, all of which expands our connectedness to deeper dimensions.

We can also dialogue with our bodies. Years ago, I tried this one night when I couldn't get to sleep. I asked my body why she wouldn't settle down, annoyed as I was with her, and like a shot, she came right back at me, "Because I'm sick and tired of you bossing me around." (The control paradigm is actually something I know quite well.) I inquired what she'd like to do, and that's all I remember until I woke up the next morning, well rested.

Through dialogue, we can connect with our inner support network.

Dialoguing with outer worlds. But we can also expand our dialogue to include social systems, whose job it is to support us without. Social systems need to hear our voices, because they need our feedback in order to do their jobs well. They need to know where we are and what we need, and they need to know how we're experiencing their rules, roles, and structures.

Communicating our feelings, experiences, and perceptions to our systems makes them more humane—more sensitive to the beings they exist to serve. Dialoguing with social systems serves the truth of everyone involved.

That's why, for instance, a handful of schools around the country are asking students to help run them. "Some public high schools now allow their students to interview prospective faculty; others include students in judging their peers' readiness to graduate. And in at least one school, students voted on their own graduation requirements."[20] The students at Rochester's School Without Walls have had suffrage for over eight years and are well represented on the school's planning team. Communities were skeptical at first, but both graduation and college acceptance rates have become exceptionally high—and drop-out rates exceptionally low—in schools that involve students in their management and operations.

By drawing our shared systems into a dialogue with us and our lives, we make sure that the communication is two-way. We reclaim our social systems as a rewarding expression of our interbeing. Through dialogue, we provide them with the perspectives *they* need to support *our* evolution, which is why we have them in the first place. Instead of being something that damages us, our connectedness with social systems serves the truth of who we are and what we want to do with our lives together.

Awake to our connectedness, we're ready for action: living the truth.

NOTES TO CHAPTER 8

1. Coleman Barks, trans., *Delicious Laugher: Rambunctious Teaching Stories from the Mathnawi* (Athens, GA: Maypop Books, 1990), 82.
2. Joanna Macy, *World as Lover, World as Self* (Berkeley, CA: Parallax Press, 1991), 12.
3. Idries Shah, *The Hundred Tales of Wisdom* (London: The Octagon Press, 1978), 104.
4. Thich Nhat Hanh, *The Heart of Understanding: Commentaries on the Prajnaparamita Heart Sutra* (Berkeley, CA: Parallax Press, 1988), 3, 10.
5. Gene Weltfish, *The Lost Universe* (New York: Ballantine, 1965), 70–71.
6. Claude Lévi-Strauss, *Myth and Meaning* (New York: Schocken Books, 1978), 3–4.
7. Gottfried Wilhelm Leibniz, *Discourse on Metaphysics*, VIII, IX, trans. Peter Lucas and Leslie Grint (Manchester, England: The University Press, 1953), 13, 14.
8. Larry Dossey, *Recovering the Soul: A Scientific and Spiritual Search* (New York: Bantam Books, 1989), 179.
9. Connie Leslie, "You Can't High-Jump If the Bar Is Set Low," *Newsweek*, 6 November 1995, 81.
10. David C. Korten, *When Corporations Rule the World* (West Hartford, CT: Kumarian Press, and San Francisco, CA: Berrett-Koehler, 1995), 111. See also Cynthia Enloe "The Globetrotting Sneaker," *Ms.*, March/April 1995, 10–15.
11. Peter Senge, *The Fifth Discipline: The Art and Practice of the Learning Organization* (New York: Doubleday Currency, 1990), 17–26.
12. Larry Dossey, *Space, Time, and Medicine* (Boston: Shambhala Publications, 1982), 83.
13. Miriam Greenspan, "Out of Bounds," in *Common Boundary: Exploring Psychology, Spirituality, and Creativity* (July/August 1995), 53, 55, 58.
14. Richard Carlson and Benjamin Shield, eds. *Healers on Healing* (Los Angeles: Jeremy P. Tarcher, 1989), 49.
15. Riane Eisler and David Loye, *The Partnership Way* (San Francisco: HarperSanFrancisco, 1990).
16. Larry Dossey, *Space, Time, and Medicine*, 84.
17. Dossey, *Space, Time, and Medicine*, 90.
18. Dossey, *Space, Time, and Medicine*, 88.
19. Dossey, *Space, Time, and Medicine*, 87.
20. Kevin Kennedy, "When Students Help Run the Schools," American News Service, reprinted in *Doing Democracy*, Winter 1995 (Brattleboro, VT: Center for Living Democracy), 5.

CHAPTER 9

Connected Action

Living the truth
Ninth of the Twelve Cycles of Truth,
the Iroquois Peace Confederacy Tradition

Ask within, and when that Presence directs you,
whatever you do will be right, even though
externally it may seem wrong. Don't curse the oyster
for having an ugly, encrusted shell. Inside,
it's all pearl. There's no way to ever say
how we are with phenomena.

Rumi[1]

THE SUPERCONNECTEDNESS OF ACTIONS

Awake to our connectedness, we feel differently about what we do. We feel the consequences of our actions as they ripple out from us. Sometimes the feeling is full of joy and promise; other times it's packed with pain and remorse.

Near-death experiences of connectedness. Those who've had near-death experiences witness their connectedness and what they've done with it. They feel everything they ever did but from the perspective of those on the receiving end. Seldom are they left unchanged by their near-death insights into the superconnected nature of actions.

Dannion Brinkley, who in 1975 was struck by lightning so severely that the nails in his shoes melded with the nails in the floor, experienced a life review in his near-death experience, which he recounts in *Saved by the Light:*

> The Being of Light engulfed me, and as it did I began to experience my whole life, feeling and seeing everything that had ever happened to me. It was as though a dam had burst and every memory stored in my brain flowed out.[2]

But his was no blissful romp down memory lane:

> From the moment it began until it ended, I was faced with the sickening reality that I had been an unpleasant person, someone who was self-centered and mean.... As I relived [the] incident, I found myself in his body, living with the pain that I was causing.... As I reviewed my life in the bosom of the Being, I relived each one of those altercations, but with one major difference: I was the receiver...I felt the anguish and the humiliation my opponent felt.[3]

When Brinkley recovered, he was powerfully transformed by the experience and committed himself to helping others. As it happened, he had a second NDE years later due to heart failure. This time his experience of what he'd done with his connectedness was different:

> The first twenty-five years were bad, but the next fourteen were of a changed man. I saw the good that I had accomplished with my life. One after the other, events both great and small were reviewed as I stood in this cocoon of light. I watched myself volunteering at nursing homes, perform-ing even the smallest duties, like helping someone stand up or comb her hair. Several times I watched as I did jobs no one else wanted to do, like clipping toenails or changing diapers....
>
> The life review that came with this second near-death experience was wonderful. Unlike my first, which was filled with mayhem, anger, and even death, this one was a pyrotechnic display of good deeds. When people ask me what it is like to relive a good life in the embrace of the Beings of Light, I tell them it is like a great Fourth of July fireworks display, in which your life bursts before you in scenes that are spiced with the emotions and feel-ings of everyone in them.[4]

However we experience the consequences of our actions—and it's nice if we don't have to die to do it—acknowledging them gives us the feedback we need to learn, evolve, and then be creative with our connectedness. We sensitize ourselves to the interconnected universe on a daily, practical, and interpersonal level—and to ourselves as active participators in all of it.

The power of butterfly wings. If connectedness is as profound as physics, spiritual teachings, and NDEers claim it is, then no one, no action, not even any thought is insignificant. Nothing is without effect. We're all involved in weaving the fabric that holds us, and every weaving we introduce, no matter how slight it may seem, alters the tapestry.

As a result, connectedness is anything but static. Any change made anywhere alters the totality, precisely because interconnectedness is so profound. In his book *Synchronicity*, physicist F. David Peat explores how something as slight as the beating of a butterfly's wing can change tomorrow's weather:

> Edward Lorenz, a pioneer in researching the dynamics of weather, has spoken of the "butterfly effect." Since the nonlinear equations involved in describing weather are so extremely sensitive to the slightest change in initial conditions, tomorrow's weather, he suggests, may be drastically changed by something as slight, but as critical, as the beating of a butterfly's wings today.[5]

Such implications are staggering. We can't do anything without affecting everything, however imperceptible the effect may be. Because no action is without consequence, we're never alone when we act.

A beautiful pattern. Waking up to the action implications of connectedness can cut two ways. On one side, it can give us the faith, hope, and vision we need to keep going—to realize that our lives have impact beyond what we know or see. We can create something beautiful with our connectedness, and we don't have to be saints to do it either.

For instance, we've all seen Frank Capra's Christmas movie classic *It's a Wonderful Life*, and we know that small acts of kindness can have big effects. In Charles Dickens's *A Christmas Carol*, Fezziwig, the boss of young Scrooge, had that effect on Scrooge, which Scrooge valued "as if it cost a fortune." To the Ghost of Christmas Past, Scrooge said of Fezziwig:

> He has the power to render us happy or unhappy; to make our service light or burdensome; a pleasure or a toil. Say that this power lies in words and looks; in things so slight and insignificant that it is impossible to add and

count 'em up: what then? The happiness he gives is quite as great as if it cost a fortune.[6]

Fezziwig bosses live today. Robert Naegele, former chairman of Rollerblade—a company that saw its sales go from $500,000 in 1985 when Naegele came on board to $260 million in 1994—joined with his wife, Ellis, "to play Santa" to Rollerblade's 280 employees just before Christmas of 1995. Naegele, having sold his 50 percent share of the company, made a whopping profit, which he could, of course, have kept. But instead, as he wrote in Christmas cards to his employees, he'd reaped those rewards because of their hard work, and as he told his product marketing director, "This is not mine. It is a gift I had to share." Though Santa and his wife revealed no totals, estimates are that they gave away $1.5 million, averaging $160 per month of service per employee. For most employees, that came to thousands of dollars, and longtime employees found checks in the mail ranging from $10,000 to $25,000. By the way, the Naegeles paid the federal taxes on the money, so that each check would be a tax-free gift.[7]

Then there's Aaron Feuerstein, the seventy-year-old owner of Malden Mills in Methuen, Massachusetts, who kept his textile factory in New England when many competitors were closing their American plants and moving south or to Asia for "cheap labor." When the plant burned two weeks before Christmas of 1995, Feuerstein remained committed to his employees. The morning after the fire, "he gave every worker a paycheck, gave each a $275 Christmas bonus and a $20 coupon for groceries," promising them wages and benefits until the factory could be rebuilt and production could resume.

> "I don't think there's another man in the world like Aaron Feuerstein," mill worker Steve Kay said of the man who eats lunch in the company cafeteria and likes employees to call him by his first name. "I know personal examples where he's helped people buy houses. He buried my best friend's son because my friend didn't have any money. And now the fire, and instead of running off [with money from insurance], what's he do? Give us Christmas bonuses."*

"After the fire: Mill owner tells crew he won't desert them," Minneapolis *Star Tribune*, 20 December 1995. It's an amazing story, which was retold on *CBS Sunday Morning*, 14 January 1996.

We didn't hear these stories in the eighties, but we're hearing them now: Fezziwigs are making a comeback.

Or a tangled knot? But acts of selfishness, greed, power addiction—i.e., unresolved traumas surfacing as everyday acting-out—can have big effects too. The defensive shell called "looking out for number one" can escalate to epidemic proportions.

Even when we're simply minding our own business, we can do harm we never intended. Connectedness won't stop and won't go away. We can't turn it off when we're having a bad day or feeling unusually thorny.

That's the other side of waking up to the super-connectedness of actions: it can make us want to hide under the covers. What if we make a mess with our connectedness? What if we're making a mess and don't realize it? What if we realize the mess we're making and still don't change?

Case in point, we're making an awful mess of the environment—one that's life-threatening to every species including ours. On his television programs, Jacques Cousteau worries out loud that, unless we do something radical to change our overfishing and ocean dumping, the earth's oceans will die. As Dr. Sylvia Earle documents in her book *Sea Change*, the entire chain of ocean life, from amoebas to whales, is in danger.

Yet even when we acknowledge what we're doing to our ecological connectedness, we're slow to alter our behavior. In fact, the basic structures— e.g., generating energy by burning fossil fuels, making chemicals that function as bioterrorists, and creating mountains of trash with superfluous packaging and throw-away products—haven't changed.

Acting on our connectedness, we can create a beautiful tapestry or a tangled knot. We can do things with connectedness that make life a joy to experience or a nonstop nightmare. How do we create more tapestry and less knot, more joy and less nightmare?

OUR SOUL NEED TO CONNECT

If philosophy, spirituality, and recovery together tell us anything, it's that the way to beauty and out of knots is through soul-connecting. Our capacity to take responsibility for our role in connectedness comes from our souls, since they're our deepest awareness of connectedness. Listening to our soul nature and acting from it is how we live the truth. It's also how we create the kind of world that our souls want and need.

To soul or not to soul? But the nagging fear keeps cropping up: If we each act on our souls, won't we have anarchy? Don't we have to check our souls at society's door and conform in order to avoid conflict?

The answer depends on what we think the soul is. If we assume, along with Thomas Hobbes, the Puritans, Freudians, and behaviorists, that the soul is selfish and out for itself, then the less soul, the better. In *Banished Knowledge*, Alice Miller tackles this view, which in psychoanalytic theories focuses on the nature of "the normal infant." She quotes psychoanalyst Edward Glover:

> The perfectly normal infant is almost completely egocentric, greedy, dirty, violent in temper, destructive in habit, profoundly sexual in purpose, aggrandizing in attitude, devoid of all but the most primitive reality sense, without conscience or moral feeling, whose attitude to society (as represented by the family) is opportunist, inconsiderate, domineering and sadistic. And when we come to consider the criminal type labeled psychopathic it will be apparent that many of these characteristics can under certain circumstances persist into adult life. In fact, judged by adult social standards the normal baby is for all practical purposes a born criminal.[8]

And we thought the doctrine of original sin was annoying! If this is our soul's nature as we come into the world, then soulless connecting followed by soulless acting are precisely what we want for an ordered society—and what control-paradigm rules of child-rearing, schooling, marriage, religious obedience, political loyalty, and job training give us. What we carry within is not only socially unacceptable, but even dangerous to society.

Connected nonetheless. Some organized religions may agree, but spiritual philosophies don't share this view of the soul, nor does Alice Miller. True, the ego or personality can be as wounded as they come—and wounded animals bite. We're born into systems that assume the worst about us—as Edward Glover's portrait proves—and then treat us accordingly.

As a result, because our experiences of each other are interconnected, it's not long before our world of connectedness is all knots. Kicked around by control-paradigm systems, we find ourselves behaving in ways that vindicate the worst that Hobbes or the Puritans, Freudians or behaviorists ever said about human nature. Tangled ourselves, we make tangles of our connectedness.

But we're more than tangles—more than so many traumatized fragments. The part of us that feels abuse *as* trauma and not as what we deserve gives evidence of a soul awareness that persists in spite of culturally reinforced knocks to our souls. Our core—the inner presence behind all the trauma and system screwiness—gives us the desire to connect with something greater and more true to who we are.

Needs for connectedness. That's our most basic need, from which all other needs grow. Born in a connected universe, our foremost need is to connect—with ourselves and those around us; with the environment that includes the food chain and life-support systems; with family, educational, economic, and political systems; with ideas and human evolution; with meaning and purpose. Experiencing our connectedness to its fullest is what being alive in a connected universe means.

Our need to experience our connectedness—and to act in ways that affirm it—doesn't mean we're inherently selfish or criminal. It simply shows that we understand our existence to be woven into expanding patterns, without which we cannot exist. Far from making us behave selfishly, cultivating an awareness of our connected existence affirms us as an integral part of larger tapestries.

BIG-PICTURE CONNECTEDNESS AS THE CONTEXT OF ACTIONS

Connected across time, space, and egos. Our awareness of connectedness touches the essence of who we are. According to Tibetan Buddhism, for instance, our essence is a stream of luminous knowing. This stream isn't broken into our knowing others or their knowing us; it's knowing-going-on.

We experience this knowing stream as our own thoughts, but the reality is an unbroken knowing field that flows through everyone and embraces the universe of connectedness. Hawaiian kahuna philosophy refers to our participation in this field as our "High Self" or that dimension of us that's both superconnected and superaware of connectedness.

Unlike our ego personalities, which are geared to more immediate, short-term connections, our High Self sees our connectedness within the big picture. And not just connectedness around the corner. On some level, we know what's going on across time and space. As past-life therapy indicates, some part of us knows our distant past as well as the ever-shifting quantum possibilities for our futures. What's more, this deep knowing affects what we do. Past-life experiences come out in our health and how we conduct our relationships.*

Learning about connectedness. From our High Self, we know all this. We know that, since every action ripples out to affect the totality, anything we do to others, the earth, or the cosmos, we do to ourselves. Chief Seattle's famous speech makes the point:

> All things are bound together. All things connect. What happens to the Earth happens to the children of the Earth. Man has not woven the web of life. He is but one thread. Whatever he does to the web, he does to himself.†

But on an everyday, time-space-matter level, we're still learning the lesson. For instance, we've spent the last fifty years learning that the DDT we spray on crops, we end up ingesting through the air, water, and food. We can't drop a nuclear or biochemical bomb on someone else without having the fallout drift back home.

Interpersonal connectedness works the same way. Paul Kivel says that every shaming comment, every taunt makes the world unsafe for all of us. Violence is more prone to occur. Our thoughts, words, and actions have an effect in creating a world that we also live in.

Dannion Brinkley discovered this in his NDE: what others felt as a result of his actions, he also felt. His enemies' experience of him became his own experience of himself. The lines separating "us" from "them" aren't what they seem. As Joanna Macy put it, a superconnected universe means we don't stop with our skins.

Karma and the learning universe. When it comes to actions, this can be scary, and no concept brings this point home more than *karma* in Eastern philosophy. Big-picture connectedness as the context of actions is what

---

*Among the excellent books on past-life therapy, see Brian Weiss, *Through Time Into Healing* (New York: Simon and Schuster, 1992), and Bruce Goldberg, *Past Lives, Future Lives* (New York: Ballantine Books, 1988).

†*How Can One Sell the Air? The Manifesto of an Indian Chief,* eds. Eli Gifford and R. Michael Cook (Summertown, TN: Book Publishing Company, 1980). We know there's controversy as to the authorship of this speech. But whoever its author was, the speech comes straight from Native American philosophy.

karma is all about. Karma describes the universe as an all-encompassing learning process. To learn, we need feedback. Connectedness guarantees that we get it: our actions boomerang.

This being so, actions pose the challenge to use our connectedness to evolve. We need not only to connect but more to be supermindful of how we connect, since it's all coming back to us. Because the universe is super-connected, karma advises us to be mindful of connectedness when we act and to pay attention to the feedback we get when our actions mirror back.

The question is, how painful does that learning have to be? What, for instance, are the top managers of Union Carbide, who cut corners and reduced safety standards in their Bhopal plant, going to feel? On a life review, what would it be like to experience between 2,500 and 7,000 traumatic deaths and between 70,000 and 600,000 long-term injuries (depending on who counts them)*—all caused by the decision to risk other people's lives in order to maximize profits?

The need to narrow the focus—and the dangers of doing so. Granted, it's a bit daunting to keep up with all of our connections every time we move, so we learn to narrow our focus. When others suffer, we learn not to feel their pain but to focus instead on what affects us directly. After all, we can't walk around in pain for all the suffering in the world. If we don't zone out to some extent, we can't watch the news or read the paper without getting depressed. For convenience, efficiency, and self-protection, we narrow ourselves.

Yet we've gone a bit overboard on shutting out pain. The pain-making connections we push aside tend to flood back in, and usually in inconvenient, efficiency-confounding, and life-threatening ways. Precisely for convenience, efficiency, and self-protection, we need to watch the ripples moving out from us into the universe body.

Short-term—that is, long enough for a business to turn a profit—some actions seem harmless enough. But extended to all their implications, we

---

*The figures on deaths and long-term injuries due to the December 3, 1984, chemical accident at the Union Carbide Plant in Bhopal, India, are all over the place, depending entirely on who's counting. See Peter Stoler, "Frightening Findings at Bhopal," *Time*, 18 February 1985, 78; Steve Lerner and Mary Ellin Barrett, "What You Haven't Heard About Bhopal," *Ms.*, December 1985, 85–88; and Joshua Karliner, "To Union Carbide, Life Is Cheap: Bhopal—Ten Years Later," *The Nation*, 12 December 1994, 726–28.

find another story, as we're discovering the hard way about so many actions we've taken in medicine, agriculture, industry, education, politics, and everyday business.

The drug thalidomide, for example, is an effective sedative and may help with leprosy, tuberculosis, and some potentially fatal side effects of bone marrow surgery. But when used during pregnancies, thalidomide also causes babies to be born without arms or legs. Apparently, thalidomide acts on more systems in the body than we realized. Whereas the United States has strict restrictions on its use, some countries do not. Brazil, for example, has recently had forty-six new instances of birth defects caused by thalidomide. As one Brazilian cleaning woman said on seeing her newborn, "When I saw him with only a head and a torso, I was devastated. I wanted to kill myself."[9]

Connectedness holds all sorts of surprises. To cut down on the number of painful ones, we're learning about connectedness fast. How can we do something creative with the connected universe, instead of hanging ourselves with it?

Knot-tying actions

Connected action takes us straight into the issue of responsibility: In a connected universe, what does it mean to act responsibly or irresponsibly?

Acting for power. The control paradigm turns out to be the model of irresponsibility. According to it, the universe of connectedness is a playground for asserting power. Connectedness is valued only insofar as it furthers control conquests. Acts of domination serve as mood-altering comforters: they prove how great our power is, since if we can hurt others and get away with it, we *must* be powerful.

Profit-taking actions. In businesses, for instance, executives who give themselves golden parachutes when they switch jobs acknowledge their connectedness to a company that can pay stratospheric sums but don't acknowledge how their actions affect the solvency of the company or how they impact those working at minimum wage.[10] Perhaps they're using connectedness to offset low self-worth: someone who gets that much money *must* be worth something. Or perhaps they're using connectedness to offset fear and isolation, as if money brings security. But whatever the reason, they're tying knots in the universe of connectedness. Companies can endure only so much profit-taking before they go bankrupt.

Or what about the owners and managers who choose to do nothing about the conditions of workers in Mexico who slave in their affiliated *maquiladoras* (factories) and live in shacks with no running water surrounded by human and toxic waste? When workers get sick from contact with toxic chemicals or are injured by accidents on the job, they're often simply fired and replaced. This is what many Americans lost their jobs for?

These aren't things that manufacturers advertise. Instead, they tell us— to take one case—about their "environmentally sensitive" trash bags sold under in-house labels (from Thriftys to Kmart) made at Plásticos Bajacal, a factory owned by Carlisle Plastics, a Boston-based company.[11] Carlisle Plastics uses the idea of environmental connectedness to sell its products, but it looks the other way on its connectedness to working conditions out-lawed in the United States as the source of its profits.

Acting to concentrate power. Using positions of power to exploit con-nectedness is acting out on a grand scale: those who had their souls knocked senseless return the favor by doing it to others, and they use businesses, cor-porations, universities, churches, and governments to do it. "What we haven't begun to admit," writes Gloria Steinem in *Revolution from Within*, "is the degree to which world leaders are motivated by vengeance, rage, and the need to act out on a national and international stage the pain and humilia-tion they experienced when they too were dependent and vulnerable."[12]

Reacting from original pain, these people obviously aren't thinking in terms of a learning universe, nor do they take seriously the idea that actions boomerang. Only power counts. To have power means to be able to hurt others—to make them do what you want, no matter what it costs them. Then you're powerful, and both you and others know it.

According to the control paradigm, what's the point of having power if you don't use it? If you have the power to take millions from a company, you'd be a fool not to take it. If you have the power to make people slave under inhuman working conditions in order to make yourself wealthier, you should do it. If you have the power to pass laws that legitimize exploitive actions, pocketing PAC money along the way, you should.

Making the universe of connectedness serve the concentration of power and wealth is what life is about. That's control-paradigm reality. And that's what directs actions. Eighteenth-century economist Adam Smith summarized what he called "the vile maxim of the masters of mankind" with these words: "All for ourselves, and nothing for other People."[13]

This way of acting is many things, but it's not responsible within the universe of connectedness. We've tolerated its knots for millennia. We've even believed that the knots were necessary to hold society together. But now we're rethinking. The knots it ties are nooses.

ACTING FROM OUR SOULS

The way to act responsibly in the universe of connectedness is not to dominate it—or try to—but to act from our souls. And for three reasons. First, as we've said, our souls are our link to big-picture connectedness. They sensitize us to the impact of our actions. Second, who we are in our bones is whole-connected and guides us as to what's ours to do. As Rumi put it:

> When you do things from your soul,
> you feel a river moving in you, a joy.
>
> When actions come from another section,
> the feeling disappears.[14]

Third, because of this, our souls act creatively in ways that the control paradigm never allows.

1. Our link to the whole. It is on deep levels of consciousness that we experience big-picture connectedness. Connectedness is our core reality, and the closer we are to our core, the more we're conscious of this. Explaining the teaching of the "Great Smoking Mirror" used by the Mayans, Cheyenne, and Pawnee, for instance, Jamie Sams discusses the "life-form to life-form" connectedness: "The Mayans say, 'I am another one of Yourself.' In this manner the Mayans stress that every life-form reflects every other life-form and that all originate from the same Original Source."[15]

If we regard others as "another one of Yourself," then we'll support and nurture them. Connectedness is a one-word paraphrase of the Golden Rule. We treat others the way we'd like to be treated—or don't treat them in ways we wouldn't like—because we're connected, and to treat others well or badly is to treat ourselves well or badly. Because our existence is rooted in a common ground of connectedness, to violate this ground is to hurt ourselves.

Our souls know this, because it's their reality. The more we're attuned to our souls, the more we bring an awareness of connectedness up to our conscious, active lives. We tap a resource of knowing that's turning out to be essential for our survival as a species.

The effect can be powerful. "The Smoking Mirror's concept of unity can eliminate all types of grandiose/elitist ideas that evolved in the Fourth World of Separation," Jamie Sams writes. "If every Two-legged would see all other humans as unique expressions of oneself, we would have no basis for quarreling or war."[16]

When we're attuned to our souls, we're sensitized to our deep connectedness, as psychologist Win Wenger discovered. Specializing in conflict resolution, Wenger uses free imaging to break deadlocks in negotiations. He discovered that on intuitive levels, polarized factions often agree on how to resolve their differences. In meditative states, their imaging patterns are amazingly similar and open to common resolutions. On a soul level, polarized parties already know how to achieve mutually beneficial solutions. The trick for Wenger lies in persuading their conscious minds to back off from polarized positions and to be guided by their own intuitions of common ground.[17]

Listening to our souls attunes us to our interbeing. Our inbuilt knowledge of connectedness inspires us to act responsibly. We strive either to maximally benefit or at least to minimally harm those touched by our actions. If we eat meat, for example, we don't raise animals in hellish conditions or treat them brutally. We express gratitude and respect for fellow beings who have sacrificed their lives for our nurturance. Soul-connected, we care about the universe of connectedness and take responsibility for our participation in it.

2. Trusting our souls' purposes. Acting from the essence of who we are inspires responsible action in another way. It connects us with our life's purpose. Acting from our souls means acting from why we were born.

Spiritual traditions say we're all here for purposes. Every life-form is. These purposes are encoded in our being and link us to the whole. They're put in us from our origin in the holomovement and guide us to do what's needed within the big picture. When we're doing what gives us joy and meaning, we're connecting with our souls' purposes, and this puts us in a relation of mutual benefit with larger processes.

Far from our being a threat to society, who we are is important to the whole tapestry. Embedded in who we are is a special quality that's unique. We each contribute perspectives and talents that support evolution in the grand scheme of things, and no one else can do this precisely as we do. If we abandon our souls' calling, we leave a hole, a vacuum, that diminishes the connected universe.

Trained to discount our souls' purposes. This message is the opposite of what control-paradigm systems give us. They say that our actions don't count, that we're a dime a dozen, and that who we are is of no special value to systems. The students in our college classes believed that there was no place for them in society after they graduated—no jobs, no affordable houses, but most of all no voice in the structures affecting their lives. They were unwanted and expendable. To win a place, they'd have to become whatever their employers wanted. Or if they wanted to live their souls' longings, they'd first have to make a pile of money by doing something else (usually something boring, stressful, unpleasant, or even illegal).

We're needed. Our souls don't buy it. They put us at odds with control-paradigm systems for a survival reason: social systems need us, since without us, they go downhill fast. They can't survive without our grounding and soul-connected energies. We're all that our systems have to offset the control paradigm's agenda—that of domination and power instead of the common good. The control paradigm, by its nature, creates soulless, self-destructive systems, despite the fact that the only true reason any such systems should exist is to serve us.

As we act from our souls, we discover exactly how much our systems need us to keep them sane servants to human welfare. Acting from our souls proves this by continually bringing systems back to their original purposes. Who we are is essential—the *sine qua non*, or "without which nothing"—to making our systems work. Soul-guided acting makes our actions maximally responsible, because then we do what our connected systems most need.

3. Tapping our souls' creative powers. Acting from our souls is maximally responsible for a third reason: by doing so, we access our creative powers and therefore create options that wouldn't otherwise exist. Following our souls' purposes and carving new niches takes creativity, and plenty of it.

According to spiritual traditions that focus on God as Creator, we're in luck: creativity is in our bones. Created "in God's likeness," we're creative by nature, and we participate in reality's nature when we're open to creativity and ready to run with it.

Creativity has all to do with seeing old things in new ways, jumping levels to take a new perspective, and restructuring relationships so that old problems don't exist. We're not, for instance, still trying to find a better way to remove tons of horse manure from the streets; creativity made that problem obsolete. Einstein's creative genius lay in leaving behind the Newtonian world and imagining how the universe would appear if he were traveling on a beam of light. His creative perspective-shift revolutionized physics.

Creativity enhances our responsibility, because it makes us better able to respond to problems. Creativity expands our options for weaving the tapestry of our connectedness. Whereas control-paradigm systems control our decisions by limiting our options (e.g., Sir Humphrey's three-card trick, which in business boils down to "Do what I say, or you don't have a job"), creativity generates alternatives. Faced with office problems, perhaps we can look beyond office roles to the real-life people, perhaps we can get a dialogue going among co-workers, perhaps we can rotate jobs, or if none of these options inspire us, perhaps we can start our own business.

The more we're connected to our souls, the more we're open to creativity and the options it presents. All the "shoulds" and "don'ts," the "no ways" and "that's impossible" strictures that control-minded systems impose fall away. By now, our souls are bored stiff with such responses. What we really care about is creating beauty, joy, and happiness: e.g., creating products and services that are of real benefit to people, creating meaningful as well as dynamic and fun relationships, creating governments that honor the freedom to be creative, creating interesting and diverse communities, and creating healthy environments.

SOUL ACTORS

People who've acted responsibly to change abusive systems have done so from their souls. Nothing less could have given them the strength to challenge control-paradigm institutions. Soul actors listen to the universe of connectedness as their souls reveal it; they let themselves be guided by their souls' purposes; and then they rely on their souls' creative powers.

Gandhi. Gandhi, for instance, had no possessions or political power, no particular standing in the community, nothing but his own soul-connectedness to go on. Many times it seemed that the South African and then British governors had beaten him. They held all the cards—the armies, the resources, the police, the laws—and they used them. At those times, Gandhi withdrew to contemplate—to reflect on the big picture and to reconnect with his purpose within it.

When he went back into action, the originality of his plans both exposed injustices and advanced a new understanding of self-government that revolutionized India. And his plans always took power-over types by surprise: "Salt? Gandhi is marching to the ocean to make salt? It takes more than a little salt to bring down the British Empire," the British governor boasted in Richard Attenborough's film *Gandhi*. He was wrong. Gandhi's creativity in effecting political change was unprecedented. He not only ended colonial rule in India, but expanded the world's options for how political transformation can occur—as Martin Luther King Jr. demonstrated in the civil rights movement.

Frank Fools Crow. Nor is Gandhi alone in using creative powers to change systems. All his life, Frank Fools Crow, the great Sioux holy man and healer, was forced to rely on his soul resources and from them to be creative in standing against the control-paradigm powers of the United States government and the Bureau of Indian Affairs. Fools Crow's childhood at the turn of the century saw Native Americans herded onto reservations, their sacred languages, cultures, and spiritual traditions outlawed, and their way of life disrupted, even constantly assaulted. Nonetheless, Fools Crow remained dedicated to the traditional way of life and became the Ceremonial Chief of the Teton Sioux, a position he used to champion Native American culture.

As life on reservations went from bad to worse—and Fools Crow himself suffered under these, being poor most of his life and robbed of all his possessions in the last year of his life—Fools Crow retained his dedication, his dignity in the face of injustices, and his commitment to "all my relations," a Lakota phrase he often used. His life inspired many Native Americans who were ready to give up, and his character and work offered alternatives to reservation life at its worst—alcoholism, hunger and unemployment, anti-Indian education, and crime.

Fools Crow's outstanding healing work showed the efficacy of traditional healing methods. But he also turned his creative energies to political change, mediating between the FBI and American Indian Movement (AIM) activists at Wounded Knee in 1973 and testifying before Congress to return the Black Hills to the Native Peoples. After Fools Crow's death in November 1989—at age ninety-nine—AIM leader Russell Means eulogized him, crediting him with the return of the Spirit Keeping and Sun Dance ceremonies (outlawed by the U.S. government in 1890, the year of Fools Crow's birth) and leaving "a legacy showing how beautiful the Native Americans have been as a race."[18]

Though not everyone has the life of Gandhi, King, or Fools Crow, human interest stories in the media are full of cases of "ordinary" people walking out from under control-paradigm models and using their creativity to put soul, meaning, and responsibility back at the center of their worlds. It's our birthright to act from our souls. Where there are no options for doing this, we create them. That's what human beings do most naturally.

Flexing our powers. When we combine (1) our awareness of connectedness, (2) the unique gifts embedded in who we are, and (3) our powers to be creative, control-paradigm systems haven't a chance of stopping us. Even the knots don't stop us.

AA's Ninth Step—we "Made direct amends to such people wherever possible, except when to do so would injure them or others"—focuses our powers to be creative, particularly in untying knots. Armed with soul-awareness, we can make amends for whatever wrongs have been incurred by us or by our systems. We can do something with the universe of connectedness that's healing, world changing, and life transforming. And because we're part of the connected universe, claiming our power to do this heals and transforms us in the process.

NOT BEING FOOLED BY "BIGNESS"

So what goes wrong? Why does acting from our souls seem hopelessly - ineffective? How are we fooled into surrendering our creative powers and tolerating gross knots all around us as school, business, church, or government as usual?

The "big" smoke screen. From ancient times, control-paradigm systems have kept themselves in power by convincing all but a few that "we the people" are utterly powerless. How? With a smoke screen: big counts, little doesn't. Quantity counts, quality doesn't. Therefore control counts, transformation doesn't. Big businesses, big institutions, and big governments—and the people sitting at the top of them—have power. We're little; the top is way up there; we have no chance of reaching it; therefore, we have no power but to do our little number in our little corner of the very big world. Why waste our time trying to change systems? They're just too big for us.

"Big is overpowering" has been drummed into us for millennia. The Assyrians had bigger armies than anyone had ever seen (at least in that neighborhood). The Egyptians had the biggest monuments. Diocletian's version of the Roman Empire had the biggest bureaucracy. Constantine had the biggest religion—and the biggest statues of himself. Europe's empire-minded nobility had all of the above plus the biggest titles. The current "masters of mankind" own the biggest banks, the biggest agribusinesses, the biggest estates, the biggest yachts, and the biggest buildings to house their biggest-on-the-globe corporate conglomerates.

The point of bigness is not productivity. Anyone who's worked in big military institutions, big corporations, big religious hierarchies, or big government knows that very little gets done. Rather, the point is intimidation. Bigness is designed to make potential challengers—defined as the rest of humanity—feel small and helpless by comparison. We're supposed to be cowed into letting the movers and shakers run the world.

Overwhelmed by the size of problems. Unfortunately, the smoke screen works more than it should. Big gets to us, and we start thinking that way. By buying the big lie, we put ourselves right where control-paradigm systems want us: under their domination with the belief that we can't do otherwise.

The effect is that we feel overwhelmed by the sheer size of everything—both the problems and the dynamics that cause them. We see misery everywhere, and we feel powerless to stop it. We see big institutions behaving irresponsibly, and we haven't the time, energies, or resources to stop them. It's hard enough grieving our own wounding, but where do we start to grieve and then heal the wounding of the world?

What's more, if the movers and shakers can't fix things, how can we? If they oppose our efforts toward change, what chance do we have? And if, as we suspect, they haven't the remotest interest in fixing the environment, changing working conditions in Mexico, or getting rid of poverty here in America, then it's hard not to be immobilized with despair. We've all been there.

Removing the smoke screen. Immobilizing despair, as annoying as it is, can be useful. It tells us we've bought the smoke screen. There are no big movers and shakers in the connected universe. Some people seem big and powerful only insofar as we've bought the control paradigm and allowed them to use the universe of connectedness to appear big and powerful. But it's an illusion.

And it's an illusion whether we're one person or several billion.

JoAnn Tall is one woman. She's Lakota, she has eight children, she suffers debilitating rheumatoid arthritis, and she lives on the Pine Ridge Reservation in South Dakota, situated in the poorest county in the United States. Hers is not a mover-and-shaker profile. Yet she's moved and shaken many powerful institutions:

> Inspired by the Lakota tradition of respect for the land, she participated in the 1973 occupation of Wounded Knee by the American Indian Movement (AIM) and in 1978, helped to raise awareness on the reservations about the health hazards of uranium mining. Since that time, Tall helped stop nuclear weapons testing in the Black Hills and prevented a hazardous waste dump from being located in Pine Ridge and the neighboring Rosebud Reservation.... Tall has worked on many other issues, including leading the fight to stop an experimental hepatitus vaccine from being tested on Lakota children.[19]

That's the power of one soul-connected person. But if it's numbers we want, Gandhi laid the numbers-reality on the line: several hundred thousand British couldn't oppress several million Indians if the Indians refused to cooperate. If the earth's economically and politically disenfranchised peoples—that's 99 percent of us—decided tomorrow that we'd had enough, the so-called movers and shakers would be lucky not to have their heads handed to them. And the peoples of the earth are much closer to doing just that than the mighty few would like to admit.

In *Your Nostradamus Factor*, famed and much studied psychic Ingo Swann describes what's ahead of us, as best he can discern. By the way, this is someone who predicted *that* the Berlin Wall would fall—and *when*—at a time when no one could imagine such a thing. He writes:

> [I predict] that 1998 will be the year in which the future becomes irrevocably detached from the past. The completeness of the failure of most twentieth-century systems, mind-sets, and affiliated institutions will be clearly visible by then....
>
> Twentieth-century system failures will result in a great sense of betrayal and great, unifying anger. It is out of this great anger that the centralizing, reempowering highest values and objectives of the third millennium will arise. These values will not remotely resemble those of the twentieth century.*

LEVERAGE FOR CHANGE

The trim-tab effect. If Swann is right that sweeping system changes are just around the corner, how is this going to happen? Swayed by the myth of bigness, we fall into thinking that action has to be big to bring about big changes.

But that's not how a connected universe works. Like the beating of a butterfly's wings—or a pebble tossed into a lake—small actions have big effects; they initiate ripples that keep moving out.

An image first used by Buckminster Fuller (and explored, for instance, in Harold Willens's 1984 book *The Trimtab Factor*) is the trim tab on a rudder. To change the direction of a really big ship or airplane, we need a really big rudder, in fact, too big. The power of the currents of air or water, combined with the size of the rudder, make it almost impossible to move the rudder without breaking it. The solution is to put a tiny rudder, called a trim tab, on the big rudder. The tiny trim tab moves easily, because it's small. But as it does, it causes the currents to shift, which makes it easier for the big rudder to move, which makes the even bigger ship change its course. The physical mass of the trim tab is a tiny fraction of the weight of the ship or plane, yet the trim tab determines the vehicle's course.

---

*Ingo Swann, *Your Nostradamus Factor: Accessing Your Innate Ability to See into the Future* (New York: Fireside/Simon and Schuster, 1993), 23–25. Swann predicted the fall of the Berlin Wall to an audience in Detmold, West Germany, in April 1988, and he predicted it would happen within eighteen to twenty-four months. It happened nineteen months later.

The American Revolution illustrates the trim-tab effect. The revolution didn't happen because the majority wanted it. In the early 1770s, only a handful of radical intellectuals were thinking the unthinkable of breaking with the biggest naval power on the planet. Even by 1776, support for independence was by no means unanimous or even the majority. Strong elements within the middle and southern colonies wanted to keep the economic and military protection of Britain. Loyalists to the Crown were everywhere. It's estimated that only 11 percent of the population was actively involved in making the American Revolution happen.*

Today's revolution. Another revolution is now in the wind, only this time it isn't just political. All systems are involved. And more than 11 percent of the population is on board. Preliminary results of a study conducted by the Institute of Noetic Sciences in conjunction with the Fetzer Institute suggest that as many as forty-five million adults, roughly 24 percent of the adult population, have adopted "new paradigm" values and ideas. These new-paradigm values include altruism, creativity, tolerance, openness, interest in spiritual development and higher consciousness, desire for positive cultural change, feminism and racial equality, optimism about the future, preference for holistic health care, environmental and social concern, drives for self-expression and self-actualization. According to the study, these values aren't merely espoused; they're "affecting behavior and changing lifestyles."†

Frances Moore Lappé, known for her 1971 classic *Diet for a Small Planet*, appeals to the trim-tab powers of individuals with a new citizen-action project, the Center for Living Democracy, which she co-founded with her husband, Paul Martin Du Bois. Defining the purpose of the Center in its newsletter, *Doing Democracy*, they appeal to the power of "regular citizens" in bringing change from the ground up:

---

*Though figures are hard to come by, contemporary historian Forrest McDonald mentions the support issue in *E Pluribus Unum* (Indianapolis: Liberty Fund, 1979), 45–46, but the famous Beards—Charles and Mary—already gave telling figures in their classic 1944 work, *The Beards' New Basic History of the United States* (Garden City, NY: Doubleday, 1960), 121–22, supported by Harry Carman and Harold Syrett's respected work, *A History of the American People, vol. 1, to 1865* (New York: Alfred Knopf, 1952), 156–57.

†*Noetic Sciences Review* (Winter 1995), no. 36 (Sausalito, CA), 5. The Institute of Noetic Sciences generously sent us a copy of the preliminary study, "The Integral Culture Survey," by Paul H. Ray, Ph. D., October 1995.

Despite all the bad news, something extraordinary is happening in America: A profound shift in attitudes and expectations is reshaping our culture from the bottom up. Living Democracy is what we call this broad awakening to the essential role of regular citizens in solving America's toughest problems. Millions are now learning that public life is not just for officials and experts, but part of a rewarding life for each of us. The Center's mission is to dramatically accelerate the emergence of Living Democracy.[20]

Doing Democracy is full of examples of people doing just that, from using civil suits to shut down crack houses to passing city ordinances that require businesses to pay a "living wage" of $6.10 an hour. The center has even started its own news service, the American News Service, whose purpose is to "break through despair with practical insights and real-life stories."

In other words, "we the people" are getting wise to the control-paradigm myth of "big is too big for us" and taking seriously what anthropologist Margaret Mead said: "Never doubt that a small group of committed citizens can change the world; indeed it's the only thing that ever has."*

---

*Quoted in yet another innovative news service devoted to reporting on women and women's issues, the *WorldWIDE News*, Winter 1993.

NOTES TO CHAPTER 9

1. Coleman Barks, trans., *Delicious Laughter: Rambunctious Teaching Stories from the Mathnawi* (Athens, GA: Maypop Books, 1990), 28.
2. Dannion Brinkley with Paul Perry, *Saved by the Light: The True Story of a Man Who Died Twice and the Profound Revelations He Had* (New York: Villard Books/Random House, 1994), 10.
3. Brinkley, *Saved by the Light*, 10–11.
4. Brinkley, *Saved by the Light*, 148, 152.
5. F. David Peat, *Synchronicity: The Bridge Between Matter and Mind* (New York: Bantam Books, 1987), 44–45.
6. Morton Dauwen Zabel, ed., *Charles Dickens' Best Stories* (Garden City, NY: Hanover House, 1959), 106.
7. "It was a surprisingly green Christmas for Rollerblade employees," Minneapolis *Star Tribune*, 3 January 1996.
8. Qtd. in Alice Miller, *Banished Knowledge: Facing Childhood Injuries* (New York: Anchor Books, Doubleday, 1990), 42.
9. Christine Gorman, "Thalidomide's Return," *Time*, 13 June 1994, 67.
10. Kevin Phillips, *The Politics of Rich and Poor* (New York: Random House, 1990), 180–82.
11. See, for example: *Ms.*, January/February 1994, 12–15.
12. Gloria Steinem, *Revolution from Within: A Book of Self-Esteem* (New York: Little Brown, 1991), excerpted in "Self-Esteem," *Ms.*, November/December 1991, 26.
13. Qtd. by Noam Chomsky, "Notes on NAFTA: 'The Masters of Mankind,'" *The Nation*, 29 March 1993, 412.
14. Coleman Barks, *We Are Three* (Athens, GA: Maypop Books, 1987), 44.
15. Jamie Sams, *Sacred Path Cards: The Discovery of Self Through Native Teachings* (New York: HarperCollins, 1990), 291.
16. Sams, *Sacred Path Cards*, 291.
17. Sheila Ostrander and Lynn Schroeder, *SuperMemory: The Revolution* (New York: Carroll & Graf Publishing, 1991), 152–53.
18. Thomas E. Mails, *Fools Crow: Wisdom and Power* (Tulsa: Council Oaks Books, 1991), 197. See also Thomas Mails, *Fools Crow* (Lincoln: University of Nebraska Press, 1979).
19. "1993 Goldman Environmental Prize: Three Women Among Winners of This Prestigious Prize," *WorldWIDE News: A Special Newsletter on Women, Environment and Development*, special ed., Spring 1993, 12.
20. *Doing Democracy*, Winter 1995 (Brattleboro, VT: Center for Living Democracy), 7.

CHAPTER 10

Conspiring Ongoing Paradigm Evolution

Working the truth

Tenth of the Twelve Cycles of Truth,
the Iroquois Peace Confederacy Tradition

The breeze at dawn has secrets to tell you.
Don't go back to sleep.
You must ask for what you really want.
Don't go back to sleep.
People are going back and forth across the doorsill
where the two worlds touch.
The door is round and open.
Don't go back to sleep.

Rumi[1]

HAVING A PARADIGM AND EVOLVING TOO

What are we looking for in this book? The right paradigm? The one that can solve all our problems? The one we can use to restructure our systems and then forget about all this paradigm stuff? That'd be nice, maybe, but it's not actually what we're after, mainly because we don't believe it's possible or even desirable.

The yin and yang of paradigm evolution. The goal here isn't to end up having one paradigm but rather to engage in the process of evolving through paradigms. This process has two faces, like the two complementary processes of yin and yang described in Chinese philosophy.

The yang face of paradigm evolution is when we're operating within a paradigm and developing its possibilities. We assume a paradigm and run with it. We're confident that our mental model serves us well and that it organizes our lives in useful and meaningful ways. Everything has its place, and we're able to specialize our role and function within the big-paradigm picture. When problems arise, our paradigm solves them, and we're satisfied with how. In Kuhn's language, this is normal science. It's a period when we tend to forget about paradigms, since they become second nature to us.

But paradigms, which are limited, aren't the last word on reality, which is unlimited. Doing things in specialized ways has its limits. Either we get bored with the specialized roles, or we reach the limits of their effectiveness. Behavior that once "worked" and that we found meaningful no longer has the same effect.

At this point, the yang of paradigm evolution gradually gives way to the yin phase, when we confront the limits of our paradigm. The paradigm has taken us as far as it can. To continue evolving, we need to restructure.

During the yin stage, we step into the void of a paradigm shift. We're no longer confident about our paradigm, so we pull it out of the background to take a good look at it. We don't take things for granted anymore. We don't assume our specialized roles are the right ones or that our paradigm-defined ways of handling problems are the best. Instead, we're aware of the assumptions we're making—as much as we can be (more yin for you)—and we're aware that they may not be helping us as much as we thought they were. This is the extraordinary-science phase.

Like yin and yang, both phases of paradigm evolution are important, just as both legs come in handy for walking. In balance, they set up a rhythm that works. We establish structures in the yang phase, and then we step back and reflect on the process in the yin phase. By doing both, we can have our paradigms and evolve too.

Yang heavy. But as the Chinese discovered, it's easy to get yin and yang out of balance. Specifically, we love the yang phase, because that's when we're ready to take on the world, and we've got the paradigm to do it. Yang is "productive." It's the sun, warmth, action—the "go get 'em" feeling. It's what we hope we'll feel every morning when we wake up. When we're in normal science, our paradigms give us a sense of being on top of things. We're in the groove.

For a culture that leans heavily on the control paradigm, normal science is *the* phase. It's the phase when we can be experts and authorities, when we can make money and get the job done. We look good in the yang phase, at least by control-paradigm standards, because we know what's what and we're certain about it. We've adapted ourselves to a specialized function within the established order of things, and it works. We don't have any problem giving orders, managing things, and telling people what to think and do. We've got it all figured out.

But what if we don't? And what if our specialized role isn't working as well as we'd like to think. These are yin questions.

Yin questions: Philosophy's role. Paradigm-pushing questions are also the questions of classical philosophy, going back to Socrates and before. Philosophical skepticism doesn't mean being a nihilist or stonewalling every effort to think things through with a glib, "Yeah, but you don't *know* that." It means being aware of paradigms and their limits. It also means being aware of the process of shifting paradigms and sensing when it's time for a shift.

As we've mentioned, Socrates viewed himself as a midwife—that's definitely yin—in helping his fellow Athenians give birth to the good, the true, and the beautiful. Since goodness, truth, and beauty are without limit, Socrates had his own brand of job security (though without pay). With always more of the good, true, and beautiful to be expressed through our paradigms, he as a philosopher had plenty of midwiving to do. Expanding our mental containers for holding ideas and values was more interesting to him than propounding one fixed container. That's what the Sophists did, and Socrates found it thoroughly tedious.

The best philosophies, he believed, help us stay loose in our paradigms. We keep the yin-yang rhythm foremost in our minds, so we don't get stuck or become dogmatic. Questioning, dialoguing, exploring, thinking, and rethinking are the yin contributions of philosophy to paradigm evolution.

And the tradition stuck, from Cicero to Leibniz. The Roman philosopher Cicero (106–43 B.C.E.), for instance, observed that whereas geometricians demonstrate a proof and then never do it again, philosophers think things through from the ground up regularly. They go back to basics and start fresh.[2]

Leibniz was a great one for doing this. Every time he wanted to work through a subject—even one he'd thoroughly analyzed before—he'd start from scratch and write a new thesis on it. Of course, rumor has it that he did this because the top drawer of his desk, where he stuffed all his writings, was so messy that he couldn't find what he'd written before.*

"Beginner's mind." Eastern philosophy teaches the wisdom of balancing yang processes with yin ones to produce ongoing evolution. As one Chinese saying puts it, "There's a time for fishing, and a time for drying nets." Contemporary Taoist Master Ni Hua-Ching writes, "Life is a continual process of evolution, and if experienced this way, it allows no room for fixation of any kind."[3] Gandhi took the same yin approach, stating, "Constant development is the law of life."[4]

Yin is the art of being continually open to development and ready to go with it. In Zen philosophy, this readiness to evolve is called "beginner's mind." A beginner's mind has an openness that an expert's doesn't. In *Zen Mind, Beginner's Mind*, Zen master Shunryu Suzuki explains this:

> If your mind is empty, it is always ready for anything; it is open to everything. In the beginner's mind there are many possibilities; in the expert's mind there are few....
>
> In the beginner's mind, there is no thought, "I have attained something."... When we have no thought of achievement, no thought of self, we are true beginners. Then we can really learn something....
>
> So the most difficult thing is always to keep your beginner's mind.... Even though you read much Zen literature, you must read each sentence with a fresh mind. You should not say, "I know what Zen is," or "I have attained enlightenment." This is also the real secret of the arts: always be a beginner.[5]

The great benefit of yin-openness, of course, is that we're able to perceive meaning that yang-ers locked in a given paradigm don't. In *Synchronicity*, physicist F. David Peat distinguishes a yin mind that's open to synchronicity—that is, meaningful coincidences—from a yang one that isn't:

---

*While visiting from England, G. H. R. Parkinson, a scholar on Leibniz told this story about this philosophical giant of the late seventeenth and early eighteenth centuries.

Synchronicity will appear very naturally to a mind that is constantly sensitive to change.... A mind that remains flexible and sensitive will be in a constant process of creative change and will respond to the overall patterns of nature so that the individual can enter into these patterns in new ways.

When the mind, and its worldview, become fixated upon...forms and relationships in space and time, the overall meaning of synchronicity tends to be lost. In this way, knowledge becomes fragmented and the ability to see deeply into the structure of things is impaired by the failure to perceive wider patterns and contexts.[6]

Yin's challenges in yang-dominant systems. Of course, we don't put "beginner's mind" first on resumés. We keep our yin face—our doubts, uncertainties, and questions about paradigms—to ourselves. Yin's beginner's mind isn't welcome during the expert-driven, yang phase of any paradigm, but it's an absolute pariah to the control paradigm at full tilt. Yin questions are exactly what control-paradigm practitioners don't want to hear, because they register them as suggesting imperfect control.

Nor are yin periods particularly easy on us. Questioning the unquestioned can get us into a peck of trouble. Perhaps the hardest thing about the yin phase, though, is that just when we're moving into the void of a paradigm shift, we often get cold feet. We lose confidence that yin is what's needed. Yin leanings don't carry much weight in control-paradigm systems—not any, in fact. Insofar as we've been raised to have all the facts on the tip of our tongues, know what we're doing at all times, and be on top of things no matter what, the uncertainty of the yin phase doesn't sit well. Our inner critic—the one that would just as soon we forget about paradigm shifts—nags at us, wondering when we're planning to look respectable again.

So we mistrust yin leanings and push them aside. We read them as signs that we're inadequate, incompetent, or "losing it." Yin leanings sprout up spontaneously as we reach our paradigm's limits, yet we avoid them. They'd move us toward a paradigm shift, and that's a nuisance to the established—and familiar—order.

PAEDOMORPHOSIS, NEOTENY, AND THE INNER CHILD

So what's the appeal of yin? Evolution. We can't develop without it. Doing only the yang of paradigm development, we get boxed in fixedness. The paradigm sits on us like a prison, for once we've developed all we can in it, we don't see a way out. We keep doing more of the same—and more and more, louder and louder—when what we really need to do is switch tracks and branch off in a new direction.

In *Janus: A Summing Up*, Arthur Koestler compared the dynamics of human evolution to biological evolution and came up with some remarkable analogies for how the yin phase works.

Trapped in dead-end overspecialization. Evolution stalls, Koestler observed, because we get locked in fixed paradigms of behavior. We become overspecialized in our relation to our environment, which means we lose adaptability. Yang gets too yang, and normal science gets too normal.

People who do a specialized job for years and then find themselves out of work know the problem. So do women who spend twenty years raising children and managing a home. Or men who spend their work lives being efficient, important, and managerial and then retire to do...what?

Social systems get overspecialized as well. The defense industry still depends on the perception of military threats to get contracts from Congress and foreign governments, though the people of the planet—who pay the price of having their communities turned into high-tech war zones—are moving away from the armed and dangerous model. By their very structure, schools continue to treat students as if they're headed for life on the assembly line, though we've long since moved into the information age, when the ability to think, adapt creatively, and be self-motivated are prime assets.

Overspecialization isn't just boring, it's deadly. It locks us in patterns adapted to reality-of-the-past, while present reality has moved on. Skill at cracking a buggy whip won't make a car move, nor will physical force solve computer problems (though throwing the thing out the window does have its appeal from time to time). Applying old models to new worlds, even if the old model made us king of the castle, courts disaster. Koestler writes:

> The principal cause of both extinction and stagnation appears to have been over-specialization with its concomitant loss of adaptability to changes in the environment....
>
> The human paradigm of over-specialization is the pedant, the slave of habit, whose thinking and behavior move in rigid grooves—a predestined victim of any unexpected calamity. His equivalent in the animal kingdom is the pathetic koala bear, which specializes in feeding on the leaves of a

particular variety of eucalyptus tree and on nothing else; and which has hook-like claws, ideally suited for clinging to the bark of the tree—and for nothing else. All orthodoxies tend to breed human koalas.[7]

Backing up to go forward. How do we break out of the box? By going back to the evolutionary stage when we were still flexible, namely, to when we were a child or even a fetus. If we're an adult sea cucumber, for instance, that means going back to the larva stage. A free-floating larva has more possibilities for adaptation than an adult. Whereas the adult sea cucumber has life all figured out, the larva is still learning—it has beginner's mind.

This zig-back to zag-forward pattern of evolution is called "paedomorphosis"—undoing evolution to redo it, de-specializing to re-specialize or, to use the French phrase, *reculer pour mieux sauter*, that is, step back to take a better leap forward.[8] Koestler explains:

> What this amounts to is a process of "juvenalization" and de-specialization—a successful escape from a dead-end in the evolutionary maze....
>
> Sir Gavin de Beer compared the process to the re-winding of a biological clock when evolution is in danger of running down and coming to a standstill: "A race may become rejuvenated by pushing the adult stage of its individuals off from the end of their ontogenies, and such a race may then radiate out in all directions."
>
> The record from palaeontology and comparative anatomy does indeed suggest that this retracing of steps to escape from the blind alleys of over-specialization was repeated at each major evolutionary turning point....
>
> Paedomorphosis—or juvenalization—thus appears to play an important part in the grand strategy of evolution. It involves a *retreat* from specialized adult forms to earlier, less committed and more plastic stages in the development of organisms—followed by a sudden advance in a new direction.[9]

In fact, Koestler says, the adult human resembles the embryo of an ape far more than it resembles the adult ape: "The 'missing link' between ape and man will probably never be found—because it was an embryo."[10]

Zigzagging cultural evolution. Koestler applies this concept to how cultures evolve, and he describes the same process that we're exploring with paradigm shifts:

> Biological evolution is to a large extent a history of escapes from the blind alleys of over-specialization, the evolution of ideas a series of escapes from

the tyranny of mental habits and stagnant routines....

But the new theoretical structure which emerges from the breakthrough is not just added to the old edifice; it branches out from the point where the evolution of ideas has taken the wrong turn. The great revolutions in the history of science have a decidedly paedomorphic character. In the history of literature and art, the zigzag course is even more in evidence; we have seen how the periods of cumulative progress within a given "school" or technique end inevitably in stagnation, mannerism, or decadence, until the crisis is resolved by a revolutionary shift in sensibility, emphasis, style.[11]

In other words, cultures get stuck in overspecialized forms—the yang phase. Instead of pushing into greater specialization—doing yang/normal science more and more—cultural evolution occurs when people or disciplines back up to when they were more open in their thinking. From that flexible stage, they then branch off in new directions.

Neoteny: Lifelong juveniles. The flexibility of the juvenile stage is so valuable to evolution that different species have developed different ways to capitalize on it. Some species cut off the adult form, and individuals spend their lives as juveniles. Humans, for example, may be immature apes. We never became adult apes but kept the juvenile form, which was more flexible, hence more open to evolution (not to mention less hairy). This pattern of retaining juvenile flexibility into adulthood is called "neoteny"—in control-paradigm terms, "goof-offs."

In evolution terms, though, immature is good because the options for developing in different directions remain open. Immature stages haven't decided yet how they're going to meet their evolutionary challenges, and they're not afraid to experiment.

Not that mature stages don't serve their role in evolution as well. But in human evolution, we all know the kind of mature that's a pain in the neck, namely, the kind that has no sense of humor, that takes itself superseriously, that's cross, cranky, and hates to be interrupted, that justifies its own mistakes but has no tolerance for the mistakes of others, that weighs everything in terms of money, in short, that's just too important to have fun, relax, or yield—yin.

When adults overdo the mature form, it's because they conceive of being an adult as settling into a fixed relation to the environment. They forget that there's also something valuable about being a juvenile—having the options for what kind of adult we become left open to us.

In biological evolution, neoteny is the remedy for overmature adults. When adult forms become too fixed, species can evolve past the fixedness by eliminating the adult end of the life cycle and doing all the living and reproducing as juveniles. From the juvenile stage, new patterns emerge, which lead to new "adult" forms.

Prolonged dependence on parents. Another trick that species use to maximize the evolutionary capacity of their young is to extend the period in which the individuals remain juveniles. By prolonging the juvenile period in the normal life cycle, the species increases the possibilities for creative adapting. When individuals aren't thrust into adult roles, they have more time to cook up alternative adult patterns. The more intelligent the species, the more time it allows its new members to do the kind of creative experimenting that juveniles do. They don't force beginner's mind out.

If, for example, children in contemporary societies had only until puberty to be non-adults and were forced into meeting survival needs and raising families at twelve or thirteen, they'd have little time to reflect on their parents' lives—to see what it's like to be an adult—and to react accordingly, which often means rebellion. Rebellion to fixed adult patterns is a pain in the neck if we're the adults, but it's important not only to the individual's development—and to the adults'—but also to the creative evolution of our species. We'd be shortsighted specieswise to truncate our juvenile period, which is why, for example, laws prohibiting child labor were and are a good idea, not only here in America but around the world.*

---

*For the treatment of children by foreign companies, see David C. Korten, *When Corporations Rule the World*. For instance, he reports, "In Bangladesh, an estimated 80,000 children under age fourteen, most of them female, work at least sixty hours a week in garment factories. For miscounting or other errors, male supervisors strike them or force them to kneel on the floor or stand on their heads for ten to thirty minutes. It isn't only the garment industry. In India, an estimated 55 million children work in various conditions of servitude, many as bonded laborers—virtual slaves—under the most appalling conditions.... Former Indian Chief Justice P. M. Bhagwati has publically testified to observing examples of boys working fourteen to twenty hours a day: 'They are beaten up, branded [with red-hot iron rods] and even hung from trees upside down.' The carpet industry in India exports $300 million worth of carpets a year, mainly to the United States and Germany. The carpets are produced by more than 300,000 children laborers working fourteen to sixteen hours a day, seven days a week, fifty-two weeks a year" (231–32).

These are some of the evolutionary innovations that species have used in the past to maximize the flexibility of the juvenile stage.

Inner child work: Evolutionarily revolutionary. Now there's another innovation on the evolutionary horizon: What if we can integrate the juvenile with the adult, so that as adults we can be as open to creating new models as we were as juveniles? In other words, what if by tapping our young/yin/beginner's mind consciousness, we profoundly enhance our capacity to evolve as adults?

That's what's going on in recovery. Those who have reached some crisis in their adult lives, often precipitated by various forms of addiction, found the overspecialized roles of adults unacceptable. All the control-paradigm messages they received growing up put them on a course of development that didn't work—that didn't bring happiness, well-being, or peace. Self-destructive behavior is one way to change the situation, but not the best one obviously, especially insofar as our species' evolution is concerned.

The revolutionary alternative—evolutionwise—has been to step back to leap forward in a new direction. By reconnecting with what went on while we were growing up—rediscovering our inner child—adults withdraw from overspecialized roles, go back to when stifling patterns started and before, and branch out on a new course of evolution. We consciously cultivate the fluidity, openness, malleability, creativity, joy, freedom, and spontaneity that we experienced as children. Then we use that childlike consciousness to give birth (Socrates again) to new patterns now.

Mike Nichols's film *Regarding Henry*, written by Jeffrey Abrams and starring Harrison Ford and Annette Bening, showed the power of this process. Harrison Ford's character was overspecialized in making money—a thoroughly offensive lawyer, husband, father, and person. His turnaround came when he was shot in the head during a robbery and lost his memory and motor skills. He had to begin again and relearn everything. This time, though, his character developed along a different course. His childlike qualities came out, sensitizing him to the people around him and to a different set of values. He reverted to childhood and, as a result, he found the inner plasticity to develop into a completely different person.

Going back to develop anew. Going back to our own childhood means allowing ourselves to feel what we felt not through the fixed, judgmental adult categories that parents, teachers, bosses, or clergy had—or that we now may have—but through the receptive, undefined, sensitive-to-the-environment categories that we possessed as children. We reexperience what it's like to be a child and what it was for us to experience life as we did.

Doing this reawakens many things. It reawakens, for instance, the pain we felt when we ran head-on into control-paradigm conditioning. In *Banished Knowledge*, Alice Miller tells about the German tradition of taking children to see Saint Nicholas. The children prepare songs or poems for Saint Nicholas, not realizing that their mothers slip him notes detailing all their shortcomings. When the children come before him—delighted to finally meet the good saint—Saint Nicholas publicly scolds the children, even with the implied threat that if they don't do better, he'll stuff them in his sack and take them away. The children go into the "celebration" with joy but come out stricken with fear and shame, many too humiliated to remember the songs or poems they'd painstakingly prepared.[12]

Such painful experiences can set us on a particular course of development—one in which we become fear-driven, obedient to authorities, and controllable by the promise of external rewards. This, in fact, is precisely what such experiences are designed to do to us: to choose for us the course of our development. Going back to them and acknowledging what happened—the legitimacy of our joy and the illegitimacy of the shaming—gives us the opportunity to evolve a different response from the one we evolved when we were so vulnerable. We reclaim the power of choice that we possessed as juveniles of the species—the power to choose a different course of evolution.

Besides pain, inner child work also reawakens the free and open consciousness that we had as children. That's when everything lay before us, and when we weren't committed to doing things one way or another. We didn't identify with one paradigm. We didn't have decades of choices to defend or mistakes to justify. We weren't stuck in grooves that would take a major crisis to jolt us out of. We could grow into whomever we wanted, and we didn't have a zillion arguments or expectations to stop us. By recovering our inner child, we recover our capacities to evolve.

A worldwide movement to reconnect with our inner child and to let this child help us evolve new forms of adulthood is nothing short of revolutionary. It says that, by reintegrating our child consciousness, we're opening ourselves to ongoing evolution. We're claiming our innate capacities to evolve, and we're not going to persist in paradigms that aren't working, even if we are adults. That's powerful, world-changing, species-evolving stuff.

Yin and the juvenile. In yin and yang terms, the child or juvenile form of the species expresses yin, while the adult is yang. Like yin, the child is flexible, less formed, less defined, more sensitive to the environment, and empty of fixed ideas. Chinese Taoism, a yin-oriented philosophy, uses the image of the uncarved block to symbolize yin, since many forms could be carved from it. Taoism even uses the image of a baby to describe the sage—one who is flexible, natural, ready to flow with changes, effortless in action, and open to development.

"Don't be childish!" But again, yang-ers in the rhythm of paradigm evolution, especially control-paradigm ones, don't appreciate yin dynamics, precisely because they invite paradigm change. Even the words *baby, child, childish,* and *juvenile* are often used pejoratively: "Don't be such a baby!" "How childish!" or "You're being juvenile!" Being a baby, a child, or a juvenile isn't a good thing in a control-paradigm culture.

Jesus, by contrast, told his disciples to let children sit around him "and forbid them not: for of such is the kingdom of God…. Whosoever shall not receive the kingdom of God as a little child, he shall not enter therein."[13] Jesus' comments make sense on a model of ongoing spiritual evolution, though that's not how they're often interpreted. Instead of suggesting that we be open to evolution as only children can be, his comments are rendered to mean that we're supposed to be obedient to church authorities, just as good children are supposed to be obedient to parents and teachers—a control-paradigm mangling of spiritual teachings if ever there was one.

The general disdain for the juvenile stage of our species and a rejection of our own childhood as raising too many painful memories combine to make people less than enthusiastic about inner child work. We'd like to forget that we ever were a child, and, in some cases, it's hard to imagine that someone ever was. As one person put it, "You mean that by playing with toys on the floor, my wife and I can get along better?"

Reclaiming evolutionary processes. The person who said this is a kind, sensitive, good-hearted man who had no idea how to deal with the emotional and physical pain he'd endured growing up. He wanted to let go of the past and get on with his new married life, but it wasn't working out the way he'd hoped. The very intimacy of the new relationship made it safe for original pain issues to surface in ways they hadn't done before. The same thing happens in many marriages, as it did in ours.

The major obstacle to going back to our juvenile stage is our idea of what it means to be an adult: "Real adults don't develop." "I'm an adult now; how can thinking about child stuff help me?" "It's been hard enough to get to where I am; I'm not about to undo it." This fixed-as-an-adult attitude accords with the officially adult/yang/make-the-paradigm-work response: "Forget about the processes that brought you to where you are and just make the best of things." "What's happened, happened." "That's all water under the bridge." "You can't change the past, so why bother with it?" "Grow up and get on with your life!"

These instructions are great for trying to make a failing paradigm work, even at cost to our happiness and relationships, but they're not good for evolution. They're exactly what makes adult forms rigid and locked-in. If we ignore the dynamics that brought us to where we are and just focus on fixing outcomes, we'll always be fixing, and neither the paradigm nor the dynamics that produce those outcomes will change. Significant evolution won't occur.

Paedomorphosis says that if you're caught in an adult paradigm that isn't working, go back to the roots of your evolutionary processes and from those roots evolve along a different course.

CYCLING AND RECYCLING THROUGH

Deganawidah, who founded the Iroquois Peace Confederacy, knew about paedomorphosis—cycling and recycling through a process to bring profound evolution. After all, he taught the Twelve *Cycles* of Truth. They map not a linear program to be done once and forgotten but an ongoing process of paradigm evolution, or, as the Tenth Cycle of Truth says, of "working the truth." The parallel to Step Ten of AA is uncanny: we "Continued to take personal inventory and when we were wrong promptly admitted it."

"Working the truth" or continuing to cycle through AA's Steps means engaging in evolutionary processes—consciously cultivating a yin-openness to paradigm shifts. Instead of boxing ourselves in overspecialized "adult" forms, we continually cycle and recycle through to maximize our powers to evolve.

That's what the Cycles of Truth do. They engage us in a paradigm-evolving process. How?

1. *Learning the truth* begins the process by making us look at where we are. We're invited to learn the truths that an established paradigm may not want us to acknowledge. Specifically, *we come out of denial about pain.* Whereas ignoring pain protects the paradigm-in-charge, learning the truth of what's going on holds the paradigm accountable for the pain it's causing.

2. *Honoring the truth* suggests that there's more to truth than one paradigm embodies. Ultimately, our paradigms must *answer to reality as a whole.* They can't arbitrarily choose to leave out pieces that are relevant to our existence. When a paradigm does, whole truth asserts the dimensions that are being overlooked, which we may experience as crises or addictions.

Specifically, if our paradigm accentuates our analytic, rational powers at the expense of our intuitive, meaning-oriented powers, we experience over-compartmentalization and fragmentation, as well as a loss of meaning and connectedness. It's not so much that something's wrong with *us* when paradigm worlds start to unravel—though it seems that way—as that we're ready to make a leap in paradigm evolution, and that requires our full attention.

3. *Accepting the truth* expands the context in which we explore truth. Paradigms define the playing field. As long as we stay within paradigm-defined limits, we'll end up playing the paradigm's game. To evolve, we need to push the limits and *redraw the context.* From the perspective of spiritual teachings, there's no better way to do this than to appeal to the whole context as our ultimate context. That way, we bring a wider perspective to any specific paradigm.

To borrow the terms used by Dietrich Bonhoeffer, the Lutheran theologian executed by the Nazis, we don't confuse "penultimate" contexts with "ultimate" ones. Making money within the business world is a penultimate context. It's not ultimate. Regarding the welfare of humanity as our business is also a penultimate one, but one that points us in the direction of the ultimate context, because it trains us to think in wholeness and connectedness. When we mistake penultimate contexts for ultimate ones, we constrict evolution; the penultimate context becomes our whole world. By contrast, when we open ourselves to the ultimate context, we invite evolution. The ultimate context urges us to look beyond the limits of a given paradigm—"What's on the other side of that fence?"

4. *Observing the truth* brings paradigm evolution home to where we live. Paradigms aren't "out there"; they're us, all of us. We embody them through every thought, desire, and action, as well as through every rule, procedure, and policy. Through self-observation, we *notice the paradigm filters* that both we and our systems are using, and that's knowledge we need before we can change paradigms.

5. *Hearing the truth* says it's wise to admit what's wrong, whether it's on a personal, system, or paradigm level. Through *self-disclosure*, we open our paradigms to examination. If, however, we identify with a paradigm and defend it as if our image is at stake, we'll pretend we have no paradigm commitment: "Who me? What paradigm? I don't have a paradigm! I'm just doing what every parent/boss/teacher/senator/reporter/minister/scientist has to do." Such "defensive routines," as Senge calls them, hide our paradigm commitment, which means we're not open to having it questioned. Self-disclosure—hearing the truth—gets paradigm evolution going again. We open our inner processes to investigation, which moves us into the yin phase.

6. *Presenting the truth* grounds paradigm evolution on the bedrock of who we are. Paradigms that tromp all over our reality for some paradigm-justified reason are unacceptable. Yet that's what the control paradigm does. Those who are one-down in power or authority deserve to be treated as inferiors, which means they can be abused or exploited with impunity. Children fall in this category, for example, as do students, employees, women, minorities, poor people, middle-class people, new rich, Jews, Catholics, Hindus, Muslims, the "dumb masses," foreigners, and all animals—in fact, 99.99 percent of the life-forms on the planet are one-down for some goofy reason or another.

Presenting the truth says this will never do. For a paradigm to work, it has to *build on who we are*—all of us. We can't be factored out of a paradigm and still create a harmonious world with it. We need "Soul force," as Gandhi put it, at the center of our paradigms for them to do their job in creating humane rather than inhuman social structures.

7. *Loving the truth* cultivates a yin attitude through *dialogue*. Treating each other as equals, suspending our paradigm commitments, and interacting with

a genuine spirit of inquiry, we create an open system for evolving. We don't impose closed-system conditions or limits on how we develop, as if we can mastermind evolution. We simply love the truth and follow where it leads.

8. *Serving the truth* opens our paradigm evolution to the universe of *connectedness.* We learn how profoundly linked we are and how our paradigms can't afford to ignore this. We need paradigms that embrace connectedness and put us in a healthy relation to it—that help us serve the truth of connectedness. We don't need paradigms that tell us that the only way to survive is to make the connected universe serve narrow, elitist, and destructive ends.

9. *Living the truth* takes paradigm evolution down to the level of action: How can we *act mindful of our connectedness?* How can we make something beautiful of our connectedness and not something nightmarish? The more soul-connected we are, the more we're in touch with our personal hotline to the universe of connectedness. Aware in our bones of our connected reality, we're attuned to connectedness and do everything we can to keep it healthy. To do anything less, as karma teaches, is to harm ourselves.

10. *Working the truth* engages us in *ongoing paradigm evolution.* Instead of fixing on one paradigm, we can have paradigms and evolve too. We keep the yin–yang rhythm of development going.

A META-PARADIGM

What emerges from this process is a rough sketch of a meta-paradigm, which is a paradigm for evolving paradigms. Using the cycles to describe this meta-model, the meta-paradigm

1. keeps us open and ready to acknowledge what's really happening and how it relates to the established paradigm;
2. depends on the exercise of our whole minds;
3. invites us to continually expand our paradigm context;
4. makes us aware of the paradigm filters we're using;
5. encourages us to disclose our paradigm and its limitations, since that's how we either refine our paradigm or realize that it's time for a shift;
6. grounds us on the touchstone of accepting who we are and staying soul-connected as the core of paradigm development;

7. sets basic rules for dialoguing about paradigms, so that we don't get locked into closed-systems ways of thinking;
8. keeps whatever paradigm we consider within the universe of connectedness;
9. applies the paradigm's treatment of connectedness to actions, so that we act mindful of our connectedness;
10. conceives of paradigm evolution as an ongoing process.

This meta-paradigm gives us the promise of evolving paradigms that are both worthy of us as True Human Beings and worthy of reality as greater than any one paradigm can capture—"walking the truth."

NOTES TO CHAPTER 10

1. John Moyne and Coleman Barks, trans., *Open Secret: Versions of Rumi* (Putney, VT: Threshold Books, 1984), 7. Also in Coleman Barks with John Moyne, A. J. Arberry, and Reynold Nicholson, trans., *The Essential Rumi* (San Francisco: HarperSanFrancisco, 1995), 36.

2. Michael Grant, trans., *Cicero: On the Good Life* (New York: Penguin Books, 1971), 62.

3. Master Ni, Hua-Ching, *8000 Years of Wisdom: Conversations with Taoist Master Ni, Hua Ching, Book I* (Malibu, CA: The Shrine of the Eternal Breath of Tao and Los Angeles: College of Tao and Traditional Chinese Healing, 1983), 127.

4. Louis Fischer, ed., *The Essential Gandhi* (New York: Vintage Books/Random House, 1962), 184.

5. Shunryu Suzuki, *Zen Mind, Beginner's Mind* (New York and Tokyo: John Weatherhill, 1970), 21–22.

6. F. David Peat, *Synchronicity* (New York: Bantam Books, 1987), 178–79.

7. Arthur Koestler, *Janus: A Summing Up* (New York: Random House, 1978), 216.

8. Koestler, *Janus*, 219.

9. Koestler, *Janus*, 217–19.

10. Koestler, *Janus*, 218.

11. Koestler, *Janus*, 219–20.

12. Alice Miller, *Banished Knowledge: Facing Childhood Injuries* (New York: Doubleday, 1990), 13–20.

13. Mark 10:14–15, also Luke 18:16–17.

CHAPTER 11

Walking or Sleepwalking, Philosophy or Trance?

Walking the truth
*Eleventh of the Twelve Cycles of Truth,
the Iroquois Peace Confederacy Tradition*

You ask the embryo why he, or she, stays cooped up
in the dark with eyes closed.
Listen to the answer.

*There is no "other world."
I only know what I've experienced.
You must be hallucinating.*
Rumi[1]

"I'M AWAKE"

Awake to what is. Our goal isn't to settle on one paradigm but to keep evolving them. But that's not the end of it. Beyond evolving paradigms is the goal to live conscious of reality and not to live from narrow, control-paradigm programming. That's why we have paradigms in the first place—to develop a clearer awareness of what's going on.

That's also the thrust of spiritual teachings. The spiritual path is the quest to be awake to what is. When someone asked the Buddha who he was, that's how he answered: "I'm awake."

Awake to who we are. Why is this important? Being awake to reality includes being awake to *our* reality, and that makes all the difference for how we live. We perceive options that control-paradigm systems say are off-limits to us, and we discover resources we never thought we had.

At the beginning of chapter 1 under the heading "Going for the gold," we quoted some poems of Rumi that give a far bigger sense of human beings than we ordinarily grant ourselves:

> A True Human Being is never what he or she
> appears to be. Rub your eyes,
> and look again.[2]

> Some human beings no bigger than a water trough
> scooped out of a log are greater glories
> than the universe full of stars.[3]

Now it's time to cash this in. Who are we really? That's the big mystery. Is Rumi hallucinating when he says things like this, or are we hallucinating when we don't experience ourselves or others this way? If we're the ones hallucinating, we're sitting on a gold mine, and we're selling ourselves every day for—what? No wonder Shankara, the great ninth-century Hindu saint and philosopher, said, "The realization of the Supreme Self should be the goal of all who seek peace and the Highest Good."[4]

Nor are Rumi and Shankara alone among the world's spiritual thinkers to suggest something magnificent about our real nature. The famous passage from one of John's letters in the New Testament suggests much the same: "Now are we the sons of God, and it doth not yet appear what we shall be; but we know that, when he shall appear, we shall be like him; for we shall see him as he is"[5]—and presumably see ourselves as we are too.

In his introduction to the *Katha Upanishad*, Shankara describes "Atman" or the true Self as one "whose nature is incomprehensible to the ordinary understanding. It is the unchanging Consciousness present in man, and the Witness of his waking, dream, and dreamless states."[6] The *Katha Upanishad* puts it simply:

> Concealed in the heart of all beings is the Atman, the Spirit, the Self; smaller than the smallest atom, greater than the vast spaces. The man who surrenders his human will leaves sorrows behind, and beholds the glory of the Atman by the grace of the Creator.[7]

The *Chandogya Upanishad* affirms this view: "There is a Light that shines beyond all things on earth, beyond us all, beyond the heavens, beyond the highest, the very highest heavens. This is the Light that shines in our heart."[8] According to the beings of light that Dannion Brinkley encountered on his two NDEs, we're great spiritual beings, all of us, endowed with tremendous spiritual capacities, and heroes just for being here.[9]

Learning to use what we've got. But mystics and people who've been dead for twenty-eight minutes aren't the only ones to wax eloquent about our powers. If we talk brain language, our brains have immense capacities that we haven't begun to tap. In fact, our brains are some sort of evolutionary enigma. Arthur Koestler writes of their appearance:

> The evolution of the human brain not only overshot the needs of prehistoric man, it is also the only example of evolution *providing a species with an organ which it does not know how to use;* a luxury organ, which will take its owner thousands of years to learn to put to proper use—if he ever does....
> The evolution of the brain overshot the mark by a time factor of astronomical magnitude....[10]
>
> Only in the case of homo sapiens has evolution anticipated his needs by a time factor of such magnitude that he is only beginning to utilize some of the unexploited, unexplored potentials of the brain's estimated ten thousand million neurons and their virtually inexhaustible synaptic cross-connections."[11]

Koestler compares learning to use our brains to that of an illiterate shopkeeper in an Arab bazaar who prayed to Allah for an abacus. Instead, he got the latest PC with a stack of instruction manuals, which he couldn't read. After fiddling with the thing, he ended up kicking the computer and some numbers popped up on the screen. By trial and error, he could make it function as an abacus. He had something that could derive Einstein's equations and predict the orbits of planets and stars for thousands of years to come, and he was using it for an adding machine.[12]

"Unimaginable potentials." That's our predicament. Nor is this a secret. Superlearning specialists Sheila Ostrander and Lynn Schroeder report what brain-mind researchers are discovering:

- Psychologist Jean Houston says: "We are just beginning to discover the virtually limitless capacities of the mind."

- Mathematician Charles Muses states: "The potentials of consciousness remain well-nigh the last reachable domain for man not yet explored—the Undiscovered Country."
- Brain specialist Frederic Tilney predicts: "We will, by conscious command, evolve cerebral centers which will permit us to use powers that we now are not even capable of imagining."
- Based on the "hard scientific research" of neuroscientist and engineer Dr. Manfred Clynes, it seems "that we are at the stage where we can develop new emotions, genuinely new states we've never before experienced."
- Psychologist Patricia Sun suggests: "We are at the point of developing talents we haven't got words for."
- Psychophysical expert Jack Schwarz estimates that "We are hoarding potentials so great that they are just about unimaginable."[13]

Where's the commitment to learning? These statements were made in the seventies. Have our schools changed since that time? "'A teacher from 1890 could step out of a Winslow Homer painting and feel right at home in a 1990 classroom,' says Ellen Dempsey, president of Teachers Network. 'What other business could remain in existence exactly the same way for one hundred years?'"[14]

True, more alternative schools are popping up around the country, and home schooling is becoming popular with many parents who either can't find or can't afford good alternatives for their children. But where is the societywide commitment to cultivating the innate abilities that all human beings have? As Howard Gardner, the psychologist who identified the seven different learning styles, observes, the state of modern schooling amounts to nothing short of "educational malpractice."

If we want to be bottom liners about it, tapping our mind's powers makes business sense. To stay at the forefront of change, businesses depend on lifelong learning. They don't need employees traumatized every time they have to take a course to keep up-to-date with fast-moving fields. Learning should be fun and exciting, since that's when learning seems effortless. Yet for the vast majority of children and adults, learning is stressful; we're lucky if it's only boring. Again, where is the commitment to ending this waste of our minds? Ostrander and Schroeder write:

As never before, we need the know-how to bring more of our abilities on line—that supposed 90 or 95 percent of human potential we don't usually connect with. A hundred years ago William James calculated we use only about five percent of our innate ability.

"It's more like three percent. Few of us use even five percent of our capacity," insists Dr. Raymond Abrezol, who has trained hundreds of Olympic stars.[15]

The bottom line is, if you've got a human brain, you're a genius. If you're not feeling like a genius, it's not that you've got a lemon upstairs—or a pea. It's just that you haven't figured out how to turn the thing on, especially given a culture that seems hellbent on keeping it turned off.

"WALKING THE TRUTH" VS. SLEEPWALKING

Sleepwalking. "It is indeed miserable to be born into the world a victim of ignorance…and experience the suffering of old age, disease, and death."[16] That's from the *Kena Upanishad*, but it could also be from a text of Buddhism—or from anyone who's having enough of a bad day to sit down and think about it.

We're not walking the full truth of who we are because we're sleepwalking—unconscious of our immense abilities. Even the most advanced people on the planet, whoever they may be, aren't scratching the surface of what we all are and can become.

"Becoming 'that dumb little kid.'" Instead, we've come to believe that such abilities don't exist for us. In *Babies Remember Birth*, David Chamberlain recounts the loss of wisdom expressed to him by one young woman:

> Linda…remarked at sixteen, after recalling her birth, that when she was born she felt "wise" and knew a lot. By the time she was three, however, she had become a conventional child fitting into the role expected of her. She said she became "that dumb little kid" everybody thought she should be and had to grow up and become wise again.[17]

Even people who are highly educated at the "best schools" experience a loss of "the magic." Physicist Fred Alan Wolf writes of his own education:

> I paid a price for my learning. A dear price that I hadn't even realized at that time. Somewhere in all of that education, I had lost the magic. I simply

accepted the physics education as an indoctrination. I can't say I really understood physics even after getting my Ph.D. I knew how to manipulate the math and logically prove whatever needed proving according to the rules of physics, but I hadn't understood it at all.

I had become a kind of physics machine, and even though I did have some creative moments solving academic problems, I really didn't know how physics fit into the total scheme of things.[18]

The advantage for power-over institutions is obvious. "Physics machines" don't indulge in big-picture thought. They do the calculations; they don't assess the impact of what they're calculating. Control-paradigm systems want the human brain to be an obedient machine, not a mind.

But why, having experienced this, do we perpetuate the loss by becoming agents of wounding social systems? "That's not abuse; that's schooling," we tell ourselves, or, "That's not violating our rights; that's business," or, "That's not undermining representative democracy; that's getting reelected," or, "That's not toxically shaming; that's the Word of God." After a boom in recovery books during the 1980s, why are we still tolerating—as adults—social systems that function abusively?

Our bet is that a big piece of the answer to this one is philosophical—or more accurately, a con using a philosophy cover.

Philosophy or Trance?

The control paradigm posing as a philosophy. The dumbing down—becoming less than who we are—brings us face to face with one of the control paradigm's most powerful devices for achieving control. The control paradigm presents itself as a philosophy, as if it's innocently telling us what's what. It even insists that its mechanistic, materialistic, control-measured picture of reality depicts the "real world" and tells us how to be practical in the world of facts and things, dogs eating dogs and sharks eating whatever.

The more our reality can be reduced to objects, this philosophy tells us, and the less we trouble ourselves with ideas, values, and other intangibles, the more we understand the "realities" of the control universe. If we as an object are big enough, we can control other people-objects. The unpredictable quality of our inner lives is made predictable by the pursuit of external rewards, control being the biggest reward. We're inducted into the control world, in which we either control others or they control us.

Adopting this philosophy as the most practical way to maximize our personal sphere of control, we don't notice that we're made controllable in the process. To buy the philosophy is to become controllable by its values of external rewards and suggested into a view of ourselves that's not true to our nature and potential as True Human Beings.

Nonetheless, in spite of the less-than-humanizing messages, we're led to believe that a control philosophy helps us live more realistically, which means more successfully by control standards. When you become a "responsible adult," that's how you learn to think. "It's not my fault that that's the way things are. I'm just telling you this for your own good. Forget about inner mucking around. Make some money! Whoever made a fortune on ideas?" Socrates certainly didn't; he was nearly penniless when he drank the hemlock.

But that's the con, the disguised mechanism of control. The control paradigm isn't a philosophy. It doesn't encourage free thought or dialogue. It doesn't develop our minds or souls. Nor does it invite inquiry into its core assumptions, strategies, responses, and goals.

Instead, it functions as a mind-control trance. A big trance, almost a global trance, but a trance nonetheless. We think it's a philosophy and act as if it's one we chose freely as we became adults. But the choice was not so free. The control paradigm comes across as *the one way* to experience reality, and it doesn't make room for alternative perspectives. To do so would go against the control agenda. Consequently, the control paradigm has little in common with philosophy and much in common with propaganda and mind-control methods—trance-inducers, the kind Hitler was skilled at using.

Trance guises. To work, mind-control methods must be hidden or pass as something acceptable. The trick to a manipulative trance—as opposed to a therapeutic one—is that it remains unnoticed. The trance-inducer needs a good guise.

Some trance-inducers disguise themselves as advertising, some as news,* some as schooling, some as textbooks, some as pep slogans written on the walls of office buildings, some as sermons. As Alice Miller points out,

---

*For news as propaganda, see Ben H. Bagdikian, *The Media Monopoly* (Boston: Beacon Press, 1993) and Carl Jensen, *Censored: The News You Need to Know*, 1994 ed., the *Project Censored Yearbook* (New York: Four Walls, Eight Windows, 1994).

"Conditioning and manipulation of others are always weapons and instruments in the hands of those in power, even if these weapons are disguised with the terms *education* and *therapeutic treatment*."[19] The control paradigm uses all of the above, but ultimately philosophy is its greatest cover. Philosophy lends the control paradigm an air of authority.

If we recognized mind-control methods, saw through their disguises, and named them as such, they'd lose their effectiveness. We'd say to ourselves, "Oh, they're trying to use my emotions (mostly fear, guilt, and desires) to sell their products, make me work harder, get me to fall in line, and be obedient. I see how they're doing it, I'm feeling the emotional reactions they're trying to elicit, but I also know they're not *my* emotions; they're implants. Now I have a choice what to do about it."

That's what Vance Packard and later Wilson Bryan Key—both pioneers in research into subliminal suggestions and their grotesque use in both news and advertising media—discovered: recognizing subliminals as such reduces their influence on us.[20] The more Key's students were aware of subliminals, for instance, the less they were affected by them. By contrast, those who didn't believe in subliminals or believed they were above being affected were the ones most influenced.

Awareness of trance-inducers destroys their cover and, therefore, cuts their effectiveness. Being as aware as we can—the Buddha's "I'm awake"—is the best protection. It's also the ticket to getting out of a trance and connecting with who we are beyond it.

For openers on the path of awareness, what is a trance?

The anatomy of a trance

Selective focus that bypasses the critical faculty. Dave Elman, who started as a stage hypnotist and went on to teach thousands of doctors and dentists how to use hypnosis to reduce or even replace anesthesia, defined the hypnotic or trance state as when *our minds voluntarily choose to bypass their critical faculty and focus selectively*.[21] In the words of psychologists Milton Erickson and Ernest Rossi, "Trance is a condition wherein there is a reduction of the patient's foci of attention to a few inner realities; consciousness has been fixated and focused to a relatively narrow frame of attention rather than being diffused over a broad area."[22]

We become so focused on one thing, such as imagining ourselves sitting by the ocean, that we don't notice a dentist's drill or a surgeon's knife. It sounds impossible, but that's exactly what happens, indicating the enormous power of our minds to both selectively focus and selectively ignore.

Suggestibility. One reason we can do this is that when we bypass our critical faculty and narrow our focus, we're highly suggestible. Our critical minds go off duty, and suggestions made to us go straight into our internal operating systems. In fact, some practitioners—such as the mentalist Kreskin—believe that a focused openness to suggestion is all that's needed to get past the critical faculty. Instead of a formal trance state induced by a hypnotist,* our own receptivity to suggestibility is enough to let almost anything in. When we watch television or go to movies, for example, we open ourselves to a barrage of suggestions, so that filmmakers from Hitchcock to Spielberg can get almost any emotional response from us they want. In other words, we don't need *an expert* to put us in a trance. Many circumstances and perceptions can render us highly suggestible. Once we're in such a state of suggestibility, the usual doorman isn't there to decide what gets in and what doesn't. When Dave Elman suggested to someone having a tooth pulled that he didn't feel a thing, he didn't, not a twinge.

Psychologists—or earlier versions of them—have been developing an understanding of the trance state and our suggestibility for several centuries. In this century, Milton Erickson advanced the therapeutic uses of hypnosis. It's now used for physical and psychological healing, memory enhancement, learning, stress management, performance, as well as consciousness research.

"I'm not in trance!" Some hypnotherapists—those who agree with Kreskin—say hypnosis is not a *state* at all but a *process* of selective focusing that we choose to engage in, since many of the characteristics of the trance state apply to other states of consciousness as well. In fact, when people are

---

*In *Secrets of the Amazing Kreskin* (Buffalo: Prometheus, 1991), Kreskin criticizes the notion of a formal "hypnotic trance state," noting that with imagination, concentration, willingness, and faith in the prestige of the practitioner—or in the case we're making, the control paradigm—people can be made to do almost anything. See pp. 69 to 82, as well as his examples in other chapters of how subtle cues and suggestions can influence, even control people's minds and behavior.

in the trance state, many swear they're not. "They have no sense of altered consciousness when responding to hypnotic suggestion and, therefore, do not believe themselves to be in *trance*."[23]

Yet they very much are. And they discover that the trance process, whether they believe in it or not, is a potent reality-changer. Time, for instance, becomes distorted. A half hour watching TV or playing with the cat can seem like five minutes. Perceptions are altered as well. We think that having a tooth pulled is painful, but suggestions can change that. Suggestions made during the trance period stick whether we're in trance or not.

Michael Talbot, an engaging new-science writer who unfortunately died several years ago, told a fascinating story about the trance process. At a party, a man named Tom was given a post-hypnotic suggestion that when he came out of trance, his own daughter would be invisible to him. Sure enough, when the hypnotist brought Tom out of trance and his daughter walked into the room, Tom saw all the other people in the room, but didn't see his daughter, even though she was standing right in front of him and giggling her head off. But it gets even more weird. The hypnotist pulled an object out of his pocket and held it hidden behind the daughter's back so no one could see it. Then he asked Tom to identify it. Tom seemed to peer straight through his daughter's body and said it was a watch. He even was able to read the inscription on the back of the watch, which neither Tom nor anyone in the room except the hypnotist had ever seen or read before.[24]

Trance as a tool of oppression

The dark side of trance. That's mind-bending stuff. But the very power of the trance when used for healing or even for amusement suggests its potential as a tool of oppression—for making us less than who we are. As it is, we're just now learning the *positive* uses of hypnosis. A *healing* trance and our *awareness* of the trance render the process only useful. Indeed, it can't make us budge an inch from our moral basis, but it can help us learn, stop smoking, lose weight, or be more creative.

But *negative* trance conditioning is very different. The mind-control uses of the trance process are millennia old and permeate control-paradigm institutions.

Let's go back to four of the leading characteristics of trance—(1) bypassing the critical faculty, (2) selective thinking, (3) high suggestibility, and (4) lack of awareness of the trance process—and see how two master oppressors, Hitler and Eichmann, used them in the concentration camp experience. Psychiatrist Viktor Frankl, who himself endured years in the camps, including Auschwitz, analyzed the induction of prisoners into a trance of dehumanization.

1. Eliminating the critical faculty. First, concentration camp prisoners were taken from their homes, deprived of all possessions, stripped naked, shaved head to toe, and mass showered. They were treated as if they were subhuman criminals who deserved harsh treatment, even though no crime had been committed, like the prisoner in Kafka's *The Trial*.

The impact was that all the *assumptions* they'd ever made no longer applied. As Frankl said, "I struck out my whole former life."[25] Every sense of right and wrong, as well as every assumption about human dignity, was violated. Inmates went into shock, and their ability to think shut down. Having lost autonomy, even of their own bodies, they realized that critical thinking made no difference in prison life. It was utterly irrelevant, since nothing made sense. "Beatings occurred on the slightest provocation, sometimes for no reason at all."[26]

The critical faculty was gone: step one of imposing a trance.

2. Narrowed focus on survival. Second, the brutality of camp life made everyone think only on the barest survival level. Every thought focused on how to get a crumb of bread, how to stay warm, or how to avoid the moody wrath of the guards.

In other words, thinking became highly selective. Tremendous thought would go into planning the simplest details of survival, which may or may not work, since, at a whim, the guards would switch routines. No one could form any reliable *strategies*. Only the guards had that luxury. If inmates challenged the guards' actions in the slightest way, such as wiping away filth thrown in their faces, they could be killed.

Selective thinking was established: step two.

3. Normal emotions removed and camp ones implanted. Given the shock of all this, emotions shut down. "Disgust, horror and pity are emotions that our spectator could not really feel any more. The sufferers, the dying, and the dead, became such commonplace sights to him after a few weeks of camp life that they could not move him any more."[27] Apathy took over—the inability to care about anything. The prisoners gave up their normal ways of *responding*. They couldn't afford to be angry, to defend themselves, or to be indignant.

Instead, new responses were implanted ("suggested"): the desire to save one's life, to not antagonize the guards, to submerge into the crowd, even to do favors for the guards in order to gain a favored position. The responses that the guards wanted from the prisoners—unquestioning obedience, abject submission, having no will but what the guards indicated—were the responses they got.

Suggestions were implanted to the effect that human beings have no intrinsic worth, only extrinsic usefulness to authorities: step three.

4. Aware of the trance or not? At this point, as Frankl saw it, the prisoners had a choice. Either they could descend into the trance of being degraded humans and succumb to despair and hopelessness, or they could recognize the trance induction and resist it. They could maintain their own sense of meaning and *purpose* in spite of their degrading, dehumanizing treatment.

Those who bought the trance—as if the way they were being treated reflected their real worth—didn't last long, even if they had been of superior physical build. They were "doomed."[28] They didn't see that they'd been put into a trance whose purpose was to destroy their inner lives, so they let their inner lives die. Those "who allowed their inner hold on their moral and spiritual selves to subside eventually fell victim to the camp's degenerating influences."[29] Their bodies soon followed.

The trance of dehumanization overcame them without their conscious awareness or resistance: step four.

Alternatively, some prisoners recognized that a trance was being imposed on them and resisted it. Their treatment as if they were subhumans did not convince them that they were subhuman. The trance didn't take. Frankl wrote:

> The experiences of camp life show that man does have a choice of action. There were enough examples, often of a heroic nature, which proved that apathy could be overcome, irritability suppressed. Man can preserve a vestige of spiritual freedom, of independence of mind, even in such terrible conditions of psychic and physical stress.

We who lived in concentration camps can remember the men who walked through the huts comforting others, giving away their last piece of bread. They may have been few in number, but they offer sufficient proof that everything can be taken from a man but one thing: the last of the human freedoms—to choose one's attitude in any given set of circumstances, to choose one's own way.[30]

By recognizing the trance imposed by the structure of concentration camp life, those few held on to their inner lives and survived against staggering odds.

TRANCES OF DEHUMANIZATION

A legacy of dehumanizing trances. Nazi concentration camps are an extreme case of mass induction into a trance that negates us as "True Human Beings." They represent the control paradigm naked and unrestrained. We could dismiss concentration camps as representing insanity, a fluke in human history, except that our global control culture has produced comparable structures that induce dehumanizing trances—and continues to do so.

- Slavery also imposed a trance of dehumanization, and it was an institution that stretched back to the ancient Greeks and Romans, even to ancient Sumer 6,000 years ago. The American Constitution allowed this dehumanizing institution to exist until 130 years ago—a blink of the eye, evolutionarily speaking.
- The brutal attempts to impose a trance of dehumanization on Native Peoples in America, as well as around the world, provide examples that surpass the brutality of Hitler's concentration camps. Far more than six million people have been involved, and the dehumanizing trance induction continues today through government agencies (legislatures and courts) here and around the world.* What's hard to grasp is that we're not talking about Nazi Germany for ten years half

---

*Among the many sources documenting centuries of dehumanizing treatment, see Russell Means with Marvin J. Wolf, *Where White Men Fear to Tread: The Autobiography of Russell Means* (New York: St. Martin's Press, 1995); Richard Erdos, *Crow Dog: Sioux Family Saga* (New York: HarperCollins, 1995); Wallace Black Elk and William Lyon, *Black Elk: The Sacred Ways of a Lakota* (San Francisco: HarperSanFrancisco, 1990); James Axtell, *The Invasion Within: The Contest of Cultures in Colonial North American* (New York:

a century ago; we're talking about "the land of the free and the home of the brave" for centuries up to and including the present.

- China, which enjoys MFN (Most Favored Nation) trading status with the United States, has torture camps for Tibetans and its own people that Asia Watch and Amnesty International worry may be even worse than Hitler's. China's invasion of Tibet, recently declared illegal by the U.S. Congress on advice by international legal authorities, has resulted in over a million and a half dead and the destruction of an ancient culture.

- South Africa's policy of apartheid for white supremacy brutally oppressed the native African population, reducing them to slave labor until recently. Yet for most of the century the world didn't oppose this corporate and governmental racism; it made the racists super-wealthy by buying their diamonds and gold.

- As David Korten documents in *When Corporations Rule the World*, corporations are creating concentration camp–style workplaces all over the southern hemisphere. The clothes and shoes we wear bearing labels made in India, Mexico, Indonesia, or China may well be made under conditions of terrible human suffering. Impoverished nations are populated with "subhumans," in the eyes of wealthy corporations, since that's exactly how they treat their foreign workers.

- Back at home, modern prisons, which are now big business, regularly induct millions into similar dehumanizing trances—trances which apparently "take" given the high rates of recidivism.† Prisoners accept the "you're a subhuman criminal" trance and carry it back onto the street.

Oxford University Press, 1985); Rex Weyler, *Blood of the Land: The Government and Corporate War Against Indigenous America* (Philadelphia: New Society Publishers, 1992); and Dee Brown, *Bury My Heart at Wounded Knee: An Indian History of the American West* (New York: Holt, Rinehart & Winston, 1970/Bantam, 1972), and, of course, Vine Deloria Jr., *Custer Died for Your Sins* (New York: Avon, 1969), *God Is Red* (New York: Delta, 1973), and (the most recent of his fifteen books) *Red Earth, White Lies: Native Americans and the Myth of Scientific Fact* (New York: Scribner, 1995).

†*The New Encyclopedia Britannica*, (Chicago: Encyclopedia Britannica, 1987), vol. 9, p. 977b, suggests that from one-half to two-thirds of those imprisoned in the United States and Europe have served previous sentences.

- Our college students, on reading Frankl's book in our classes, found the psychological environment of concentration camps familiar. They'd experienced a schoolroom version of it: frequent but unpredictable humiliation, fear-instilling tactics, disempowerment, absolute control by authorities, lack of self-determination, constant surveillance and senseless punishments, inequities and abuse of power, as well as the hostility, bullying, and suspicion among fellow students created by favoritism and competition. Students whose innate humanity seeks cooperation for learning are penalized and forced into competitive models: "I hurt myself if I help you learn this material."

- Even unioned American employees, especially those low on the ladder, cope with induction into a "you're not worth much," "you might steal from me," "you're an idiot," "do what I tell you" trance regularly, while those above suffer a similarly dehumanizing induction: "If you step on them, that proves you're better than they are."

- As recovery literature documents, children are regularly treated as subhumans—lesser beings deserving less-than-human treatment. According to a 1995 Gallup poll, 85 percent of 1,000 parents surveyed said they shout, yell, or scream at their children; 47 percent hit their children on the bottom with a bare hand; 25 percent hit using a belt, stick, or some other hard object; while 25 percent believed that praising children too much "may go to their heads."[31] "These findings," says company chairman George Gallup Jr., "will shock you. They will anger you. And they will sadden you."[32] Children don't have rights, only privileges. If a child is being abused at home, where can he or she go? What would be considered assault if done to an adult is considered good discipline if done to a child. To challenge this treatment of children, Robert Kennedy advocated that the voting age should be lowered significantly, and that still wouldn't create the full child suffrage that Deganawidah instituted in the 1500s.

Indeed, the fact that Frankl's book became an international bestseller suggests that his insights tell a truth about life that goes far beyond those who have suffered the most extreme circumstances. There's a dressed-up, "civilized" version of the same trance induction into becoming less than who we are, less than a True Human Being. This trance induction parallels the concentration camp experience:

1. Setting aside the critical faculty. Whether through childhood traumas, stresses at school, or fears about making a living, we're inducted into social systems through traumatic experiences. The *assumptions* and sensibilities we bring into this world as babies get zapped. Instead of being welcomed as special beings, worthy of respect just for who we are, we get the message that, to survive, we must obey authorities and do what's expected without question. Our right to think for ourselves is undermined systematically.

"Theirs not to make reply, Theirs not to reason why, Theirs but to do and die."[33] Tennyson's poem "The Charge of the Light Brigade" was meant not as a critique of a foolish tragedy but as a credo. That's how we're taught: bypass your critical faculty, if you want to fit in.

2. Selective thinking enforced. With our critical faculties put on permanent hold, we're told to think selectively. We bypass healthy *strategies* that affirm our worth and focus instead on gaining external approval and rewards. Then we're schooled into specialization and compartmentalized thinking. "The whole is too big for you; here, just think about this little piece; that's all you can handle." Highly selective thinking makes acceptable graduate theses; theses that integrate disciplines do not.

On the job, we do the few things we're told to do and don't do anything else. When Johann Sebastian Bach was hired as the organist for Duke Wilhelm Ernst, he was forbidden to compose his own music and reprimanded when he composed anyway. Being an organist was all he was officially allowed to do.

3. Suggested into becoming less than who we are. As with Bach, the impact is that we're "suggested" into being less than who we are. The cultural structures suggest us into conceiving of ourselves narrowly. We have no other options except what they offer us, so we *respond* the way they demand. We become what the social structures say we must be.

We get the respect that institutions put behind our names only if we play their games to their satisfaction. As mere humans without the right titles, degrees, or positions, we're cattle—just another one of the "degraded majority," to use Viktor Frankl's terms, as opposed to the "promoted minority." We don't count, nor do we have special gifts to offer. We're just one more human using up scarce resources on an overcrowded planet.

4. It's not a trance; it's reality. This is the control-paradigm trance in a nutshell. Yet we don't perceive ourselves as being in a trance; we're just coping with "the real world." If anything, we think we're succumbing to illusions when we nurture feelings of compassion, altruism, idealism, or hope. If we act on these feelings and work toward our own higher *goals*—which may entail disobeying the directives of superiors—we can lose our jobs. The trance carries the day as the no-trance way of life, which only affirms how effective the culture's induction of the population into the control-paradigm trance has been.

COMING OUT OF TRANCE TO WALK OUR TRUTH

Breaking the trance. Psychologist Stephen Wolinsky, working from twenty-three years of therapeutic practice, including Ericksonian training, eighteen years of meditation practice, and six years of living in a monastery in India, has the background to distinguish what's a trance and what isn't.

In his view, his clients walk into his office in a trance, and it's his job as a therapist using hypnotherapy to get them out of it, since the "Deep Trance Phenomenon," as he calls it, is at the root of their symptoms. The trance holds all the symptoms together. Break the trance, and the symptoms disappear. "The job of the hypnotherapist," he writes, "was no longer to *induce* a trance but rather to *de-hypnotize* the individual out of the trance [he or she] was already experiencing."[34]

He came to this conclusion because he observed that "what was currently being called 'therapeutic trance' in the hypnotherapy community was really similar to the *no-trance state* in which a person's perceptions and observations flow unobstructed in the Eastern practice of meditation."[35] When people do hypnotherapy—which is indeed a modern form of an ancient meditative practice—they access levels of knowing that go beyond the control paradigm's trance conditioning. They glimpse themselves and their life's processes from a no-trance perspective. Even that glimpse can be powerfully transforming, because it says it's possible to live our lives outside the trance.

This, of course, is what Socrates told the ancient Athenians, and what the Buddha wanted the Indians to do. It's also essentially what Frankl argued. By holding fast to their inner lives and pursuing the search for meaning, prisoners could resist the deadly hopelessness of the concentration-camp trance. We can do the same.

How do we break the trance? With the help of three friends of humanity:* (1) philosophy, (2) prayer and meditation, and (3) psychology and recovery processes.

1. Philosophy: Reawakening our critical faculties. We need our critical faculties back, and philosophy is the discipline devoted to helping us do it. Philosophy—the love of wisdom—is all about freedom of thought and exercising our powers to explore ideas. It's about connecting with our inner authority and listening to it even when external authorities oppose it. For Socrates, philosophy was about remembering the wisdom we bring into this world but have somehow forgotten.†

Philosophy invites us to investigate and question everything we can imagine. In his *Consolation of Philosophy*, the fifth-century philosopher Boethius—writing from a dungeon awaiting execution—described philosophy as "the queen of all disciplines." Above all, philosophy invites us to reflect on the big picture, namely, our paradigms—our assumptions, strategies, responses, and goals—since doing so calls our critical faculties into play. We ask such questions as the following:

- What do we *assume* about ourselves and our abilities? about our social institutions and the way society must run? about children and who we are when we're born? about other people and human nature in general? about the earth and other life-forms?
- What *worldviews and strategies* flow from our assumptions? What are the rules we talk about, and what are the unspoken ones? How do we feel about the strategies we're living? Do they help us blossom into who we are, or do they narrow us and make us cynical or depressed? Can we imagine a different worldview with strategies that free us to be different people?
- How do we *respond* to experiences? Are our responses coming from a sense of isolation, including the fear and insecurity that goes with

---

*Control-paradigm systems try to claim each of these friends and use them to oppress humanity further by deepening the control-paradigm trance—and what they can't claim, they discredit—but if so, it's time for us to claim these friends back.

†Remembering was Socrates's theory of knowledge explored in Plato's dialogue *The Memo*, where Socrates drew out of an uneducated slave boy the knowledge of basic concepts of geometry.

it: trance responses? Or are we bucking trance narrowness by engaging in a dialogue with the universe of connectedness, which includes listening to how that universe talks back?

- What are our *goals* and where are they taking us? Are our goals as big as we are, worthy of True Human Beings, or are they little goals that make us little when we pursue them? The control-paradigm trance loves little goals and ridicules big ones, and that's why so many philosophers in history who had the effrontery to live big goals got martyred. We once made a list, starting with Socrates, and were amazed at how many philosophers had their writings destroyed, were imprisoned, tortured, burned at the stake, exiled, and otherwise eliminated. Many are famous, but many more are not.

Philosophy and trance-inducers don't go together, which may be why philosophy is not taught in lower, middle, or high schools (though big questions are on people's minds at these ages) and why little funding goes into philosophy departments at higher levels. Engineering, yes; football, yes; philosophy, no. What's the agenda here? Trance defense, since no medicine is more potent against trance-inducing systems than philosophy. As long as we're flexing our philosophical muscles, our critical faculties stay on line, and trance-inducers can't get to first base.

2. Prayer and meditation: letting our minds roam the big picture. Prayer and meditation counteract the second feature of trances: selective thinking. As long as we keep ticking away on a narrow track, we stay in the trance, focused on details and trivia, deadlines and schedules. The big picture never comes up, which means we stay narrowly focused. The trance runs the show.

Prayer and meditation intrude on this arrangement, which is why they're built into AA's Twelve Steps. Step Eleven says: we "Sought through prayer and meditation to improve our conscious contact with God *as we understood [God]*, praying only for knowledge of [God's] will for us and the power to carry that out."

Prayer and meditation invite us to contemplate ourselves, our lives, and the universe from as wide a perspective as we can. They give us relief from trance narrowness—a no-trance glimpse of ourselves. In prayer and meditation, we're free to let our consciousness open as wide as it wants, as a lotus blossom opens from the muddy swamp (no, we didn't make that up—it's a

Hindu-Buddhist image). Instead of nine-to-five mouse vision, prayer and meditation invite eagle vision. Rumi said:

> Wait for the illuminating openness,
> as though your chest were filling with Light,
> as when God said,
>
> > *Did We not expand you?*
> >
> > (*Qur'an*, XCIV:1)
>
> Don't look for it outside yourself.
> You are the source of milk. Don't milk others!
>
> There is a milk-fountain inside you.
> Don't walk around with an empty bucket.
> You have a channel into the Ocean, and yet
> you ask for water from a little pool.
>
> Beg for that love-expansion. Meditate only
> on THAT.[36]

Prayer and meditation show us our "channel into the Ocean." They draw us out of the dehumanizing trance long enough for us to dream our reality as spiritual beings, heroes on earth, and to choose walking our dreams over walking the trance.

In the language of brain states, prayer and meditation move us out of beta. That's the mode that's good at fight or flight, act and react, make decisions, answer the phone, do this and don't forget that. The more we're in beta, the more we're focused on immediacies and externals. We're so projected "out there" that we don't notice "in here" messages.

Prayer and meditation settle us into alpha—an open, receptive, but also creative state precisely because it's not so focused. In alpha, the lines dividing our thoughts into compartments aren't so solid, and we see connections that busy, specialized thinking cannot notice.

The powers we have in alpha are enormous. In fact, most of the comments made earlier about our mind's potential were made from research into the alpha state. Knowing things we didn't know we knew or being able to heal ourselves in ways we'd thought impossible become possible in alpha. It is, as Wolinsky described, a "*no-trance state* in which a person's perceptions and observations flow unobstructed."

3. Psychology and recovery processes: Correcting dehumanizing suggestions. With consciousness liberated from trance ruts, we're able to correct and remove the dehumanizing suggestions implanted in us about who we are. That's where psychology, therapy, Twelve Step programs, and recovery processes come in. We clear out the demeaning, shaming, put-downing messages we've absorbed. We may not know who we are now, but we'll know better as we take off the layers of trance programming that have bombarded us since birth. Unless we take the initiative in getting rid of control-paradigm suggestions implanted along the way, they shadow us.

After Dannion Brinkley was struck by lightning, he became psychic to an extraordinary degree. Just by touching someone, he could see their past, present, and future. As he soon discovered, such a gift carries a burden, since it exposed him to the inward suffering people bear from all the negative suggestions implanted in them:

> I began to realize that people have almost a need to feel guilty, wrong, or inferior, and that this need seems to overwhelm any consideration that they are spiritual beings. Instead, they see themselves as being trapped in a reality that is controlled and manipulated by everybody else. I often wondered how much the system had to do with their low self-opinions—institutions from government to religion are always expressing people's inadequacy. And amazingly, people seem to accept that judgement.[37]

There's work to do in recovering from years of living in a society run by a control-paradigm trance, and we all have it to do. Why is this work so important? Because, Wolinsky explains, trances blind us to our resources. We experience ourselves as trances say we are—as not smart enough, successful enough, or good enough. Brinkley observed that "rarely did the people whose thoughts I was picking up focus on what great and powerful spiritual beings they were."[38] Thanks to both selective thinking and control-paradigm suggestions, we're like genies in a bottle. We don't see our power to act differently from how the trance sets us up to react.

Yet the work of uprooting dehumanizing suggestions doesn't have to be overwhelming. If Wolinsky is right, once we break the trance, the symptoms dissipate. Only the trance holds them together. Then we begin to discover our true potential.

De-suggesting cultures. That's true for us personally, and it's true for systems and cultures as well. Only the control-paradigm trance keeps our shared interactions stuck in dehumanizing patterns. Once we break the trance for ourselves, our participation in shared patterns changes. We don't give dehumanizing trances our assent or energies.

For instance, the man who stood alone in front of the army tank in Tianenman Square was not in a control-paradigm, fear-and-submission trance. Apparently his no-trance response also broke the trance of the army driver inside, who didn't—at that time anyway—run over him. So, too, with the Berlin Wall: the wall symbolized a political control-paradigm trance for almost half a century. But once the communist version of the control-paradigm trance broke, the wall came down almost overnight.

Social systems can change on a dime. We just have to break the trance that holds them in dehumanizing patterns.

4. Expanding awareness. With the help of philosophy, prayer and meditation, and psychology and recovery, we can break the trance—personal and cultural—which we do simply by being aware of it. According to psychiatrist M. Scott Peck, those "who have been deprogrammed by psychotherapy or one of the twelve step programs...no longer fit into the traditional cultural program."[39] Once we're aware, we're awake, and we have choices: trance or no-trance.

Granted, waking up from the control-paradigm trance isn't what a trance society encourages. Family, educational, religious, corporate, and government institutions depend on our remaining in appropriate trances for their perpetuation. They don't welcome a no-trance look at them.

Yet if we're embarking on an expanding spiral of awareness—as a no-trance quest invites us to do—the "traditional cultural program" is not an issue. We've set our sights on giving birth to a new consciousness and with it new worlds—"being grateful for the truth." Against the power of our awakening, trances can't stand for long.

Notes to Chapter 11

1. Coleman Barks, trans., *We Are Three* (Athens, GA: Maypop Books, 1987), 10. Also in Coleman Barks with John Moyne, A. J. Arberry, and Reynold Nicholson, trans., *The Essential Rumi* (San Francisco: HarperSanFrancisco, 1995), 71.
2. Coleman Barks, trans., *Delicious Laughter: Rambunctious Teaching Stories from the Mathnawi* (Athens, GA: Maypop Books, 1990), 65.
3. Coleman Barks, trans., *One-Handed Basket Weaving—Poems on the Theme of Work* (Athens, GA: Maypop Books, 1991), 116.
4. Swami Nikhilananda, trans., *The Upanishads*, vol. I (New York: Ramakrishna-Vivekananda Center, 1949), 175.
5. I John 3:2, King James version.
6. Nikhilananda, *The Upanishads*, vol. I, 173.
7. Juan Mascaró, trans., *The Upanishads* (New York: Penguin Books, 1965), 59.
8. Mascaró, *The Upanishads*, 113.
9. Dannion Brinkley with Paul Perry, *At Peace in the Light: The Further Adventures of a Reluctant Psychic Who Reveals the Secret of Your Spiritual Powers* (New York: HarperCollins, 1995), 16.
10. Arthur Koestler, *Janus: A Summing Up* (New York: Random House, 1978), 275.
11. Koestler, *Janus*, 277.
12. Koestler, *Janus*, 276.
13. Qtd. in Sheila Ostrander and Lynn Schroeder, *Superlearning 2000* (New York: Delacorte Press, 1979), 3–4, 88.
14. Ostrander and Schroeder, *Superlearning 2000*, 11.
15. Ostrander and Schroeder, *Superlearning 2000*, 4.
16. Nikhilananda, *The Upanishads*, vol. I, 240.
17. David Chamberlain, *Babies Remember Birth* (New York: Ballantine, 1988), 192.
18. Fred Alan Wolf, *The Eagle's Quest: A Physicist Finds the Scientific Truth at the Heart of the Shamanic World* (New York: Touchstone/Simon and Schuster, 1991), 35.
19. Alice Miller, *For Your Own Good* (New York: Noonday/Farrar, Straus, Giroux, 1990), 277.
20. Vance Packard, *The Hidden Persuaders* (New York: Pocket Books, 1957), 228, and Wilson Bryan Key, *The Age of Manipulation* (New York: Henry Holt, 1989), 37.
21. Dave Elman, *Hypnotherapy* (Glendale, CA: Westwood Publishing Co., 1964), 16.
22. Milton Erickson and Ernest Rossi, *The Collected Papers of Milton Erickson on Hypnosis I. The Nature of Hypnosis and Suggestion* (New York: Irvington, 1976/1980), 448.
23. E. A. Barnett, M.D., *Analytical Hypnotherapy: Principles and Practice* (Glendale, CA: Westwood Publishing Co., 1989), 19.
24. Michael Talbot, *The Holographic Universe* (New York: HarperCollins, 1991), 141.
25. Viktor Frankl, *Man's Search for Meaning* (New York: Washington Square Press, 1984), 33.
26. Frankl, *Man's Search for Meaning*, 42.
27. Frankl, *Man's Search for Meaning*, 40.
28. Frankl, *Man's Search for Meaning*, 95.
29. Frankl, *Man's Search for Meaning*, 90.
30. Frankl, *Man's Search for Meaning*, 86.

31. Reported in the media 7 December 1995 by *The New York Times*, B16; *USA Today*, 3A; and *The Christian Science Monitor*.
32. *USA Today*, 7 December 1995, 3A.
33. Alfred Tennyson, *The Charge of the Light Brigade and Other Story Poems* (New York: Scholastic Book Services, 1969), 10.
34. Stephen Wolinsky and Margart O. Ryan, *Trances People Live: Healing Approaches in Quantum Psychology* (Falls Village, CT: The Bramble Company, 1991), 6.
35. Wolinsky and Ryan, *Trances People Live*, 6.
36. Coleman Barks and John Moyne, *This Longing: Poetry, Teaching Stories, and Selected Letters of Jelaluddin Rumi* (Putney, VT: Threshold Books, 1988), 70. Also in Coleman Barks with John Moyne, A. J. Arberry, and Reynold Nicholson, trans., *The Essential Rumi* (San Francisco: HarperSanFrancisco, 1995), 255.
37. Dannion Brinkley with Paul Perry, *At Peace in the Light*, 38.
38. Brinkley, *At Peace in the Light*, 38.
39. Qtd. in Charles H. Simpkinson, "The Importance of Being Civil," *Common Boundary*, vol. 11 (March/April 1993), 22.

CHAPTER 12

Changing the Consciousness Grid

Being grateful for the truth
Twelfth of the Twelve Cycles of Truth,
the Iroquois Peace Confederacy Tradition

If you've opened your loving to God's love,
you're helping people you don't know
and have never seen.

Is what I say true? Say *yes* quickly,
if you know, if you've known it
from before the beginning of the universe.
Rumi[1]

WHAT'S OUR PURPOSE WITHIN THE BIG PICTURE?

Nothing big, just changing the world. What's our role in the big-picture paradigm shift? That brings us back to what Margaret Mead said: "Never doubt that a small group of committed citizens can change the world. Indeed it's the only thing that ever has."[2] Yet it's hard not to doubt. Not only are we few among billions—and not the mover and shaker few either—but also we have jobs, children, friends with problems, not to mention our own problems. "Committed citizen" has a hard time getting on the schedule even in election years.

On top of that, the magnitude of the problems intensifies doubts. On an old activist model, we'd have to wave signs around the clock to get our social systems back on track, and even then it may not do the trick.

Fortunately, new activists, following Gandhi, are getting more creative—and subversive. Frances Moore Lappé and Paul Martin Du Bois explore the new activism in *The Quickening of America*, and their book is full of examples:

- "Workers at Weirton Steel buy the company and apply knowledge from their direct experience to make the company profitable."
- "Citizens in St. Paul devise their own neighborhood network to help the elderly stay out of nursing homes."
- "Sixth graders in Amesville, Ohio, don't trust the EPA after a toxic spill in the local creek, so they make themselves into the town's water quality control team."[3]

Elsewhere we hear about cities turning their garbage problems into booming methane businesses, mothers getting MADD about drunk driving, parents setting up their own homeschooling programs, a young boy named Trevor taking his own blankets to the homeless on the winter streets of Philadelphia, or a professor tackling the advertising business by exposing often misogynous, usually sexually explicit, and always anatomically correct subliminals.

Where do we fit in? But still there's the question, what should *we* do? We're not necessarily in positions to do these things, plus we don't feel as if they're necessarily *ours* to do.

That's the purpose issue raised in this last chapter: How can we be awake to who we are not as isolated seekers but as beings integrally connected to the transformation that's occurring on the planet? Is it possible that our presence counts—that we make a difference in the thick of our species' evolutionary crisis?

As we know from the Chinese ideogram, "crisis" involves both "danger" (a character depicting a person standing on a precipice) and "opportunity" (something that seems small but is the way out of danger). How can we participate in moving away from the precipice and discovering that small, even invisible factor that's our greatest opportunity?

One-dimensional purposelessness. For old-paradigm thinking, such questions trigger alarm bells of grandiosity. The mechanistic paradigm, which focuses on quantifying physical objects, says there's no way we count, and we're delusional if we think we do. We're cosmic dust that flickers in and out without any meaning beyond what we invent for ourselves to pass the time. In the grand scheme of things, there is no meaning, no significance to our lives. In fact cosmically speaking it doesn't matter one iota whether we ever lived or not. If that depresses us, the control paradigm suggests we should just take some drugs, until we can grow up and accept it.

This familiar credo of materialist science is not, however, a fact of reality. It reflects only a working definition of it—one that works for people driven by the burning question: What can we measure around here? According to this definition, only measurables are real. They alone count as factors in science and medicine; nothing else does, not if we're being "scientific."

"Anything which fits the definition [of reality given by science] is acceptable," Lyall Watson writes, "anything which doesn't fit is impossible and must be rejected." "What is being ignored," Watson goes on to explain, "is the point that our definition of reality is a theory, not a fact."[4]

Consider the source. It's an odd theory from which to make *any* comments about meaning and purpose, one way or the other, because its definition of reality excludes them outright. We can't measure meaning or purpose, because they're not physical objects. Of course we see no meaning when we put on measuring glasses—they're meaning-blockers.

This particular paradigm of science is dehumanizing *by definition*, because it arbitrarily defines out of existence the very thing that's most meaningful to human beings: consciousness. It's absurd to have such a paradigm dominate a culture, at least a human one. On an object-only view, for instance, there's not much difference between an alive person, one in a coma, and a corpse, yet somehow we perceive a difference. Without the factor of consciousness, there's no awareness at all and certainly no awareness of meaning or purpose—or science.

This goofy theory says far more about what some scientists are willing to discuss than about reality itself. Part and parcel of the control paradigm, the matter-only theory is designed to limit our thoughts to the one dimension that's externally controllable and to ignore the inner, consciousness dimensions that can't be so easily controlled.

The very irrationality of such a paradigm—irrational, that is, if it's supposed to help us understand *human* existence—suggests that its hold on the global mind-set has less to do with reason and more to do with trance. Trances are tenacious by nature anyway, but when they're touted as the official, no-trance, last-word arbiter of truth, they're monsters.

CONSCIOUSNESS IS HERE TO STAY

A theory that carves up reality to serve a control agenda—that makes truth fit its terms, especially by excluding consciousness as a dimension of reality*—is not a theory that's "grateful for the truth." Assuming that truth is more than our theories about it, being grateful for the truth means being grateful for the whole ball of wax, even the dimensions that don't fit our theories. That's the original spirit of scientific inquiry—science before the control paradigm twisted it.

Consciousness is back in science. And it's what many scientists, starting with Einstein, have been doing this century, so much so that the matter-only model is obsolete. (It's just dying a slow death in the cultural mind-set.) As a result of their open inquiry, insights from relativity theory, quantum physics, and biology converge to put consciousness back on the map of science. Consciousness is now recognized as central to reality as we know it. It won't be written off.

Specifically, prompted by Werner Heisenberg's uncertainty principle, quantum physicists are forced to take consciousness into account in their theories. Our perspective as conscious beings makes all the difference—not just as observers but as participators in bringing certain aspects of reality

---

*Watson reports the research of sociologists Harry Collins and Trevor Pinch, who studied how parapsychology was treated by its critics in mainstream scientific journals: "They found straightforward statements of prejudice; pseudophilosophic arguments to the effect that parapsychology ought to be rejected simply because it conflicts with accepted knowledge; accusations of fraud without evidence to support them; attempts to discredit scientific parapsychology by association with cut and fringe activities; and emotional dismissals based only on grounds that the consequences of its acceptance would be too horrible to contemplate. And they concluded that the ordinary standards and procedure of scientific debate were being seriously violated" (Lyall Watson, *Beyond Supernature: A New Natural History of the Supernatural* [New York: Bantam Books, 1989], 232).

into focus, even into existence. We're not outside reality looking in. We're players, participating in creating reality as we go. If we want to understand reality, consciousness can't be factored out.

In *Recovering the Soul*, physician Larry Dossey explores "that single fact which, more than any other I can think of, has the capacity to redirect our vision and restore our ability once again to feel life: the absolute status of human consciousness—consciousness as fundamental and not derivative of the physical; consciousness as infinite in space and time."[5]

This may seem radical for physicists, doctors, and other scientists to say, yet it's something we experience all the time: consciousness creates reality as we experience it. Businesses come into existence because of people's decisions to start them, and they prosper or fail because of other people's decisions to work for them or to buy their products or services. Political systems live or die according to the ideas and values we put into them, as do our religious and educational systems. Consciousness is very much a factor. Our choices call different realities into existence, and we're choosing every moment. If we choose differently, different realities—like different storylines—unfold.

Consciousness never left Eastern philosophies. That consciousness is the bottom line for reality is no news to Eastern philosophies. In fact, they go the whole nine yards to say everything is consciousness. Consciousness is a better description of the bottom-line stuff of the universe. What we experience as matter is just a more dense or focused form of consciousness.

The focused forms are things we've had a hand in creating, precisely by focusing on them. If we focus on certain interpersonal activities, for instance, in nine months the focal point known as babies follow. If we focus on exercising, our bodies take a different shape. If we focus on building a business or developing a career, businesses and careers follow. Forms follow focus.

Forms serve as symbols for consciousness, giving us one of many languages to express ourselves. They also give us feedback. We bump into forms distilled from the consciousness that are beyond our particular perspective, and thanks to the bump, our perspective expands.

Our lives are peopled with all sorts of forms, but it's consciousness that calls them into existence. Nobel Prize–winning biologist George Wald concurs. Having wondered for years what made the universe favorable for the development of life, he wrote:

> A few years ago it occurred to me…that mind, rather than being a very late development in the evolution of living things, restricted to organisms with the most complex nervous systems—all of which I had believed to be true—that mind instead has been there always, and that this universe is life-breeding because the pervasive presence of mind had guided it to be so. That thought…so offended my scientific sensibilities as to embarrass me. It took only a few weeks, however, to realize that I was in excellent company. That line of thought is not only deeply embedded in millennia-old Eastern philosophies—but it has been expressed plainly by a number of great and very recent physicists [Eddington, Schrödinger, Pauli among others].[6]

Nonlocal consciousness fields interacting

Consciousness is nonlocal. The implications of this paradigm shift from matter-centered to consciousness-centered models are enormous, and we're only beginning to digest them culturally.

Right off the bat, we notice that consciousness is not a time-space phenomenon the way objects are. Consciousness isn't bound by the laws of matter. As NDEs indicate, our physical bodies can be dead, but our consciousness can be very much alive—and live to tell what happened right down to the details of technical medical procedures used to resuscitate the body during the flatliner period.

From his experiences with consciousness in healing, Dossey describes consciousness as "nonlocal." Consciousness isn't boxed in our heads but operates nonlocally, across space and time. Through consciousness, we have access to information that our bodies by ordinary physical means couldn't possibly pick up.

For instance, parents often know when a child is in danger, even though the child may be miles away. In a case reported several times on television, a mother woke from a dead sleep and yelled the name of her son, who was a soldier in Vietnam. Somehow in Vietnam, he "heard" her call his name and paused, perplexed long enough to avoid walking onto a minefield that killed those with him on patrol.

Animals' consciousness operates nonlocally as well, and stories of it won't quit. In *The Language of Silence*, J. Allen Boone tells of a troop of monkeys that had settled into an area to play in the trees over where Boone was sitting. All of a sudden, they bolted. Boone checked his watch but stayed where he was (we'd have followed the monkeys). After a while, some hunters came by looking for monkeys to shoot. Boone asked them when they decided to come hunting in this direction, and it was the exact time that the monkeys took off.*

Consciousness fields. If consciousness isn't boxed in our heads, how can we picture it? A less local, less material image is that of fields. Biologist Rupert Sheldrake defines "fields" as "non-material regions of influence," using gravitational and electromagnetic fields as examples. But there are many more fields than these: "All around us there are countless other vibratory patterns of activity within the field which we cannot detect with our senses; but we can tune in to some of them with the help of radio and TV receivers."[7]

Just because we can't see fields doesn't mean they're not there or not affecting us. "Fields are the medium of 'action at a distance,' and through them objects can affect each other even though they are not in material contact."[8] To use the gravitational field as an example, the sun, earth, and moon all affect each other at a distance; they're not in material contact. Or, to consider the emotional field surrounding two people in a marriage, both the spouses and their children are powerfully affected by the invisible field, even when the family members aren't in physical contact. Parents may be long dead, but children can still be affected by their emotional field.

"According to modern physics," Sheldrake says, "these entities [fields] are more fundamental than matter. Fields cannot be explained in terms of matter; rather matter is explained in terms of energy within fields."[9] We usually think of fields forming around things, so that the thing is primary, but it's more accurate to put it the other way, as Einstein used to in his physics classes: fields form things.

The Language of Silence was published posthumously by Boone's wife based on his notes and partially completed manuscript, and it's a hard book to find. We lent our copy years ago and haven't been able to replace it, but we both seem to remember the story this way. For other amazing stories on the nonlocal functioning of animals' consciousness, see Bill Shul, *Animal Immortality* (New York: Fawcett, 1991) and *The Psychic Power of Animals* (New York: Ballantine Books, 1977).

On this analysis, our brains aren't so much originators of consciousness as receivers of consciousness, and we each tune in to different fields. We may be in the habit of tuning in to certain frequencies, like listening to the same radio station on the way to work, yet nothing but habit prevents us from switching the dial and tuning in to other fields.

Interconnecting consciousness fields. In fact, fields naturally tap into each other, because they don't have sharp borders. Fields theoretically extend to infinity, each overlapping and intersecting with all others. "If the mind is nonlocal in space and time," Dossey writes, "our interaction with each other seems a foregone conclusion. Nonlocal minds are merging minds, since they are not 'things' that can be walled off and confined to moments in time or point-positions in space."[10] We're interconnected to a profound degree through consciousness, participating in each other's awareness and development. "If nonlocal mind is a reality," Dossey continues, "the world becomes a place of interaction and connection, not one of isolation and disjunction."[11]

Einstein took this idea very seriously. In an interview with Michael Toms, Dossey, who's studied how scientists talk about consciousness, reports: "Einstein...certainly had the idea that his consciousness was connected with that of everyone else's.... He had no idea of himself as a separate entity. He felt that he was hooked up with everyone else."[12]

Einstein's perception echoes Claude Lévi-Strauss who said, "I appear to myself as the place where something is going on, but there is no 'I,' no 'me.' Each of us is a kind of crossroads where things happen."[13] Biologist Lyall Watson, as we mentioned in chapter 2, had the same perception.

Nor was Einstein the only physicist to take the nonlocal field-nature of consciousness seriously. Physicist Erwin Schrödinger argued that the Upanishadic thinkers of Hindu philosophy were right. The appearance of many separate minds is an illusion. Whereas "separate" is a time-space concept, consciousness is ultimately one unbounded field, which means, in his words, "there is only one mind."*

---

*Erwin Schrödinger, *Mind and Matter* (Cambridge, England: Cambridge University Press, 1958), 53. According to Dossey, Schrödinger wrote this book in the 1920s but was so concerned about the backlash from matter-only scientists that he wouldn't allow it to be published for thirty years.

Patterns within the one consciousness field. Though one, consciousness isn't an undifferentiated "one." "The One" is also "the many," just as one person has many facets and talents. There's a wholeness to the consciousness field, but there's also diversity. Psychologist Carl Jung referred to this diversity as universal archetypes or "innate psychic structures"[14]—structures that we all draw on in virtue of being part of universal consciousness.

Paradigms are another way of talking about patterns within consciousness. Paradigms serve as focusing devices. Through them, we focus our consciousness to call certain realities into existence. With a different paradigm, our focus shifts, and the forms shift with us.

A paradigm shift isn't, therefore, just a new way of thinking, while things roll on as before. It marks a shift in reality as well. We use a new blueprint to build new worlds.

Plato's Ideas. Plato discussed patterns within consciousness in terms of "Forms" or "Ideas." Ideas bring the one consciousness into focus and give it form—enough form at least to guide our development. By focusing on truth, beauty, and the good, or on wisdom, courage, temperance, and justice, we open our personal consciousness field to interact with the universal consciousness field.

In fact, as Plato's teacher Socrates suggested, we're ideas too, in that we're the one consciousness focused in a specific way. Ideas are the essence of who we are, and by exploring ideas, we discover our souls. In *A Blue Fire*, psychologist James Hillman has a powerful passage on ideas and how they permeate our identity:

> The soul reveals itself in its ideas, which are not "just ideas" or "just up in the head," and may not be "pooh-poohed" away, since they are the very modes through which we are envisioning and enacting our lives. We embody them as we speak and move. We are always in the embrace of an idea.... No one concerned with soul dare say, "I am not interested in ideas" or "Ideas are not practical."[15]

IDEAS ALONG THE SPECTRUM OF CONSCIOUSNESS

Platonic philosophy: Static or developing? One of the standard criticisms of Plato is that his philosophy depicts an absolute world of ideas that is static. Ideas are eternal and unchanging, therefore critics assume that Plato allows no room for evolution and change.

Yet if that were so, why would Plato rely on dialogue as the way to explore ideas? Dialogue is a process, one that fosters evolution. His dialogue medium sends a message of thinkers-in-process.

Also, if Plato were a static thinker, why would he be a skeptic, arguing that the beginning of wisdom is to know that we don't know? Plato claimed that no one would know what he really thought from the dialogues he wrote, because he viewed the dialogues as journeys into ideas that could go on forever and had no stopping point other than a practical one: time to eat. Treating Plato as a static philosopher preaching static perfection is to mistreat him—badly.

Ideas serving consciousness evolution. Process, change, and development are integral to Plato's philosophy of ideas, but from another perspective—ours. Ideas have their own dynamics, which we're constantly exploring, and this exploration spurs us to evolve. Indeed, we may well say that evolving consciousness is *the* point of Plato's philosophy. He wrote to challenge readers to think—and in new patterns.

Not all ideas serve the same function in our evolution, of course. Different patterns occur along the spectrum of consciousness.

North Star ideas. Some ideas, such as truth, beauty, and the good, tell us about the patterns within the one consciousness, and, relative to us, they seem unchanging. We have some growing to do before we can appreciate the dynamics that express the one consciousness, just as children perceive adults as unchanging until they grow up.

In his classic 1947 book *Human Destiny*, biologist Pierre Lecomte Du Noüy compared the role of ideas such as love, truth, or justice in our development with the role of the North Star in guiding ships on the ocean. Relative to where we are, ideas seem like absolutes. That's not to denigrate our position in the cosmic scheme of things (it takes a diehard one-up/one-downer to get competitive with Plato's ideas) but to help us get our bearings. We can set our course and approximate nearness to the ideal. It doesn't break a seaman's heart that he can't land on the North Star; it's actually more useful to him if it stays where it is, always a bit beyond reach. That way, he can set a course.

So, too, instead of claiming to attain truth, a good Platonic philosopher—like a good quantum physicist grounded in Heisenberg's uncertainty principle—endeavors to approximate truth and to keep approximating it.

Down-home ideas. But not all ideas are North Stars to us. Others are closer to home, and we experience them as the warp and woof of our lives. Love, truth, and justice have down-home versions that we wrestle with every day. They're not "up there," though we can always deepen our sense of them.

The ideas we embody ourselves or that get embodied in our families or businesses tell stories about change, transformation, and evolution. They show how we're approximating love, truth, and good in our lives—and there are countless ways to do it.

According to Hillman, ideas are life; they're never separate from us and our life's experiences. When an idea grabs us, everything about us shifts:

> Ideas remain impractical when we have not grasped or been grasped by them. When we do not get an idea, we ask "how" to put it in practice.... But when an insight or idea has sunk in, practice invisibly changes. The idea has opened the eye of the soul. By seeing differently, we do differently....
>
> Ideas are inseparable from practical actions;... there is nothing more practical than forming ideas and becoming aware of them in their psychological effects. Every theory we hold practices upon us in one way or another, so that ideas are always in practice and do not need to be put there.[16]

Consciousness embraces the spectrum of ideas. Ideas describe patterns within the consciousness field, but they're not all on the same level or telling the same kind of story. The stories to tell about how consciousness evolves are infinite, as are the ideas to help us tell them.

The consciousness grid. What we're calling "the consciousness grid" is on the closer-to-home level—the consciousness field that's made up of all of us here on the home planet, all involved in process, change, and evolution. The consciousness grid reflects where we are: our collective stage of evolution.

Because the consciousness grid is made up of all of us, it's always changing. It's like the ocean with all the currents in it, only a very subtle ocean that senses every movement within it. If atmospheric conditions can change because of something as slight as the beating of a butterfly's wing, the consciousness field can respond to the slightest shifts as well. The intercommunication isn't obstructed by the limits of time or space.

Since consciousness participates in creating reality, this home grid is all-important for the kinds of worlds we experience. It's the formative field or blueprint from which our social systems emerge. Just as personal paradigms provide the blueprint for personal lives and business paradigms provide the blueprint for businesses, the consciousness grid—made up of everyone's paradigms together—provides the blueprint for human societies.

As the blueprint goes, so go the worlds that follow.

Big change—really big

Bigger than the evening news. If ancient prophecies as well as modern seers are right, we're in the throes of a major blueprint shift. And we don't have to be psychic to pick up on it. But what we tend not to grasp from ordinary perception is the magnitude of the shift. From an evening-news perspective, major earth-shaking change means having a third political party, discussing national health care (not changing anything, just discussing it), or legislating maternity and paternity leave that's more than a few weeks—things that are old-hat in other affluent countries.

These changes are not, however, what intuitives and psychics—from the famous "sleeping prophet" Edgar Cayce early in the century to Paul Solomon, Lazaris, and Paul Shockley in the present—are describing. Somewhere in the consciousness grid are rumblings of mind-boggling shifts.

Once in eighty-seven million years. One image that's stayed in our minds for years comes from Robert Monroe, the engineer, journalist, and radio and television producer, who one night found himself floating out of his sleeping body. In the years since, Monroe has devoted himself to the study of OOBEs or "out of body experiences." He and other researchers have made OOBEs so popular that there's now a T-shirt that says, "Out of body—back in five minutes."

Monroe himself has been popping out for decades to investigate the consciousness fields that, though he uses his own language to describe them, sound quite similar to the ones described in Hindu and Buddhist texts.

On one trip that he recounts in his second book, *Far Journeys*, he went far beyond Earth's atmosphere and noticed a great gathering of beings around him, all looking with great expectancy at Earth. It turned out that in their view, Earth is experiencing "a very rare event" that "may occur once every 87 million years." It is "the conflux of several different and intense energy fields arriving at the same point in [our] time-space." Perhaps one of these energy fields is the photon belt due to pass through our solar system, about which there's been considerable speculation among scientists, especially in Eastern Europe.

Whatever fields are involved, this rare event, full of both danger and opportunity, "will offer the human consciousness a rare potential to emerge rapidly into a unified intelligent energy system that will range far beyond [our] time-space illusion, creating, constructing, teaching as only a human-trained graduate energy is able to do."

Many other-dimensional beings are watching with intense interest, Monroe was told, because how this transformation goes "may alter not only [our] time-space but all adjoining energy systems as well."[17]

Monroe's image of planetary change reminded us of time-lapse pictures of a cell growing. For a while, the cell gets incrementally bigger, until all of a sudden, it starts shaking frantically. When it settles down, the cell has jumped a level: one cell has become two. Perhaps our planet's consciousness grid is shaking like a huge cell mutating to a new level, which accounts for the bumpy ride.

THE THREE FACES OF CHANGE

Change is also here to stay. Actually, maybe the news perspective of change is right. Reforming our health care system, getting insurance companies to budge, restructuring education, redistributing wealth, cleaning up the environment, revitalizing self-government, and treating children and animals as conscious beings worthy of respect would make a passing photon belt seem tame by comparison. But however we view change, it's here to stay.

According to the pre-Socratic philosopher Heraclitus, change is the only constant in the universe. The trick for us is to understand the dynamics of change, so that we can move with it instead of having it flatten us.

Impermanence, as we mentioned, is also the starting point of Buddhist philosophy. We experience suffering, the Buddha taught, when we become attached to things that are by nature impermanent. From mountains to personalities to social institutions, everything is in constant flux. Mindful of this, we don't develop expectations that set us up to suffer. Instead, we move with change.

Whatever other patterns may be in the cosmic blueprint, change is one to take seriously. How does change work from a consciousness-field perspective?

1. Field-generated change. We usually picture change in terms of objects and forces, people and events: Who did what to make the change occur? What event (the more catastrophic, the more change) caused people to alter their behavior? If we don't have much money or the right connections, on this view, we're not likely to make much of a dent.

But from a field perspective, change is field-generated. The changes we experience reflect shifts in the consciousness grid. Forms distill out of fields. When the fields change, the forms follow suit.

Field-generated change is how Rupert Sheldrake discusses biological evolution. Shifts in the morphogenetic fields—which work like biological information fields or biological blueprints—cause new strands of DNA to appear, which create new species. Fields initiate changes in how matter gets organized. Organisms simply follow the new blueprint.

From this perspective, the urgings for change that we feel in ourselves, our paradigm, and our social systems are our responses to shifts in the consciousness grid. The field moves and, because we're all part of it, we all sense the new currents—current events.

But what changes the grid? Where do new currents in the field start?

2. Fields changing fields. The consciousness grid isn't "out there." Because we're all part of it, we all contribute to it with every thought and action. We respond to changes in the consciousness grid, but we also participate in making those changes happen. The action is two-way: the grid to us, and us to the grid.

One way we contribute to changing the grid is through our interactions. Our planet's consciousness grid is made up of billions of subfields—all life-forms, all social structures, even the earth itself, if James Lovelock's Gaia hypothesis is right. Fields don't exist in isolation but constantly overlap. As they do, they exchange perspectives and evolve. This overlap leading to evolution may look like falling in love, cross-cultural dialogue, interspecies communication—or even members of the same species communicating.

The more fields interact, the more each expands to incorporate new perspectives. Using idea language to talk about consciousness fields enriching each other, Hillman writes: "the more ideas we have, the more we see, and the deeper the ideas we have, the deeper we see.... ideas engender other ideas, breeding new perspectives for viewing ourselves and world."[18]

Neurologist Eric Kandel describes in brain language the creative power of interconnecting fields. Each thought we have changes our neural networks by introducing new patterns. Just by thinking, we create new brains for ourselves:

> ...even during simple social experiences as when two people speak to each other, the action of the neuronal machinery in one person's brain is capable of having a direct and long-lasting effect on the modifiable synaptic connections in the brain of another.[19]

The more we interact with each other and explore ideas, the more we feed earth's consciousness grid with new patterns.

But there's another, even more potent way that we participate in changing the consciousness grid.

3. Grounding a higher-dimensional field. From a spiritual perspective, we're more than the human consciousness grid focused. Ultimately, we're the one consciousness field focused. That's a field interpretation of what the Bible may mean in the first account of creation when it says that man, male and female, is made in the image and likeness of God.[20] Other spiritual teachings say as much: a True Human Being brings many dimensions into focus. We make our appearances on a time-space dimension, but our origin and nature encompass many other dimensions.

If that's so, we have the capacity to ground consciousness fields higher than the totality of human thought at any one time. By opening our personal consciousness fields to the whole—perhaps by focusing on Plato's ideas, or on our High Self, our Buddha nature, the Christ consciousness, or perhaps by simply being open—we provide a means for higher-dimensional insights to intersect the consciousness grid and expand it.

That's what Einstein did with physics. He didn't come up with his ideas about relativity in 1905 by talking to other physicists. He was a patent clerk daydreaming about what it would be like to ride on a beam of light—how time and space would appear differently at the speed of light. He tapped a higher dimension of understanding time and space, and then he grounded that understanding through his theories, which he then explored with others. Yet even after his initial breakthrough, accounts of Einstein's character suggest he was always half or even three-quarters somewhere else. He may not have been an Edgar Cayce–type channel, but his consciousness field was by no means limited to the consciousness grid.

We don't have to be geniuses in physics, though, to ground higher-dimensional consciousness fields. We ground such perspectives when we allow ourselves to feel empathy for other living beings or when we refuse to tolerate abusive norms. When we seek a deeper relatedness than what traditional roles allow, we ground a higher consciousness of intimacy, even though it may take emotional pain, confusion, and turmoil to do it. Doorways to a higher awareness are all around us, and it's our nature as human beings—as the whole focused—to want to explore them.

Where we come in

So back to our original question: Where do we come in? What's our role in big-picture change? What, if anything, should we do?

Being who we are changes the consciousness grid. Given these perspectives about consciousness, fields, and change, our first and most powerful contribution to world change is to be who we are. That's not trite; it's a life or death challenge.

Who we are comes from the whole and brings many dimensions to earth's consciousness grid. Who we are is what the one consciousness, the infinite field, brought into focus for some reason. Our very being is a force for transformation, because we embody higher dimensions—dimensions that have the power to overturn systems, as Einstein overturned physics and Gandhi overturned British colonialism in India. We're encoded with a whole-awareness that's exactly what's needed for consciousness to evolve—ours and everyone else's.

This whole-awareness that we are—in contrast to the role images that control systems would reduce us to—carries great power, true power. If the beating of a butterfly's wing changes the weather, our existence or nonexistence changes the character of the consciousness grid—and the worlds that follow from it. What if Arthur Schindler hadn't lived his soul's truth, or

Chiune Sugihara, known as the Japanese Schindler, hadn't? For six weeks during the summer of 1940, Sugihara, the Japanese consul in Lithuania, "acted against orders from Tokyo and issued visas to some 6,000 Jews who sought to flee Nazi Europe."[21]

The connected universe needs us to live who we are because, to paraphrase Claude Lévi-Strauss, we are the universe coming together in a unique way so that transforming experiences can happen. If we don't live our souls, what could have happened doesn't.

Frank Capra's vision in *It's a Wonderful Life* is right: being who we are calls different realities into existence. With George Bailey, the town grew into the prosperous village of Bedford Falls; without him, it became the crime-ridden gambling town of Pottersville. George Bailey perceived his own consciousness as small and invisible, as having no particular impact, even as being worth more dead than alive. Yet his "invisible" contribution as a savings and loan banker moved the crisis of the Depression away from danger and toward opportunity. Acting from who he was—even though it didn't mean becoming an architect and traveling the world—changed the consciousness grid.

Not being agents for the control paradigm. Being who we are, of course, means not being agents for the control paradigm. Refusing to participate in abusive systems, we have the power to make them obsolete.

George Bailey, for instance, had to make the decision not to work for Mr. Potter. Cogs in control-paradigm systems—packaged units of obedience and conformity longing for approval and controlled by money—aren't who we are, nor do these roles do much for the consciousness grid. To be less than who we are diminishes the consciousness grid. Gandhi wrote, "We are…children of one and the same Creator, and as such the divine powers within us are infinite. To slight a single human being is to slight those divine powers, and thus to harm not only that being, but with him, the whole world."[22]

It's hard, though, to buck control-paradigm roles and reclaim ourselves. Materialism may say we have no purpose, so the control paradigm steps in to give us plenty: "Your purpose is to do what you're told, accumulate external rewards, and fulfill the expectations put on you by other people and systems."

That's why the recovery movement, far from being a fad of the 1980s, is a revolution that's here to stay. It's about saying "No" to Mr. Potter wherever we find him, within and without. AA's Step Twelve moves us in a subversive, revolutionary direction: "Having had a spiritual awakening as the result of these steps, we tried to carry this message to alcoholics [and other addicts] and to practice these principles in all our affairs."

George Bailey did this naturally. He didn't have to go on a crusade to be revolutionary; being who he was brought a revolution. Indeed, nothing could be more revolutionary than if today every person on the globe did precisely that and claimed his or her from-the-whole nature. That'd be a show worth waiting eighty-seven million years to see.

Being grateful for who we are. Being grateful for reality in all its dimensions leads us to be grateful for who we are in all our dimensions. Who we are is something precious and wonderful, something worth living, and something our world very much needs. But most of all, who we are is something immensely powerful: it changes the blueprint, the consciousness grid, that creates our reality.

Nelson Mandela, now president of the Republic of South Africa, expressed this eloquently in his 1994 inaugural speech:

> Our deepest fear is not that we are inadequate. Our deepest fear is that we are powerful beyond measure. It is our light, not our darkness, that frightens us. We ask ourselves, who am I to be brilliant, gorgeous, talented and fabulous? Actually, who are you not to be? You are a child of God. Your playing small doesn't serve the world. There's nothing enlightened about shrinking so that other people won't feel insecure around you. We were born to manifest the glory of God within us. It's not just in some of us; it's in everyone. And as we let our own light shine, we unconsciously give other people permission to do the same. As we are liberated from our own fear, our presence automatically liberates others.[23]

On one hand, this suggests that we don't have to do something else to participate in consciousness change; being who we are already does something—the biggest thing. We ground a different consciousness from what the control paradigm gave us, and that different consciousness permeates not only everything we do but also the consciousness grid. As Rumi said, we're affecting people we "don't know and have never seen."

On the other hand, being who we are doesn't mean we have to spend our lives sitting in a room blissed out and gathering dust. Being who we are may also mean being activists, teachers, meditators, parents, friends, lovers, animal lovers, secretaries, businesspeople, ministers, bankers, janitors, representatives in government, assistants, administrators, managers, artists, journalists, actors, editors, writers, counselors, monks, healers, naturalists, farmers. It may mean exploring archetypal patterns—Innocents, Orphans, Warriors, Caregivers, Magicians, Fools, Creators—as well as countless ideas, spiritual teachings, and philosophies. Being who we are means exploring anything and everything that who we are may include.

Whatever we do, we're automatically forces for transformation, because we live not from the control paradigm's definition of us but from our essence, that core of us that the whole field called into existence for a purpose. Rumi said:

> This is how a human being can change:
>
> There's a worm addicted to eating
> grape leaves.
>
> Suddenly, he wakes up,
> call it Grace, whatever, something
> wakes him, and he's no longer
> a worm.
>
> He's the entire vineyard,
> and the orchard too, the fruit, the trunks,
> a growing wisdom and joy
> that doesn't need
> to devour.[24]

Notes to Chapter 12

1. John Moyne and Coleman Barks, trans., *Open Secret: Versions of Rumi* (Putney, VT: Threshold Books, 1984), 69.
2. Qtd. in chap. 9 from the *WorldWIDE News* (Winter 1993).
3. Frances Moore Lappé and Paul Martin Du Bois, *The Quickening of America: Rebuilding Our Nation, Remaking Our Lives* (San Francisco: Jossey-Bass Publishers, 1994), 65.
4. Lyall Watson, *Beyond Supernature: A New Natural History of the Supernatural* (New York: Bantam Books, 1988), 265.
5. Larry Dossey, M.D., *Recovering the Soul: A Scientific and Spiritual Search* (New York: Bantam Books, 1989), 8.
6. Qtd. in Willis Harman and John Hormann, *Creative Work* (Indianapolis: Knowledge Systems, 1990), 102.
7. Rupert Sheldrake, *The Presence of the Past: Morphic Resonance and the Habits of Nature* (Rochester, VT: Park Street Press, 1988, 1995), 97.
8. Sheldrake, *The Presence of the Past*, 97.
9. Sheldrake, *The Presence of the Past*, 99.
10. Dossey, *Recovering the Soul*, 7.
11. Dossey, *Recovering the Soul*, 7.
12. Hal Zina Bennett, ed., *Larry Dossey in Conversation with Michael Toms* (Lower Lake, CA: New Dimensions Books, Aslan Publishing, 1994), 54.
13. Claude Lévi-Strauss, *Myth and Meaning* (New York: Schocken Books, 1978), 3–4.
14. C. G. Jung, *Two Essays on Analytical Psychology* (London: Routledge and Kegan Paul, 1953), 188.
15. James Hillman, *A Blue Fire: Selected Writings by James Hillman* (New York: HarperCollins, 1989), 53–54.
16. Hillman, *A Blue Fire*, 53–54.
17. Robert A. Monroe, *Far Journeys* (New York: Doubleday, 1985), 231–32.
18. Hillman, *A Blue Fire*, 53.
19. Eric R. Kandel, "Small Systems of Neurons," *Scientific American* 241 (September 1979), 66–76.
20. Genesis 1:26–27.
21. *Christian Science Monitor*, 16 November 1995.
22. Mohandas K. Gandhi, *Gandhi: An Autobiography: My Experiments with Truth*, part IV, chap. 9 (Boston: Beacon Press, 1957), 276.
23. Qtd. in *Noetic Sciences Review* (Winter 1995), no. 36, 48. Nelson Mandela used this text in his speech, but it has since come to light that he was quoting the inspirational writer Marianne Williamson.
24. Coleman Barks, *Delicious Laughter* (Athens, GA: Maypop Books, 1990), 127. Also in Coleman Barks with John Moyne, A. J. Arberry, and Reynold Nicholson, trans., *The Essential Rumi* (San Francisco: HarperSanFrancisco, 1995), 265.

THE PARADIGM CONSPIRACY: THE DYNAMICS OF SHIFTING PARADIGMS

Recovery as a paradigm shift / The elements of a paradigm	1. Where are we? Where are we going? / Confronting pain	2. How do we get to where we want to go? / Spiritual awakening	3. Taking the step and making the shift: "Make it so!" / Creativity
(a) Assumptions	CHAPTER 1	CHAPTER 2	CHAPTER 3
	Pain and the power of shifting assumptions	Power in whole-minded shifts	Power in shifting the context
	learning the truth	honoring the truth	accepting the truth
(b) Strategies	CHAPTER 4	CHAPTER 5	CHAPTER 6
	Self-knowledge: knowing our paradigm filters	Self-disclosure: breaking through paradigm defenses	Self-acceptance: building systems on who we are
	observing the truth	hearing the truth	presenting the truth
(c) Responses	CHAPTER 7	CHAPTER 8	CHAPTER 9
	Dialoguing our way to social order	Dialoguing with our connectedness	Connected action
	loving the truth	serving the truth	living the truth
(d) Goals	CHAPTER 10	CHAPTER 11	CHAPTER 12
	Conspiring ongoing paradigm evolution	Walking or sleepwalking, philosophy or trance?	Changing the consciousness grid
	working the truth	walking the truth	being grateful for the truth

INDEX

wholeness-change, 98–100, 135
wholeness principle, 80–84, 98, 106; and
    control systems, 83–86; and control
    thinking, 97; surrender to, 135
Wholeness Principle, The (Lemkow), 80
who we are, 360–63; being all that this
    includes, 362–63; being grateful for,
    362–63; force for transformation,
    360–61, 363; is the whole focused for
    a purpose, 360–61, 363. *See also*
    human nature, human potential, soul,
    True Human Beings
Who Will Tell the People? (Greider), 57, 92
Wiens, John, debunking competition
    among animals, 228n
Wilson, Bill, 19
Wolf, Fred Alan, 325–26
Wolinsky, Stephen, 337, 340, 341
women: in power-over systems, 123–24;
    salaries of, 123; work at home,
    123–24
Woodman, John (Nike), 263–64
Working Ourselves to Death (Fassel), 46
work issues: conditions of workers in
    southern nations, 289, 334; forced to
    work overtime, 11; losing livelihood,
    111; stress of, 121; taboos at work,
    177–78; unfairness of rewards, 46–47.
    See also Bill of Rights, competition,
    employees, human rights, slavery

World as Lover, World as Self (Macy), 252
worldview, *see* paradigm, philosophy
WorldWIDE News, 300n
wrongs, admitting, 182–83, 186–87

XYZ
yang, *see* yin and yang
Yergin, Daniel, 262
Yes Minister, 229
yin and yang, 303–7; compared to child
    and adult stages, 314; yang-heavy cul-
    ture, 304–5; yang phase of paradigm
    evolution, 304, 7; yin phase, 305–7;
    yin's challenges in yang-dominant
    systems, 307
You Just Don't Understand (Tannen), 150
Your Nostradamus Factor (Swann), 297
Zen, 66–67, 306
Zen Mind, Beginner's Mind (Suzuki), 70,
    306
zig back to zag forward, 309; applied to
    cultural evolution, 309–10
Zohar, Danah, 82
Zukav, Gary, 108

ABOUT THE AUTHORS

Denise Breton and Chris Largent, a wife-husband writing and teaching team, have done freelance teaching in colleges and universities for over twenty years, focusing on philosophy and comparative religion. Their first book, *The Soul of Economies—Spiritual Evolution Goes to the Marketplace*, explores how a philosophical and spiritual perspective changes our concept of business and what economies are all about. It was described by *Publishers Weekly* as "perhaps the clearest, best written book in that newest of genres, religion/business." They have also done editorial consulting and managed their own small publishing company.

Currently, Denise and Chris do philosophic counseling, assisting clients in integrating the philosophic dimension of personal and system change. They also run community education programs oriented to investigating the transforming power of both philosophy and spirituality in everyday life, using the history of both disciplines as resources.